OLYMPIC DREAMS

CHINA AND SPORTS
1895–2008

✦ ✦ ✦ ✦

XU GUOQI

Harvard University Press
Cambridge, Massachusetts
London, England
2008

Library of Congress Cataloging-in-Publication Data

Xu, Guoqi.
Olympic dreams : China and sports, 1895–2008 / Xu Guoqi.
p. cm.
Includes bibliographical references and index.
ISBN 978-0-674-02840-1 (alk. paper)
1. Sports—China—History. 2. Sports—Political aspects—China.
I. Title. II. Title: China and sports, 1895–2008.
GV651.X78 2008
796.0951—dc22
2007   041329

To my two great teachers,
Akira Iriye and Yang Shengmao

CONTENTS

FOREWORD

WHY ARE SPORTS IMPORTANT? Why does Boston collectively rise, fall, then rise again with the fate of the Red Sox? How have Yao Ming, the NBA star, and Chien-Ming Wang, the Yankees pitcher, come to be national heroes in the People's Republic and Taiwan, respectively, even though they ply their (quite different) trades an ocean away? And how have the Olympic Games, created to promote the ideal of international sportsmanship, become such a lightning rod for demonstrations of nationalist pride?

There are no simple answers to these questions, but with the 2008 Beijing Olympics at hand, it is an opportune moment to address the political history of sport in modern China. That is the purpose and the achievement of this book. For the history of *organized* sport is coterminous with the history of the modern Chinese state, which has been formed and re-formed on international models over the course of the past century.

China is home to a great and ancient civilization. But "China" as a political entity is much newer, founded on the ashes of the Qing empire in 1912. The great (and largely successful) quest of China's twentieth-century rulers was to make a Chinese-led nation-state out of what had been an enormous multinational and multicultural dynastic realm. Thus China's drive to participate in the international diplomatic arena as a respected nation-state coincides almost exactly with the rise of the modern Olympic movement and the growth of spectator sports as an international cultural phenomenon.

There is a great myth that China "opened its doors" only in the last thirty years. This is not true. Rather, the years of isolationism (ca. 1960– 1972) are the great exception to the rule of China's international engagement in the past century. The country became a republic with a series of constitutions modeled on international norms; Chinese capitalism and then Chinese socialism developed with international partnerships from Wall Street to Moscow; Chinese higher education was molded by American, European, and Soviet models; and China survived as a nation-state not least because of its political and military partnerships with Germany, the United States, and the Soviet Union.

In the creation of this new country, sports played a role that has grown in importance. The modern Olympic Games may have aspired to diminish national rivalries, but they have also helped to create and reinforce new national identities. The 1904 Games, played in conjunction with the great Louisiana Purchase Exposition in St. Louis, allowed Qing leaders to mount an exhibit portraying the dynasty as a conservator of Chinese culture (although no athletes from the region participated). By contrast, when the Nationalist Revolution brought the Guomindang to power in 1927, its early plans for its new capital city of Nanjing included an Olympic-scale stadium, and it sent China's first athletes to the Olympic Games in 1932 and 1936.

As Xu Guoqi shows, in China politics and sports have been linked from the beginning: China's first (and, in 1932, only) Olympic athlete was sent by Nanjing in part for fear that he otherwise might have competed for Manchukuo, the Japanese puppet state. In 1936, the sixty-nine-member Chinese delegation was both a symbol of China's growing self-confidence, and, almost surely, its close relationship with its German hosts. During the Communist period, participation in the Olympics was subject to political constraints—with the Republic of China on Taiwan initially retaining its recognition by the international Olympic movement—and sporting events were secondary to political friendships. Drawing from materials only recently made available, Xu illuminates here a history of match-fixing and tanking, on the orders of Premier Zhou Enlai himself, that would do the 1919 Black Sox proud, even if the only gambling was in the arena of diplomacy.

Today, the sports are cleaner but the politics remain. The controversy over Taiwan, which has persisted in international forums like the United Nations, has repeatedly flared in the Olympic context because of the unique history of Taiwan's involvement in the international Olympic movement—and is one of the more pressing concerns of the 2008 Beijing Games. As just one measure of the anxiety this "two-China" issue has caused, the Olympic torch will not pass through Taiwan (which was forced to reenter the Olympics through the back door as "Chinese Taipei") because no one can agree on just what, exactly, the political relationship is between Beijing and Taipei.

Historians, journalists, and others interested in the rise of organized sports in modern China will learn much from this book. The next generation will learn from it as well. This book is, as Xu argues, above all a history of modern Chinese elite attitudes toward sport. Yet we have entered an era of mass participation and mass consumption, in China as elsewhere, of sporting competitions. Now—as a "new Beijing," built on and beyond the old Qing capital, welcomes a "new Olympics"—is the perfect time to look back on the history of China's intense, and only recent, involvement with Western organized sports.

WILLIAM C. KIRBY

Geisinger Professor of History and Director,
Fairbank Center for Chinese Studies
Harvard University

Note on Romanization

This book employs the pinyin system for the transliteration of Chinese names, with the exception of names such as Confucius, Mencius, Sun Yat-sen, and Chiang Kai-shek, whose established spellings are familiar in the West. In citing Western-language sources that use older spelling systems, references to persons and places have been left unchanged.

OLYMPIC DREAMS

INTRODUCTION

The country is being drained of strength. Public interest in martial arts is flagging. The people's health is declining with each passing day. . . . Our country will become even weaker if things are allowed to go unchanged for long.

Mao Zedong, 1917

WHAT IS CHINA? Who are the Chinese? What is China's role among nations of the world? For centuries, people both in China and abroad have asked these questions and tried to address them from many different perspectives. But in recent decades, as China has sought to participate actively in the international community, these concerns about Chinese national identity, nationalism, and internationalization have become more urgent.

Sports, perhaps more than other modern cultural activities, provide a useful perspective on—and may even help shape—how national identity is developed and internationalization is achieved. As Eric Hobsbawm has pointed out, sports have proved "uniquely effective" in defining national identity and the sense of belonging.[1] Adrian Smith and Dilwyn Porter also argue, "Sport supplies a mirror that a people holds up to itself."[2] Jacques Barzun even famously maintained, "Whoever wants to know the heart and mind of America had better learn baseball."[3] These scholars make the same point from different backgrounds—namely, that sport defines a country's national identity and internationalization because it inspires solidarity and self-reflection. For outsiders wishing to understand modern

Chinese society, then, the history of sports in China can offer valuable insights.

By internationalization, I mean the ways that the Chinese people actively engage in and are engaged by international ideas, forces, and trends—a process that has compelled China to associate with the outside world and the international system. As I have argued elsewhere, internationalization has been driven by shifts in the flow of social, intellectual, economic, ideological, and cultural resources between China and the wider world, as well as by a new Chinese interest in foreign affairs and their position among nations.[4] Now that globalization has further integrated China into the world system economically, and China is eager to play a more active role in international affairs, the country's long process of internationalization has become clearer and more important in its search for a new national identity.

Over the course of the twentieth century, five words figured prominently in Chinese public discourse: nationalism, internationalization, socialism, revolution, and imperialism. Internationalization, though rarely mentioned directly in the first half of the century, nevertheless functioned as a driving force behind China's foreign policy and social change. Since the 1980s this term has become one of the most popular words in the Chinese public vocabulary. Individuals, enterprises, and government agencies, newly obsessed with the idea of internationalization, have asked themselves or have been asked whether they are in step with international trends or norms. At the same time, words like revolution and imperialism have progressively lost their usefulness; moreover, nationalism, frequently invoked in the first half of the twentieth century, seems to have lost favor with the Chinese people.

But it would be misleading to discount the ongoing importance of nationalism in China since, like internationalization in the early twentieth century, it has started to play a major behind-the-scenes role in recent years. Internationalization and nationalism, in other words, have simply traded places in Chinese social and political discourse and development. This book will explore the important relationship between internationalization and nationalism in China and examine how those Chinese obsessed with internationalization in fact have served the causes of nationalism. Since nationalism and national identity make sense only in an international context, where nations are striving to distinguish and prove themselves, nationalism and internationalism are essentially two sides of the same coin.

Sports, and the Olympics in particular, show well how nationalism and internationalism come together in China: Chinese participation and interest in modern sports are largely motivated by nationalism, but by importing sports from the West and taking part in world competitions, China has also engaged the world community. A 1994 editorial in the *Guardian* observed, "Sport may be the quintessence of nationalism on many occasions, but it is also one of the most effective means yet devised of uniting the global village."[5] In China, too, sports serve as an expression of internationalism that in some sense transcends nationalistic tendencies. This study will examine how the global reach of China's sports and sports figures has affected the country's relationship with the outside world. It will explain how the Chinese embrace of sports at the turn of the twentieth century was motivated by the same "fighting spirit" that influenced Americans then—and why Chinese enthusiasm for the Olympics and Western sports resembles Japanese cultural borrowing in the wake of the Meiji Restoration.

★

Every society is, to a great extent, an "imagined" one.[6] Historians often pay far more attention to elite members of a society, allowing them to play a disproportionately large role in articulating national identity. But a consideration of sports brings a much larger segment of the population—rich and poor, educated and less educated—into the story. From this perspective, sports have represented the broad Chinese determination to achieve national independence and rejuvenation and has served as an expression of defiance at critical moments—when China suffered through a national crisis at the turn of the twentieth century, during its long war against the Japanese, and as the country began its ascent toward global power in the

1990s. Sport as a collective experience crosses the social and political divisions of everyday life, and the study of it offers a unique window into larger historical processes. It is an effective vehicle for studying society-to-society, people-to-people, and culture-to-culture interactions. It allows us to examine how the Chinese relate to the rest of the world and how they negotiate the tricky matters of self-perception and perception by others as their national identity evolves.

Many books have been written about Chinese nationalism and China's internationalization from the perspective of political, diplomatic, and governmental issues. But few have considered communally charged popular activities such as sports. To date no study has systematically combined the issues proposed here. Current works on sports in China, too, either focus on sports per se, or on certain periods or themes.[7] None has presented a broader explanation of how sport has tied into China's developing self-representation in the world. None has used an international history approach to address this topic.

Sports in China continue to serve as an agent of social change and legitimacy, as well as a source of international recognition, national prestige, and an engine of nation-building. Looking at how and why sports and sports institutions reflect and engage Chinese society in relation to the world community further emphasizes how sports can be a bridge from a nation's internal reality to the external world. The materials I consult here come from libraries and archives in mainland China, Taiwan, Hong Kong, Canada, the United States, Switzerland, and elsewhere, and many of these sources became available only very recently. This book is the first to use these new materials to examine many important yet rarely studied issues such as Beijing's involvement in the 1952 Helsinki Olympic Games, the two-China issue, Mao Zedong's decision to use Ping-Pong to influence world politics, and the importance of the 1976 Montreal Olympic Games. In other words, with these new materials and perspectives, I aim to offer a new approach to understanding the formation of China's modern national identity and its sometimes ambivalent embrace of internationalization. Given the attention the world will focus on China in connection with the 2008 Beijing Olympic Games, the study is also intended to give journalists, sport scholars, and policymakers the tools they need to appreciate this enormously significant global event in context.

★

When people from different areas of the world come together for athletic contests, the games and competitions become in effect cross-cultural exchanges. In a sense, the International Olympic Committee (IOC) and other transnational organizations are stimulating cultural flows as well as managing sports competitions. Major events such as the Olympic Games and soccer World Cups are inevitably international and national activities, social and political events as well as gatherings of nations and cultural exchanges. Some commentators have pointed out connections between sport as popular culture and larger issues in the international realm. They argue that by linking sport to globalization we can better analyze sport as part of an emergent global culture, as contributing to the definition of new identities and to the development of a world economy.[8] To some, sport as a cultural phenomenon reaches far beyond its traditional boundaries; it expresses a new understanding of culture.[9]

This kind of cultural approach can add nuance to our understanding of nationalism and internationalization, which have traditionally been conceived as political. Sports as popular culture has in many ways shaped the historical landscape of modern China—including its foreign policy and relationship with the wider world. And in fact modern sports, especially the Olympic Games, have played a crucially expressive role in the wider developments of world history. It is only natural to wonder what effect the 2008 Games in Beijing will have on China and its image in the world. Will the Olympics stimulate Chinese nationalism? Will the embracing of world sport encourage China to take its place peacefully among the powerful nations of the world? How will the increased international attention affect China's political system and social stability? Will the Olympic Games change the way Chinese see themselves and how the rest of the world sees them? Will the Games be a "coming out party" bringing political legitimacy to the Chinese communist regime, or will the event be a catalyst for political reform and a serious challenge to the existing political order? Although few scholars have addressed all these questions, they are crucial for those studying China and its relations with the outside world.

China's past experience necessarily provides the framework to help us understand the potential significance of an event like the 2008 Olympic Games. While we cannot predict the future, we can consider some possible outcomes on the basis of how sports affected both popular opinion and policy on earlier occasions. A central focus here will be the history of the twentieth century, when the Chinese became obsessed with their country's international status and their own identity as Chinese. As I have pointed out elsewhere, the problem of just how China would join the world community as an equal member has been a key concern since the turn of the twentieth century. One can write modern Chinese history from many perspectives and approaches, but this fixation is vital to understanding China today.[10]

Chinese attitudes toward modern sports seem to perfectly mirror the anxieties of the Chinese regarding national pride. For the Chinese, sporting events represent something deep and fundamental—a validation of their nation's long labors toward international acceptance, a sign that China has overcome its "century of humiliation and shame" to become a full member of the community of nations. Chinese exuberance at hosting the Olympics clearly demonstrates the depth and significance of the Chinese passion for international prestige as well as the importance of sports in China's embrace of internationalism. The official slogan for the 2008 Beijing Olympic Games, "One World, One Dream," clearly reflects this drive.

Finally, this book will take an international history approach. As master historians like Akira Iriye brilliantly demonstrate, this perspective goes beyond the national level of analysis, using the entire world as a reference point. It explores the connections between popular culture and politics and between society and individuals. It emphasizes interactions between the national dreams and international reality and communications between different cultures and political orders. For this study, the international history approach will allow me to explore the relationship between the international political system and China's cultural outlook, explain the interactions between nationalism and internationalism, and highlight the connections between Chinese domestic politics and international affairs. The approach seems a reliable compass with which to examine China's engagement with the rest of the world through sports. By linking culture and sports with a study of nationalism and international relations, I hope to cross some of the boundaries that previous scholarship has erected and demonstrate both the continuities among different regimes in China and the similarities between China and other countries.

★

This book is not a general history of sport in China, but rather an account of broader themes that interlock and overlap. For purposes of clarity, however, each chapter focuses on an individual theme, necessarily leaving certain related elements unexplored. For instance, I rarely discuss the role of women in Chinese sports, although in contemporary China, female athletes hold up more than "half of the sky."[11] In the 1980s the Chinese women's volleyball team was both a national and an international sensation due to their performances in world competitions. In the next decade, the Chinese women's soccer team, lovingly called the "iron roses" by many fans, dazzled the world with their skills and determination to win. Even today, Chinese women outshine Chinese men in many world sports.[12]

This book, by necessity, also leaves out detailed discussions of Chinese indigenous sports such as martial arts and other types of physical exercises, although these indigenous physical activities too have played a role in articulating Chinese national identity and promoting China's internationalization. Nor is this a book about mass sports. Rather it is a study of Chinese competitive sport undertaken on a national level. Accordingly, the book largely focuses on Chinese elite society. After all, Chinese society from 1895 to the present has been controlled by and operated under elites who played the leading role in debating and articulating a modern Chinese national identity and internationalization. Sports activities developed on a national level, especially after 1949, remained largely elite pursuits, controlled and managed by the state and often subject to marked political influences.

As Chapters 1 and 2 show, modern sports in China are a completely invented tradition; their role in nation building, internationalization, and nationalism is more obvious and important than in many other countries. When the Chinese embraced Western sports, they were motivated more by the project of building an image of strength and accomplishment than by personal enjoyment. This was the case from the late Qing dynasty, into the early Republican period, in Nationalist China, and throughout the Maoist era; it remains the case as China enters the twenty-first century. Chapter 3 focuses on the role of sports in Chinese nationalism. It examines issues such as how members of the Chinese elite developed the links between training strong bodies, strengthening the race, and saving the nation; how the burning desire to compete spurred the Chinese to embrace Western sports; and how and why winning gold medals in world sports competitions has become a national obsession in China.

Chapter 4 explores the issue of China's national representation through sports, especially the Olympic movement. It demonstrates how both Beijing and Taipei fought for their respective international legitimacy within the Olympic movement from the early 1950s until the early 1980s. Although Beijing's first major political and diplomatic battle for national representation was fighting for the right to take part in the 1952 Olympic Games, it was the Nationalist government of Chiang Kai-shek rather than Beijing's Communist regime that first strongly opposed the two-China representation in the Olympics. This chapter also points out that China's paramount leader, Deng Xiaoping, first articulated or at least practiced his theory of "one country, two systems" in responding to Taipei's and Beijing's participation in the Olympic movement during the late 1970s. The chapter demonstrates that Beijing, Taipei, and the International Olympic Committee all made serious mistakes in handling the issue of China's representation in the Olympics. I also maintain that despite all the differences between Taiwan and Beijing, from the early 1950s to the 1980s, they had common ground regarding the issue of China's national representation.

For many Westerners, it is difficult to understand why Beijing was so concerned about Taiwan's membership in the Olympic family. Beyond Beijing's hopes for its own international legitimacy was the so-called one-China principle. The PRC's obsession with the one-China principle explains why even today the Taiwan issue is still potentially the most dangerous one surrounding the 2008 Olympic Games.

The relationship between China and Taiwan has long been complicated. According to the PRC's official version of China's modern history, the period beginning in the 1840s and ending in 1949, the start of the Chinese revolution, was a century of shame and humiliation for the Chinese, because during this time they were subject to many unequal treaties under Western and Japanese imperialism. Therefore, the hoped-for reunification of Taiwan with the PRC is directly linked to the long struggle of the Chinese against foreign imperialist pressure. The middle kingdom syndrome— that is, the idea that China is the cultural and political center of the region—also propels Beijing's determination to bring Taiwan back to the motherland. Many Chinese have believed in the ideal of the middle kingdom and that Taiwan's current separation from the mainland occurred first because of Japanese imperialism and then due to American intervention in the Chinese civil war. Because of these deep-rooted and widespread notions, the Communist regime has felt compelled to fight Taiwan's efforts to become more fully independent even at the risk of canceling the Olympic Games. Hosting the Olympics for the party may bring glory and legitimacy, but losing Taiwan would eclipse that honor.

Chapter 5 tells the story of ping-pong diplomacy. It explains why the common ground that Mao and Nixon worked so hard to find turned out to be the small white Ping-Pong ball. This chapter also examines the American version of ping-pong diplomacy through its detailed study of the Chinese table-tennis team's visit to the United States in the spring of 1972. No other studies have ever paid attention to this second act of ping-pong diplomacy, although from a scholarly perspective, it was more important in the sense that individuals and nongovernmental organizations interacted in new and significant ways. If we argue that Mao's act of ping-pong diplomacy set the stage for better diplomatic relations with the United States, the Chinese ping-pong visit of 1972 kicked off a healthy and fast-developing trend toward expanded cultural exchange between the two countries.

Chapter 6 uses materials that have become available only very recently to study, in the most comprehensive manner attempted to date, how the two-China issue affected the 1976 Montreal Olympic Games and international politics at the time. The controversy led not only to a threat by the IOC to cancel the Olympic Games and by the United States to boycott the Games, but also an almost universal condemnation of the Canadian government.

Chapter 7 studies how since the 1980s sports have once again become a key tool in China's all-out campaign for international prestige, status, and legitimacy. It explains the reemergence in China of the close link between sports and national honor, and between nationalism and internationalization. It also demonstrates the close relationship in the minds of the Chinese between winning gold medals in sports and achieving glory for the nation. This obsession with winning has turned China into a country whose citizens feel they cannot afford to lose a major international sports competition.

Why did it take the Chinese a hundred years to achieve their dream of hosting the Olympic Games in Beijing? Why did the Communist party put its credibility on the line and try so hard to bid for the Games? Why did Beijing lose its first bid? What kind of influence will the 2008 Games have on Chinese national identity and internationalization? Chapter 8 considers the Beijing 2008 Olympic Games from a comparative historical perspective. It explains that the Games present both dangers and opportunities to the Chinese nation and the Communist party. For the nation, it might be the beginning of a wonderful journey to self-confidence and democratic development, while for the party it could represent the beginning of the end.

★

No matter what happens to China in connection with the 2008 Olympics, the Games will be a major milestone: the selection of Beijing as the host city is, for many, an acknowledgment by the world that China has become a major international power. For generations of Chinese who have been part of the country's drive for both a new national identity and a place in the international community, a century-long dream of sponsoring the venerated Olympics has finally been realized—and a larger goal of achieving international respect seems at hand.

STRENGTHENING THE NATION WITH WARLIKE SPIRIT

★ ★ ★ ★

National power relies on [its citizens'] warlike spirit. . . . [We] should use sports to save the nation. Together [the Chinese] can achieve their heroic national ambition.

Chiang Kai-shek, 1933

The important thing in the Olympic Games is not winning but taking part.

Pierre de Coubertin

UNTIL THE LATE 1890S, the modern Mandarin phrase *tiyu* (sport or physical education) did not exist in China.[1] Moreover, the term took a long time to mean what it does today. Once the term had been imported from Japan, it referred more to personal hygiene and general health than physical exercise. And in 1902, when Liang Qichao and others first used *tiyu*, their discussions focused more on preparing the mind and body for war with militarized physical training *(shangwu)*.[2] The phrase *tiyu* consists of two Chinese characters—*ti* means body, and *yu*, cultivation. But when the Chinese began to embrace modern Western sports, *tiyu* developed a significant new meaning: the possibility and mission of nation-strengthening. Its appearance coincided with Chinese ambitions to forge a new national identity and assume a role in the international scene at the turn of the twentieth century.

Throughout this book, I use "physical culture" and "sports" interchangeably with the Chinese expression for several reasons. First, the two represent a very close translation of the Chinese phrase. And second, by using physical culture or sports here, I mean to convey something more than physical training. In the Chinese context, *tiyu* also involves culture, especially public culture—a forum where, as Thomas Bender claims, "power in its various forms is elaborated and made authoritative."[3] For many Chinese who started to embrace *tiyu* at the turn of the twentieth century, this turn to physical culture reflected or responded to a national cry for renewal and a desire to be recognized as a respected power among other nations of the world.

Sports in China before 1895

When Beijing applied to host the 2000 Olympic Games, it emphasized the historical development of sports in China.[4] Doing so was somewhat misleading, because traditional sports in China were not really relevant to the modern Chinese obsession with sports and the Olympic Games. Nevertheless, the culture of physical fitness has had a long history in China. For example, physical education was an important part of Confucian teaching. Confucius and many other sages of the ancient period emphasized cultivating both an individual's intellectual and physical accomplishments. For Confucius, in order to be an educated and useful person, one must develop physical strength in tandem with moral values and intelligence. Physical accomplishment was clearly emphasized as part of the core Confucian curriculum, the so-called Six Arts of ritual mastery, music, archery, horsemanship, literature, and mathematics.[5] Mencius, who lived in the fourth century BC and was another key Confucian figure, also advocated the importance of *lao qi jin gu,* or the significance of enduring physical challenges for creating a great man. In the eras of Confucius and Mencius, Chinese people seemed to realize the linked importance of mental and physical skills. A two-thousand-year-old silk painting from an imperial tomb shows a group of people engaged in fitness exercises.[6] As early as the Warring States era, which lasted from the fifth century to the third century BC, *weiqi,* or Chinese chess (which the Japanese later borrowed and called *go*), was very popular, and many people were also devoted to an ancient version of soccer in the Warring States period and Han dynasty (206 BC–220 BCE) periods.

Other games were also popular in ancient times. According to one historical record, Liu Bang, the founding emperor of the Han dynasty, was surprised to discover after building a luxurious house for his father in the capital that his father was not very happy there: he missed playing a game called *cuju* with his hometown friends.[7] This game, similar to today's soccer, remained popular among both high-society members and the lower classes in Song China (960–1279). An ancient form of polo, called *jiju*, *jiqiu*, or *daqiu*, was also developed during this early period. Sports were visible enough that they attracted the attention of the Han historian Ban Gu, who, in his famous history *Han Shu*, devoted a chapter to individuals talented in a certain sport or martial art or demonstrated other types of exceptional skill.[8] Indeed, the Chinese played soccer and polo with great devotion in the Tang and Song periods.[9]

The origins of some of these early games provide a glimpse of what an international crossroads China had become. During the Tang dynasty (618–907) people from many countries came to the powerful empire's capital, Chang'an, for work, travel, or study. Some scholars have suggested that polo in Tang China might have been brought in by the Persians. In the Song dynasty, a game called *chui wan*, which means "to strike the ball with a stick," similar to modern golf, became popular within elite circles.[10] It is well known, too, that the Chinese have practiced *wu shu* (martial arts such as *tai ji*) and other types of physical exercise for many centuries.

From ancient times to the beginning of the modern period, then, the Chinese people, due to the openness of Chinese society, enjoyed a wide variety of sports. Mongolian wrestling and horse racing, Tibetan foot racing, and Manchurian skating, among other activities, were practiced at different times. One might speculate that these different sports may have also helped shape Chinese views of prowess and influenced the development of specifically Chinese physical arts in the long run.

Nevertheless, China's long history of sport does not necessarily mean that sports were an important part of the Chinese way of life. Although some sports had powerful fans, by and large, few Chinese became skilled in physical games. In fact, prior to 1895, Chinese attitudes in general toward the body and physical training were ambivalent, to say the least. Chinese high culture downplayed the importance of personal physical fitness

vis-à-vis so-called moral cultivation for both men and women. This was especially the case after the Song dynasty, with the rise of neo-Confucianism,
institutionalized civil service examinations, and foot-binding. After the
Song period, games like polo, golf, and soccer gradually disappeared, and
Chinese high culture further emphasized values associated with civilian
rather than military expertise and disparaged the physical activities that
many members of the Chinese elite thought were linked to the common
people, or *lao li zhe* (people who rely on physical strength). Ideas such as
he wei gui, or "harmony and peace are most precious," and *junzi dong kou
bu dong shou* (the gentleman uses words, not fists, to settle disputes) became widely accepted as preferred social norms. Although Mencius talked
about the link between *lao qi jin gu* and the great man, overall his idea that
"those who use their minds and brains rule, and those who use their physical strength are ruled" encouraged the Confucian scholars who led society
and the government to look down on physical education. Consequently,
during the eighteenth and nineteenth centuries, Chinese elites generally
considered sports undignified—a robust body was not consistent with the
idea of the cultured gentleman.

The civil service examination institutionalized since the Tang and Song
dynasties and based on Confucian ideas of merit also effectively led to the
general degeneration of elite men's bodies. The examination system, which
lasted into the early twentieth century, kept Chinese men preoccupied with
Confucian texts and exam preparations and discouraged most of them
from paying attention to "ungentlemanly" physical education.[11] Chinese
men under the influence of this system and of neo-Confucianism idealized
the delicate, indoor genteel life and looked down on the merits of strong
bodies and a warlike spirit.

If the culture of the civil service examinations had worn down the ro-
bustness of elite Chinese men, its most damaging influence was inflicted on
Chinese women in the form of foot-binding.[12] It is perhaps no coincidence
that foot-binding became widespread in the tenth century, at the fullest
flowering of the civil service examination culture and neo-Confucianism,
and was not banned until the examination was itself abolished in the early
twentieth century. During this thousand-year period, and especially in the

Qing dynasty (1644–1912), nearly all Han Chinese women had their feet bound and were therefore physically disabled. We still do not completely understand why foot-binding lasted so long and spread so widely, or just what its social, cultural, economic, and even physical implications were for the Chinese people. Perhaps as Chinese male elites became feminized through a lack of physical exercise after the tenth century, they indirectly forced or at least preferred Chinese women to become "hyper-feminine" through the practice of foot-binding.

The dynasties that followed the Song, despite their differing ethnic and cultural origins and the fact that they all took power on horseback, tended to emphasize an interest in high culture and moral values rather than coercion to govern. The general result was that Chinese society, for nearly one thousand years, was characterized by physical weakness, even frailty. Rarely did Han Chinese elite society encourage physical training. Traditional Chinese novels in early modern times idolized the white-faced bookworm type and women were praised for being as "fragile as a willow." Popular sayings like *wan ban jie xia pin, wei you du shu gao* (everything else is inferior to preparation for the civil service examination) or *hao nan bu dang bing, hao tie bu da ding* (a good man should not become a soldier, just like high-quality iron should not be used for making nails) largely reflected the general mindset that underlay the denigration of physical strength in traditional Chinese society.

The Boxer Rebellion (1898–1900) was a rare exception; during this period a machismo subculture within the larger society used physical skill in a way that strongly influenced Chinese national identity and internationalization. The group was dubbed "boxers" by foreigners. Among themselves, however, they were called Yihequan (Fists united in righteousness) and almost all of their members were poor young male farmers from northern China who had suffered enormously from foreign incursions (later there were female members called Red Lanterns). The Boxers were interesting in that they practiced martial arts, which they believed were animated by the possession of spirits, and showed a strong anti-foreign attitude—especially in their attacks on Christians (both Chinese and foreign) and missionaries. After the Qing court decided to transform the Boxers into an officially sponsored militia and encourage them to target foreigners, the rebellion triggered an international military response, which successfully quelled the uprising. The Boxer Rebellion had a long-lasting effect on Chinese politics and foreign relations. The uprising reinforced negative European perceptions about China and its people—their purported hostility to Christianity, resistance to modern technology, and xenophobia. And the defeat and humiliation suffered at the hands of the international expeditionary forces soon led to the Qing's final fall in 1912.[13]

By participating in the downfall of the Qing, the Boxers precipitated developments that would lead to much broader changes, though this was not their intention. The Boxer Rebellion was the last powerful cry of advocates of traditional martial arts and religion for undertaking political change through the old style of armed rebellion. Although their efforts ended in tragedy, one might argue that the Boxer Rebellion marked a new trend in which physical education was increasingly linked with China's national identity. Prior to 1895, those Chinese who believed in the value of physical exercise were generally focused on personal enrichment. Only after 1895 did the Chinese begin to associate physical training and the health of the public with the fate of the nation. To understand this change, we will want to examine China's relationship with the world at the turn of the twentieth century.

The "Sick Man" and a New World

The year 1895 was a turning point in both Chinese and world history. Leading up to this point, the major European powers were moving closer to the first global war. And China, which called itself "the celestial empire" or "the middle kingdom" (despite having been reduced to peripheral status in the 1840s with the Opium War), was clinging to its middle kingdom dream. China's sound defeat in the first Sino-Japanese War (1894–1895), then, was for the Chinese a shock—a wake-up call that China had to come to terms with a new reality. As a consequence of China's defeat in that conflict, most Chinese elites became convinced that only by giving up its traditional imperial identity and becoming a nation-state could China endure—

and more importantly, only by joining the emerging world order dominated by Western powers did China have any hope of recovering its past
glory.[14] In other words, China finally was ready to learn from the West and
negotiate a new national identity based on Western ideas and practices.
Ideas such as Social Darwinism and survival of the fittest, introduced at
this juncture, prepared the Chinese mentally for their embrace of Western
sports.

Chinese interest in Western sports was directly linked to their rethinking of China's national fate. For many Chinese after the first Sino-Japanese
war, their country had become a "sick man" who needed strong medicine.
The first person to coin the phrase "sick man" was Yan Fu, an influential
scholar and translator of Western books at the turn of the twentieth century. Yan had received an excellent education in both Chinese traditional
culture and foreign affairs, and had spent several years in Britain as a military student. In March 1895, in an article in Tianjin's *Zhibao* titled "Yuan
qiang" (On the origins of national strength), Yan wrote, "A nation is like a
human. If an individual is not active physically, the body will be weak. If a
person is active physically, the body will be strong. This is common sense.
How about a sick man? If he wants to transform his sick body into a
strong one overnight, he is bound to overdo. Pursuing this strategy to become strong will actually speed up his death. Does today's China look like
a sick man?" In Yan's view, the country did seem sick, and to make China
strong again, Yan argued, the Chinese had to improve their physical shape,
intelligence, and moral values. He put physical strength at the top of the
list. He strongly criticized Chinese habits of opium smoking and foot-binding. For Yan Fu, only a healthy mother could produce strong children.[15]

Yan also blamed the civil service examination system for China's frail
condition.[16] If the Chinese really wanted to be strong and rich again, Yan
argued, they had to be physically fit and energetic; a country of weak people could only become a sick nation.[17] As Benjamin Schwartz has written,
for Yan Fu physical strength was "closely associated in his mind with the
psychological values of physical courage and the power of physical endur-
ance. In some ways, the affirmation of man's physical powers and what

might be called the physical virtues would provide the most dramatic man-
ifestation of the new transformation of values."[18]

At some point after Yan had characterized China as a "sick man,"
foreigners started to use the same expression. For example, in 1896 the
Shanghai journal *Shiwubao* published an article translated from a British
journal that labeled China in this way.[19] Since then, this label has haunted
and humiliated the Chinese. Chen Tianhua, in his famous 1903 article
"Jingshizhong," wrote, "Shame! Shame! Shame! This great China, which
for many centuries was hailed as The Celestial Empire by neighbors, is
now reduced to a fourth-rate nation! The foreigners call us the sick man of
East Asia, call us a barbarian, inferior race."[20] In 1904 the writer Zeng Pu
took as his pen name "Dong Ya bing fu" (sick man of East Asia) for his
novel *Nie hai hua* (Flowers in a sea of sin) in part to motivate the Chinese
to reflect on their condition and make efforts toward self-renewal. Although the phrase "sick man of East Asia" may have only rarely had serious currency in Western thinking, for the Chinese, the idea has been part
of their cultural background since the turn of the twentieth century.

The image of China as a sick man motivated many Chinese to think
hard about how to "cure" their nation and eventually led to the introduction of modern sport as one prescription for the Chinese national crisis.
From this perspective, the year 1895 was pivotal. Elites began to question or even repudiate their old identity and culture, including traditional
physical activities. For many elite members of society, sports now meant
Western sports, activities imported from abroad. As Xu Yixiong, a distinguished sports scholar in Taiwan, has pointed out, the adoption of modern sports in late imperial China was fueled by the idea of saving the Chinese race and self-strengthening.[21] Even the conservative reformer Zhang
Zhidong concluded in his influential article "Quan xue pian" (Exhortation to learning) that physical training and China's national survival were
closely linked. Zhang argued that to make the nation strong the Chinese
must rely on *wu gong*, or Western-style exercise and military training.
Liang Qichao, an important reformer and writer, wrote in his 1902 article
"Xin min shuo" (On new citizenship) that "to be civilized, citizens need a

warlike spirit that serves as the essence of a nation. Without this warlike spirit, a nation can not stand." For Liang, this animus was the key factor behind the power and strength of the Western powers and Japan.[22] Liang argued that China had lost this spirit a long time ago; it had become a country of "sick people and as a result a sick nation."[23] Clearly the shame that the Chinese felt about their nation being labeled the "sick man of East Asia" motivated many of them to advocate Western sports. Xu Yibing, a student who returned from Japan, established China's first school of gymnastics in 1908, giving it the motto "Zeng qiang zhong hua minzu tizhi, xi shua dong ya bing fu chi ru" (Strengthen China's physical condition, remove the shame of being Asia's "sick man"). Xu contended that China could only compete with the West when its people paid attention to sports.[24] Even Sun Yat-sen, founding father of the Republic of China, acknowledged that "today we advocate physical exercise because it is crucial for us to strengthen our race and protect our nation." He further stated, "If we want to make our country strong, we must first make sure our people have strong bodies."[25]

At the turn of the twentieth century, then, in the name of making China strong and rich, many Chinese started to push hard to ban foot-binding and abolish the civil service examinations. Indeed, Chinese women's liberation began with this idea of "national salvation": a healthy mother with natural feet was considered vital to the country's goal of producing strong and healthy children. By the early twentieth century Chinese women began to unbind their feet or stopped binding those of their daughters, and left the inner chambers to seek an education and even to exercise. Qiu Jin was an exemplar of this new type of woman. She not only went to Japan to study, but also enjoyed fencing, horseback riding, and other types of exercise.[26] By 1905 both foot-binding and the civil service examinations had been legally abolished.

Jun guomin zhuyi (societal militarism) and *shangwu* (a warlike spirit) were also popular ideas for how sports could be used to save China in this period. Individuals like Liang Qichao, Cai E, and many others all advocated that the Chinese cultivate *shangwu*. In a sense, *jun guomin zhuyi* and *shangwu* were two sides of the same coin. As Zhang Jian pointed out,

"Promoting education that will militarize our citizens is the same as promoting a warlike spirit."[27] Cai Yuanpei, the first minister of education in the new Republic of China and a returned student from Germany, stated even more clearly that the *jun guomin* doctrine not only was appropriately part of physical education, but also was all about the military spirit (*shangwu*) and could be understood as a worldview.[28] He said, "National strength is based on citizens. The people's strength is decided by their physical strength. The physical strength comes from their warlike spirit."[29] Although before the emergence of Confucianism in China important affairs of state had centered on worship and warlike activities (*guo zhi da shi, wei si yu rong*), modern advocates of *shangwu* believed that the practice had been neglected for too long.[30] Interestingly, Avery Brundage, who served as the IOC president during 1952 and 1972 and was not particularly famous for his intellectual observations, wrote in the 1930s about this issue:

> It has come to be my conviction that there was more than a coincidence between the corruption of sport and the ruin of ancient cultures. . . . China offers a splendid modern example pointing to the conclusions I arrive at among the ruins of Mediterranean civilizations. In this most ancient and veritable civilization—the Chinese—physical fitness and its national organization have been neglected. The highly intellectual citizens of China have allowed themselves to be plundered by their own bandits for generations. Nations which have developed physical fitness through the hardships of their environment and constant conflict, with the discipline thereby built up, have done as they pleased with China for generations.[31]

In a context of many unequal—and humiliating—treaties with other nations, many Chinese felt that now was the time for China to reawaken its warlike spirit. Physical education was believed by some to be the only solution to the nation's crisis.[32] China needed to institute national games not only to promote sports but more importantly to help revive the national spirit.[33] Indeed, after the first national games were held in Nanjing in 1910, the government issued the following statement: "[China] is living under multiple threats from abroad; it will have trouble surviving as a nation if most of its citizens have no war-like spirit."[34] In 1914, when China held its second national games in Beijing, organizers welcomed spectators to attend so they could observe the progress the country had made in sports and "show their appreciation and admiration for the war-like spirit [of the competitors]."[35]

The ideal of *shangwu,* which many Chinese elites shared, grew from observing the rapid rise of Germany and Japan during the late nineteenth century. Chinese who went to Japan concluded, as one article noted in 1904, that Japan had succeeded where China had not because it had "a warlike spirit."[36] As for Germany, according to Liu Shuya, a scholar in the early Republican era, the main difference between a weak China and a strong Germany was that "Germans practiced warlike education" but China did not.[37]

Even the young Mao Zedong was completely taken with the *shangwu* idea. In his first published article, "Tiyu zhi yanjiu" (On physical culture), published on April 1, 1917, in the influential journal *Xin Qingnian* (New youth), Mao began by stating that "among today's civilized powers, Germany really stands out; fencing is widespread there, while in Japan, the samurai spirit was very influential. . . . It is absolutely right to say that one must build a strong body if s/he wants to cultivate inner strength." In Mao's view, "Physical education or exercise . . . should be the number one priority." Like Mao, many Chinese were very clear about the national and international implications of sport. One *Shenbao* author wrote about the 1921 Far Eastern Championship Games this way: "The spirit of struggle in athletics is the same as in war. If one is defeated in war, territory is lost. If one is defeated in athletics, reputation is lost. And of territory and reputation, no one yet knows which is more important. . . . We need to be able to perform in athletics before we can talk of war. A nation needs to be able to fight before it can talk of peace. World peace begins with athletics."[38]

The sports referred to here were clearly of the Western variety. Hao Gengsheng, in his book *Physical Education in China,* published in 1926 and "dedicated to a China wise and strong," wrote that the model of physical education pursued at the turn of the twentieth century had been introduced from the West.[39] But what had happened to traditional Chinese sports? Liang Qichao, like other advocates of a modern sports regime, simply dismissed them as having nothing to do with the ultimate goal of cultivating solidarity, moral strength, and a warlike spirit.[40] By contrast, modern sport was believed to create harmony among body, mind, and spirit and could serve as a sort of religion. This belief was not new; it could be found in records of the ancient Olympic Games. For the Greeks, "the idea behind the Olympic games was the development of the complete man, the old idea of the mind in an active and alert body." The concept that sport draws from high culture and physical culture, and that it contributes to one's physical, moral, and mental development, was also obvious in the thinking of Pierre de Coubertin when he decided to revive the Olympics. For him, the Olympic movement aimed to develop understanding among all peoples, as well as cultivate the "complete man."[41] Coubertin, like the Chinese, observed that the German empire was built on "military athletics."[42] He noted the "close correlation between frame of mind, ambitions, the tendencies of a people and the way in which they understand and organize physical exercise."[43]

The thinking of the early twentieth-century Chinese elites thus shared more with the ancient Greeks and Coubertin than with Chinese philosophers and statesmen of antiquity. For advocates of Western sports in China, aligning one's arguments with foreign thinking was a natural outgrowth of a new international mindset.

In the early 1890s, just as Chinese elites were realizing that through Western sports they could take the first steps toward reinvigorating their country, world sport entered a new phase with the revival of the Olympic movement. The hosting of the first modern Olympic Games in Athens in 1896 thus coincided with China's awakening to the new international reality. But the founding of the modern Olympics was also clearly a result of a broader trend toward internationalization. It was German scholars who excavated the ancient Olympic site and Frenchman Pierre de Coubertin who led the campaign for the revival of the Games. In Coubertin's view, bringing back the Olympic Games would encourage "peace among na-

tions," with the participating athletes acting as "ambassadors of peace."
Significantly, Coubertin tried to bring about an "enlightened internationalism by cultivating a nonchauvinistic nationalism."[44] As John MacAloon,
Coubertin's biographer, argued convincingly, Coubertin's "very identity
was wrapped up as fully in his internationalism as in his patriotism."[45]

On June 23, 1894, at the founding congress of the modern Olympic
Games in Paris, Coubertin officially announced the birth of the modern Olympic movement and chose the words "Citius, Altius, Fortius"
(faster, higher, stronger) as its motto. At the dinner that closed the founding congress, Coubertin made the following toast, "I raise my glass to the
Olympic idea, which has crossed the mists of time like a ray from the all-
powerful sun and is returning to shine on the gateway to the twentieth century with a gleam of joyful hope."[46] On April 6, 1896, the first modern
Olympic Games were held in Athens. Coubertin noted, "The important
thing in the Olympic Games is not winning but taking part."[47] The beginning of the modern Olympics thus marked the start of a new era of international engagement.

For Chinese elites, who were looking for direction for their nation,
modern sports and the Olympics with their mix of nationalism and internationalization seemed a possible solution to their problems. The Olympic
Games, as John Lucas wrote, "are both a vision and a search for the extraordinary."[48] This kind of vision was precisely what the Chinese were after. We do not know exactly when the Chinese heard about the revival of
the Olympic movement and the first modern Games, but one thing is clear:
the Olympic call to be "faster, higher, stronger," and to participate in the
world as an equal, matched the ideals that motivated the Chinese most at
that time. After all—theoretically—the new Olympics and other international sports events provided the proverbial level playing field where every
nation, large or small, could take part and be judged by the same rules and
standards. As one scholar has noted, "The first laws ever to be voluntarily
embraced by men from a wide variety of cultures and backgrounds are the
laws of sport."[49] The Chinese not only wanted to compete in sports, but
also—and more importantly—saw the modern Olympic movement as co-
inciding with their broader plans for national renewal.

Internationalizing China through Modern Sports

At the first modern Olympics in Athens, a woman approached Coubertin and asked him whether his Games would be a theatrical reproduction of the ancient Olympic Games with nude actors. No, he replied; these games would be real and worldwide. "Oh, then," she asked, "will we see Indian, Negro, and Chinese performers?"[50] Coubertin did not respond then, but on other occasions he expressed high hopes for the development of sports in Asia. The "yellow men," according to Coubertin, were "ready collectively, because their young imperialism, which has not yet had its fill of domination, will impel them to taste the fresh joys of athletic victories, as well as the honor this brings to their national flags."[51] Coubertin of course had no idea what the thinking was in China about Western sports. In fact, it was the Young Men's Christian Association (YMCA), not the IOC, that was responsible for introducing the Chinese to these games. To be sure, Western sports were first introduced in Chinese territory in the 1840s by foreigners in the wake of the Opium Wars, but at that point they were only played by foreigners, and the Chinese were not encouraged to follow suit. Mission schools also played a role, albeit a limited one, in spreading sports to China. Still, into the late nineteenth century, only foreigners or mission school students participated; most Chinese elites and the general population showed no interest. This situation changed dramatically with the arrival in 1895 of the YMCA representative David Willard ("D. W.") Lyon. The YMCA could not have chosen a better time to encourage the Chinese to play Western sports; that very year China had suffered a defeat at the hands of the Japanese and had begun to wrestle with the issue of nation-building and adapting to the new international situation. The Chinese of the 1890s, like the Americans of the same period, seem to have suffered from what Richard Hofstadter called a "psychic crisis," even though the backgrounds to their respective crises were fundamentally different.[52] The prominent Chinese linkage of *tiyu* with national self-strengthening was clearly fostered in this climate through the efforts of the YMCA in major cities around the country.

With arrival in Tianjin of Lyon, a recent graduate of Wooster College in Ohio, the YMCA started to promote modern sports in China with its coherent and collective effort.[53] In 1899 a Shanghai branch was set up, and by 1922, forty branches were operating across China. From the very beginning, then, the YMCA played a pivotal role in China's modern sports development. The organization successfully promoted modern sports by sponsoring games, journals, and lectures. After J. H. Gray arrived in Shanghai in 1920 to be director of the YMCA's physical education department, he issued a report to the International Committee of the YMCA about the state of physical education in China. He wrote, "A good start was made in the beginning, which showed that China was in the early stages of a great physical renaissance in which the old ideals of the body and of living were being rapidly changed for new and different ones."[54] It was under the YMCA's leadership that the first Chinese national games took place in 1910. The idea of the games came from an American, M. J. Exner, a YMCA official sent to China to provide physical education leadership in 1908. Major officials and referees for the 1910 games were foreigners, and the official language of the games was English. In 1923, when the Far Eastern Games took place in Japan, the leader of China's team was none other than Gray, who delivered a speech to the games on behalf of China.

Interestingly, some YMCA officials understood and even shared the new Chinese obsession with *shangwu*. Charles Harold McCloy is the best example of this group. McCloy worked in China for more than ten years, between 1913 and 1926, and spoke Chinese. Among his other accomplishments, he made the argument to the YMCA office that foreign sports educators in China should speak the local language.[55] In the 1910s McCloy was excited by the new Chinese interest in physical education and in one of his reports wrote, "There is work enough now at hand for fifty men [of the YMCA] to keep busy for fifty years. . . . We just can't do it with the men we have at present."[56] With his writings, lectures, and teachings, McCloy was instrumental in bringing China to international sports both as a YMCA official and later, as a professor. According to another YMCA official, Eugene E. Barnett, "McCloy was more than the activist, the innovator, the promoter; he was also the researcher and the scholar."[57] In one of his many publications, McCloy pointed out that from ancient times, there had been two different cultures: the militaristic and aggressive, and the civilized and passive. Although it was difficult to say which was better, the militaristic and aggressive culture often enjoyed an advantage. McCloy thus reached the same conclusion as many Chinese: if China wanted to survive and win in this dangerous world, it had to follow the militaristic and aggressive model.[58] McCloy's influence in this regard was so great that when he resigned his professorial post in 1926, the acting president of China's National Southeastern University wrote that his departure marked a "loss to the whole field of physical education in this country."[59]

Although some Chinese claim that soccer and golf originated in China, modern sports obviously came from the West. Basketball was introduced in 1895 by an American and volleyball about ten years later. Ping-Pong, an import, eventually became one of the most popular sports in China. Foreigners (especially YMCA officials) and Chinese returning from abroad often introduced Western sports to the Chinese public. (Americans were especially key in this regard.) And under YMCA sponsorship, many future leaders of Chinese sports had an opportunity to study abroad, including Wang Zhengting, the first Chinese member of the IOC; Zhang Boling; Dong Shouyi; Hao Gengsheng; and Ma Yuehan. In fact, until the 1920s, foreigners, especially Americans, remained the driving force behind Chinese interest in sports. No wonder Jonathan Kolatch in his pioneering book *Sports, Politics, and Ideology in China* called the period from 1895 to 1928 "The YMCA era."[60] Only in the late 1920s, when China was striving to recover its national sovereignty, did the influence of the YMCA decline.

But the YMCA was only one of many international agencies that played a role in the development of sports in China. Japan was also instrumental. Sports that were popular in the West, including gymnastics, fencing, rifle shooting, riding, and skiing, had been introduced to Japan after the Meiji restoration in connection with government attempts to modernize the military.[61] In 1903, the Qing court of China adopted this Western-influenced Japanese curriculum as part of its first modern educational system. The Qing's new education model stipulated that all schools establish physical education classes, and as in Japan, these featured not so much sports as military-style exercise. This emphasis became even clearer in the Qing's 1906 revised regulation, which maintained that all school textbooks should promote militarization of citizens and emphasize the idea of *shangwu*—imperatives that were soon inherited by the Nationalist government. After the Chinese Communists came to power in 1949, elements of the Russian system were also introduced into the schools' sports curriculum. Internationalization thus continued under the Communists, even though China changed dramatically in other respects.

Modern physical education, an import from the West, was thus fundamentally different from the old tradition of *tiyu*. But even as the Chinese adopted Western sports, they also gave them new meanings. Sports, for the Chinese, were one avenue to national renewal and equality among the nations of the world, and a means to achieve their desire to be recognized as a respected power. As Andrew Morris recently pointed out, early Republican China's discourse on physical education "was clearly part of the project to reinsert 'China' into an international narrative of history and progress." Morris is correct to argue that "the modern physical culture so quickly accepted as *tiyu* was novel for its systematic" effort to link "individual strength, discipline, and health" with the military, industrial, and diplomatic "strength" of the national body.[62] For the Chinese, *tiyu* not only conveyed a distinct sense of sports, but also the idea that through the forum of sports as public culture, they could articulate Chinese nationalism, the national identity of China, and even the meaning of being Chinese.

Nothing could be a better vehicle for China's international recognition than the modern Olympic Games. Not surprisingly, it was through the YMCA that the Chinese learned of and understood the revived Games. As early as 1907, YMCA officials systematically introduced the modern Olympic movement and the coming London Olympic Games to Chinese audiences. According to the YMCA journal *Tiantsin Young Men*, Zhang Boling, future president of Nankai University, gave a stirring speech about the Olympics and China at a gathering organized by the YMCA on October 24, 1907. He briefly described the history of the Olympic Games in the West and expressed the hope that China could send teams to the Olympic

Games someday. To prepare for entry, he suggested that China first hire Olympic winners from the United States as coaches. Zhang was perhaps the first Chinese national to talk seriously about the Games and articulate the Chinese ambition to take part in them.[63]

Another article published in *Tiantsin Young Men* in May 1908 included similar sentiments. According to the author, although nobody knew how long it would take for China to take part in the Olympic Games, the day would come. It was the duty of the Chinese to make China ready for the moment when the country could not only take part in the Olympic Games, but also host the Games in China.[64] A lecture organized by the Tianjin YMCA in 1908 also fueled these interests. It focused on three questions: (1) When would China be able to send a winning athlete to Olympic contests? (2) When would China be able to send a winning team to the Olympics? and (3) When would China be able to invite the world to come to Beijing for an Olympic Games?[65] According to a YMCA document at the time, "This campaign grips in a remarkable way the heart and imagination of Chinese officials, educators, and students."[66] But China's Olympic dream would have to be deferred for a long time.

The level of sports competition in Asia was generally poor at this early date. Even the Japanese did not take part in the Olympic Games until 1912 and their performance then was not impressive. The first Japanese IOC member, Jigoro Kano, was chosen in 1909 at the IOC's Berlin sessions. To narrow the gap between China and the rest of the world in modern sports and prepare for eventual Chinese participation in the Olympic Games, some Chinese played crucial roles in the founding of the Far Eastern Athletic Association (FEAA). Wu Tingfang, a distinguished Chinese diplomat, served as the president of the association in 1915.[67] The FEAA sponsored the Far Eastern Championship Games, also known as the Far Eastern Games, which took place every two years.[68]

During this period, the American influence continued to be strong. Americans were central to the founding of the FEAA; the Philippines, the launching pad of the Far Eastern Games, was then an American colony. The first games were held in 1913 in Manila; the second games, held in

1915, were in Shanghai. For several years, Hong Kong teams represented China in these games. Among them, the Hong Kong football team was most important and won several championships for China.

In 1934 the Japanese tried to legitimize its control of Manchukuo in Chinese territory by proposing that Manchukuo be made a member of the Far Eastern Games. The Chinese rejected the Japanese proposal and withdrew from the meeting. The regional athletic initiative that had lasted over twenty years dissolved with the Chinese withdrawal, but after World War II, it was replaced by the Asian Games.[69]

Coubertin considered the Far Eastern Games to be a kind of Olympic kindergarten in Asia. On behalf of the IOC, Coubertin contacted the FEAA in the 1910s and wrote enthusiastically about the organization: "Now that the prestige of the IOC had reached their shores, [they] showed themselves quite eager to place their 'Far Eastern Games' under its wing. They felt called to regenerate China, Japan, and Siam."[70] The organizers of the Far Eastern Games agreed with Coubertin that the FEAA was a preparation for better performances in the IOC later. Remnants of Westerners' confused and outdated notions about Asia's potential were still evident, however. In expressing his hope for a sports movement in China, Coubertin explained: "Sport is the apanage of all races. It is not so long since Asiatics were actually considered excluded by nature."[71]

Although few scholars have noticed, China planned to be associated with the IOC as early as the 1910s. According to the minutes of the IOC's Paris session from June 15 to 23, 1914, just before the fatal shot in Sarajevo was to start World War I, China was one of thirty-three countries, including the United States and Great Britain, to receive permission to take part in the 1916 Games scheduled to take place in Berlin.[72] The same minutes also indicated that the Chinese minister to France had attended the official celebration of the twentieth anniversary of the IOC. In its 1919 session, after a period of inactivity during the Great War, the IOC decided that only member nations had the right to send athletes to the Games, although for the short run the 1920 Olympic Organizing Committee might invite nonmember nations outside of Europe to participate. It also confirmed that only national Olympic committees (NOCs) could send athletes

China marches toward the world. The PRC delegation, shown here at the
opening ceremony in Albertville, France, went on to win sixteen gold
medals at the 1992 Winter Olympic Games.

to the Games.[73] Perhaps prompted by the new regulations and under the
sponsorship of the YMCA, the China National Amateur Athletic Federation was established in 1921 and was subsequently, in 1922, recognized by
the IOC as the Chinese Olympic committee. Also in 1922 Wang Zhengting
became the first Chinese member of the IOC (the second member from
Asia); his election symbolized the beginning of China's official link with
the Olympic organizing body.[74]

China and the Shared World of Modern Sports

The Chinese obsession with militarizing its citizens through physical education was not unique. It had surfaced in many other countries and during
many other eras. The ancient Greek Olympics itself was rooted in part in
military training that was then under way in Athens and elsewhere; the

games "were often shaped by considerations of war, and the two institutions had close associations in origins, ideals, and language."[75]

During the early twentieth century, too, the moral panic that the Chinese were feeling about the declining physical condition of their men was similarly affecting many other countries' military self-image. The British, for example, had become concerned about the "fitness" of their young men. When Britain was surpassed by the United States in both amateur sprinting and the strength of their economy, British elites feared for the future of the country. They believed, like the Duke of Wellington, that the Battle of Waterloo had been won on the playing fields of Eton. Thus the inadequate physical condition of men now presenting themselves as military recruits was an obvious cause for concern.[76] The Parliament and the British Medical Association even launched commissions to inquire into the causes of, and solutions to, this problem.[77]

As mentioned earlier, the Chinese understanding of *tiyu*, like the American concept of Social Darwinism at the turn of the twentieth century, emphasized militarizing the national spirit and physical training, rather than an idea of sports as we know it today.[78] The Chinese defined sports as *shangwu* or "fighting spirit"; and Alfred Thayer Mahan, a representative theorist of American expansion in the late 1890s, argued, "No greater danger could befall civilization than the disappearance of the warlike spirit (I dare say *war*) among civilized men."[79] Like Mahan, Liang Qichao and other Chinese thinkers influenced by Social Darwinism linked sports, national identity, and national survival very closely. They argued that Chinese citizens needed to be prepared to defend themselves from foreign invasions if the country were to recover its lost glory. To train the nation's youth for war, the state needed to encourage sports.

The American commitment to this fighting spirit has been brilliantly demonstrated by Kristin Hoganson in her book *Fighting for American Manhood*. For Hoganson, nations have always stressed manliness as a way to survive and compete, and sport has been considered one way to cultivate manliness. Henry Cabot Lodge, an influential American politician at the turn of the twentieth century, clearly linked sports with nation-building. He even exhorted Harvard University, his alma mater, to bolster its athletic program: "The time given to athletic contests and the injuries incurred on the playing-field are part of the price which the English-speaking race has paid for being world-conquerors," he said.[80] Theodore Roosevelt, president of the United States from 1901 to 1908, was a firm believer that men and nations could build themselves through strenuous endeavor.[81] "Greatness means strife for nation and man alike," he declared. Roosevelt despised the men and nations that lacked strength of character: "We respect the man who goes out to do a man's work, to confront difficulties and overcome them, and to train up his children to do likewise." "So it is with the nation," he continued. "To decline to do our duty is simply to sink as China has sunk."[82] Roosevelt proclaimed that "all the great masterful races have been [strenuous] fighting races, and the minute a race loses the hard fighting virtues," it loses its "proud right to stand as the equal of the best."[83] Other Americans also singled out China as an example of a country that had lost the fighting spirit. A contemporary of Roosevelt's, Senator Albert Beveridge, claimed that China's degeneration had resulted from its complacency and lack of a warlike disposition: "There was a time when China was heroic, masterful, consolidated, militant, devotional."[84]

At the turn of the twentieth century, many Americans worried about the perceived decline of the United States and looked for ways to rejuvenate the country. General Palmer E. Pierce concluded, "History shows that a healthy state requires a healthy citizenry," and as soon as "the inhabitants of a country begin to degenerate physically, decay sets in all around and the existence of the state is endangered." Such concerns with physical fitness and national preparedness had, according to sports historian S. W. Pope, "a profound influence on the American sporting culture."[85]

Here again, the development of sports was to a great extent linked to the military, which played a key role in popularizing the causes of physical vitality and the American sporting spirit. In the United States "this vision linking sport and the military was a newly invented" institution. Starting in the 1890s, mandatory physical training was introduced to improve muscular fitness but more importantly to produce "the heroic spirit" across the American military. The Spanish-American War also played an important role in the American embrace of sport and athletics as the most efficient means to cultivate national vitality, citizenship, and the martial spirit, and to restore social order and patriotism.

Americans' experience in World War I further accelerated the development of a national sports culture in the United States. According to one commentator, that "war did much to legitimize sport in the public mind, both at home and abroad, and revealed the utility of physical education to the armed services and to the masses of Americans." The YMCA was actively involved in sports programs for American military during that time and stressed the importance of building "physical manhood."[86]

The Japanese also embraced sports as a means to promote a number of national goals. They adopted a paramilitary version of physical education in the schools in the 1910s. In 1917 the Diet promulgated "Propositions on the Promotion of Military Gymnastics," which stipulated that every middle-school student "be trained to be a soldier."[87] Even in the interwar period, the government showed a persistent concern for patriotism and military preparedness in physical education, a focus that intensified during the Pacific War. From the late nineteenth century until the 1930s, the Japanese used as a model the American approach; from then until 1945, they followed the German example.[88]

Clearly the Chinese desire to achieve *shangwu* and to militarize its society followed world trends quite closely. Modern sports in China were more than amusement or play; they were considered vital to the future of the nation and its position in the world. As we will see, China's efforts to reinvigorate its national identity by embracing Western sports competitions were integral to its more serious game: challenging both its old self and the existing international system on diplomatic playing fields of the new world order.

REIMAGINING CHINA THROUGH INTERNATIONAL SPORTS

The main issue in life is not the victory but the fight; the essential is not
to have won but to have fought well.

Pierre de Coubertin

PARTICIPATION IN SPORT can be an expression of an individual's national identity, political orientation, or culture. To a certain extent, one
even can claim that the way a sport is played and promoted is iconic of an
entire nation's character, reflecting some essential aspects of its culture and
history. It allows us to see that nation in a new light and understand its
self-perception and relationships with the outside world.

Sport is a prominent institution in almost every society because it
draws on and celebrates widely valued characteristics; it commands a distinctive appeal perhaps shared only by religion. The socialization of athletes at competitions around the world, too, fosters the kinds of transnational exchanges that lead to greater understanding among far-flung
populations. The founder of the modern Olympics, Coubertin, put it this
way: "The Olympic movement gives the world an ideal which reckons
with the reality of life, and includes a possibility to guide this reality toward the Great Olympic Idea."[1] The same can be said about soccer's
World Cup. As Franklin Foer wrote recently, soccer is more than a game,
or even a way of life; it is a perfect example of how to successfully navigate
the crosscurrents of today's world. Consequently, the game seems "much

further along in the process of globalization than any other economy on the planet."[2]

Nothing better exemplifies the Chinese obsession with its place in the international arena than its responses to modern sports. For the Chinese, *tiyu* was a vehicle by which they could not only strengthen the sense of nationalism, but also promote an international presence. As Andrew Morris points out, "Without the international context there would be no need to create a modern Chinese nation, and without the nation and its need to impress itself on the minds of all modern citizens, no one ever would have thought to organize, participate in, or pay to view institutions like the Olympics or the Far Eastern Games."[3] Thus sports, especially the Olympic Games and the World Cup, are a form of popular culture that can offer a fresh perspective on modern China, its foreign policy, and its relationship with the wider world. They also provide a clear point of reference for discerning some important experiences that China shares with the rest of the world.

Sports and National Presentation

Involvement in international sport requires membership in networks of transnational organizations, and victories in major sports can become a measure of political legitimacy, modernization, or a people's resolve. All countries use sports to affirm their distinct identity, especially in the case of major international events such as the World Cup and the Olympic Games. No matter how bad the political, economic, or social situations may be, sports such as soccer give a diverse population something to share in the name of national solidarity. This is true even when a nation is in serious trouble, when its politics and economy are in a state of dissolution or divided by regional segregation and rivalries. A recent example is the Ivory Coast's qualification for the World Cup in 2006, which brought together factions and helped end three years of civil war. Here, sports helped unify the country under a single identity, and symbolized hope for a brighter future. Similarly, in the 1950s a wrestler named Riki Dozan brought millions of demoralized Japanese men to their feet by beating much larger, meaner, brawnier foreigners in the ring. That he was in fact Korean was conveniently left unsaid.[4]

A loss in a major sports event, meanwhile, can have a negative effect. For example, a new study shows that when a country's soccer team loses a World Cup elimination match, its stock market, on average, loses nearly half a percentage point in value the following day.[5]

Although modern sports have played a significant role in constructing identities and ideologies since their gradual emergence in the mid-nineteenth century, the political functions of sports became even more pronounced during the twentieth century. In some circumstances, sports have even played an important role in the rise and fall of political systems, as Tara Magdalinski wrote in her study of East Germany. Magdalinski points out that sport in East German history "illustrates the cultural production of a mass historical consciousness, a precursor for national identification," as backed officially by the authorities and sports organizations.[6] For East Germany, it seemed that all major sports events were occasions to demonstrate the country's status and personality on the international stage.

Earlier, the exclusion of Germany from the Olympic Games immediately after the two world wars was a clear statement of German defeat and international isolation. In Nazi Germany in particular, sports had been unabashedly political. To Nazi officials, nonpolitical sportsmen were unthinkable in the new Germany. All athletes during this period had to be trained as fighters for Nazism and tested for their political reliability; no athlete's training was complete until he or she had mastered the details of Hitler's career, along with Nazi principles and racial theories.[7]

If defeat on the battlefield brought exclusion and isolation on the playing field, success in sports could herald a renaissance. Germany's first World Cup victory in Switzerland in 1954 helped lift the country out of the ashes of war. The German victory at home in the 1974 World Cup finals over the Netherlands demonstrated Germany's rising self-confidence, and another victory in 1990 was heralded euphorically as a sign of reunification. The 2006 World Cup finals were calculated to show off the new Germany.[8]

Germany has had a long and complicated journey toward normalcy.

The tragic attack on Israeli athletes by Palestinians during the 1972 Munich Olympics reopened wounds that Germany was desperately trying to heal. In his memoirs, Chancellor Willy Brandt captured the feelings of many Germans after that "Black September" incident: "My disappointment at the time was intense" largely "because the Olympics on which we had expended so much loving care would not go down in history as a happy occasion—indeed, I was afraid that our international reputation would be blighted for many years." As Christopher Young comments, "Both the order of Brandt's regrets (which prioritize the self over the other) and the list of key words—history, international reputation, loving care, and happiness—are telling. Munich was Germany's chance to showcase its rehabilitation as a peace-loving, democratic state."[9]

Sports have also played an important role in how the United States has presented itself to the international community. The world heavyweight boxing prize fight on June 22, 1938, between the (African) American Joe Louis and German Max Schmeling at New York's Yankee Stadium lasted only 124 seconds, but its influence was long-term and widespread. According to David Margolick's recent book on this fight, "No single sporting event had ever borne such worldwide impact. . . . It implicated the future of race relations and the prestige of two powerful nations—which, only three years later, would be at war." For many Americans, the prize fight was more than a sports event. It was a fight between democracy and Nazism, between freedom and fascism. Louis represented democracy in its purest form—the African American who could become a world champion regardless of his race, creed, or color—while Schmeling represented a country that did not recognize this idea and ideal.[10]

Sometimes the behavior of American spectators and athletes colored the perception that foreigners had of the United States. Coubertin wrote of the 1908 London Olympic Games, "From the very first day, King Edward had taken exception to the American athletes because of their behavior and their barbaric shouts that resounded through the stadium. I just could not understand [U.S. delegation leader] Sullivan's attitude here. He shared his team's frenzy and did nothing to try and calm them down."[11] Even today some American behavior regarding sports triggers amusement or annoyance elsewhere. One example is the American habit of calling the national baseball championship a "world series" though it is really a North American series. According to Alan Bairner, "The course of American sport history has been characterized by a tension between expansionism and isolationism."[12] S. W. Pope also maintains that turning Thanksgiving Day from a religious holiday into a holiday strongly linked to football games in the late nineteenth century "connected an Americanized game with the sacred ideals and customs of a nation just one century old."[13]

Many countries, the United States included, invest sports with their political and social values. During the Cold War period, both the United States and the Soviet Union used sports as an arena in which to demonstrate the superiority of their political systems. If the connection between sports and national presentation is very close in these countries, the influence of sports in China is even deeper and greater.

The Nationalist Regime and the Olympic Games

Nothing can bring the world closer than modern sports. Sports organizations such as the International Olympic Committee and the International Federation of Football (FIFA) have more members than the United Nations. (At the start of the 2006 World Cup, FIFA had 207 members and 203 national Olympic committees had joined the Olympic family, while the United Nations had only 191 members.) These sports organizations consider themselves symbols of internationalism. The Olympic flag with its interlocked rings was designed by Coubertin in 1913 to symbolize bringing the people of five continents together, and the lyrics of the Olympic hymn promote international cooperation.[14] Sport like nothing else helps give shape to the single-world idea, in which the same rules and standards apply to everyone regardless of nation of origin, religion, or wealth. Modern sports in theory require that every country's team be treated equally and that no country be excluded from participation.

Fueled by forces of global capitalism, sports have become perhaps the most visible symbol of modern internationalization. Walter LaFeber's book on Michael Jordan clearly demonstrates the power of sport to internationalize.[15] Grant Jarvie and Joseph Maguire have suggested that "dominant, emergent, and residual patterns of sport and leisure practices are closely intertwined with the globalization process."[16] John Sugden and Alan Tomlinson in their study of world soccer wrote, "FIFA can be viewed *both* as a transnational body which promotes globalization (and transnational capitalism), and as a locus for resistance to entrenched forms of imperialist domination, and emergent forms of international and capitalist power."[17]

It was precisely the role of sports in internationalization that most captivated the Chinese. After all, since the turn of the twentieth century, many Chinese elites had been obsessed with how China would fit into and engage with the outside world. Accordingly, China had begun to associate with the international community, driven by flows of social, intellectual, economic, ideological, and cultural resources between China and the wider world, as well as by new Chinese interest in foreign affairs. Modern sports provided yet another area of engagement for China, another opportunity to exercise agency in the process of its own internationalization.

China's participation in the Olympics in the 1932 Los Angeles Games gave a huge boost to this process. Chinese involvement in 1932 had more to do with its determined efforts at internationalization than with a love of the games. Moreover, the country's first appearance on the Olympic stage nearly didn't happen. As late as May 1932, China's official sports body had decided not to participate in the Games due to lack of funding. It planned to send Shen Siliang just to observe, as it had sent Song Ruhai to the 1928 Games. According to Shen, the recently established Nanjing government had even refused to provide any financial support for his trip.[18] But on June 12, 1932, *Shenbao,* an influential Shanghai newspaper, published the shocking news that the Japanese puppet state in China's northeast, Manchukuo, might take part in the Los Angeles Games. On June 17 there was further news in *Shenbao* indicating that Manchukuo would send Liu Changchun and Yu Xiwei to the Games to give the Japanese occupation there international legitimacy. Liu Changchun was China's best short-distance runner and Yu Xiwei, its best long-distance sprinter. Japanese propaganda even claimed that the Los Angeles Organizing Committee had accepted this plan.

This claim would later prove false. Under the terms of the Stimson Doctrine, the United States would not recognize Manchukuo, and the Los Angeles Olympic Organizing Committee, backed by the IOC, refused to allow the puppet government to send a team. But it was clear that the Japanese had planned for Manchukuo to attend the Games by sending the two Chinese athletes to compete.

When the Chinese learned of the plan, they were outraged at this attempt by the Japanese to gain legitimacy for their invasion of Chinese territory. In the uproar that ensued, China's sports organization decided to take part in the Games after all, sending Liu and Yu in China's name. Liu, who had moved to Beijing after the Japanese occupation of Manchuria, issued a statement exclaiming that as a patriotic Chinese he would never play for the puppet state.[19] In the end, only he was available to go to represent China in the Los Angeles Games. Yu Xiwei was quickly put under house arrest by the Japanese to prevent him from leaving to represent China.

Once the members of China's sports federation concluded that China would take part in the Games, they had to act quickly since the deadline to inform the Los Angeles Organizing Committee, June 18, had already passed. On June 26, the committee accepted the Chinese plan to enter the Games.[20] After securing the entry paperwork, Chinese social elites started a public fund-raising campaign that was wildly successful. Zhang Xueliang, Manchuria's chief warlord, donated eight thousand yuan, and Beiping (Beijing) mayor Zhou Dawen presented Liu with a new suit. Indeed, several figures played leading roles in China's participation in the 1932 Games, prominent among them former Tianjin mayor Zhang Xueming, chief secretary of Northeastern University Ning Encheng, and Hao Gengsheng.[21] Zhang Boling, Wang Zhengting, and other important Chinese social and political celebrities also supported the idea that China should send an athlete to Los Angeles to represent the nation.[22]

Liu left Shanghai for the United States on July 8 with Song Junfu, who acted as his coach. Before Liu left for Los Angeles, Wang Zhengting, president of China's National Amateur Athlete Federation, presented him with the Chinese national flag and several National Amateur Athlete Federation flags at a send-off ceremony. Wang reminded him that because this was the first time a Chinese athlete would take part in the Olympics, all eyes would be on him to win glory for China. In keeping with the enormous symbolism of the event, Wang told him it was important that the national flag of Republican China fly among the flags of other nations.[23] When Liu boarded the ship to Los Angeles, people cheered at a special ceremony, sending their hero athlete to the Games with three cries of "Long Live the Republic of China!"[24] Liu arrived at Los Angeles on July 29, just one day before the opening ceremony.

Even Americans understood the significance of China's one-man team. The official Olympic report described Liu Changchun as "the lone representative of four hundred million people."[25] The *Los Angeles Times* reported, "The one-man teams from China and Colombia gathered lots of applause. The Chinese athlete had four officials with him, while Jorge Perry of Colombia was alone."[26] One spectator commented, "China! There's a boy that gets my cheer. All by himself, with a couple of coaches."[27] Liu ran the 100-meter and 200-meter races, but did not even place in the top six. Upon his return to China on September 16, Liu expressed his disappointment that he had won no medals and had thus failed to gain glory for his country.[28]

The 1932 Olympics is often glossed over in world history and especially in American history, since the world was at that moment consumed by the Great Depression. Perhaps as his way of acknowledging the gravity of the economic situation in the United States or his disinterest in the Olympic Games, President Herbert Hoover, contrary to custom, refused to attend. Instead, he sent Vice President Charles Curtis to Los Angeles to welcome the assembled athletes and "warmly hope that the Games may be in every way successful."[29] Nonetheless, Liu's participation in the Games was important for the Olympics and for the Chinese. As Hao Gengsheng explained in a statement issued before Liu went to Los Angeles, China's sending a team to the Games served four purposes: (1) It thwarted the Japanese plot to use the Games to legitimize its puppet state, (2) It signaled the

Liu Changchun was the only Chinese athlete to take part in the 1932 Los Angeles Olympic Games. The official report of the Games called him "the lone representative of four hundred million people."

beginning of a new era, one of Chinese participation in the Games, (3) It promoted exchanges and cooperation among world athletes, and (4) It allowed China to observe and learn from the world's athletic champions. Moreover, while at the Games, Liu could tell the world about Japanese aggression in his hometown of Manchuria and seek the support of world public opinion for China.[30] While in Los Angeles, Liu frequently interacted with people from the United States and other countries and so in a sense brought China to the world. Liu's participation was also important for bringing the experience of the Olympic Games home to the Chinese. During the Olympics, Liu kept a diary that was published in a Chinese newspaper.

Liu himself seemed to be proud of his role in China's internationalization. He later wrote that although he did not win any medals, his "initial intention was to strengthen China's international status" and his "trip served the purpose."[31] Shen Siliang perhaps expressed this significance even better from his perspective of close personal involvement in the 1932 Games. He wrote, "When the Xth Olympiad took place in Los Angeles, the whole world was surprised and amazed to find the Chinese national flag and delegate . . . with the Chinese national flag flying at the games, . . . the whole world realized that China retains a youthful spirit and the determination to compete in the world. China's participation in the Games indicates that it will never give up and will fight against any invasion."[32]

China's participation in the 1932 Olympic Games was thus a turning point in its efforts to enter the international arena. No one could turn back the clock to the earlier days of isolation, not even the relatively inward-looking Communists when they came to power in the second half of the twentieth century. It was true that some Chinese were so disappointed about Liu's performance that they argued China should give up on the Western Games. An editorial in Tianjin's newspaper, *Dagongbao,* for example, suggested that rather than take part in the Olympics, the Chinese should work out their own style of national physical education *(tu tiyu)*. The author went on to argue that Western sports were not appropriate for a poor country like China. The Chinese could not win a world competition.[33]

Yet this defeatism reflected more the Chinese desire for a quick victory than the true national attitude toward Western sports. In fact, the very writing of such an editorial indicates how seriously the Chinese took the event and modern sports generally. After all, victory is not the most important thing in the Games. The essence of the modern Olympic movement is participation, and through participation, the claiming of international stature. In the wake of the 1932 Games, most Chinese who paid attention to sports were realistic about the competitive level of Chinese athletes and did not expect them to place. Instead they set their eyes on diplomatic gains: the chance to express their own national pride, and recognition by the world community. In this sense, Chinese expectations were a good match with Olympic goals. As Coubertin put it, "The main issue in life is not the victory but the fight; the essential is not to have won but to have fought well."[34]

The Chinese appearance in Berlin in 1936 generated even more excitement at home. The Nationalist government's strong interest in the Berlin Olympics clearly indicated their enthusiasm for international engagement through sports. This time the Chiang Kai-shek government was determined to send a large delegation, both for diplomatic reasons and because it genuinely believed in the value of sports for cultivating modern Chinese citizens and a strong nation. Chiang's government funded the entire cost of the Chinese delegation, and sixty-nine Chinese athletes participated. Interestingly, many members of the Chinese delegation came from Hong Kong. For instance, among the twenty-two soccer players, seventeen were Hong Kong Chinese.[35]

Besides its delegation to the Berlin Games, China also sent a forty-two-member study group to Berlin and other European cities to study sports in Europe. Led by Hao Gengsheng, the group included nine government officials, twenty-three representatives of higher education, nine participants from nongovernmental sports organizations, and one military delegate. Their trip lasted over forty days and took them to Germany, Sweden, Italy, Denmark, Czechoslovakia, Austria, and Hungary.[36]

Even with a much larger delegation of participating athletes, the Chinese won no medals at the Berlin Games, although they impressed the world with their brilliant demonstration of martial arts. Many Chinese

Chinese swimmer Yang Xiuqiong from Hong Kong with Hungarian
swimmer Magda Lenkei at the 1936 Berlin Olympics.

Members of the Chinese delegation demonstrate their martial arts skills at
the 1936 Berlin Olympic Games.

were crushed by their loss to Japan in basketball; the Chinese media had
proclaimed that China could lose to any other team, but not to Japan,
which had invaded China.[37] The Chinese basketball team's performance
thus was criticized strongly at home.

Not everyone was unsupportive, however. Lin Sen, a high-ranking official in the Nationalist party, observed, "We should not blame our athletes
for their failure to win medals. This outcome is directly linked to our people's [poor] physical education. . . . If we want to revive the nation, . . . we
have to fundamentally improve our people's health."[38] More importantly,
some Chinese agreed that a medal was not the only objective. As Shen
Siliang remarked after the Games had concluded, during the Games "the
Chinese flag was on all the stands, and in the streets it was plainly seen
with those of other nations. The sight of our delegation, marching in orderly array, training as others trained, participating in games, was all good
propaganda. At least other people are now aware we are a nation to
be counted." Shen insisted, "The achievement of international recognition alone is worth millions to us as a nation and more than justifies the
amount [of money] spent on the tour. . . . I believe [the athletes] have ac-

complished more for China than several ambassadors could have achieved in years."[39]

One government report also pointed out that the main purpose of China's participation was "to encourage Chinese patriotic and nationalistic spirit, and enhance China's international status."[40] By taking part in the 1932 and 1936 Olympics, the Chinese wanted to show the world a new face, a new identity—as well as defiance in the face of the Japanese invasion.

Even with a civil war raging at home, China still managed to take part in the 1948 London Olympics. Once again, the Chinese delegation came up empty-handed in terms of medals. But consider the conditions: this time the delegation was poorly funded and unlike any of the other teams could not afford to stay in the Olympic Village; the athletes eventually ended up staying in an elementary school and cooking their own meals.[41] The Chinese team even had to borrow money to purchase return tickets to China, which luckily, the head of the delegation, Wang Zhengting, managed to do.[42] Given this unfortunate situation, simply taking part in the Olympics was important enough that the Chinese persevered, demonstrating the country's motivation to stay engaged in the world through sports.

Sports and World Revolution: The Chinese Communist Regime

The Chinese Communists and Nationalists were political rivals, with radically different ideologies. But both understood the value of sports for nation-building, expressing Chinese nationalism, and international engagement. Consequently, there were an amazing continuity of participation and interest in sports across the 1949 political divide. True, the Communists were not interested in sports per se when they first came to power. In a report issued in 1953, the party's highest office dealing with sports pointed out that many cadres not only did not understand the importance of sports but "have even ignored sports."[43] Yet the Communists were quick learners, especially when that learning came from "Elder Brother," the Soviet Union. He Long, one of China's top generals at the time, served as the first head of the newly established sport commission in 1952. In that capacity, he declared that China would "learn from the Soviet Union" by translating Russian sports books into Chinese, by sending Chinese athletes to Russia, and by inviting Russian teams to visit China.[44] Largely through its Russian mentor, Communist China seemed to be off to a good start in getting its foot in the door of the IOC and entering the Olympic Games in 1952. Unfortunately, this would be the only Olympic Games in which the Chinese Communists took part until the 1980s because the PRC soon became consumed by the two-China problem. As Chapter 4 examines in detail, Beijing subsequently withdrew from the Olympic movement and other major international sports federations in 1958 to protest Taiwan's membership there.

But the Communist regime continued its efforts to internationalize through sports even after its self-imposed isolation from the IOC. For many years under Mao, sports became a tool of world revolution and remained a key means of cultivating friendly relations with other countries. American legendary football coach Vince Lombardi's maxim "Winning isn't everything, it's the only thing" never occurred to the Chinese; instead Mao and his followers used sports (and other cultural activities) to serve politics and revolution.

Indeed, from the 1950s to the early 1980s, China frequently used sports as part of foreign-policy initiatives. With the slogan "Friendship first, competition second," the Chinese emphasized friendship and camaraderie in their sports exchanges with other countries, playing down the competitive angle. Although the practice is not unique to China, the Chinese have shown unbridled enthusiasm for using sports for political purposes, most especially for strengthening the ruling party's legitimacy and as a means of garnering international prestige.[45]

The best example of "friendship first, competition second" can be found in the sports exchanges between China and North Korea. The Chinese and Koreans described their relationship as being as "close as lips and teeth," and in fact in the early 1950s Beijing fought a war against the United States to save the Korean Communist regime from collapse. It was quite well known that during the 1971 world table tennis championship in Japan that Beijing and the United States launched their famous ping-pong diplomacy, but few know what happened between Beijing and North Korea during and after those games. Prior to the 1971 Ping-Pong championships, North Korea had had reservations about its participation due to concerns about the hostile attitudes of Koreans who lived in Japan and worries about its team's performance. Beijing encouraged North Korea to take part anyway; it promised to help the North Koreans score a victory or two to impress the 600,000 Koreans who lived in Japan.[46] This meant that when the Chinese players were playing the North Koreans, they were supposed to lose some important games to them. But the leader of the Chinese delegation, Zhao Zhenghong, was a military man and not very adept politically. After all, from a military perspective, defeating the opponent was a basic requirement. So he coached the Chinese players to, as the traditional Chinese saying goes, "baxian guo hai, ge xian shentong," or "try your best." The Chinese team included some of the best Ping-Pong players in the world, despite the negative influence of the Cultural Revolution on Chinese sports; consequently, in due course the Chinese defeated the North Koreans 3–0 and eliminated the chances of a North Korean victory in men's singles. In the friendship games between China and Japan, too, the eight Chinese players defeated all eight of the Japanese competitors.

Normally players and teams would be congratulated for victories. But China was not a normal country and this was not an ordinary time. When the team returned to Beijing, Premier Zhou Enlai sternly criticized the team for its victories over Korea and for beating up Japan in the friendship competitions. Zhou took the issue so seriously that he not only forced Zhao Zhenghong to write a self-criticism report; he also insisted that a delegation go to North Korea to apologize. The delegation included the vice minister of the Foreign Ministry, Han Nianlong; the poor head of the Ping-Pong delegation, Zhao Zhenghong; and the miserable Chinese player Xi Enting, whose only mistake was that he won the game against North Korea. Zhou also personally apologized to the North Koreans on April 17 and May 1, 1971, when he met with Korean sports delegations and admitted that China had made a mistake in Nagoya.[47] Later, during the apology mission when Zhao Zhenghong personally apologized to Kim Il Sung, the Korean leader stopped him. As the head of the Ping-Pong team, Kim said,

Zhao had reason to win. "It is common sense that everyone wants to win in a game. Even father and son do not give the other special treatment when they are playing chess. In the world championship game, no country wants to intentionally lose to the other country's team. It does not sound right." But Kim did express satisfaction that the Chinese had apologized; he told the Chinese delegation, "I appreciate Comrade Mao and Comrade Zhou Enlai's effort to strengthen the Chinese-Korean friendship."[48]

Ironically for China, the North Koreans, although appreciating the spirit of "friendship first" that the Chinese offered, rarely passed up any opportunity to beat the Chinese. Perhaps the first time the Chinese learned this lesson about friendship in sport from the North Koreans took place in 1979, as China prepared to take part in the next year's Olympic Games. In the soccer qualifying competitions for the 1980 Olympics, China, Japan, and the two Koreas were fighting for two slots to play in the next round against the two Western Asia winners. North Korea and China plotted to help each other win by secretly agreeing to end with a tie score of 3–3 when they played each other. The idea of the 3–3 draw came from the North Koreans, and the Chinese accepted immediately since China had not completely awakened from the dream of "friendship first" between these two socialist countries. When the score reached 3–3, the Chinese players understandably took it easy. But the North Koreans suddenly scored again, making the tally 4–3. When the Chinese tried to come back, the North Koreans played hard, preventing another goal and sticking the Chinese with a defeat. According to one Chinese source, with this game the Chinese realized that "there is no such thing as friendship in games," even with a socialist brother country like North Korea.[49] But this awakening happened only after the Mao years had ended.

If its revolutionary friendship games took ironic turns, China's plan to advance its international status through the so-called Games of the Newly Emerging Forces (GANEFO) also did not succeed. In 1962 the fourth Asian Games took place in Indonesia. Beijing tried hard to convince the host country not to invite Taiwan to attend. The Indonesian government wanted to please Beijing and therefore agreed to keep Taiwan out. But refusing to invite Taiwan risked eliciting opposition from most members of the Asian Games since it was Taiwan, not Beijing, that was a member of the Asian Games Federation. Eventually the host decided to play a trick. Instead of sending Taiwan the blank identification forms, it sent blank paper instead. When the Taiwanese realized something was wrong, they decided to send veteran sports official Hao Gengsheng to Indonesia to find out what was going on. Hao planned to enter Indonesia by pretending to be a member of the Thailand team. But Beijing informed the Indonesian government of Hao's scheme in time and the Indonesian authorities stopped him at the airport. Indonesia then used Hao's attempted deception, a violation of Indonesian law, to prevent all Taiwanese from entering the country during the Asian Games period.[50] The IOC strongly criticized Indonesia's decision to bar Taiwan and Israel from the Asian Games. It refused to recognize the games and suspended the Indonesian Olympic Committee's membership in the IOC "for its complicity in this outrageous violation of Asian Games and Olympic principles."[51]

Angered by the IOC's decision, the Indonesian president Sukarno announced that the developing countries had had enough bullying from the IOC and would organize their own games, GANEFO. He also stated that the existing organization of world sport was outdated and should be completely revamped, that sport could never be separated from politics, and that international competitions should be handled by government politicians. Beijing could not have been happier with this development and immediately promised full cooperation and financial backing.[52] One source has even suggested that Sukarno's idea of organizing the new games came from Chinese president Liu Shaoqi, when he had visited Indonesia in the spring of 1963 and discussed the IOC censure. On April 20, 1963, Liu and Sukarno issued a joint declaration that in part stated, "The Chinese government strongly denounces the IOC's irresponsible decision to suspend Indonesian rights to take part in future Olympic Games. The Chinese government reiterates its strong support for President Sukarno's proposal to organize games for newly emerging forces. The Chinese government will try its best to make contributions to turn this proposal into reality."[53]

In the end, Beijing did more than it promised. Although in 1963 China had not yet recovered from Mao's disastrous economic policy, the "Great

Leap Forward," which had brought about a famine that killed more than 30 million Chinese, the Chinese government provided enormous financial and material support for the newly established games. When the first such games took place in 1963, China not only sent a large delegation; it also offered to pay the expenses of any "newly emerging nation" that was unable to attend due to financial difficulties.

Before the Chinese delegation left for the games, foreign minister Chen Yi instructed the Chinese athletes that they should not take all gold medals in badminton even though the Chinese team was stronger; they should make sure the Indonesians won some.[54] As a further gesture of Chinese support, vice premier He Long went to Indonesia to attend the games. Since he had a heart problem, his doctor only allowed him to watch the games from the television in his room. When he found out that the Chinese contestant was leading by a large margin in the badminton championship match against his Indonesian opponent, He Long quickly ordered the Chinese player to lose in the spirit of "friendship first." The poor Chinese competitor, of course, had to obey and moreover had to figure out just how to lose since he was far ahead of his opponent. The only thing he could do was to intentionally hit the ball either out of bounds or too low. Even the Indonesian announcer was astonished that the Chinese player suddenly did not know how to play. The Indonesian won the match, but the games themselves were the ultimate victor.[55] On August 18, 1963, Zhou Enlai met with the Indonesian sports team in Beijing and told them that although the games of the newly rising forces were not yet of the level of other international competitions, they were sure to have a great future.[56]

China became involved in the GANEFO so that it could champion developing countries and revolution on an international stage. At the second council meeting of the GANEFO Federation, held in Beijing in 1965 with Zhou Enlai attending, the Chinese government announced through He Long, who was also head of the sports commission,

No matter what may happen in the world, the Chinese people will never shirk their international duty of aiding and supporting peoples of the world in their revolutionary struggle against imperialism. We are determined to unite with all anti-imperialist peoples and carry forward to the end our revolutionary struggle against the imperialists headed by the United States and their lackeys. However desperately and frantically it may struggle, U.S. imperialism can never save itself from doom. Just as Chairman Mao Tse-tung has said, the days of imperialism are numbered. The prospects for us newly emerging forces are infinitely bright.[57]

The tragedy for China was that these new games did not last long and the cooperative relationship with Indonesia soon turned hostile. Beijing's intention to start an alternative sports federation to challenge the Western-dominated IOC and project a revolutionary image to the world ended in vain. But Communist China's idea of using sports to create a different kind of world order did achieve one objective: it garnered the attention of the entire international community.

MODERN SPORTS AND NATIONALISM IN CHINA

Serious sport has nothing to do with fair play. It is bound up with hatred, jealousy, boastfulness, and disregard of all rules and sadistic plea-
sure in witnessing violence: in other words it is war minus the shooting.

George Orwell, 1950

AT THE DINNER THAT CONCLUDED the founding congress of the
modern Olympic movement in 1894, the movement's founder, Pierre de
Coubertin, expressed high expectations for the twentieth century internationalism that would be realized through his Games. But he also acknowledged that nationalistic sentiments were also likely to have a profound influence on the new Olympics, telling the gathered members, "As you toil
on behalf of sport, rest assured that you are working on behalf of your native country!"[1]

Coubertin's motives to found the modern Olympic Games thus "were
a mixture of nationalism and internationalism."[2] Indeed, Coubertin became convinced "that patriotism and internationalism were not only not
incompatible, but required each other."[3] This fact is evident even today in
individual states' responses to the Games and the displays of emotion by
the athletes and audiences whenever their national flag is raised and their
national anthem is played to honor a winner.

The Chinese obsession with both sports and nationalism is not unique
to China; nor is it truly a departure from China's drive toward internation-

alization. After all, only a strong nation will be accepted as an equal in the arenas of global politics and world sports. To associate effectively with the rest of the world, then, China had to first become confident in its own abilities and resources.

A World Shared through Sports and National Pride

From ancient times to modern societies, states have encouraged their youth to participate in sports so they would be ready for the possibility or eventuality of war. For example, as mentioned earlier, modern sports took a giant step forward in the United States when the country became involved in World War I.

Countries have also used sports events to punish other countries for launching a war. After the Great War, for instance, both Belgium and France, hosts of the 1920 and 1924 Olympic Games, respectively, refused to invite Germany to take part. It was not until 1928 that the Germans returned to the Olympic Games, and only in 1931 did the French and German soccer teams again compete. Similarly, after World War II Germany and Japan were not invited to take part in the 1948 London Olympics.

Sports have even been used to take revenge for losses on the battlefield. A good example is the soccer match between Argentina and England after the two countries fought over the Malvinas, or Falklands, in 1982. In the next World Cup after the British military victory, in 1986, Argentina's team defeated England's and went on to win the championship. The star of the Argentine team, Diego Maradona, later wrote in his autobiography *Yo soy el diego:* "More than defeating a football team, it was defeating a country. Of course, before the match, we said that football had nothing to do with the Malvinas War, but we knew a lot of Argentinean kids had died there. Shot down like little birds. This was revenge. It was like recovering a little bit of the Malvinas."[4] During the Cold War era, too, rival teams frequently brought political and ideological hostilities to the arena.

Wars are waged for nationalistic interests, and sports can reflect, strengthen, and even create that nationalism. As James G. Kellas asserts, "The most popular form of nationalist behaviour in many countries is in sport, where masses of people become highly emotional in support of their national team."[5] Grant Jarvie agrees: "It is as if the imagined community or nation becomes more real on the terraces or the athletics tracks." As Jarvie sees it, "Sport often provides a uniquely effective medium for inculcating national feelings; it provides a form of symbolic action which states the case for the nation itself."[6] John Hoberman takes a possibly more nuanced view: "Sportive nationalism is not a single generic phenomenon; on the contrary, it is a complicated sociopolitical response to challenges and events, both sportive and non-sportive, that must be understood in terms of the varying national contexts in which it appears."[7] As Eric Hobsbawm notes, "The imagined community of millions seems more real as a team of eleven named people [of a soccer team]. The individual, even the one who only cheers, becomes a symbol of his nation himself."[8]

Political rivalries can flare dramatically when representatives of opposing governments challenge each other in sports. During the Cold War, when Russians defeated either the American basketball team or the Canadian hockey team, some American commentators reacted as though they were witnessing the collapse of Western civilization.[9] In the 1956 Melbourne Olympics, a water polo match between the Russians and the Hungarians was turned into a version of the Hungarian revolution. The Hungarian team won in a brutal contest for the gold that left the pool streaked with blood. Iran's soccer riots of October 2001 that followed its 3–1 defeat by Bahrain in the World Cup qualifying match represented the largest mass disturbance in the country since 1979. Rioting during an El Salvador–Honduras game in 1969 led to their hundred-hour "soccer war" two weeks later, with two thousand casualties. In 1969, less than one year after Soviet tanks crushed the independence movement known as the Prague Spring, Czechoslovakia beat the Russians in the ice hockey finals in Stockholm. The meaning of the game and its victory went beyond a regular sports competition: as Ian Buruma wrote, "On a night like that, when a humiliated people enjoy a moment of pride, revenge can taste sweet."[10]

And the World Cup finals of 1966, particularly the final match itself, have become part of "the collective memory of the English."[11] That event, like Britain's position in World War II, has since largely engaged its national imagination. Some British fans chant "Two World Wars and one World Cup" whenever England and Germany meet.[12]

In many cases, sports served the cause of nationalism by uniting a population behind a single national competitor. A classic example was the match between the Irish-American boxer John Heenan and the English champion Thomas Sayers in 1860, when the American union was in danger of collapse. Heenan emerged victorious after an exhausting forty-two rounds. The match, as Elliott Gorn commented, by "deflect[ing] internal divisions onto an outside enemy," allowed fans to "experience a rush of patriotic fervor precisely" when the country was perilously close to dissolution.[13]

The 1984 Los Angeles Olympics likewise combined American nationalism and anti-Soviet propaganda. According to Bill Shaikin, the most common complaints about the Los Angeles Games were generated by "excessive displays of U.S. nationalism and the allegedly meaningless domination of U.S. athletes. . . . Spectators found an official 'Olympic Cheering Card' inside their program. The letters 'USA' appeared on the placard in red, white, and blue, and fans were instructed to 'show your colors with pride' by waving the card 'proudly for all the world to see.' . . . It was of little concern to Olympic sponsors if some spectators did not happen to be Americans or did not plan to root incessantly for the home team."[14]

U.S. boosterism was not simply a Cold War phenomenon. It resurfaced as the country became the sole superpower in the world politically and militarily. In 2006, to prepare for a strong showing at the 2006 Winter Olympic Games, the American Congress swiftly passed a provision that would allow Tanith Belbin, a Canadian ice dancing champion who has lived in the United States only since 1998, to immediately gain American citizenship; President George W. Bush signed the bill as soon as it reached his desk. Belbin and her partner, Ben Agosto, became the U.S. ice dance champions and went on to finish second at the 2005 world championships;

they were considered strong contenders for a medal at the 2006 Winter Olympics, in an event that U.S. athletes had never won.[15]

The Soviet Union's history in this area is also interesting. For many years after the Bolshevik Revolution, the Soviets refused to take part in international sports competitions such as the Olympic Games, following a precedent set very early by Soviet leaders, who considered sporting events too bourgeois.[16] Eventually, after the Soviet government realized the value of sports for promoting its political causes, the country's attitude toward sports underwent a complete about-face. They decided not only to join the so-called Western games, but also to win at any cost. Soviet journalists frequently wrote, "Each new victory is a victory for the Soviet form of society and the socialist sports system; it provides irrefutable proof of the superiority of socialist culture over the decaying culture of the capitalist states."[17] Once the Soviets joined the Olympics in the early 1950s, sport was officially considered "another sphere, another criterion for evaluating the advantages of the Soviet political system. . . . Competitions are not just sports events. They carry a tremendous ideological and political charge, they demonstrate the aspirations of the Soviet People." Soviet athletes go out and win medals "for the motherland, for the Party."[18]

Even Canada, a country never known for its strident nationalism, has not been able to resist the temptation to associate sports achievement with national prestige. Take the case of Ben Johnson, a naturalized Canadian citizen from Jamaica. Johnson's victory over Carl Lewis of the United States and his world record performance in the Seoul 1988 Olympic Games set off celebrations across Canada, "including a nationally broadcast congratulatory telephone call from Prime Minister Mulroney."[19] As sport sociologist Steven J. Jackson observes, "Johnson's mediated representation during his reign as world champion, an achievement which brought Canada international recognition and prestige, reveals a temporary displacement of his racial identity." Johnson had become "Canadian," not "Jamaican-Canadian" and definitely not "Jamaican." He embodied a "Canadian" work ethic and achievement orientation and his successes on the track had been translated "into a symbolic representation

of Canada's pride, strength, and independence and a national identity."
When Johnson tested positive for anabolic steroids in the Seoul Olympics,
however, Canada felt ashamed. As Jackson points out, "Following the initial shock, disbelief, denial, and shame, there appeared to be a wave of
abandonment and resentment." According to Jackson, even Johnson's Canadian identity was called into question.[20]

This same process of co-opting athletes occurred during the 1930s,
when the militarist Japanese government used sports competitors of other
origins to promote Japanese nationalism.[21] During this period, after Japan
had turned Korea into a colony, the Japanese generally treated Koreans as
second-class subjects. But when Sohn Kee-chung of Korea competed in
Berlin as a member of the Japanese delegation under his imposed Japanese
name, Kitei Son, and won the marathon, the Japanese were happy to claim
his glory as Japan's national honor.[22]

Of course, the close link between national honor and sports is only ad-
vantageous if the home team wins: indeed, governments can feel the need
to pacify the public if an international match ends in defeat. The most recent example of this defensive posture occurred in 2006 after Iran failed to
qualify for the second round of the World Cup finals: both the coach and
the head of the soccer federation were fired summarily by the government,
which then issued an apology to its citizens for the embarrassment caused
by the team.[23] Such concern is not without foundation; sports certainly
have been the catalyst for uprisings in Eastern Europe and elsewhere that
eventually led to regime change. In the so-called Red Star Revolution,
for example, the Belgrade soccer fans played an important role in top-
pling Slobodan Milošević's regime. Sports also played an important role in
the Paraguayan revolution, which destroyed the Alfredo Stroessner dictatorship.

Although the Olympics were designed to be nonpolitical games between individuals rather than competitions between countries, they have
been employed repeatedly for political ends. The Chinese not only participated in this world trend, mixing sports with nationalism; they brought it
to a new level by defining sports almost completely in terms of nationalism
and politics. As established earlier, the Chinese have long identified sports

with a warlike spirit, and in so doing have equated sports with aggressive nationalism.

Strengthening the Race and Saving the Nation

The introduction of Western sports to China at the turn of the twentieth century clearly indicated the cross-border movement of ideas between China and the world, and provided an index of its emerging internationalization. This progressive movement was not imposed by others; on the contrary, the Chinese chose to pursue it. As explained in earlier chapters, China was looking for ways to make itself, the "sick man of East Asia," healthy and strong again. For many among the Chinese elite, Western sports were considered a possible solution. The logic seemed obvious: "countries where physical education was widespread were progressive and strong, while physical education was less widespread in weak and poor countries."[24] As Tianjin's influential *Dagongbao* explained in a 1920 editorial, "Encouraging physical training among the Chinese is essential to saving the nation and strengthening the race *(jiuguo qiangzhong)*."[25] *Shishiyuebao* (Current events monthly), an important magazine based in Nanjing, the new capital of the Nationalist government, similarly noted, "The purpose for our advocating physical education focuses on removing national shame and supporting national survival and national renewal."[26] In the 1930s, "training strong bodies for the nation" became a widespread slogan and even a guiding sports ideology. Zhang Boling, president of Nankai University and an influential leader of the Chinese sports organization, wrote,

> China has been called a sick man for a long time; only recently have the Chinese tried to discover the reason for China's sickness and for other countries' health and strength, in hopes of finding a prescription for China. This is good. I recently went to Japan to attend the 9th Far Eastern Championships and witnessed the remarkable progress the Japanese have made in their physical education. It will take a long time for China to catch up with them. However, where there is a will, there is a

way. . . . Let me recommend two ways to improve our physical education. They include a long-term solution and a short-term fix. In the long term we need to have mandatory physical education from elementary school on and must encourage the whole nation to develop a lifelong habit of physical fitness. The short-term fix is to organize many games and competitions between Chinese and foreign teams. This type of direct competition may help the Chinese learn not to fear competing. If we carry out both these suggestions, with effective and quality training, we may achieve very good results down the road.[27]

Many other members of the elite shared Zhang Boling's views. On May 10, 1932, General He Yingqin, who had served as Chiang Kai-shek's minister of defense, suggested that the education ministry and government should encourage physical education and instill a military spirit in the public.[28] The 1930s slogans *jiuguo qiangzhong* (save the nation and strengthen the race) and *tiyu jiuguo* (use sports to save the nation) were popular across China. Liu Shencheng wrote in his influential article "Tiyu jiuguo lun" (On using physical education to save the nation), published in Shanghai, that the Chinese nation had reached a dangerous juncture, due to the Japanese invasion and domestic problems, and that only sports could save the nation. He explained that his *tiyu jiuguo* idea consisted of two parts: using *tiyu* to improve the personal character of the Chinese, and revolutionizing physical education across China. His goal was, through physical training, to make the Chinese brave, determined, and decisive.[29]

Launching a sports program to save a nation may sound naive, but Chinese intellectuals were willing to try anything and everything to defend their country against the impending invasion. The war with Japan was a total war, and victory would be decided both on battlefields and on the home front. It was in these pressing circumstances that the idea of *tiyu jiuguo*, like *jiaoyu jiuguo* (use education to save the nation), became a rallying cry. Not until after the long war with Japan ended in 1945 did the expression *tiyu jiuguo* disappear from the public vocabulary.

Of course, not everyone was a big fan of Western-style athletics. A few influential Chinese argued that the nation should focus on its traditional sports (*guoshu*) instead of blindly imitating the West. Chen Dengke, who

had studied in Germany in the early 1930s and admired German militarized sports, was one who took this position. But regardless of whether
traditional or Western sports were pursued, the objective was the same: a
stronger China. When Chen argued that the essence of *minzu tiyu* was to
encourage every citizen to engage in physical training *(quan min tiyu hua)*
and to militarize sports *(tiyu jun shi hua),* he was advocating that the Chinese "should exercise for the state, exercise for the nation."[30] He also
pointed out that *minzu tiyu* might come to include foreign sports, once the
Chinese had turned them into their own.

Echoing Chen Dengke's appeal for strength, Wang Zhengting wrote in
1930 on the significance of the Olympic Games: "If people want to pursue
freedom and equality in today's world where the weak serve as meat on
which the strong can dine, they first must train strong and fit bodies."[31] In
1928, the Central Academy of National Sports was established to fortify
the nation and race, and rid the Chinese of the hated "sick man" label.[32]

During the 1930s and early 1940s, Chinese scholars, educators, and
politicians put their nation-saving ideas about sports into practice locally
and nationally. Chiang Kai-shek's unification of China and the establishment of a national government after the long disunity that followed the
fall of the Qing made this possible. Chiang, a military man, immediately
raised the profile of sports in government policy when he became the national leader. His Nanjing government, established in 1928, passed the first
sports law in Chinese history the next year. Called *Guomin tiyu fa* or the
Citizens' Physical Education Act, the law's very first clause stated, "It is the
responsibility of every young man and woman of the Republic of China to
pursue physical exercise."[33] Several years later, on November 28, 1936, the
law was expanded to include the young and the old; its first clause stated
that improving one's physical condition is "every citizen's responsibility to
the nation."[34] In 1941 another revised sports law was enacted that dealt
more with practical issues such as budgets and teacher training. If the first
sports law was motivated by the urgent need to build the nation, the second focused more on national defense.[35] Wu Zhigang was perhaps right to
call the period from 1927 to 1937 the "Golden Period" of physical education and athletics in modern China; during the Nanjing Decade "many

new athletic records were established and sound school physical education programs were provided."[36]

To make sure local officials paid attention to the new law, the Nanjing government issued instructions about the importance of physical education. One such missive from the Ministry of Education stated, "Physical training is the key to make both citizens and the nation strong. Recently with the encouragement of schools, students have made substantial progress in their physical training. Yet the non-student citizens have not paid enough attention to their physical condition. The ministry hopes each provincial board of education will take physical education seriously and promote it."[37] In October 1932 the Nanjing government went a step further, publishing bylaws governing a special physical education committee within the education ministry that was to direct and facilitate all national sports-related activities.[38] Also in 1932, the Nationalist government organized a national conference on physical education in order to emphasize the link between a strong race and a strong nation, between physical exercise and national revival. The conference declared, "The rise and fall of every nation in the world depends on its citizens' physical situation, weak or strong. That is why this government strongly pushes for our citizens' physical education in order to improve the overall health of our citizens and further revive our national spirit."[39] The organizers of the 1933 national games, in the notice they sent to local and provincial governments about the games, wrote, "At this moment of national crisis, China cannot survive without national unity, the nation cannot be saved if we cannot develop a new national spirit. Since the Great War every European nation has made efforts to advocate sports because their citizens' physical condition is closely related to their national rise and fall." Indeed, the national games in China at this critical juncture were meant to draw Chinese attention to sports and advance the country's chances of survival.[40] In the games' opening ceremony, the organizers again reminded the participants, "We must understand that the most important thing for the Chinese is that we create a healthy people if we want a strong nation."[41]

Even the Nationalist party organization got involved in the drive to promote physical education. At its fifth national congress in November

1935, Wang Zhengting and other members submitted a proposal for the assembly's consideration titled *Jiajin tichang quanguo tiyu, yi shuli fuxing minzu zhi jichu an* (A measure to immediately promote physical education nationwide to establish a foundation for national revival). The proposal began, "The rise and fall of a nation depends on its citizens' capacity to defend their country, its citizens' physical strength, and how united they are. For the last couple of years, competition among the great powers has escalated and therefore the need for [China's] renewal and transformation becomes more urgent and the responsibility to defend and protect the country becomes greater." The proposal further stated that when the great powers emphasized the importance of their citizens' physical strength, weak countries like China should take note, and its citizens should develop a sense of urgency about improving their physical condition. The document proposed three measures for improving Chinese fitness: (1) increase the budgets for physical training, (2) nominate officials from all levels of government to become specialized in training citizens to be more physically fit, and (3) establish more centers to train physical education specialists.[42]

The government and Nationalist party were pressured by members of the social elite to take this issue seriously, through groups such as Guomin canzheng hui (Association for citizens' participation in politics). This association included elites in many different fields such as higher education and industry. In early 1939, association members Shen Junru, Liang Shuming, and others submitted a proposal to the central government called *Tichang shangwu jingshen yi gu guo ji er li kang zhan an* (Measures for promoting a warlike spirit to strengthen the nation's foundation and aid in the anti-Japanese War). The proposal noted that "bad habits and customs over thousands of years have made the Chinese physically weak. They have jeopardized both the individual's body and national survival." Now as the Chinese were fighting a prolonged war with Japan, "It is important for us to encourage a warlike spirit."[43]

The implementation of any government policy largely depended on Chiang Kai-shek, who ran China as a strongman. Chiang, a military man, was the perfect person to promote physical education. From 1928 to 1945, he made many speeches about the importance of citizens' physical condition to the nation's destiny. For instance, Chiang addressed the Fourth National Games, held in April 1930, three separate times to impress the participants and their local sponsors with the central government's attention to sports.[44] And on March 2, 1935, Chiang issued a telegram statement to local governments and other government branches pronouncing that "Physical training . . . is one of the most important elements strengthening the race and saving the nation." He declared that the government would promote sports aggressively and make sure that physical training was embraced by everyone who worked for the party, the government, the military, or the schools.[45] Chiang sent a second telegram message one month later (April 1935) that again stressed the importance of citizens' physical training to the nation's future.[46] And at a national conference of Chinese youth leaders, Chiang made another speech on the importance of physical exercise. He asked, "Why do foreign aggressors dare to look down on China?" and went on to answer: "Because the Chinese are weak physically and inferior to them. The decay and weakness of our citizens' physical condition has been our nation's greatest shame." He told his audiences, "From now on, we have to work hard to make our country strong, if we don't want to be despised by other nations, and our foremost task is to emphasize physical education and work on it."[47] He continued to make many of the same points in a long address to the national conference on sports and physical education organized by the central government in October 1940. Leaders of the conference responded by issuing the *tiyu* declaration that clearly linked sports and physical training with the nation's fate and national development.[48]

Chiang Kai-shek's government policies were not just empty talk. When Chiang first came to power, his government turned "training strong bodies for the nation" into one part of his New Life Movement (xin sheng huo yun dong), which was launched in the 1930s. Robert Culp in a recent article argued that "during the Nanjing Decade, military training classes became a fundamental part of physical education and civic training at high schools, colleges, and professional schools. Military training was introduced and developed through a complex interaction among educators,

Symbols of Republican China's Sixth National Games, Shanghai, 1935.
The top two symbols are the commemorative buttons issued for this event;
at the bottom are pictures of medals given to the winning athletes.

party and government leaders, and the students themselves."[49] Producing a militarized body citizenry had been an obsession among China's elite since 1895, but only with the establishment of the Nationalist government in 1928 did this militarization become a coherent part of national ideology and government policy.[50] The New Life Movement aimed to create a new type of citizenship that would cultivate courage and the "warlike spirit."

Unfortunately, the movement failed under pressures from the all-consuming war efforts against Japan and the Communists; even so, the Nanjing government's other sports initiatives enjoyed some success. For instance, in 1942, the Nationalist government announced that September 9 would be celebrated as physical training or sports day. On this day, each agency was to organize games and other types of physical fitness events, funded by education boards at each level of government. As Chiang explained: "The purpose of establishing a physical education day is to make sure that everyone in China—men and women, old and young—understands the importance of physical exercises and practices them regularly. . . . If we want China to be an equal member in the family of nations, our citizens must be healthy and strong."[51]

Even while the Nanjing government was at war (first with Japan and then with the Communists), it succeeded in organizing several national games. The Chinese National Games had been initiated in 1910 under the auspices of the YMCA. Between 1910 and 1948, when the Nationalists organized the last games held on the mainland, seven National Games were held. The first two occasions were controlled by foreigners, namely YMCA officials, but the third was organized by the Chinese themselves and motivated largely by nationalism. Nationalist China also actively took part in the East Asian Olympic Games, which were held ten times from 1913 to 1934.[52] In addition, the Nationalist government in mainland China participated in the 1936 and 1948 Olympic Games.

Sports and Chinese Nationalism in Practice

For a country like China where sports have long been largely controlled by the state, sports are a means of politics and national presentation. Indeed, Chinese interest in sports and the Olympic Games in particular has more to do with the Chinese desire to be rich and strong, and to show the world that China is the equal of other nations, than with a love of the Games. In this sense sports and Chinese nationalism are difficult to separate. The clear articulation of the link between sports and patriotism was a major development of the Republican era. As one Chinese wrote in 1914, "If we want to instill nationalism [in our citizens], it is absolutely necessary to have sport competitions."[53] Wang Huaiqi, a physical education specialist, wrote in the early Republican period that regimens of physical education may help students gain awareness of China's national and international struggles.[54] Sun Yat-sen also saw the clear link between sports and nationalism. Sun had argued several times that only a physically active and fit people could make the nation strong and powerful.[55] The only way for the Chinese to prove themselves, as some Chinese writers have noted, "is to win at sports." In this sense, sports victories equal national honors. If the Chinese win, the nation wins. If they lose, the nation is humiliated.[56]

Fueled by this feeling, any games, including the games sponsored by schools, were taken seriously in a political sense. For example, on May 21, 1915, Jiangsu Province's No. 2 Women's Normal School sponsored a sports competition that had two slogans with obvious nationalistic spirit: "Let us use the spring rain to wash away the shame," and "Let us mobilize and never forget May 9."[57] (May 9 was considered a day of national shame because it was on that date, in 1915, that the Chinese government was forced to accept most of Japan's infamous Twenty-one Demands.[58]) One teacher even invented a flag exercise called *wu yue jiu ri xin qi cao* (new flag exercises of May 9). The inventor of this exercise arranged the flag holders to follow the lines of the characters "May 9" to remind students and teachers of the national shame and motivate them to make China strong enough to take revenge. To remind students of the importance of national unity, another educator of the early Republican era created a game called *wuzu gonghe* (peace and harmony among the five nationalities), which emphasized the brotherhood of China's nationalities, a shared spirit of bravery, and a fighting mentality.[59]

Perhaps the best example of the Chinese nationalistic obsession with sports can be seen in the first book in China about the Olympiad. Its author, Song Ruhai, who worked both for the YMCA and China's amateur athletic association, transliterated Olympiad as *wo neng bi ya* or "I can compete!" for two reasons: *wo neng bi ya* sounds much like "Olympiad," and the Chinese expression conveys the encouraging idea that the Chinese can compete if they have the determination and courage.[60] In his 1929 preface for the book, Wang Zhengting wrote that ever since China had been dragged into the international political and cultural arenas, "the Chinese have been known in the world as culturally non-militaristic and physically weak. Only in recent decades have some Chinese educators learned the value of a healthy body to intellectual development and started to emphasize sports."[61] Yu Rizhang also wrote in 1929 in his preface to the book that "the neglect of physical training is one of the most important factors behind China's decline."[62]

In the 1920s, the drive for *tiyu,* according to Andrew Morris, "became a widely accepted component of future Chinese nationalisms of all stripes."[63] Modern sports in China may have been largely defined by an internationalist character, but it was the strong link between modern *tiyu* and China's nation-building, the blending of nationalism and internationalization in sports, that made it so compelling. During the early 1920s, especially during the period of 1922–1924, a widespread anti-YMCA sentiment developed in China, which reflected a general push to recover national sovereignty, including control over sports and education. In July 1923, the Chinese decided to create a new organization, called the Chinese Athletic Association (Zhonghua tiyu xiehui), in opposition to the YMCA-dominated China Amateur Athletic Union. The YMCA was denounced as an agent of America and accused of "training running dogs of imperialism."[64]

The Chinese were not the only ones to make an association between sports and American imperialism. Decades later the Canadian sports historian Geoffrey Smith commented, "In most global sport—so much of it Americanized—we behold a new and insidious form of imperialism." This so-called imperialism was especially insidious for its "absurd monetary stakes" and its attractiveness to "millions around the globe."[65]

If nationalism strongly colored the Chinese embrace of modern sports, it also continued to be bound up with overcoming the "sick man of East Asia" label. One famous physical educator linked Chinese performances in international games to that hated label.[66] In addition, important athletic victories by Chinese individuals and teams were pointed to as evidence of a reinvigorated China. During the YMCA-sponsored track and field games in Shanghai in 1905, for example, when the Chinese runner Ma Yuehan surged past his Japanese competitors, Chinese fans first cheered for him, but then, as he went for the win, switched to "Go China! Go China!"[67] Similarly, after the November 1926 football playoff in Shanghai between the Shanghai American School and two Chinese teams, which the Chinese won, the American school's cheerleading squad dedicated a transnational cheer to the victors:

> What's the matter with China?
> She's all right!
> Who's all right?
> Who won the game?
> China![68]

In this episode we see that even winning a school game was regarded as an omen for the future of the nation. These examples are not unique. The Chinese often treated sports competitions, especially between China and Japan, like battles between two rival nations. For the Chinese, *tiyu* not only strengthened the national spirit, but also represented new possibilities for improving China's international stature through victories on the playing field.

Despite the PRC's vigorous insistence that it had made a total break from the past, the new regime linked sports with nationalism and nation-building much like its predecessors had. The Communists even continued to promote the warlike spirit in sports. In 1952, when the PRC finally decided to establish a national sports commission, it chose a military man, He Long, as its first leader.[69] In Communist China, athletes who defeated Japanese competitors were hailed as national heroes, and their performances were praised as expressions of Chinese national honor. In the minds of many Chinese, if their countrymen won, the nation won. If they lost, the nation was humiliated.[70] The famous Chinese Ping-Pong player Zhuang Zedong remembered that when he took part in the Twenty-sixth World Table Tennis Championship, he considered his "every shot against the Japanese players revenge for the Chinese [who had suffered from the Japanese invasion]." He strove to "win honor for the whole nation, and for Chairman Mao." Before the championship games between the Chinese

In 1959, PRC leaders attended the PRC's first National Games,
held in Beijing. From left to right (seated): He Long, head of the Chinese
National Sports Commission, Lin Biao, Zhou Enlai, Zhu De,
Mao Zedong, and Liu Shaoqi.

and the Japanese, one senior Chinese official told Zhuang that if he defeated the Japanese, he would be celebrated as a national hero.[71]

A similar attitude prevailed in November 1981 when the World Women's Volleyball Championship games took place between the Chinese and the Japanese. The Chinese team was destined to win the championship because they had defeated the Americans in an earlier game, so at first they did not play their hardest against their Japanese opponents. But their enraged coach, Yuan Weimin, screamed at them during a timeout: "Do you understand whom you are playing against today? You represent the Chinese nation! The people of the motherland want you to play hard! . . . They want you to win every game [against the Japanese]!"[72] In March 1981, too, when the Chinese men's volleyball team defeated the South Koreans, students in Beijing were so excited that they shouted the slogan: "Unite and renew China!"[73]

In a similar way, throughout the 1980s the whole nation was obsessed with the heroic victories of Nie Weiping, the Chinese *weiqi* player, over his Japanese opponents (*weiqi* is better known in the West by its Japanese name, *go*). The new sense of nationalism had become deeply rooted even in this traditional form of chess. According to Nie, he benefited greatly from support he received from top leaders of the country such as the foreign minister Marshal Chen Yi and Deng Xiaoping. Chen Yi frequently told Nie that he should develop his skills well enough to defeat Japanese players and "win glory for the nation."[74]

One can even argue that when the Chinese followed the practice of "friendship first, competition second" during the Mao eras by intentionally losing to opponents, they did so because they had developed such confidence in their athletic superiority that they could afford to treat the outcome of a match as a political gambit. In other words, their intentional losses did not hurt China's national honor; instead, they enhanced China's prestige, because everyone recognized that the Chinese team was giving away the win.

From the late 1950s to 1966, the year the Cultural Revolution began, the Communist party was careful to maintain control over Chinese sports. According to the PRC's official policy since its founding, sports were to fall under the party's leadership, athletic teams were to follow the party line, and, in certain major sports, China was to strive to catch up with and even surpass the world's top levels of performance in three to five years.[75] On February 11, 1954, Zhou Enlai said at a state council meeting that "we must understand the link between sports and the nation's future."[76] At this point, the winning of gold medals, the raising of the national flag, and the sounding of the national anthem at awards ceremonies were considered essential to China's rise as a nation and its prestige in the world. In 1955, Beijing sponsored its first Workers' Games and He Long made a speech in the opening ceremony claiming that sports were an important political task for the new regime.[77]

Only during the Cultural Revolution did China break away from its obsession with sports victories. The radicals during that period claimed that the Chinese policy toward sports, with its emphasis on chasing medals, had moved in the wrong direction. Their draconian solution was to put the sports programs under military control. During this traumatic era several world-class athletes such as Rong Guotuan, the renowned Ping-Pong player, committed suicide. But as we will see, what happened to sports during the Cultural Revolution was an aberration; themes of nation-building and defense soon resurfaced to influence the next stages of the history of Chinese sports.

THE TWO-CHINA QUESTION

Zilu [Confucius's disciple] asked: "If the ruler of Wei [state] were to entrust you with the government of the country, what would be your first initiative?" The Master [Confucius] said: "It would certainly be to rectify the names. . . . When language is without an object . . . the people do not know where they stand."

The Analects (13:3)

FOR PIERRE DE COUBERTIN, the modern Olympiad was established in a spirit of "all games, all nations."[1] In a dispute over the participation of Bohemia and Finland in the 1912 Games, Coubertin reminded the parties that there existed a "sports geography" that was quite "distinct from the political geography."[2] Thus he preferred to allow Bohemia and Finland—which belonged to the Austro-Hungarian and Russian empires, respectively—to participate as independent entities. But Coubertin was perhaps naively optimistic in his outlook. Individual governments usually did not buy his high idealism when political interests and issues of legitimacy were involved. Some states, though not all, did as they pleased when it came to dealing with the Olympic Games and movement, as when Great Britain refused to allow Ireland to participate independently in the Seventh Olympiad in 1920, and the Irish athletes refused to compete under the British flag.[3]

Until perhaps the early 1990s, then, the IOC purposely claimed that it recognized national Olympic committees, not nation-states. Thus the IOC in principle can certify a national Olympic committee for any territory. For instance, there are three national Olympic committees that are

U.S. territories: the U.S. Olympic Committee, the Puerto Rico National Olympic Committee, and the Guam National Olympic Committee. The British territories also encompass multiple IOC-certified national committees, including Hong Kong's. Perhaps the best examples of IOC independence regarding jurisdiction are its inclusion of two Korean (North Korea and South Korea) and two German (East Germany and West Germany) national committees.[4]

When it comes to the participation of Beijing- and Taipei-based athletes in the Olympic movement, however, the well-established IOC principle has stumbled. For thirty years after the founding of the PRC in 1949, when the Nationalist government fled to Taiwan, Beijing and Taipei used sports as an important vehicle for proclaiming their political legitimacy to the world. Both governments claimed to represent China and did everything possible to block the other from membership in the Olympic family. Heated disputes surrounding their respective membership claims plagued the international Olympic movement for many years. The problem was so serious that IOC chancellor Otto Mayer complained, "The quarrel of the 'two Chinas' has been, from 1954 on, the main burden of Olympism."[5]

Why is the Chinese case so problematic for the IOC? Although it would be impossible to explore the whole range of reasons here, the Chinese situation was distinctive in two ways. First, from 1949 to the late 1970s, both Beijing and Taipei believed that there was only one China and both strongly opposed the other's membership in the Olympic family. The key dispute between them was over who truly represented the Chinese nation. Each side declared that it was the legitimate government of China, while the other was a mere pretender, and both swore that their own legitimate government would never allow the "rebel" government to play a role in international organizations.

Second, both linked membership in the Olympic movement with political legitimacy and seemed to ignore or not to understand the Olympic principles and the IOC rules. Consequently, both claimed membership in the Olympic movement and Olympic Games and were intensively engaged in the fight for membership. The IOC's inconsistence and incompetence in handling the "two-China" problem only made it worse.

Who Represents China? The Beijing Position

The year 1949 was a turning point in Chinese history; the Chinese Communists had come to power and sent the Nationalists packing. From the perspective of the PRC, the Republic of China ceased to exist when the Communist government took over the mainland; Taiwan was merely a renegade province that did not—and could not—belong to the international sport federations or Olympic family.

When the Communists first came to power, they did not know much about the Olympics. They had no idea that China had been a member of the Olympic movement for many years, and they were not even aware that of the three Chinese IOC members, one, Dong Shouyi, chose to remain on the mainland after 1949.[6] The top Communist leaders were so busy consolidating their power, building their nation, and fighting the United States in the Korean War that the upcoming 1952 Helsinki Olympics was not even on their radar screen. Had the Soviet Union not intervened, the PRC might not have thought about the Olympic movement or the Olympic Games until much later. But luckily for Beijing, the Soviets brought up both issues early enough for the Communist government to take part (although, as we will see, its team arrived too late to compete).

Although Beijing had not even set up a sports commission, the government used the Communist Youth League as a sort of facilitator for sports. Only after Beijing had taken part in the 1952 Helsinki Olympic Games did the Chinese establish a separate sports federation under the new regime. The Chinese Communist Youth League representatives, upon their return from Finland, prepared a report on China's participation in the Helsinki Games for Liu Shaoqi, second in command of the Communist system, suggesting that Beijing establish a ministry-level sports commission headed by a high official such as a vice premier. This suggestion was accepted and He Long, a top military man, assumed leadership.[7]

Why was the USSR interested in Beijing's involvement? International politics. After World War II, the USSR had decided to compete in every area, reversing its former refusal to join corrupt capitalist sports events (as a way of demonstrating the so-called superiority of the Russian political system and society). In 1950 the Soviet Union's official sports organization was accepted as a national Olympic committee by the IOC, and the 1952 Helsinki Games were Communist Russia's first Olympic appearance.

The participation of the Soviet Union in the Olympic movement was important both for sports and for international politics. Avery Brundage, president of the IOC from 1952 to 1972, wrote in his unpublished memoir that "for the first time in forty years the Russians participated—and the large and well-organized team from the Soviet Union which came to Helsinki astonished the world by its outstanding performance."[8] The significance of their athletes' performance was not lost on the Soviets themselves. A 1953 editorial in a Russian newspaper expressed how pleased Russians were about the 1952 Helsinki Games. It proclaimed, "The Russian people are ready to open their doors . . . the Iron Curtain will be lifted for all sportsmen from all over the world." Brundage also noted, "That the first raising of the Iron Curtain should be in the field of sport is not without international significance—and a great tribute to the power of the indestructible Olympic idea."[9] Brundage did not realize that with the USSR's entry into the Olympic movement—and the Soviets' subsequent push for Beijing to become a member of the Olympic family—the IOC would be forced to deal with the two-China issue even before the IOC and Beijing's own sports organization were ready. The Soviets had every reason to demonstrate their solidarity with the new Communist regime in China and to groom it to be a close ally in the spirit of the Cold War struggle.

The Russians seem to have brought the Olympics issue to Beijing's attention in 1951. Beijing's foreign ministry was informed by Helsinki, the 1952 host, which was strongly influenced by the Russians politically and diplomatically, that Finland would like to have Beijing take part in its Olympic Games. Finnish enthusiasm for the PRC's participation made then IOC president J. Sigfrid Edström uneasy; he had no desire to get embroiled in the tricky China issue.[10]

At first Beijing, not being familiar with world sports, did not take Finland's invitation seriously.[11] But a sharp prod from the Russians the next year quickly sent Beijing into action. On February 2, 1952, the Soviet ambassador to Beijing made an urgent inquiry as to whether Beijing would send a delegation to the 1952 Games and whether the new China would join the Olympic movement and attend the IOC meeting on February 15, 1952. The Soviet ambassador requested an immediate reply. On the same day, after meeting with the Soviet ambassador, Feng Wenbin, secretary of the Chinese Communist Youth League, wrote a report to Premier Zhou Enlai about China's potential participation in the 1952 Games. This report, which has become available to scholars only recently, explains that the Russians had asked Feng to tell the Russian embassy immediately what China's attitude was toward Olympic participation. According to the report, the Soviets were under the impression that Beijing was not a member of the Olympic family, and that Taiwan was. The ambassador reminded Beijing that participation in the Olympics was an important political issue, and he even suggested that his government was willing to train Chinese athletes so the Russians and Chinese could attend the Games together.

Through most of the 1950s, Beijing's official policy was to learn from the USSR, so this inquiry and suggestion from Beijing's "Elder Brother" carried a great deal of weight. The report from Feng spurred Zhou Enlai to meet with him on February 4 about the Olympics issue; Zhou then forwarded Feng's report to Liu Shaoqi with his own recommendations that same day. Zhou told Liu that, based on his discussion with Feng Wenbin, he believed Beijing should send a telegram to the IOC in the name of the All-China Sports Federation, which then existed only in name, to declare that Taiwan could not represent China in the Olympic family. He suggested they demand that the IOC allow Beijing to attend its February meeting and the coming Olympic Games. Zhou also told Liu that the telegram had already been sent, due to the pressing deadline. With no understanding of China's past involvement with the Olympic movement, the telegram dashed off to the IOC claimed that Beijing had just organized a national Olympic committee and requested the IOC's certification so Beijing could participate in the 1952 Games. Zhou further reported to Liu, "I estimate that if the IOC does not allow us to attend its February meeting, then we will not attend the July Olympic Games to avoid running into the delegation from Chiang Kai-shek's bandit organization. [But] if the IOC invites us [not Chiang] . . . to attend the February meeting, the situation is favorable to us politically. Moreover, since the Games will take place in Helsinki, we may attend. Even if we don't do well in the competition, it is not important." Liu quickly approved Zhou's suggestions.[12]

This report, then, which details the developments behind Beijing's early interest in the Olympic movement and the 1952 Games, shows that Beijing chose to fight its first major battle for international legitimacy through its membership in the Olympic family and Olympic Games.

Once a decision had been made, Beijing acted quickly and with determination. As IOC president Edström wrote in June of 1952, "The Communist Chinese organizations are making all kinds of efforts to take part in the Olympic Games in Helsinki."[13] The Chinese ambassador to Finland, Geng Biao, personally made sure the telegram from Beijing was delivered to the IOC on February 5. China even sent its diplomat from Stockholm to personally visit Edström about Beijing's membership and the invitation to the 1952 Games. In a presentation to Edström on February 13 during the IOC's Oslo session, Sheng Zhibai argued that the PRC's All-China Athletic Federation represented 600 million people and should be considered the only proper participant in the Olympic movement from China. He further demanded that the IOC immediately expel Wang Zhengting and Kong Xiangxi, who were then living in exile and serving as IOC members in China, and decertify Taiwan's national Olympic committee. But Edström had had enough from the Beijing diplomat and cut him off. "My dear sir," he protested, "you are neither qualified nor entitled to give the IOC orders or instructions!"[14]

Beijing had made two mistakes. First, by its forceful intervention, the PRC had conveyed a strident politicization of sports that was off-putting to the IOC. Second, by not using Dong Shouyi, the IOC member who remained in China, to communicate with the IOC, Beijing had not only forfeited any legitimate claim to membership in the Olympic family, but also given the impression that Dong was either dead or imprisoned—even though at the time, the Communist government knew nothing of, or at least did not pay attention to, Dong Shouyi and his IOC involvement.[15] It was Dong who learned of Beijing's intentions and eventually made contact with the Chinese government.[16] Had Beijing known the IOC rules and

Olympic principles and simply asked Dong Shouyi to contact the IOC, its first official contact with the IOC might have been less stormy. Dong would then have attended the IOC first sessions in February that year—which would have been propitious timing because Wang Zhengting and Kong Xiangxi, formerly high officials in the Nationalist government, were too demoralized to go to Helsinki after the Nationalist regime had been defeated in the civil war.

Erik von Frenckell, an IOC member in Finland, informed the other IOC members that the Chinese ambassador in Helsinki had been in contact with him and demanded to know why Beijing had not yet been invited to the 1952 Olympic Games. Frenckell recommended to the IOC session that it should make a decision about the China issue before the June 1 deadline for entries. Avery Brundage, who would become the new IOC president in 1952, declared that the IOC had to establish contact with all three Chinese members before it could reach a decision. But with the civil war raging in China, all three members had lost contact with the IOC back in 1948.

The situation continued to unravel. The Taiwan side spread a rumor that Dong Shouyi, the only IOC member who stayed on the mainland, was dead.[17] In his meeting with Sheng Zhibai, however, Edström asked about Dong Shouyi and was told that he was alive and well. "His place is here in Helsinki," the IOC president told Sheng, who was shadowing the IOC session in Oslo.[18]

Since the IOC rules indicated that no athletes could participate in the Olympics unless they belonged to an international federation, Beijing tried a new tactic: in April 1952 it convinced the Fédération Internationale de Natation Amateur to accept the All-China Athletic Federation as a member by claiming that it succeeded the previous Chinese organization and by paying the affiliation dues that had been in arrears since 1949.[19] Beijing did the same with preexisting Chinese memberships in other world sports federations, including those related to the pentathlon, gymnastics, ice hockey, skating, volleyball, and football.

The so-called two-China issue would have been much easier for Beijing to manage had Beijing done its homework and sent Dong Shouyi in the first place. But because of its ignorance and its tendency to resort to high-handed methods, the Beijing government turned what should have been a simple sports issue into a major, messy political standoff. These critical mistakes strained relations between Beijing and the IOC from the very beginning. In his telegram of June 17, 1952, to Beijing's All-China Athletic Federation, Edström blustered that its Olympic committee had not yet been recognized and travel to Helsinki would be "useless."[20] He sent another telegram on July 8, 1952, to Rong Gaotang, a Chinese sports official, telling him that China was in political chaos and the IOC had decided that no Chinese athletes "may compete until difficulties are resolved." He also asked Rong to inform Dong Shouyi that his presence in Helsinki was "desired."[21]

Despite Edström's position, Beijing was determined to attend the Games and soon dispatched Dong to take part in the IOC's Helsinki session later that month. When Dong showed up at the meetings with a translator in tow, Edström sent the man out of the room since according to IOC rules translators were not allowed to attend IOC meetings. The translator refused, saying that Dong only spoke Chinese. According to an eyewitness report, Edström rapped his cane on the table and said icily, "You are lying. I spoke with him in English without any difficulties as recently as 1948! Leave the room immediately!" The interpreter left, taking Dong with him. It was obvious that Beijing did not trust Dong at that time. But it was also true that in the 1951 IOC session in Vienna, the newly elected Russian member Konstantin Andrianov had attended the meeting with an interpreter (since he did not speak English or French, a qualification for an elected member) without protest from the IOC. Only at its 1954 session in May in Athens did the IOC decide that newly elected IOC members must be fluent in French or English.[22] In any case, Dong's appearance at the IOC session was hardly useful for the IOC since he was in no position to resolve the problems surrounding Beijing's demands.

At the July 1952 Helsinki session, Edström reminded members that Beijing's athletes were waiting in Leningrad for an invitation.[23] Forced into a quick decision, the IOC executive board proposed not to accept either Taiwan or Beijing into the 1952 Olympic Games. This was obviously a dodge and not a very effective one, since, as Erik von Frenckell pointed out, Taiwan's national Olympic committee had already been recognized and so it was impossible to exclude Taiwan from the Games. Frenckell countered that the athletes of both Chinas should be allowed to take part. When the IOC session voted 29–22 to allow both teams to participate at Helsinki, the IOC put off a decision on whether Beijing could become a member. On July 18, one day before the opening ceremony of the Helsinki Games, the IOC finally extended invitations to both Beijing and Taipei.

The new PRC government was quick to understand the importance of the Olympic Games to their political legitimacy and took action with amazing speed. Having finally gotten the green light from the IOC, the PRC's three top leaders—Mao Zedong, Liu Shaoqi, and Zhou Enlai—personally approved the decision immediately (although it was not made public until July 23, after Beijing learned that Taiwan would not attend the Olympics). Late in the evening of July 24, Zhou met with delegation leaders and told them, "It is a victory for the PRC when its flag is flying at the [Helsinki] Olympic Games. Being late was not our fault."[24] The delegation left for Finland on July 25 and arrived in Helsinki on July 29, one day before the closing ceremony. It failed to take part in any competition; only one of its swimmers participated in a preliminary competition and he failed to qualify for the next round.[25] Even so, Beijing did participate in some of the Games' cultural programs. And Zhou Enlai was able to preview the program that would be performed by the Chinese entertainment acrobatic troupe when it visited Helsinki. Zhou told the acrobatic entertainers that they were China's national treasures and expressed the hope that they would win glory for the motherland.[26]

Beijing's principal interest in the Olympic Games and Olympic movement was to seek legitimacy in the world arena, especially given the West's recognition of the Nationalist government in Taiwan. As the Russians had made abundantly clear, the Helsinki Games provided an important platform for such efforts. Simply being there and seeing its flag fly with those of other countries counted as a victory for the new government in Beijing.[27]

Moreover, by setting one foot in the Olympics in 1952, Beijing again forced the IOC's hand. On August 3, 1952, the very day that the Chinese delegation left Helsinki, the Beijing government fired off a telegram to Otto Mayer, the IOC's chancellor. This telegram, sent in the name of Rong Gaotang, vice president and secretary general of the All-China Athletic Federation, declared that "the All-China Athletic Federation was formed through the reorganization of the China National Amateur Athletic Federation, which had already been recognized by the International Olympic Committee. It is the only legal amateur athletic organization in the People's Republic of China and exercises authority over sports activities throughout the country. Based on these facts, the All-China Athletic Federation should be duly recognized as the Chinese Olympic Committee." Rong expressed anger that the IOC had invited Taiwan to the 1952 Olympics:

> I cannot but protest, on behalf of the All-China Athletic Federation [the Chinese Olympic Committee], against such a decision which completely runs counter to the spirit and charter of the International Olympic Games. In order to maintain the dignity and principles of the International Olympic Committee, I resolutely demand that the sports organization and representatives of the remnant Kuomintang bloc in Taiwan . . . be expelled from the International Olympic Committee, the International Olympic Games and related international federations. I also demand that the All-China Athletic Federation, as China's Olympic Committee, be accorded its rightful place in all the international Olympic bodies and organizations.[28]

In a letter to IOC president Brundage, dated April 9, 1954, Rong, this time with the title vice president and general secretary of Chinese Olympic Committee, again requested that the IOC, at its upcoming session in Athens on May 14, formally recognize the Chinese Olympic Committee. With twenty-three votes for, twenty-one against, and three abstentions, the IOC in 1954 officially recognized the All-China Athletic Federation as China's official Olympic committee.[29] On May 26, the IOC's chancellor, Otto Mayer, officially notified Beijing about the decision. Mayer wrote, "We wish you the warmest welcome into our Olympic Family and thank you in advance for your kind cooperation in the Olympic movement in your country."[30] Beijing had again received what it wanted from the IOC.

Beijing may have won the first round of the two-China battle at the 1952 Helsinki Games, but it did not do as well in 1956. Leading up to the event, Beijing not only declared it would attend the 1956 Games; it also pressed its athletes to prepare. A front-page editorial in the *People's Daily* published on September 2, titled "Let's go to the Olympic Games," called on Chinese athletes to get ready and "win victories for the motherland at the 16th Olympic Games." Another article on the same page claimed that Beijing would welcome athletes from Hong Kong and Taiwan to join Beijing's Olympic delegation. Since Taiwan had remained a member of the Olympic family, Beijing's plan was to slip over to Australia before Taiwan's arrival in the hope that Chiang's regime would not take part when it realized Beijing was already there. But when Beijing arrived, the Taiwan delegation had already checked into the Olympic village, and its flag was flying. Beijing protested Taiwan's presence to the organizing committee and to the IOC but got nowhere. Beijing decided to withdraw from the Games in protest.[31]

Between 1954 and 1958, both Taiwan and Beijing claimed to represent "China" in the Olympic family. Having failed to keep Taiwan out of the 1956 Games, Beijing gradually concluded that the IOC, especially its president, the American Avery Brundage, was hostile to Beijing and was supporting Taiwan and a two-China policy. Consequently, in 1957, through Dong Shouyi (who as an IOC member was supposed to serve as the IOC's ambassador to the PRC, not the other way around), Beijing escalated its attacks on the IOC. In late December, Dong, obviously acting under official instructions, wrote to Brundage that the IOC "should recognize only one Olympic Committee in China [and] that should be the All-China Athletic Federation." In another letter to Brundage on April 23, 1958, Dong or other officials in his name expressed "indignation" at Brundage's "many unfriendly and distorting remarks" with regard to the situation with Taiwan. Brundage called the April 23 letter "insulting" and demanded that Dong resign from the IOC. He wrote, "Despite your obligations as a member of the International Olympic Committee, on every occasion you have attempted to introduce political questions and if you continue to violate both the letter and the spirit of our rules the only remedy will be to request your resignation."[32]

The heated dispute between Beijing and the IOC thus reached a point of no return. According to an authoritative account, on June 28, 1958, Premier Zhou Enlai met with He Long, Chen Yi, and other officials from the foreign ministry and national sport authority to discuss sports and foreign relations.[33] Obviously under top authorization, Dong replied to Brundage on August 19, 1958, "most indignantly," claiming that Brundage's attitude "fully reveals that you are a faithful menial of the U.S. imperialists bent on serving their plot of creating 'two Chinas.'" He continued, "A man like you, who stains the Olympic spirit and violates the Olympic Charter, has no qualification whatsoever to be IOC president. . . . I feel pained that the IOC is today controlled by an imperialist like you and consequently the Olympic spirit has been grossly trampled upon. To uphold the Olympic spirit and tradition, I hereby declare that I will no longer cooperate with you or have any connection with the IOC while it is under your domination."[34]

The same day that Dong announced his resignation, Beijing officially broke off its relationship with the Olympic movement. In a short letter to Otto Mayer signed by Zhang Lianhua, then general secretary of the Chinese Olympic Committee, the Chinese committee wrote to "lodge its solemn protest against the unlawful recognition of the so-called China National Amateur Athletic Federation in Taiwan by the International Olympic Committee" and declared that Beijing "ceases to recognize the IOC." The statement once again attacked Brundage personally for his anti-Beijing stand, and linked his attitude to the adversarial position of the United States government toward China.[35]

Under direct instruction from Deng Xiaoping, China's sport commission decided to summarily withdraw from the eleven international sport organizations that had accepted Taiwan's membership.[36] On August 15, 1958, the standing committee of China's national sports commission went so far as to revise its constitution and delete the phrases "China's Olympic committee" and "China's athletes take part in the Olympic Games."[37] This move makes it clear that Beijing's decision to break with the Olympic movement was made well before its official letter to the IOC on August 19.

The IOC realized that it needed to explain what was going on with Beijing. In a letter issued on September 5, 1958, to its members, national Olympic committees, and the press, IOC chancellor Otto Mayer repeated Brundage's old charges and blamed the conflict on Beijing. Mayer claimed that Beijing "did not seem to understand that the International Olympic Committee does not recognize Governments, but only sport organizations (it does not disapprove nor approve of the Governments of the countries that are recognized as long as the sport organizations follow the Olympic rules), and that one of the most important of these rules concerns the necessity of preventing political interference. It is regrettable that these principles are not better understood in such a large country as China."[38]

Both sides seemed genuinely to believe the other was to blame. Nevertheless, Beijing's withdrawal from the Olympic movement was a major blow to IOC prestige and the Olympic ideal. With this 1958 decision, an official and self-imposed isolation began that would last for over two decades. By taking this dramatic action, Beijing had wanted to convey its unhappiness with having to share the representation of China with Taiwan; instead, it had clearly lost the battle to Taiwan. From its place on the sidelines, Beijing could do little but complain about the IOC and its president.[39]

Who Represents China? The Taipei Position

Taiwan's successful efforts to remain in the Olympic family had more to do with Cold War international politics than the effectiveness of its policy. Most Western countries diplomatically recognized Taipei rather than Beijing until the 1970s, giving Taiwan powerful leverage in the IOC. Taiwan, after all, continued to represent China even in the United Nations until 1971.

Taipei also made several astute moves, one of which was to claim that its political legitimacy stemmed directly from the Republic of China, which had been founded in 1912 and had been a member of the Olympic family since 1922. In addition, after the Nationalistic government fled the mainland, Taipei immediately notified the IOC that the Chinese national Olympic committee had changed its address to Taiwan. These tactics helped Taipei to remain part of the Olympic family, no matter how hard Beijing tried to dislodge it.[40]

Even given all these advantages, however, the Nationalist government, like its mainland counterpart, made several mistakes when negotiating the issue of membership. One such blunder was its handling of the 1952 Olympic Games. The Nationalist government, which intended to send athletes to the Games, started to prepare for the competition in 1951, allocating on March 3 80,000 New Taiwan dollars for selecting and training athletes. But on May 10, 1951, Hao Gengsheng, an important sports leader who had moved to Taiwan with the Nationalists, suggested that Taiwan not participate in the Helsinki Games. He was concerned that the USSR, which would be attending the Games for the first time, might use the Olympics as an opportunity to confront Taiwan. Hao's ill-informed advice swayed the cabinet. When Taipei learned that Beijing had been invited to participate, its decision not to attend was strengthened because of the thinking of *han zei bu liang li*. In other words, the rationale of "no two Chinas" actually lay behind Taipei's thinking at this point, long before it was embraced by Beijing as grounds for its two-decades-long withdrawal from the Olympic movement.[41] In its official letter to IOC president Edström, dated July 19, 1952, the Nationalist Olympic Committee wrote, "as a protest against the resolution adopted at the plenary session of the International Olympic Committee on July 17, 1952, which compromises the right and position of the Chinese National committee as the only legal and recognized national Olympic committee of China, I beg to inform you that we have decided to withdraw our participation in the 1952 Helsinki Olympic Games." This letter was signed by Hao Gengsheng, then president of Taiwan's national Olympic committee.[42] In its official statement, Taiwan's Olympic committee protested the IOC's decision to allow Chinese Communists to participate in the 1952 Olympics, calling it "unlawful as it approves entry of competitors from China not entered by the Chinese national Olympic committee, which is the only legal national

Olympic committee of China and has been recognized as such for many years."[43] Taiwan's decision not to participate in the Helsinki Games, however, left the door open for Beijing to step in uncontested and make its debut on the stage of international sports.[44] (As explained later, Taiwan's decision not to compete also was influenced by the IOC's mixed signal to Taiwan about its participation in the 1952 Olympic Games.[45])

The Nationalists made another mistake by failing to act regarding their two IOC representatives Kong Xiangxi and Wang Zhengting, whose active involvement in IOC matters had long lapsed, leaving them facing forced resignation. Kong, who had been an IOC member since 1939, had never even attended an IOC meeting. While in theory IOC members were chosen by the IOC itself and functioned as Olympic ambassadors to the countries from which they were chosen, individual states retained a degree of influence through their national Olympic committees. Taipei would probably have benefited from having had more voices at the table during its membership war with Beijing. Brundage, who was obviously pro-Taiwan, advised Hao Gengsheng even before the Helsinki Games that "the important thing now is for Nationalist China to have its representative at Helsinki prepared to fight vigorously for its recognition by the different international federations and the International Olympic Committee. This is a very serious situation."[46] During the crucial diplomatic battle between Taipei and Beijing over membership in the Olympic family, however, the only contribution Kong Xiangxi made was to write to Otto Mayer on February 29, 1952, to oppose the IOC's recognition of the All-China Athletic Federation "because it is against the rules of the International Olympic Committee which states that the national Olympic committee of any country must be affiliated with the IOC." Kong commented, "I believe the Olympic committee of China is still in existence and functioning on Taiwan."[47]

Brundage continued to urge on the Taiwanese. In his cablegram to Hao Gengsheng on April 22, 1954, Brundage told Hao bluntly that it was "most important you have someone at Athens. Wang [Zhengting] and Kung [Xiangxi] are both delinquent according to rules and liable to forfeit [their] memberships because of repeated non-attendance."[48] But the warnings and advice went unheeded. In 1955, after prompting by the IOC, Kong finally tendered his resignation in a letter to Brundage on June 24, 1955.[49] Wang Zhengting, although more involved in the IOC than Kong, rarely took part in IOC meetings and other activities after the 1948 London Olympic Games. He sent his resignation to Brundage in 1954, changed his mind, and eventually resigned for good in 1957.[50] In other words, over the course of these crucial developments, Taipei had no active IOC members, while Beijing's Dong Shouyi was aggressively asserting Beijing's interests.

Even though Cold War politics—and the advocacy of the strongly pro-Taiwan Brundage—were helping to keep Taiwan in the Olympic family, when Beijing made the two-China issue worldwide news with its withdrawal from the Olympic movement in 1958, the IOC had to act regarding Taiwan's membership. In its 1959 Munich session, IOC members from the Soviet Union asked for a change of name for Taiwan's national Olympic committee on the grounds that "this NOC cannot possibly supervise sports in mainland China." The IOC recognized the argument had merit and asked Taipei to come up with a different designation: "The Chinese national Olympic committee having its seat in Taipei (Taiwan) will be notified by the International Olympic Committee chancellor that it cannot continue to be recognized under that name since it does not control sport in the country of China, and its name will be removed form the official list. If an application for recognition under a different name is made it will be considered by the International Olympic Committee."[51]

The IOC's insistence on the name change, however, met with harsh criticism in the United States from major media, politicians, and the general public. It seemed to the American public that the IOC was expelling Taipei from the Olympic family to please Beijing. The *New York Times* wrote in one of several editorials on this issue that "in expelling Nationalist China from the International Olympic Committee—and thus eventually from Olympic participation—the committee has yielded to the rawest sort of political blackmail." The editorial called the IOC's decision not only political, but also "cowardly, evasive and shameful. . . . The idea that Nationalist China 'no longer represents sports in the entire country of China' is unworthy of a forthright American."[52] William Theodore de Bary, a noted expert on China at Columbia University, also was dismayed. He wrote to Brundage stating, "I agree with the N.Y. Times editorial on May 30. . . . Unless this expulsion is rescinded, the Olympics will have ceased to represent anything worthwhile in sports and the American people should withdraw their support from it."[53]

The American government also felt compelled to act. As the Nationalist government in Taiwan spoke of "betrayal," the U.S. State Department officially declared the IOC decision to be "a clear act of political discrimination." The House of Representatives unanimously voted to withhold an appropriation of $400,000 for the 1960 Winter Olympic Games in California "if any free nation is barred from participation." Representative F. E. Dorn of New York declared that the "United States must not allow a friend of many years to be pushed aside by communist blackmail." Dorn called for the United States to withdraw from the Olympic movement if Taiwan were barred from the Olympic Games.[54] President Dwight Eisenhower condemned the IOC for its political behavior. And letters of protest from the American public poured in.

Brundage was under enormous pressure. He scribbled himself a note: "Everyone is getting into the Act," and later wrote that "the country seems to have gone off on an emotional binge in unprecedented proportions." He felt himself nearly alone, "confronting 175,000,000 misinformed people."[55] The best poor Brundage could do was to send out his standard reply: "Dear sir or madam: Apparently you have been badly misinformed" and explain that Taiwan had been neither mistreated nor expelled from the Olympic movement. "The IOC has simply asked Taiwan's NOC to choose a more sensible designation for itself."[56]

In this war of words, the influence of politics was apparent. An editorial in the *Christian Science Monitor* pointed out, "Now that the furor over the International Olympic Committee's withdrawal of recognition of Nationalist China has subsided somewhat, it may be useful to see how much the Olympic spirit has been trampled under the spikes of politicians, East and West." During the heated exchange of political charges over the IOC's decision on Taiwan, media outside the United States seemed to have a better sense of what was really going on. The *Manchester Guardian* wrote on June 11, 1959, "Question: when are politics non-political? Answer: when they happen to be your own. It is always the other fellow who defied the purity of your organization by being partisan." That is why, according to this article, many American politicians had become indignant when the IOC had stated what was "obvious to most people"—that Taiwan's national Olympic committee could no longer be recognized as the Chinese Olympic committee "because it does not control sports in the entire country of China." "What is perplexing to those who are not Americans," commented the author, is the conviction "that it is not political to be loyal to your ally, but is political to admit that a committee in Formosa cannot send any athletes from the mainland."

Although the harsh attack by the United States put the IOC on the defensive, it had no choice but to find a suitable name for Taiwan's Olympic committee. Heated debates would rage about which name Taiwan should use within the Olympic family; in the 1960 session in San Francisco, IOC member Jorge Vargas suggested, "Why not drop the words China and Taiwan [altogether] and call the committee the Chinese Taipei Olympic committee?" Unfortunately it took the IOC nineteen years to understand the wisdom of this suggestion and two decades to put it into effect in Montevideo, where precisely this name was adopted to resolve the longstanding deadlock.

In typically incompetent IOC fashion, the committee did not come out with a new name for the Taipei's national Olympic committee until just before the Rome Olympic Games in 1960. The name, "Taiwan," enraged the representative of the Rome organizing committee, who had already invited the "Republic of China" at the IOC's behest, and who had had all of the documents and papers printed with that original name. The organizing committee told the IOC that it would be impossible to reprint everything, but it would accept the name change provided the IOC recorded in the session minutes how the change had been implemented at the last moment. To make the situation even messier, when the IOC session voted on the proposed new name, the voting ended twice in a 25–25 tie. The IOC had no choice but to make a decision at this point, and eventually the members agreed that the team from Taiwan should take part in the Rome Games as "Taiwan," but in the future would be the Olympic Committee of the Republic of China, as the Taiwan's national Olympic committee had requested.[57]

During the 1960 Rome Games, then, athletes from Taiwan had to compete and march under the geographical designation of Taiwan, even though Taipei considered this designation discriminatory and unfair. The Nationalists, including Chiang Kai-shek himself, were determined to let the world know they were unhappy with this decision. On Chiang's instructions, the Taipei delegation marched at the opening ceremony behind a sign that read "UNDER PROTEST."[58]

The action infuriated the IOC. In a joint letter to the Taipei delegation to the 1960 Games, Brundage and Otto Mayer wrote, "We consider your gesture inelegant, political-minded and an offence to the dignity which should prevail in the Olympic Games. We think that by way of this action you have lost the last sympathy you might have had among the sportsmen of the world. We regret that we have to censure you, but we do so with the hope that in the future you will understand that you must take part in the Games under the name of the Territory over which you have jurisdiction and with a better spirit."[59]

Taiwan and the IOC had managed to humiliate each other, but the name problem remained unsolved.[60] In a letter to the IOC, Hao Gengsheng asked the committee to reconsider Taiwan's designation for future Olympic Games at its 1963 Baden-Baden session. Hao wrote, "Among the 105 recognized national committees, only the Republic of China committee has received the discriminatory and unfair treatment of being forced to use a designation . . . that is materially different from the name of the country our committee represents." Taiwan proposed that "ROC," the abbreviation of its official name, be used as its designation.[61] Brundage worked hard to get Taipei what it wanted at the Baden-Baden session. In a letter to Yang Sen, president of the Taiwan Olympic committee, dated December 9, 1963, G. D. Sondhi, an Indian IOC member, remarked, "Mr. Brundage, in his own quiet but forceful manner, was very helpful and deserves your thanks. There are some great difficulties in the way of your getting the

Taiwan's delegation, furious to be participating as "Taiwan" rather than
the "Republic of China," marches behind an "UNDER PROTEST" sign at
the opening ceremony of the 1960 Olympic Games in Rome.

designation of your country altered."[62] Finally, at the IOC Mexico City
session in 1968, Brundage managed to change Taiwan's national Olympic committee designation to the Olympic Committee of the Republic of
China.[63]

Taiwan's situation in the Olympic movement worsened after the successes of Beijing's "ping-pong diplomacy" and once the PRC had replaced
Taiwan at the United Nations in 1971.[64] Ping-pong diplomacy, which is

described in detail in Chapter 5, was Beijing's diplomatic offensive that convinced many countries to switch their diplomatic recognition from Taipei to Beijing. Xu Heng (Henry Hsu), who was chosen by Brundage's dubious methods to be an IOC member in Taiwan in 1970 without the IOC executive board's prior approval, wrote in an extremely secret report to the Nationalist government dated April 3, 1972, that Taiwan's position in the IOC after 1972 was in "extreme danger" *(ji qi xian e)* because the pro-Taiwan president Brundage was retiring; without his advocacy, many more IOC members in Europe were likely to vote with Beijing.[65] "It is extremely urgent for us to figure out how to safeguard our position in the IOC. . . . If the communist bandits' entry into the IOC becomes a reality, then Taiwan's participation in international sports would be negatively affected and it will even become difficult for us to take part in friendly games. . . . not only will our international sports activity be eliminated, but the effect on our diplomacy will also be negative." Xu Heng suggested that the Nationalist government act quickly and decisively by working closely with South Korea's IOC members, who were pro-Taiwan, and by making sure that Taipei would be represented at any international sports meetings and gatherings. The National government seemed to grasp Xu Heng's urgency and adopted his suggestions, thus establishing a high-level cross-ministry group to handle international sports issues.[66]

But the tide seemed to be turning against Taipei. Even formerly friendly nations like Japan began to question the legitimacy of Taiwan's membership in the Olympic movement as a representative of China. In response, Taiwan's IOC member Xu Heng pointed out, "Some supporters of the All-China Sports Federation may contend that there is only one China and the IOC has to make a choice between the two Chinas. As a Chinese, I deplore the fact that China is now in a divided state with two governments. But since we are gathering here as sports leaders rather than politicians, there is nothing we can do to alter this political fact of life."[67]

Taipei's position eroded further during the late 1970s. In May 1978, the IOC executive board decided that the time had come to solve the two-China problem by sending a mission to Beijing and Taipei with the goal of persuading Taiwan to remain independently recognized but change its name in the Olympic family to something acceptable to Beijing. The IOC president "reminded the members that if Taiwan refused to change its name the IOC would be obliged to go through the machinery of suspension."[68] After an impasse of over two decades, new international developments promised to force a resolution of the problem through compromise by both sides. It was still unclear, however, why the IOC had to be pushed by external forces before it dealt effectively with this issue.

Who Represents China? The IOC's Perspective

If both Beijing and Taipei made mistakes negotiating their explosive membership conflicts, the IOC itself may also shoulder a significant share of the blame. The IOC's first misstep was its readiness in 1951 to have China's national Olympic committee address changed from mainland China to Taiwan. When Hao Gengsheng, on behalf of the Taiwan's sports authority, informed the IOC that the office of the Chinese Olympic committee had been relocated from Nanjing to Taipei, the IOC bureaucrats simply recorded the change of address in the *Olympic Review* without considering the enormous political implications. Only later did Avery Brundage realize the error. Brundage commented, "The change [in address] had been made on the records in the IOC office in Lausanne as a purely routine matter, without any thought of the political significance."[69] To be fair, Edström raised the question. He wrote, "It is essential that we learn to know which is the proper Olympic Committee of China. We have had a letter from China National Amateur Athletic Federation, 147 West Gate Street, Hsin Chu, Taiwan. This federation claims to be the National Olympic Committee of China."[70] Unfortunately, however, he did not pursue the matter after being reassured by Wang Zhengting and Kong Xiangxi that the national Olympic committee in Taiwan was the right one.[71] As Edström told Otto Mayer, the IOC chancellor, "I do not want to spend more time on this Chinese question."[72]

No matter who was to blame for this careless handling of the address change, the damage was done. It was not until June 1952 that Erik von Frenckell, IOC member and chairman of the 1952 Helsinki Olympic Games organizing committee, wrote to Edström to protest the handling of the address change. He pointed out, "The change of the address of the Chinese Olympic committee from Peking to Taiwan has been a mistake, not confirmed by the Executive Committee nor by the Congresses"— and suggested to Edström that the question be "settled by the Congress [IOC session] in Helsinki."[73] Matters were not to improve soon, however: Edström's successor, Avery Brundage, chose to follow Edström's hands-off policy. As Brundage wrote to Edström in 1952, "The Chinese situation is indeed a most complicated and difficult one. As you say, it is hard to tell what to do."[74]

Due to its passivity, the IOC made another misstep, namely, its hasty decision to allow both Beijing and Taipei to take part in the 1952 Games. When Beijing broached its intention to join the Games, the IOC was not at all prepared to respond: the new sports authority in Beijing was not an official Olympic committee and Taipei was claiming to represent all of China. As Brundage told Edström at this crucial moment, "The most that we can do would be to recognize both [Beijing and Taipei] and this, of course, we have refused to do in the case of Germany. The whole situation is most difficult and it is too bad that we can't get through the next two months without taking a stand."[75]

Edström initially decided to allow neither Beijing nor Taipei to participate in the Helsinki Games and so notified them by telegram in mid-June.[76] IOC president-elect Brundage approved of this decision; he wrote to Edström, "Your action on the Chinese question in notifying both organizations that they are not eligible to participate at Helsinki, as I wrote to you before, is the correct one."[77] But Edström was not naive enough to believe that banning both teams had solved the problem. As he told Otto Mayer the very day he made his decision, "We will probably have a great fight about this matter in Helsinki with the Russian delegates and other friends from behind the iron Curtain."[78]

Indeed, attacks were soon launched from many directions. Von Frenckell protested Edström's decision, telling him that "we have been informed that FIFA, FIBA and FINA [the corresponding International Federations] have accepted the Peking Chinese as representatives of China."[79] As a matter of fact, the Helsinki organizing committee had already sent invitations to both parties to join the Olympic Games before Edström had told Beijing and Taiwan not to come.

Given the fast-approaching Olympic Games and the strong criticisms he was facing, Edström asked IOC members to vote in a general session on two possible courses of action: forbidding any Chinese team from participating, or allowing both teams to compete. The second proposal won by 29 votes to 22. The IOC executive board, however, requested an additional vote on a proposal by French member François Pietri, who wanted the IOC to approve participants only in those sports for which their national federations were affiliated with the relevant international federation. Pietri's proposal won by 33 votes to 20. To avoid conflict at the current competition, Brundage, just elected to succeed the retiring Edström, suggested that the IOC not recognize either of the Chinese national Olympic committees until later. But even that compromise, as Brundage himself admitted, "breaks our own rules . . . it is inspired by the sympathy we feel for the sportsmen who are on the way to Helsinki."[80] In fact, this delay represented a complete reversal of the original decision. The IOC seemed to be at wit's end.

The long-serving IOC president Avery Brundage was, to a great extent, responsible for many subsequent mistakes in the IOC's handling of the two-China issue. Brundage loved Chinese art and was a self-proclaimed "disciple of Lao Tzu" and "a fellow Taoist."[81] But his partisan and strident political positions belied his Daoist claim. As president of the IOC he opposed recognition of Beijing in the Olympic movement because he was strongly anti-Communist. He was not a good communicator and seemed not to grasp many important but complicated issues, such as which team should represent China. And his dispute with IOC member Dong Shouyi became quite personal.

Brundage was famous for his supposed determination to keep politics out of sports. He argued against the American boycott of the 1936 Berlin

Olympic Games, as well as against those who wanted to boycott the Tokyo Games in 1940 because of Japan's invasion of China.[82] For Brundage, the "only chance to help China in the face of aggression from all parts of the world is to teach them to lead the strenuous life of athletics, so the Chinese will be physically able to fight their own battles."[83] In his article for a Japanese newspaper dated December 21, 1971, Brundage noted, "The national Olympic Committee of China is welcome to join the Olympic movement at any time. One of the objectives, of course, is to bring together the youth of the world—and the sooner they appear, the better. However, there is no reason for eliminating the Taiwan committee, which has fulfilled all of its Olympic obligations, and is in good standing. It must be remembered that the Olympic movement is not concerned with governments, but solely with national Olympic committees."[84]

Given Brundage's notion that sports was above politics, the IOC under his leadership could only develop naive responses to the two-China issue as it emerged in the early 1950s under so-called Olympic principles. The IOC invited both Beijing and Taiwan to the Games in 1952, allowed both Beijing and Taiwan to be members of the Olympic family in 1954, and permitted both to attend the Olympic Games in 1956. The example of the two Germanys and two Koreas in the Olympic movement only confused things further. In 1968 the national Olympic committee of Eastern Germany (or the GDR) had been fully recognized as a member of Olympic family by the IOC—and Brundage could not understand why Beijing was making such a fuss about Taiwan if the two German states could join the Olympic family with no great tribulation. It never occurred to him that, given China's bloody civil war, Beijing and Taipei were destined to have much more of an emotional response to the linked issues of national legitimacy and membership in the Olympic movement than did the Germans.

Moreover, Brundage wasn't right about the Germans; even they had had deep misgivings about their dual memberships. For instance, the West German government faced a major political problem when Munich was chosen to be host of the 1972 Olympic Games. It considered all possibilities, "including declaring the city of Munich to have Vatican City status for the duration of the Olympic Games, thus effectively banishing the GDR flag. In the end, the West Germans capitulated and the way was paved for the flags of both Germanys to be paraded and celebrated for the first time at the Olympic Games."[85]

When the IOC found itself caught up with the two-China issue, Brundage at first complained that it was not the IOC's job to fix political problems. He wrote later in his unpublished memoir that "after the War more and more questions, as a result of divided countries, were raised, and the IOC was expected to settle all these thorny problems that had baffled the politicians. In a way this also was another tribute to the importance of the Olympic movement, but it led to more and more, sometimes rancorous, debate and required considerable ingenuity to find correct decisions according to Olympic regulations." He criticized all sides for putting pressure on the IOC.[86]

Yet Brundage chose to politicize the two-China issue himself. He kept Beijing out of the Olympic movement in 1960s with the excuse that many countries recognized Taiwan instead of Beijing diplomatically (using the example that Taiwan represented China in the United Nations). This argument was to cause trouble in the early 1970s when Taiwan was expelled from the United Nations and many countries switched to recognizing Beijing as the official diplomatic contact for China. Brundage's successor, Lord Killanin, wrote later in an official memorandum approved by the executive board, "I think it is important to stress that this argument was used by my predecessor and the reverse situation is now the case."[87] Killanin also commented in 1979 that "to my mind the whole of the Chinese question has been dealt with by the IOC in a political manner since the early '50s, when some of the original committee moved to Taipei and were recognized as the 'Republic of China' because they then had a seat under this name in the U.N."[88]

The most serious problem facing the IOC in general and Brundage in particular regarding the Chinese, however, was their ignorance of Chinese politics and culture. Brundage often got the PRC's official name wrong in his criticisms of Beijing's behavior, a mistake that triggered sharp rebukes from Dong Shouyi (and forced Brundage to apologize). Dong, in a letter to Brundage dated December 20, 1957, wrote, "[The IOC minutes] still mistakenly refer to my country as the 'Democratic People's Republic of China.' Once again I request that this error be corrected. The official name of my country is 'the People's Republic of China.'" Brundage replied to Dong on January 8, 1958, and promised that the error would be corrected. But he made an even worse blunder in the same letter regarding Taiwan. He wrote, "You know, and as a matter of fact, everyone knows that there is a separate Government in Taiwan, which is recognized internationally and specifically by the United Nations, consisting of most of the Governments of the world. We did not create this situation. As for Taiwan, it was last part of Japan and not of China. As a matter of fact, the natives are neither Chinese nor Japanese."[89] Since the Nationalist government and the Chinese Communists both agreed that Taiwan was part of China, this sort of statement was bound to arouse the ire of both sides, and it is possible that it was this letter that triggered Beijing's harsh judgment of Brundage and the decision to withdraw from the Olympic movement.

Mistakes of this kind continued as late as 1979. In an executive board press file issued as the IOC was finally trying to resolve the China question, for example, mainland China was still listed as the "Democratic People's Republic of China."[90]

The IOC in general has remained ignorant of China and its culture. In addition to being seemingly unable to remember the country's official name, it could not manage the names of its Chinese members. Dong Shouyi's name is frequently misspelled in almost all IOC documents.[91] Lord Killanin, Brundage's successor, was no better at avoiding such blunders. During a serious dispute with Canada over Taiwan's participation in the 1976 Montreal Games, he got the name of Taiwan's delegation head wrong; he referred to Ding Shanli (Lawrence S. Ting) as Richard Ting, and even in his memoir still referred to him by that name. Killanin wrote that when he asked Ding Shanli to consider the Canadian compromise, Ding "rejected it in a fairly unpleasant manner and I had to rebuke him for his attitude." Killanin never realized he had addressed the man by the wrong name, an especially egregious offense when discussing such a serious matter.[92]

Nor was the IOC presidency of Juan Antonio Samaranch able to shake off this incompetence. Samaranch's letter to Zhong Shitong, president of the Chinese Olympic Committee, which officially notified him about the election of He Zhenliang to the IOC, inadvertently addressed him by his first name, rather than his surname—a major gaffe in this formal context.[93] IOC director Monique Berlioux made the same mistake when she wrote to He Zhenliang, addressing him as "Mr. Zhenliang."[94] Perhaps the most embarrassing incident occurred at the new member pledge ceremony. On February 11, 1988, when the new member Wu Jingguo from Taiwan received his pledge card just minutes before the ceremony, he was horrified to notice a serious mistake regarding Taiwan's modified name.[95]

Decision-making mechanisms within the IOC during the Brundage era were deeply flawed. Brundage himself strongly resisted ideas that differed from his own, admitting at one point that "the International Olympic Committee may be undemocratic."[96] On the Taiwan issue, he made several decisions without first discussing them with other members. (Xu Heng's selection as an IOC member is just one example.) Many IOC members believed it was not right to keep the PRC out of the Olympics, but constructive discussion of the issue was difficult with Brundage in charge. Only after Brundage resigned in 1972—after twenty years as IOC president—did the IOC really begin to grapple with the thorny issue of the two Chinas. Brundage's successor Killanin admitted, "Frankly, I think it is wrong that a country of more than 800 million people is not in the Olympic movement."[97] Killanin took a personal interest in getting Beijing to rejoin the IOC and changing the name of Taiwan's Olympic committee.[98] He complained that "through my time in the IOC, the Chinese problem had dogged the Olympic movement." After two decades of personal frustration over China issues, Killanin was in a mood for change.[99]

Unfortunately for Killanin, his presidency immediately faced a major challenge regarding the two-China issue. At his first Olympic Games in 1976, the host country, Canada, refused to allow Taiwan to compete under its official name. As we will see in Chapter 6, which details this event, the hard lesson learned from the Canadian government convinced Killanin that the IOC could no longer afford to deny Beijing membership in the Olympic movement.

Around the time of the Canadian debacle, Beijing was beginning to return to international organizations after many years of self-inflicted isolation. Perhaps encouraged by the success of its ping-pong diplomacy in 1971, China's sports commission reported in May 1972 to the central government that China should return to world sports. Premier Zhou Enlai "agreed in principle," and many international sports organizations, such as the Asian Games Federation, accepted Beijing's membership as early as 1973.[100] In 1974 the International Fencing Association, the International Wrestling Association, and the International Weightlifting Association followed suit. In his letter to the president of the Asian Games Federation on August 7, 1973, Song Zhong, secretary general of the All-China Sports Federation, wrote,

> The Chiang Kai-shek clique is still illegally represented in the Asian Games Federation, usurping the seat of China. The All-China Sports Federation demands that the Asian Games Federation, acting in accordance with article six of its constitution, which states that only one national sports organization from one Asian country can be admitted, immediately annul the illegally appropriated membership of the Chiang Kai-shek clique. Under this condition, the All-China Sports Federation hereby applies for membership in the Asian Games Federation and fulfills its obligations as a member.[101]

In some ways, this letter sounded much the same as Beijing's previous communications with world sports federations, but it included a new and powerful strategy: pursuing membership under terms that would squeeze out Taiwan. Moreover, Beijing was using diplomatic initiatives to advocate for its membership in world sports federations. In 1974 the Seventh Asian Games took place in Iran, which had established diplomatic relations with Beijing in 1971. It was with Iran's help that Beijing replaced Taiwan in the Asian Games Federation.[102]

Against this backdrop, in April 1975 the All-China Sports Federation submitted its application to the IOC for Beijing's return to the Olympic family. The IOC informed Beijing it was "very happy" to receive Beijing's application, but in fact was unable to move ahead with Beijing's membership due to the unresolved debate.[103]

Yet the IOC could not postpone forever Beijing's return to the Olympic movement. On January 1, 1979, even the United States and the PRC recognized each other diplomatically and, like the United Nations, agreed that Taiwan is part of China. By this point, then, everyone was ahead of the IOC in dealing with Beijing. The pressure to fix the two-China problem and bring Beijing back to the Olympics steadily mounted, and Beijing once again tried to force the IOC's hand. Luckily for the IOC, this time the deal was more palatable: the government in Beijing had become more open and committed to pursuing internationalization.

One China, Many Members

Perhaps because of this shift in attitude by Beijing, the IOC suddenly was in a hurry to find a solution to the longstanding two-China problem. When Killanin visited Beijing from September 14 to 19, 1977, to test the waters, it marked the first time an IOC president had ever visited the PRC. Although he had "candid and serious discussions" with government officials there, he was not able to find an immediate solution and received no positive responses from Beijing.[104] This result seemed as much as anything to be a matter of bad timing, since his visit fell during the power vacuum between the Mao and Deng Xiaoping eras. Killanin spent most of his time listening to boring lectures from Lu Jindong of the All-China Sports Federation about sports in China and the importance of the Taiwan issue.[105] Lu was obviously not powerful enough to make important policy decisions.

Since Beijing was concentrating on its domestic power struggle, the IOC had to figure out on its own how to deal with Beijing's membership. A serious and heated debate on this subject broke out during its May 1978 session. During that meeting, the IOC president informed members that the PRC had applied for membership on the condition that Taiwan no longer be recognized in the Olympic movement—a condition similar to the one Beijing had laid out for its return to the Asian Games Federation. During the discussion that followed, the future IOC president Juan Samaranch, who also served as a Spanish diplomat, emphasized that the IOC "had to do everything in its power to allow the People's Republic of China to be recognized." He recommended as a first step that Taipei's national Olympic committee be asked to change its name.[106] Soviet member Konstantin Andrianov reminded the session that the PRC represented one-quarter of the world's population, and so should take part in the Games. He also pointed out that in addition to the UN, all specialized international sports organizations had already recognized the PRC—"the only exception is the International Olympic Committee." Andrianov proposed that the IOC recognize the PRC committee and immediately withdraw recognition of Taiwan's committee.[107] But many others disagreed.

The IOC seemed to still be stuck on the issue. Eventually the session decided to create a commission to study the problem further and report back.[108] The IOC did accomplish one thing during that session relevant to the Taiwan issue, however: It changed the IOC charter regarding names claimed by national Olympic committees. The new Rule 24 reads: "For the furtherance of the Olympic movement throughout the world, the IOC shall recognize as NOCs [national Olympic committees] entitled to call themselves by that name, committees that are established in accordance with the under-mentioned principles, that conform to the Rules and by-laws of the IOC, and having, if possible, juridical status."[109] Soon afterward, the IOC president himself asked Taipei to study Rule 24 and take the necessary steps.[110]

Killanin appointed Lance Cross, Anthony Bridge, and Alexandru Siperco to the commission charged with investigating the "two Chinas" situation as it affected the IOC. All three visited the PRC from October 16 to 21, 1978, but only Cross and Bridge visited Taiwan from January 22 to 27, 1979. Perhaps not surprisingly given the history of the two-China issue at the IOC, the three members disagreed so strongly about what course to recommend that they chose to issue two separate reports instead of a joint one. Cross and Bridge issued a report together on their visits to the PRC and Taiwan in which they criticized Siperco for refusing to go to Taiwan, "thus depriving himself of the opportunity to form a considered opinion of the total situation." Cross and Bridge wrote in their report that "it was apparent from the outset and throughout our discussions that there was going to be no spirit [from Beijing] of compromise in finding a solution to the present impasse." Beijing "rigidly adhered to" a policy that "there is only one China," and that Taiwan was a province of China. Their report was harshly critical of Beijing and friendly toward Taiwan. It indicated that while Beijing rejected their proposal to have two Chinese Olympic committees in the Olympic family—with one to be called the Chinese Olympic committee (Beijing), and the other the Chinese Olympic committee (Taipei)—Taiwan was "preparing to accept the compromise of a China Olympic Committee (Peking) and a China Olympic Committee (Taipei)." This view convinced Cross and Bridge "of the strength and the sincere spirit of the Olympic moment" in Taiwan—in their opinion, "it would be a travesty of justice to have this member expelled from the Olympic family; an act which could do only irreparable harm to the international Olympic movement." Significantly, they also noted that "there exists much evidence that [Beijing's] All-China Sports Federation (Olympic committee) is a state-controlled organization and is not an independent body as required under the terms of the IOC Charter. There is also evidence that full-time sports training within institutions is practiced for the purpose of preparing and developing 'elite' athletes. It is for the above reasons we suggest that before any application for affiliation is considered, the constitution submitted must conform completely with the requirements of the IOC Charter." In that spirit, the report recommended:

1. That the IOC must deal with the China problem, divorcing it from all political considerations, and taking the view that it is the IOC's responsibility as a non-governmental international organization independent of any and all government or quasi-government organizations including the United Nations to act as such and in accordance with the terms of the IOC Charter. That the political problems existing between the People's Republic of China and the Republic of China are the responsibility of those governments,

and will be determined by them alone at some time in the future, while the IOC's responsibility is to ensure that every sportsman and sportswoman in the world has the opportunity of taking a part in the Olympic movement irrespective of race, religion or political beliefs.

2. That the ROCOC [Republic of China Olympic Committee] retain its membership as at present and that the All-China Sports Federation (Olympic committee) be advised that they will be admitted to membership on condition that: a) their constitution be amended to comply fully and completely with the requirements of the IOC charter; b) that they specifically exclude from their area of jurisdiction the areas which currently come within the jurisdiction of the ROCOC.

3. In the event of the above recommendation not being acceptable, that two Olympic committees be established to administer the affairs of the Olympic movement in two separate geographical areas. These committees to be known as the China Olympic committee (Peking) and the China Olympic committee (Taipei).[111]

This report by Cross and Bridge, no matter how helpful its findings and recommendations, failed to provide a workable solution: the differences among Beijing, Taipei, and the IOC were too intractable. To make the situation worse, Siperco, the third member of the commission, strongly disagreed with the conclusions of Cross and Bridge. In his separate report dated October 24, 1978, and titled "Visit to the People's Republic of China," Siperco openly acknowledged the disagreement he had with his fellow commission members about the meaning of the term "fact-finding mission." He wrote that he considered their task to not be "restricted only to the recorded opinions of our host exposed in the official organized meetings, but also to express certain information and opinions collected from the various discussions that we had, and the impressions that we received during our visit." Siperco asked his fellow IOC members to consider, first, that the recognition of two Olympic committees for the same country was contrary to existing rules; second (using the argument used by the late president Brundage in a new way), that the United Nations now recognized the People's Republic of China as representing all of China, including its province Taiwan; and third, that the notion of a "territory" did not exist at the time in the IOC rules. Siperco concluded that "it is obvious that the IOC faces a rapidly developing process of recognition or of re-establishment of the rights of the [PRC's] national federations" by the various international federations. In essence,

> It seems that the prestige of the IOC will not be enhanced by the fact that, instead of being a guide for other international sporting bodies, it looks to be lagging behind an irreversible evolution. The fact is also to be considered that if the IOC does not re-establish the P. R. of China's recognition at the session in Montevideo, it could be placed in a quite embarrassing position at the 1980 Olympic Games of refusing the participation of athletes belonging to the national federations of the P. R. of China fully recognized by then by the majority of the [international federations]. This fact could add new embarrassments to the ones the IOC already anticipates and could harm the authority of the IOC.[112]

Killanin may have hoped that the fact-finding commission would help pave the way for Beijing's smooth entry into the Olympic family, but this feuding by the individual commission members did nothing of the sort. In 1979 the IOC devoted substantial time and attention to the China question. During its March 1979 executive meetings, the board spent most of its discussions of March 10 on the China issue. According to the minutes, Killanin opened the meeting by declaring "he felt it was well known that as far back as 1952, he had been opposed to the entry of 'Taiwan' as the 'Republic of China' into the Olympic movement. This had been accepted by the IOC shortly after the last War and he said it was regrettable that its decision had been made purely from the point of view of politics and not sport."[113] He now asked the IOC to spend as much time as necessary to find a solution to the impasse that had resulted from this early error.

The China question was discussed for two whole days again on April 6 and 7, 1979. During this session, the IOC met with representatives from both Beijing and Taipei to hear their arguments in person. Interestingly, when the IOC had first asked the PRC and Taiwan to sit and discuss the matter together, Beijing had refused and Taipei had agreed. Then, after Beijing changed its mind, Taipei decided it did not want to sit down with Beijing and instead requested a meeting with the IOC president only. Killanin refused, deciding to invite both Beijing and Taipei to a meeting of the executive board in Montevideo in April 1979. There the Taiwan delegation was asked point blank whether Taipei would accept the name of "Chinese Olympic Committee, Taipei." The head of the delegation, Ding Shanli, "acknowledged that they were in fact ready to accept this name." Siperco then asked why Taipei still claimed the right to use the old flag, name, anthem, and so on of Nationalist China if it did not claim to have jurisdiction over more than Taiwan and the surrounding islands. Ding replied that if every other country used its own country's flag, name, and symbols, he saw no reason why his country could not do the same. The discussion cooled further when the IOC asked the Taipei delegation whether they were ready to sit with the representatives from Beijing. The Taiwan side replied that "they had accepted the invitation to the Session to ask for an independent identity and area of jurisdiction and for no other discussion." With this announcement, they left the meeting.[114]

Beijing's delegation, led by Song Zhong, He Zhenliang, and Lou Dapeng, was the next to meet with the IOC. Beijing again insisted that only the PRC could represent China and expressed its interest in returning to the Olympic movement if Taiwan was removed. When delegate He Zhenliang was asked by an IOC member why Beijing had allowed Hong Kong to stay in the Olympic family but not Taiwan, he stressed that there was "a great difference between the status of Taiwan and that of Hong Kong"—Hong Kong "was a 'left-over of history' whose status had been subject to a treaty." When he was asked whether Beijing was willing to allow the Republic of China Olympic Committee to change its name, He Zhenliang replied that there could only be one national Olympic committee for China and there was only one China. Beijing was willing to accept a different name for Taiwan as a short-term compromise only if Beijing was accepted by the IOC as representing all of China in the Olympic family.

When IOC member David McKenzie asked whether Beijing would in-
sist on the expulsion of Taiwan's Olympic committee from the Olympic movement under any name as a condition of Beijing's application for
recognition, He Zhenliang replied that "it was not a question of the expulsion of one committee and the admission of another but of representation." Beijing would accept only the name "Chinese Olympic committee" for its own group, and the title "Chinese Taiwan Olympic committee"
for Taipei.[115]

Now that the IOC members had a clearer understanding of the positions of Beijing and Taipei, it was up to them to come up with a solution.
In a debate that followed, forty-two of its members, as well as the president, participated. It was almost unprecedented in IOC history for so
many members to be involved in a single issue. But so many different ideas
and suggestions were raised that the general session once again found itself
at an impasse.

Eventually the members suggested that the executive board prepare a
resolution on which the membership would vote. Soviet member Vitaly
Smirnov in particular felt that the IOC had reached the point where a decision had to be made. He reminded everyone that the Soviet Union recognized the PRC and considered Taiwan a province. This comment immediately triggered a question from McKenzie, who remembered what had
happened in the 1976 Montreal Games when Taiwan had been refused entry. He asked whether Smirnov's remark "meant that the guarantee of
entry to all NOCs at the Games in Moscow might be abrogated." The
Russian responded no, that "he was simply expressing his point of view on
bringing Peking back into the Olympic movement," and "all recognized
NOCs would be admitted" to the Moscow Games. Killanin was worried
that procedurally a session vote "would close the door for many years" to
true resolution on the issue, given that the membership was still very divided. Facing a deadlock, Killanin inquired how many of the members
wanted a decision to be made about China in the current session; the majority, forty-four members, indicated they wanted closure on the issue.

The executive board therefore met that same evening to discuss what
kind of decision should be made. After a long discussion, the board adopted

a resolution (with one abstention and one opposed) to both reintegrate the Chinese Olympic committee and continue to recognize the Olympic committee headquartered in Taipei. All matters pertaining to name, anthem, and flag would be resolved as soon as possible. The resolution was presented the next day, April 7, to the IOC session for approval. The IOC members debated its wording and even its substance, with some pro-Taiwan members proposing minor changes. Although some IOC members complained bitterly that they did not have an opportunity to fully express themselves on such an important issue, the amended resolution passed thirty-six to thirty, thus defeating the board's original resolution. The mood at the meeting now turned hostile. Killanin was upset with the minor revisions and openly expressed both "his disappointment at the lack of confidence in the Executive Board displayed by the members" and his belief that the session itself "had made a mistake in the decision it had just taken." After more serious discussion and negotiation, the session eventually agreed to give the executive board and its president the final say in resolving the two-China problem.

With an extraordinary sense of emergency, the IOC executive board in its meeting in October 1979 in Nagoya, Japan, passed its historic resolution on Taiwan. Taiwan's Olympic committee name would be Chinese Taipei Olympic Committee and it could not use its national flag, anthem, or emblem; in addition, any new versions had to be approved by the IOC's executive board. The constitution of Taiwan's national Olympic committee also had to be amended by January 1, 1980, to conform with IOC rules.[116]

After the Nagoya agreement, Taiwan was faced with the problem of having no national anthem or flag for its Olympic team to use.[117] After Xu Heng filed a lawsuit against the IOC in Switzerland, claiming the IOC's decision was illegal, Killanin asked IOC member Kevan Gosper to find out, during his scheduled meeting with He Zhenliang in China in 1979, whether it was possible for Beijing to use a different flag and anthem.[118] He Zhenliang replied, "When you have spilled as much blood and worked as hard as we have to rebuild a nation, you stand for no one else's anthem, you parade behind no one else's flag. We are Chinese, we have time."[119] In other words, there was no way the PRC would budge; Taiwan would have to make the adjustment.

Luckily for the IOC, the leadership in Beijing was growing more pragmatic under Deng Xiaoping, who wanted to put these issues behind him as much as the IOC did. Deng was no stranger to sports policy and sports. He was a big fan of soccer largely due to the several years he had spent in France as a work-study student. Further, he had been in charge of sports policy before the Cultural Revolution. Deng's final return to power coincided with his attending a soccer game between the China youth team and a Hong Kong's team on July 30, 1977.[120]

As China's new leader, Deng Xiaoping wanted his country to quickly reestablish international relationships, including those with the Olympic movement. He became deeply involved in negotiations with the IOC and personally made all of the crucial decisions on Beijing's return to the Olympic movement, including those concerning Taiwan's use of the Chinese anthem and flag.[121] On February 26, 1979, Deng Xiaoping met a Japanese journalist who asked, "The 1980 Olympic Games will take place in Moscow. Is China interested in attending the Games and even hosting the Olympic Games in the future?" Deng responded, "First, we need to solve the problem of Taiwan's membership in the IOC. When this issue is solved, of course we will join the IOC." In early 1981 Taiwan finally submitted a new flag design and emblem *(hui)* to the IOC. As some PRC officials debated whether or not to accept the new design, Deng gave personal instructions that Beijing would approve Taiwan's new design, as well as its use of the Olympic hymn if its athletes won gold medals at the Games.[122] With Beijing's blessing, the IOC happily adopted Taiwan's designs.

Taiwan did not play a completely passive role in these developments. Taiwan realized that the IOC-mandated English name, the Chinese Taipei Olympic Committee, could not be changed (Xu Heng withdrew the lawsuit), but it could play tricks with the Chinese translation of that name. Beijing insisted it should read *Zhongguo Taibei*, but Taipei made it *Zhonghua Taibei*. The one-character difference threw the two sides into a serious dispute: according to Wu Jingguo, who himself was involved in the negotiations, it implies whether or not Taiwan is subordinate to the

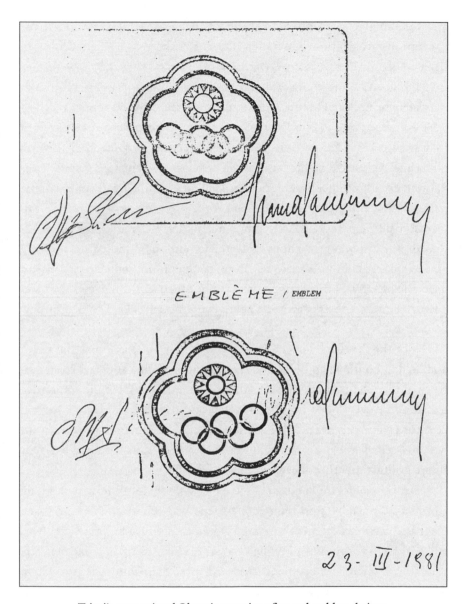

EMBLÈME / EMBLEM

Taipei's new national Olympic committee flag and emblem designs.

Chinese Olympic committee in Beijing. Several secret meetings were held in Hong Kong to work out a solution, and in the end it was Deng Xiaoping who finally decided to accept Taiwan's translation. In 1989 Beijing and Taiwan signed an official agreement that allowed Taiwan to use the contentious translation Zhonghua Taibei for the 1990 Asian Games in Beijing.[123]

Significantly, the final solution of the two-China issue in the IOC and in other international sports federations reflected Deng Xiaoping's idea of "one country, two systems." Many people know that Deng used this idea to deal with Hong Kong's return from British colonial control, but few realize that the idea was first applied in solving the Olympic dispute over Taiwan. By adopting a pragmatic attitude and avoiding the mistakes of the past, Chinese athletes from both the People's Republic of China and Taiwan can participate in the Olympics and other international events. Although Taiwan was not happy with the conditions imposed on it, being able to take part in international sports competitions conferred a sense of legitimacy that was increasingly eroding in other world forums. It was in Taiwan's interest to stay in the Games even though it had to accept new conditions.

Since the developments in 1979 and the early 1980s, although Taiwan and Beijing continue to be political rivals, both teams' athletes have competed in the Games, and Taiwan's status as a national Olympic committee has in all respects been fully maintained and respected.[124] Unlike the old zero-sum game perspective, the eventual solution has proved a win-win situation. Perhaps the hard-won IOC model could even be used as a basis for future political relations between Beijing and Taiwan.

The Taiwan formula has also served as a model for dealing with Hong Kong's IOC membership after Hong Kong was repatriated. Hong Kong was first accepted as a member of the Olympic family in 1950, when it was still a British colony. With Beijing's blessing, Hong Kong kept its membership in the Olympic movement; two days after the colony's return, Hong Kong and the IOC signed an agreement on July 3, 1997, that declared: "It is the common aim to enable the people of Hong Kong to continue taking part in the Olympic Games and generally in sports competitions everywhere as a separate and independent entity." According to the new arrangement, Hong Kong's Olympic committee would add "China" to "Hong Kong" in its committee designation, and the Hong Kong teams

A very small delegation from Hong Kong participates in the
2006 Winter Olympic Games in Turin, Italy.

would fly at all times the flag of the SAR (Special Administrative Region, a designation indicating its relationship to the PRC). The Chinese national anthem would be played on official occasions such as flag-raising and victory ceremonies. According to the agreement, the initials "HKG" would be maintained and the emblem would feature the flower Bauhinia with the Five Rings as well as the Chinese characters "Zhongguo Hong Kong," all within a circle followed by "Hong Kong" with "CHINA" underneath.[125]

Juan Samaranch, who served as IOC president from 1983 to 2001, once boasted that "we are the only international organization in the world—sports organization or other—that recognizes as full members the national Olympic committees of the People's Republic of China and Chinese Taipei." Looking back at how the IOC handled the two-China issue, however, it seems the organization has little to be proud of in this regard. Still, given the rocky early phase of their relations between 1958 and 1979, it is amazing to see how the IOC and Beijing came to be close allies, always willing to boost each other's interests.

The Sport of Ping-Pong Diplomacy

Our great leader Chairman Mao set the Ping-Pong ball in motion and moved the world.

Zhou Enlai, 1972

IN THE MODERN AGE, because of the mass appeal of sports and the nature of globalization, sports competitions have at times been used for diplomacy. The Chinese, however, have been known to take the practice to a new level. As discussed earlier, well before the Communist takeover, Chinese regimes had used sports to advance larger political and diplomatic goals. And while Mao Zedong promised a totally "new China" with the establishment of the People's Republic in 1949, the new regime actually followed previous governments in its handling of sports, although with a twist: under Mao, sports were frequently used to cultivate political alliances with fellow socialist countries.

Mao himself was no stranger to sports. As noted earlier, Mao's first published article dealt with the importance of sports to the nation. Moreover, Mao enjoyed exercise his whole life, and in particular liked to walk, swim, and hike.[1] In 1966 when he launched the Cultural Revolution, Mao staged a famous swim across the Yangtze to mark the beginning of what would become one of the most deadly political storms in China.

Largely because they approached sports as a diplomatic and political instrument, the leaders of Communist China paid special attention to sports teams and competitive events. Although Mao behaved like an emperor, avoiding the public in most situations, he met with the Chinese Ping-Pong teams several times.[2] Mao also sometimes met with visiting teams from abroad. For instance, on February 6, 1956, Mao met with the members of the visiting Yugoslavia youth football team.[3]

Under Mao's leadership, other Chinese leaders became even more deeply involved in exploring and exploiting connections between sports and diplomacy. Premier Zhou Enlai was particularly brilliant at this tactic. Despite Zhou's extremely busy schedule, he rarely missed an opportunity to meet with visiting sport teams. Once he even met with the Russian chess team. The next day he explained to Chinese sports officials that these Russian chess players were not important individuals themselves, but he had met with them to show that the Chinese were "very, very" friendly toward the Russian people.[4] On March 17, 1963, Zhou invited the Chinese Ping-Pong players to his house for dinner just before their departure to attend the Twenty-seventh World Table Tennis Championships. At the dinner, Zhou told them that "friendship is more important than the competition."[5]

Thus even before the Chinese began their famous ping-pong diplomacy with the Americans, Mao and Zhou had frequently practiced sports diplomacy. Both Mao and Zhou Enlai often listened to radio broadcasts of Ping-Pong games between China and other countries and followed them with great interest. In fact, both men took the broadcasting of the games quite seriously.[6] Once Zhou Enlai personally informed the Central China TV (CCTV) sports announcer Song Shixiong that Mao had been pleased with the way he had announced a game. And in early August 1970, Zhou, following a Politburo decision, instructed broadcasters that an important Ping-Pong game would be announced live on the radio, although the announcer was to pay attention to "politics" rather than focus on the game itself.[7]

For another game, this one between China and Vietnam in November 1970, Zhou again gave directions: "The radio and TV stations . . . must focus on pictures, voices, and acts of friendship." On December 10, 1970, when the Chinese Ping-Pong team played the Romanians, Zhou even informed CCTV that it should give more coverage to the Romanian star player, and he personally examined and approved the media's coverage plan.[8] It seems that nothing was left to chance when it came to sports in Mao's era.

This micromanagement by Chinese officials of sports-related broadcasts and publicity was to continue in post-Mao China. As Song Sixiong remembered in his memoir, it was standard practice for him to prepare a scripted narration for events such as the Olympic opening ceremonies, so that he could receive state approval before the broadcast began.[9]

Setting the Stage

China and the United States had been deadly opponents since the founding of the People's Republic of China and did not have formal diplomatic ties. But in the late 1960s both countries faced many challenges and realized they might need each other to deal with them. Although Richard Nixon was famous for his stridently anti-Communist rhetoric, he became obsessed during this period with the possibility of forging better relations with Beijing.

China was very much on Nixon's mind even before he took office as U.S. president in 1969. In a 1967 article published in the journal *Foreign Affairs*, he had argued that the United States needed to reevaluate its China policy: "Taking the long view, we simply cannot afford to leave China forever outside the family of nations, there to nurture its fantasies, cherish its hates and threaten its neighbors. There is no place on this small planet for a billion of its potentially most able people to live in angry isolation."[10]

As soon as he moved into the White House, Nixon made the China initiative his top priority. There were several reasons for this decision. First, as a presidential candidate Nixon had promised the American people that if elected, he would bring the United States out of the Vietnam War with honor, and given China's deep involvement in Vietnam, better relations with China seemed essential for realizing this goal. Nixon also needed to figure out how to negotiate effectively with the Soviet Union, since bilateral relations between the two superpowers had become one of thorniest issues American presidents had had to deal with since the end of World War II. Nixon believed that a closer diplomatic relationship with China would strengthen his bargaining position when contending with the USSR. And finally, Nixon had high expectations for himself as a politician, and was eager to be known as the one who opened up a dialogue with the PRC—thereby gaining credibility as a world-class statesman who had a bigger vision than many when it came to international affairs.

The first step in creating this new dialogue came on February 1, 1969, when Nixon asked Henry Kissinger, his national security adviser, to find a way to cultivate better relations with the Chinese.[11] But care had to be taken to send Nixon's message of goodwill to the Chinese in a way that wouldn't cause the Americans to lose face if it failed. Moreover, the United States and the PRC had no formal diplomatic relationship and their level of mutual distrust was high. Nixon was both determined and creative in his approach. Thinking through possible common ground he might have with Mao, Nixon once jotted down: "RN [Richard Nixon] and Mao, men of the people." Moreover, Nixon and Mao both had "problems with intellectuals."[12] Nixon was delighted to discover more potential commonalities in Kissinger's April 1969 report on the Chinese Communist Party's ninth congress; it seemed that Mao in his Cultural Revolution was battling to revamp educational policy. Nixon wrote in the margin: "HK: Note Mao [too] fights the educational establishment!"[13]

The Nixon administration sent out many feelers to China—"a whole series of them" according to James Lilley, who was then a CIA agent and later the American ambassador to Beijing.[14] In the early days, one attempt involved the Netherlands' minister to Beijing, J. J. Derksen, who told the Americans in early 1970 that he was willing to relay messages while preserving absolute secrecy.[15] Unfortunately Derksen proved a disappointment. As Kissinger finally admitted, "We have also been trying since the beginning of the year to open a channel through the Dutch, but I believe if we are to have any success it will be through Paris."[16]

France had diplomatic relations with both the United States and the PRC, and Beijing had an ambassador in Paris. But Nixon and Kissinger soon concluded that Paris was a risky place to conduct super-secretive diplomacy; news of their efforts could too easily reach the wrong ears. Nixon had to find a new place. In his eagerness, Nixon tried every possible channel. In the late summer of 1969, during his first around-the-world tour as president, Nixon discussed China with many world leaders and asked them to convey his goodwill to Beijing. And in October 1970, when many world leaders came to New York to mark the twenty-fifth anniversary of the United Nations, Nixon seized the moment. Knowing that Pakistan was then considered a friend by both Beijing and Washington, he arranged an October 25 meeting with Pakistan president Yahya Khan in the Oval Office. During the meeting, Nixon told Khan, "It is essential that we open negotiations with China," and indicated he was prepared to offer a high-level contact. Since Nixon knew that Khan would soon travel to Beijing, he asked him to convey this message to the Chinese leaders. The Pakistani agreed.[17]

Nixon similarly approached Nicolae Ceauşescu, president of Romania. In an October 26 meeting, he told Ceauşescu that he was very interested in establishing high-level political and diplomatic communications with the People's Republic. Kissinger the next day reiterated this point, telling Ceauşescu, "If leaders of the People's Republic of China want to tell us something through you, and your ambassador brings the communication to me, I can assure you that such communication will be confined to the White House." Ceauşescu promised that "we will inform the Chinese leaders of our conversation and if there is any communication we will pass that to you as we have in the past."[18] This was the first time an American president had used China's official name and Nixon called it "a significant diplomatic signal." In October 1970, in an interview with *Time*, Nixon declared, "If there is anything I want to do before I die, it is to go to China."[19]

Nixon backed up his words with decisive action. On September 9, 1969, Nixon personally asked the U.S. ambassador in Warsaw to contact Chinese diplomats directly and indicate that he, Nixon, wanted to begin concrete discussions.[20] At the request of the United States, talks took place in Warsaw on January 20, 1970, between Ambassador Walter Stoessel and Lei Yang, the Chinese chargé d'affaires. During their talks, Stoessel expressed the U.S. government's wish to improve relations with the PRC. One month later, again under direct instructions from the White House, Stoessel inquired further about a higher-level meeting between two countries. Still Lei Yang promised nothing.[21] Then on March 11, 1971, the U.S. State Department secretly informed its embassies abroad that "restriction on use of passports for travel to PRC automatically expires on March 15 and will not be renewed" while the restrictions on North Vietnam, North Korea, and Cuba would be extended.[22] This goodwill gesture was strategically wise; it proved very helpful when Beijing invited the American Ping-Pong team to visit in April 1971.

While Nixon was making efforts to convey a friendlier posture toward Beijing, Mao Zedong had decided that he also could realize strategic gains from better relations with the United States.[23] The insane years of Mao's Cultural Revolution had dramatically eroded all the political foundations he himself had created; the country was collapsing economically and suffering tremendously from its self-imposed diplomatic isolation. More importantly, the relationship between China and the Soviet Union had become so contentious that in 1969 the two countries had faced off in military clashes along their common border. Mao had good reason to worry about his Soviet neighbor: in 1968 the USSR had brutally suppressed the Czech revolution under the so-called Brezhnev doctrine that gave Russia the right to use military force if any socialist country dared to challenge Soviet authority. China had openly challenged the Soviets in many areas, and the Soviet Union had indeed left the door open for a possible military showdown with China by talking openly about "a system of collective security in Asia." The Soviets had even asked the United States how it might react if it attacked Chinese nuclear facilities.[24] In addition, after the 1969 border clashes the Soviets substantially increased their military presence on the borders with China, from thirty divisions in 1970 to forty-four a year later.[25]

Largely motivated by this Soviet threat, Mao, like Nixon, began to rethink Sino-American relations. As a brilliant guerrilla fighter, Mao knew that Beijing could not afford to be a mortal enemy of both superpowers now that Russia might launch an attack at any moment. Even though the

Chinese openly compared Nixon to his predecessor Lyndon Johnson, calling them "jackals of the same lair," in secret Mao hoped that Nixon would be someone he could deal with—a hope bolstered by the many feelers the American president had sent out.[26]

For Mao, better relations with the United States offered China two major advantages: some deterrence against the Soviet threat, and the possibility of bringing Taiwan back under Beijing's control.[27] It was the Soviet Union's alarming obsession with China, however, that eventually pushed the old enemies together.[28] Mao clearly understood the significance of the Sino-Russian border clashes for the Americans. During the clashes, Mao is alleged to have commented to his personal assistant: "China and the USSR have started to fight. This presents a good topic for the Americans. Now it should not be difficult for them to write the essay."[29]

As part of China's about-face on diplomatic relations with the United States, Mao personally read and approved commentators' articles on Nixon's inauguration speech and the speech itself in the *People's Daily* and *Red Flag* (*Hong qi*), the two most important propaganda organs of the Chinese Communist party.[30] In 1969, when Nixon asked Kissinger to figure out the best way to reach out to China, Mao invited four of his marshals—Chen Yi, Ye Jianying, Xu Xiangqian, and Nie Rongzhen—to assume the same task.[31] And Mao, like Nixon, personally approved the contacts and talks between China and the United States in Warsaw in early 1970.[32]

Also like Nixon, Mao used others to convey his messages to the United States. Mao's meeting and talks with his old friend, the American journalist Edgar Snow, were one example.[33] Mao's assistants woke Snow on the cold Beijing morning of December 18, 1970, to meet with Mao for several hours. During their discussion, Mao told Snow that he would welcome Nixon to China. The photo of Snow with Mao at Tiananmen with the quotation on the right top corner "The people of the world, including the American people, are our friends" was published on the front page of the *People's Daily* on December 25, 1970, through careful arrangements made by Premier Zhou Enlai.

These gestures were carefully designed as goodwill signals to Nixon.

As Mao confided to his personal aide the day he talked with Snow, he wanted to use the meeting and photo "as a trial balloon and test the American nerve."[34] Snow's role was clear; in Mao's own words, "I am courting Nixon and need a matchmaker."[35] But although Snow was the first Western journalist to interview Mao in the 1930s and had since retained privileged access to him, he was a poor choice for getting the word to Nixon because he had no access to the White House. As a result, Mao's message was not known to Nixon until Snow's interview was published in the spring of 1971. As Kissinger later noted, "Among the reasons Mao's signals had been ignored was that the Chinese had vastly overrated the importance of Edgar Snow in America. Snow, an American journalist long sympathetic to the Chinese communists, was thought by the leaders in Beijing to possess a special credibility in the United States on Chinese matters. Washington, however, thought of him as a communist tool and was not prepared to entrust him with its secrets." Kissinger would also admit that the Chinese "overestimated our subtlety, for what they conveyed was so oblique that our crude Occidental minds completely missed the point."[36] Only later did Nixon and Kissinger come to understand that Mao meant his meetings with Snow on October 1 and December 18 of 1970 to symbolize that Chinese-American relations now had his personal attention.[37]

Mao faced another major obstacle in trying to set a new tone with Washington: justifying his courtship of Nixon to his domestic audiences. For many years the Chinese people had been told that the United States was an imperialist power hostile to China. During the Cultural Revolution, political radicalism had become so deeply ingrained in the Chinese that it was now difficult to justify a more pragmatic style of diplomacy. Once when Soviet Union premier A. H. Kosygin had tried to call Mao through the hotline to discuss deteriorating relations after the border clashes, the Chinese switchboard operator called him a revisionist, told him he was not qualified to talk with the great leader Mao, and hung up.[38] In light of Mao's cult of personality, then, which he himself had been instrumental in cultivating, Mao had to move very carefully. And since there were no guarantees that his courtship of Nixon would succeed, Mao could only slowly prepare for a new era in Sino-American relations.

Mao was also not about to give up his revolutionary image abroad, which caused a great deal of confusion for Nixon. Mao's May 20, 1970, statement on the American bombing of Cambodia is a good example. In the statement, entitled "People of the World, Unite and Defeat the U.S. Aggressors and All Their Running Dogs!" Mao declared that "U.S. imperialism, which looks like a huge monster, is in essence a paper tiger, now in the throes of its death-bed struggle." Mao, of course, had to support the Cambodians due to geopolitical and ideological considerations. In a memo, Kissinger seemed to pick up on Mao's dilemma: he told Nixon that Mao's statement was actually "remarkably bland" in that it offered only "warm support" to the peoples of Indo-China, "without even the usual phrases about China being a 'rear area' for the struggle."[39] But Nixon was exasperated: "Stuff that [sic] will look belligerent. I want them to know we are not playing this chicken game."[40] In what was clearly an overreaction, he ordered every element of the Seventh Fleet not needed for Vietnam to move into the Taiwan Strait. To make matters worse for both Mao and Nixon, radicals in China continued to issue frequent denunciations of the United States.

If the Chinese under Mao sent Nixon confusing signals, the American side did much the same in return. But the underlying cause was different: for the Americans the problem was that there was no unified policy toward China. Most Americans had become accustomed to hostile relations with China and few were prepared for an about-face. Even Henry Kissinger, according to one account, initially thought that Nixon's idea to develop a diplomatic relationship with China was a "flight of fancy."[41] In addition, Nixon did not actively promote the shift; instead he was very secretive about his China initiatives, keeping even his State Department in the dark. Furthermore, serious bureaucratic infighting between the White House and the State Department at the time meant that Kissinger and Secretary of State William Rogers were frequently in conflict. This situation created muddled and contradictory messages about China that complicated Chinese efforts to understand what was going on in American policy.

Not surprisingly, these mixed signals from both sides led both Mao and Nixon to respond very cautiously to the other's initial overtures. Kissinger later wrote, "As things turned out, it proved easier to define a new architecture of relations with China than it was to implement it. The isolation between America and China had been so total that neither knew how to contact the other, or how to find a common vocabulary through which to assure the other that rapprochement was not intended as a trap."[42] Although Mao and Nixon certainly needed each other, "both parties had to tread warily, feeling their way toward each other with significant but tenuous messages and gestures, which could be disavowed if rejected."[43] After more than twenty years of mutual hatred and misunderstanding, relations could not be lightly or easily established.

Only something extraordinary could provide both Beijing and Washington with a clear signal to go forward, and that proved to be a sports event. As mentioned earlier, Mao was a sports fan, and so was Nixon, who referred to himself as the "quarterback" and dubbed the mining of Haiphong Harbor "Operation Linebacker."[44] According to the diary of H. R. Haldeman, his chief of staff, Nixon once cut short a budget meeting with top aides to watch longtime rivals Ohio State and the University of Michigan play football.[45] Interestingly, unlike Mao, Nixon enjoyed watching sports but seldom participated himself. In fact, Nixon was the least active of American presidents since Franklin Roosevelt: once he told his sports advisory council, "I really hate exercise for exercise's sake. . . . There is a tendency with television for people to just sit there with their feet up, eating pretzels and drinking and that is their participation in sports. I don't think that is bad."[46] In any case, Nixon enjoyed the beauty of sports. Consequently, when Mao suddenly proposed friendly Ping-Pong games between the two countries, Nixon was very receptive and immediately understood the implication and importance.

Mao's Initiative

Mao himself may have enjoyed sports, but his idea of using Ping-Pong games with the United States for diplomatic purposes was hampered by his own domestic initiatives. In particular, Mao's Cultural Revolution did terrible damage to Chinese sports, including Ping-Pong. Several top Ping-

Pong players committed suicide in 1967 after being humiliated and tortured by the Red Guards. Almost all participation in important international sports events was abandoned.

By the early 1970s, then, Beijing was a member of very few international sports federations. Luckily for Mao and Nixon, the PRC had retained its membership in the World Table Tennis Federation, if not the Asian Federation. Still, with the Cultural Revolution in full swing, China had missed the twenty-ninth and thirtieth World Table Tennis Championship games. The thirty-first championship would be staged in Nagoya, Japan, between March 28 and April 7, 1971. Would Beijing miss the tournament again?

Premier Zhou Enlai clearly thought that China should make an appearance as part of the nation's return to the international community, and began making plans for the team as early as October of 1970. As a first step, Zhou personally arranged to have Koji Goto, president of the Japanese Table Tennis Association, visit China in early 1971. When Koji Goto's talks with Chinese officials stalled because of Taiwan's membership in the Asian Table Tennis Association, Zhou personally intervened and sealed the deal.[47] On February 2, 1971, the *People's Daily* reported that Beijing would indeed take part in the Thirty-first World Table Tennis Championship games.

Zhou continued his personal involvement with the team. He watched the Chinese team practice on February 12, meeting with the players afterward to encourage them to do well in the coming competition. Zhou told them that their participation was a sort of "political battle" and so emphasized the ideals of friendship first and competition second. On March 8, he met with the Chinese team again to reinforce the message that politics should be the players' most important consideration. He even wrote a letter to the team the same evening to further encourage and guide their efforts.[48]

On March 11, 1971, Zhou made an amazing comment in a meeting with foreign ministry and sports officials about the issue of the Chinese encountering the American Ping-Pong team in Japan. Zhou said, "As a group, we sooner or later will have contact with them. If the American team makes progress or improves, we can also consider inviting them here for competitions. We should have [sports] competitions with the Americans. Otherwise, it does not make sense." Zhou then asked, "Our sports teams have visited West Germany in the past, then why should we not visit America? We have not yet normalized diplomatic relations with Japan, but our sport teams have been able to visit that country. . . . I hope everyone here should have some good thinking on these big world issues."[49]

Zhou was hinting at Beijing's ulterior motive for participating in the championship: the expansion of Sino-American relations. And he was an appropriate person to communicate this message: although he may not have had a final say in policy making, Zhou was at the time involved in secret communications with the White House. In addition, he knew that Mao was deeply interested in improving bilateral relations between China and the United States.

Significantly, the American government learned of Beijing's entry into the championships almost immediately. On February 3, 1971, a memorandum to Assistant Secretary of State Marshall Green from Alfred Jenkins, a state department official, mentioned the PRC's announcement that it intended to take part in the forthcoming World Table Tennis Championships in Nagoya. The memo continued, "This would be the first time the PRC, which dominated international table tennis competition prior to 1966, has sent a national team to compete in a major international sports event since the beginning of the Cultural Revolution." Jenkins commented that Beijing's decision was the natural corollary of its current diplomatic offensive and had "clear political motivations."[50] At that time, however, no one yet had any inkling that this decision was to have great significance for the development of Sino-American relations.

There were still obstacles to overcome. Developments with the Cambodians almost killed Beijing's plan. The pro-Beijing Norodom Sihanouk government had been overthrown by Lon Nol in March 1970, and Sihanouk ended up in exile in Beijing. When the Sihanouk government-in-exile learned that the Lon Nol regime was going to take part in the world table tennis championship in Japan, it asked Beijing in March 1971 not to play, in protest. The situation presented a tough choice for China. If it did not participate in the games, its diplomatic scheme of "people's diplomacy" would have to be abandoned; further, backing out would not sit well with the Japanese. But denying Sihanouk's plea might present political difficulties for Zhou, who had several times been criticized and attacked by the radicals for his dispassionate, pragmatic foreign policy.

The situation became even more complicated after the North Korean government also expressed reservations about Beijing's participation in the championships. In an effort to protect himself, Zhou asked the Chinese team members to discuss whether or not they should go, given the new developments. Zhou may have hoped that the players would support him by wanting to compete, but most members of the team, including Zhuang Zedong, their star player, chose not to support participation. Their decision was understandable, given how during the Cultural Revolution radicals had terrorized anyone they deemed less than revolutionary and negligent of politics. Everyone, including Zhou Enlai, could get into serious trouble if they were targeted by the radicals.

Although Zhou was obviously disappointed with the outcome of the team's discussion, in typical Zhou fashion, he would not decide himself but chose to play it safe by referring the decision to Mao. After all, only Mao could do anything he wanted. In his report to Mao on March 15, 1971, two days before the Chinese team was supposed to leave for Japan, Zhou explained the situation and asked Mao to make the final decision on the issue. Mao responded the same day: "Our team should go."[51] Problem solved.

On the evening of March 16, Zhou hosted a sendoff party for the Chinese team at the Great Hall of the People, where he made a long speech about world affairs and the Korean and Cambodian attitudes. He again asked the team to follow the spirit of friendship first, competition second.[52] Before the team's departure, the government issued instructions, which Mao himself approved, on how to deal with the American team at the championships: when the players met with the Americans, they were not allowed to greet them or talk with them first, and if the Chinese team played a game with the Americans, the Chinese were not permitted to exchange team flags but could shake hands.[53] In addition, the Chinese player

The Chinese Ping-Pong team enters the arena of the Thirty-first World
Table Tennis Championship Games held in 1971 in Nagoya, Japan.

Zhuang Zedong was to choose not to play against the player from Cambodia, to signal Beijing's support for Sihanouk.

Given these explicit directives, and the separate hotel and bus provided by the Japanese for the Chinese team, any communication between the Chinese and American teams would have to be initiated by the Americans. And several overtures did occur. According to a secret, official report found in the Chinese foreign ministry (and deemed reliable given the sensitivity of Sino-American relations at the time), on March 28 the American journalist Richard Miles of *Sports Illustrated* sent a letter to the Chinese team expressing his interest in interviewing its leader and world champion, Zhuang Zedong. (The Chinese did not reply.) On March 28 and 29, too, several American journalists shook hands with Song Zhong, an official of the Chinese Ping-Pong team, and expressed a desire to visit China. The same report pointed out that on March 30 the Chinese representative at the World Table Tennis Conference openly criticized the American "plot" to create two Chinas by supporting Taiwan's membership in the World Table Tennis Federation. But at the conference break, American team heads Graham Steenhoven and J. Rufford Harrison remained friendly and inquired whether China was willing to allow an American team to visit as many other teams had been invited to do. The reliability of this report can be verified from the American side. Although J. Rufford Harrison later denied that he or Steenhoven personally fished for an invitation, he did tell an interviewer from the University of Michigan's oral history project that he did not recall the Chinese approaching the Americans at the championships, and admitted, "We approached them occasionally." He also acknowledged that at the end of the table tennis association's first meeting, after the Chinese had denounced Americans regarding the Taiwan issue, he congratulated the Chinese translator on his English. And as for whether the American players had made it very apparent that they would jump at the chance to go to China, he answered:

Yes and no. . . . if somebody like Glenn Cowan went up to Sung Chung or an interpreter or anybody else and said, 'We'd like to go to China, get us an invitation,' that's not really an American group fishing for an invitation. That's one person in the American group fishing for an invitation. If Steenhoven or I had gone to the Chinese and said, 'We're wondering if it would be possible for our team to visit China on the way back home,' that would be a different matter. That would be our team fishing for an invitation. And it did not happen. We did not ask for an invitation. I'm not sure who it was, but I think somebody did say that he would like to go to China.[54]

In the long interview given for the oral history project, Steenhoven remarked about the invitation to China, "As a matter of fact, we must have said, 'Boy, we'd like to go.' I'm sure it was said." He also commented on what it felt like to learn that other teams like Canada and Colombia had been invited: as Steenhoven put it, the team was "absolutely envious."

Steenhoven also mentioned that after the Chinese attacked the Americans regarding the issue of Taiwan's membership in the World Table Tennis Federation, he and other Americans at the meeting did not respond. During the coffee break, he happened to stand next to Song Zhong and his interpreter. "I thought it proper to make some comment so I approached them and said that when I come to these tournaments I brought Kennedy half dollars; if they could accept them I'd be pleased to give them one each as a souvenir of America, and that if they couldn't accept them, I wouldn't offer them so that they wouldn't be offended. And they said yes, they could accept them . . . so my only contact with the Chinese prior to any other meeting with them was on that particular date and that friendly gesture." Steenhoven also explained that the American players paid particular attention to the Chinese team: "If you're going to watch the best, that's where you're going to learn."[55] From these stories, it seems safe to assume that the Americans repeatedly voiced an interest in visiting China once the championships had concluded.

Regardless of what happened behind the scenes, a dramatically public event was soon to bring world attention to the contact that was occurring between the American and Chinese teams. On April 4, Glenn Cowan, an American player, jumped onto the Chinese team's bus. As Zhuang Zedong later explained, when the young American hippie suddenly appeared on the bus, at first no one said anything to him. But then Zhuang remembered that Mao had told Snow in 1970 that the Chinese were hoping for warmer relations with the U.S. government and its people. He stood up and through an interpreter told Cowan that the Chinese and Americans were friends even though the American government was hostile to China. To demonstrate this friendship, Zhuang gave him a small gift: a silk painting. Cowan was overjoyed to have received even a token from Zhuang, the world champion, and the next day he reciprocated, giving Zhuang a T-shirt and expressing the hope that someday he would visit China.[56]

Kissinger felt somewhat cynical about the event: he noted in his memoir that Zhuang's gesture must have been preauthorized since "the Chinese would not have agreed had they not come to Nagoya with firm instruc-

Chinese star athlete Zhuang Zedong and American table tennis player
Glenn Cowan at the Thirty-first World Table Tennis Championship
Games, 1971. Their exchanges of small tokens of friendship, which Cowan
initiated by unexpectedly jumping aboard the Chinese team's bus, helped
renew diplomatic relations between China and the United States.

tions to befriend the Americans. One of the most remarkable gifts of the
Chinese is to make the meticulously planned appear spontaneous."[57] But
the interaction between Zhuang and Cowan was in fact completely un-
planned. Mao himself learned about it from the Western media and upon
hearing the news, personally instructed that during the competition, telephone communications between the Chinese team and Beijing be increased
from three to five times daily. Mao also asked his personal aide to read foreign press coverage of the Chinese team to him in detail every day.[58]

A secret report dated April 3 from the Chinese foreign ministry and
the sports authority informed Zhou Enlai that teams from Colombia, Jamaica, and the United States had expressed interest in visiting China af-

ter the championships. Although the Colombian and Jamaican Ping-Pong teams would be invited, in order "to enhance our political influence and lay the foundation for our sports teams to visit Latin America," the situation with the Americans was more complicated. "Some members of the American Ping-Pong team have been friendly to our team, and the head of the American team and others interacted with our team six times and made gestures of friendship," noted the report's author. But "we think that it may be not in our political interest if we allow the American Ping-Pong team to visit China first when leftist Americans and influential politicians have not yet done so. We suggest that [the Chinese players in Japan] inform the American team that it is not appropriate at this moment for them to visit us and tell them the opportunity to do so will arrive in the future." Zhou agreed with the report's recommendation, but added: "We may ask for [the American players'] addresses for future communications [if a visit opportunity arises]. However, we will seriously express to the head of the American team that the Chinese people strongly oppose the 'two-China,' 'one China, one Taiwan' plot." Zhou Enlai then forwarded on April 4 the report with his comments to Mao for further instruction.[59] On April 6, after three days' hesitation, Mao approved the report's recommendation not to invite the American team, and the matter seemed settled.

But the situation changed dramatically around midnight that same day. According to Wu Xujun, Mao's personal assistant, Mao seemed to be in deep thought that evening, and after taking his sleep medicine, became drowsy. Then he suddenly murmured to Wu that she should call the foreign ministry immediately and tell officials there that he had decided to invite the Americans after all.

At this point it was before dawn on April 7, the last day of the World Table Tennis Championship. Wu had to act quickly if she were to carry out Mao's instructions. But she faced a major dilemma: Mao had earlier decreed that his words did not count after he had taken sleeping pills. Should she ignore Mao's new instructions, possibly derailing an important diplomatic opportunity? Or should she go ahead, risking the possibility that Mao did not truly intend to invite the Americans to China?

Wu decided to ignore Mao's order for a moment to see whether he really meant it. When Mao realized that Wu was not carrying out his wishes, he ordered her to act quickly since time was running out. Wu carefully asked what order he had given her. Mao repeated his instructions to invite the American team and told her she should act even though he had taken sleeping pills. Wu, reassured, immediately telephoned the ministry, and Zhou Enlai urgently forwarded the message to Japan. Wu was understandably still nervous the next day; she worried whether Mao would forget what had transpired. It came as a great relief, then, that Mao indeed acknowledged the instructions he had given her the night before.[60] With a last-minute intervention, Mao, with Wu's help, had changed the course of Sino-American relations by welcoming the American Ping-Pong team to China.[61]

On receiving his instructions from Beijing, Song Zhong in Japan acted quickly. At 11:30 that morning he went to the hotel where the Americans were staying and found Harrison. Song asked him, "How would you react to an invitation for your team and officials to visit China?" This was a very shrewd approach from the Chinese. If the Americans reacted positively, an invitation was implied; if they responded unfavorably, no official invitation would be offered. But the Americans jumped at the opportunity. The only concern Harrison had was the cost—an understandable concern because the team's sponsor, the U.S. Table Tennis Association (USTTA), was poorly funded (some of the players had even had to borrow money to make the trip to Japan).[62] Song Zhong replied that the Chinese would pay for the trip.[63] At 7:30 in the evening on April 7, the American team officially accepted China's invitation with the additional request that China cover the $170 fee per player for the changed flight home. The Chinese agreed.[64]

The fifteen-member American Ping-Pong team arrived in China on April 10 and left on April 17. Their visit was truly groundbreaking; they were the first officially approved American group to come to the PRC since 1949. They visited Beijing, Shanghai, and Hangzhou, and held two friendship games. Zhou, a brilliant host, was personally involved in every detail of the American visit, an event that Kissinger later called "an international sensation; it captured the world's imagination, aided no little by Chou En-lai's careful state management."[65]

Zhou even gave careful consideration to what kind of entertainment the Americans should see. At the time of the American visit, only the revolutionary operas *Red Lantern (Hong deng ji), Taking Tiger Mountain by Stratagem (Zhi qu Weihu Shan),* and *Revolutionary Woman (Hong sao)* were playing in Beijing. But Zhou wanted these special American guests to see instead the spectacular production *The Red Detachment of Women (Hong se niang zi jun),* a revolutionary ballet. In the ballet, a poor Chinese servant girl escapes a wicked landlord to join an all-female detachment of the Chinese Red Army, where she comes to realize that her own suffering and desire for revenge are part of the larger problem of oppression by the landlord class and the Nationalists. Visits by foreigners to China almost invariably lead to proud performances of at least parts of this ballet, which the Chinese consider a modern dance masterpiece. As one U.S. State Department memo in advance of Nixon's 1972 visit relates, "Although the plot of the ballet is pure communist propaganda, there would be no great problem in the President or Mrs. Nixon viewing those parts of it in which the anti-Nationalist theme is least overt. However, the last act, in which the cast shouts the slogan: 'Down with the Kuomintang reactionaries!' presents a problem. There is no anti-American content or implication in the ballet."[66]

Zhou, who was determined that the American Ping-Pong players would see this ballet, attempted to have the dance troupe that was busy preparing for its foreign tour perform it especially for the Americans. Zhou even suggested the date of the performance, April 13.[67] But the plan fell through: due to logistical problems, the troupe could not perform the ballet then.

Eventually it was decided that the Americans would watch the only performance taking place on April 14: *Taking Tiger Mountain by Stratagem,* an opera set during the early stages of the Chinese civil war between the Nationalists and Communists. The story follows a Communist agent who infiltrates a group of bandits who have been co-opted into the Nationalist army. The story was controversial: a U.S. State Department memo to Kissinger on performing arts in the PRC noted that *Taking Tiger Mountain by Stratagem* "contains strongly anti-Chiang propaganda as well as some anti-U.S. propaganda. It is not suitable for viewing by the President or Mrs. Nixon."[68] (The Americans eventually did also see *The Red Detachment of Women* in Guangzhou, during their return trip to the United States.)

Zhou even oversaw development of the official American schedule printed for the Chinese, which emphasized in a bold font that during the friendship competition the Chinese audience should be instructed to applaud the American performance.[69] Before the competition, too, the Chinese and American players were to shake hands and hold hands while walking to the table, all in the spirit of "friendship first." Not surprisingly, Zhou also scrutinized how the Sino-American Ping-Pong Friendship Games would be broadcast. Before the games began in Beijing, Zhou read and corrected the draft text that announcer Song Shixiong would use for the live game coverage.[70] For Zhou, the American visit was a major diplomatic event and he left nothing to chance.

American team leader Steenhoven told the players before they left for China, "Our chances of winning our matches are not very good, but our chances of having a good time are excellent."[71] Steenhoven was right about their having a wonderful experience, but he also underestimated the Chinese team's willingness to put "friendship first." To the American players' delight, under Zhou's careful management the Americans actually won several games; the Chinese managed brilliantly to lose some matches to the Americans without letting on. As the Chinese competitor Zheng Minzhi later remembered, "I knew [the games with the Americans] would be unlike any other games I'd ever played. . . . I knew their significance and my responsibilities. I knew I was not only there to play, but more important, to achieve what cannot be achieved through proper diplomatic channels."[72]

The highlight of the American visit was meeting Zhou Enlai on April 14, 1971—an opportunity that Kissinger described as "an unfulfilled ambition of most of the Western diplomats stationed in Peking."[73] During the carefully orchestrated meeting, Zhou told the Americans "what a joy it is to bring friends from afar." He also told them that Chinese and Americans had been friendly to each other in the past, but their collegial relationship had been interrupted starting in 1949. Now, "with your visit, the door to our friendship has been [re]opened."[74] Zhou even addressed in detail a question from the eighteen-year-old, long-haired Glenn Cowan about Zhou's opinion of American hippie culture. Zhou's thoughtful answer moved Cowan's mother to arrange via a Hong Kong travel agency the delivery of roses and a telegram to Zhou, expressing her gratitude: "Many thanks to Premier Zhou for China's warm reception of Cowan and his teammates." When the Chinese foreign ministry learned about this intended gift from the travel agency, it immediately contacted Zhou Enlai for instructions. Zhou approved the foreign ministry's suggestion that the message be forwarded to Zhou, but decided that it was not necessary for her to send money for the flowers.[75]

As soon as news of Beijing's invitation to the American team broke out, the media were after the story. Tim Boggan, vice president of the USTTA, received "many bewildering offers" from publishers such as *Time, Life, Newsweek,* CBS, the *New York Times,* and even newspapers in Australia. As he recalled later, all wanted the same thing: "Write whatever [I] could, take pictures, use a tape recorder, cable, phone, wherever, whenever I could get through."[76] Almost every member of the team was bombarded with requests for interviews. Judy Bochenski, a fifteen-year-old team member from Oregon, appeared on many TV shows after she returned from China and was chosen to be grand marshal for the Rose Parade in Portland in June 1971, where she shared the spotlight with other luminaries like Bob Hope and one of the Apollo 11 astronauts. The Oregon state legislature even voted a "Judy Bochenski Day" in May 1971 and gave her "a royal reception."[77] When the American team returned to Hong Kong from its China trip, according to Boggan, six hundred reporters came out to cover them and their stories. The hippie Cowan, exhilarated after the fantastic trip, even declared confidentially, "I think I could mediate between Chou En-lai and Nixon quite easily."[78]

Not many Americans, however, understood the real significance of Beijing's ping-pong initiative. When Steenhoven was asked whether he

The U.S. Ping-Pong team, the first official American delegation of any kind
to visit China since 1949, tours the Great Wall of China in 1971.

thought the Chinese had used the American Ping-Pong team for propaganda, he answered, "No, not at all! I'm sure what they wanted was in some way for us to be friends."[79] He did not realize, of course, that Mao had used them brilliantly to initiate the bigger game he intended to play with Nixon. Even the U.S. State Department did not grasp the real meaning of Mao's move and saw it as "part of Peking's effort to present an agreeable face to the world in its drive to gain entry into the UN this autumn."[80] They were clearly missing the big picture. The little Ping-Pong ball, as Zhou Enlai pointed out, was intended to move the big ball, global politics.[81]

The American Reaction

Senator Edward W. Brooke was among the few who immediately recognized the significance of this initiative. He declared on the Senate floor on April 15, 1971, "The recent invitation to the American table tennis team, and the consistently friendly and appreciative quality of their reception, speaks louder and clearer than a hundred diplomatic pronouncements to the desire of the Mainland Chinese for more normal relations with the West. Table tennis is to the Chinese what football and baseball combined are to Americans." He called the visit "an event of historic significance," one signaling that "the log-jam of a generation has been broken."[82]

Mao's decision to invite the American Ping-Pong team in April 1971 took the world by surprise. The Soviets in particular became very alarmed; they warned Washington that Beijing's ping-pong diplomacy was a trick and worried that the Americans would be "taken in."[83] Assistant Secretary Marshall Green of the State Department admitted that "it had been a surprise to us that China should invite fifteen or more Americans to visit the mainland. After all, this was the first time that such a group had gone there in twenty-one years. Furthermore, the ping-pong match was attended by much publicity. We now have calls every day from Americans asking if we would like them to visit China."[84] News of Mao's decision to have his team play Ping-Pong with the Americans was received at the White House, as Kissinger recalled it, with "stunned surprise."[85] Nixon acknowledged, "I was as surprised as I was pleased by this news. I had never expected that the China initiative would come to fruition in the form of a ping-pong team. We immediately approved the acceptance of the invitation."[86]

They were surprised, to be sure, but Nixon and Kissinger immediately grasped the larger message of Mao's invitation. As Kissinger wrote, "In many ways the weeks following the ping-pong diplomacy were the most maddening of the entire tortuous process. Only the president and I understood the full implications of Chou En-lai's move because we alone were aware of all the communications between Peking and Washington. We knew that something big was about to happen, but we were baffled as to which channel would surface it and precisely what form it would take."[87] Moreover, Kissinger commented,

> Like all Chinese moves, it had so many layers of meaning that the brilliantly painted surface was the least significant part. At its most obvious the invitation to the young Americans symbolized China's commitment to improved relations with the United States; on a deeper level it reassured— more than any diplomatic communication through any channel—that the emissary who would now surely be invited would step on friendly soil. It was a signal to the White House that our initiatives had been noted. The fact that the players could not possibly represent a particular political tendency added to the attractiveness of the maneuver from the Chinese perspective. China would be able to make its point without any possibility of a jarring American commentary.[88]

Nixon knew perfectly well that Beijing had made a brilliant first step and the Americans could only follow that lead. As Kissinger observed, the Chinese gesture conveyed "a subtle warning to us: If Chinese overtures were rebuffed, Peking could activate a people-to-people approach and seek to press its case in a public campaign much as Hanoi was doing."[89] Luckily for Nixon, the Chinese move suited his needs exactly. By this invitation, the Chinese had confirmed their intention to work for better relations. The successful matchmaker that Mao and Nixon had worked so hard to find turned out to be the small white Ping-Pong ball.

Nixon was thrilled with Mao's ping-pong initiative since this brilliant move would help him work toward his grand vision for U.S.-China relations and implement his new blueprint for world order. Entries in the diary of Nixon's chief of staff, H. R. Haldeman, indicate the crazy process set in motion by the Chinese initiative. On Monday, April 12, for example,

Haldeman wrote that Kissinger and Nixon had agreed "our whole policy, and the current moves on China, will help to shake the Soviets up, as will Brezhnev's need to make a big peace move of some kind, which should play in our favor for a SALT [Strategic Arms Limitation Talks] agreement and a Summit conference."[90] In a handwritten note drafted April 17, Haldeman mentioned again that Nixon thought his China approach had accomplished "what no one else could do." From Nixon's perspective, with its ping-pong initiative, "China has given us maneuvering room with Russia and now we are not against the wall."[91]

In considering the potential influence of these developments on Nixon's hoped-for policies regarding Russia and Vietnam, Kissinger told Nixon, "Two months ago, we would have thought it was inconceivable." What the administration had done in Laos and other places had been judged failures, "and yet here comes the Chinese move, the ping pong team, and something more significant that pales that into nothing." What follows "can have an enormous significance." For Kissinger, "everything is beginning to fit together." Kissinger even predicted that "if we get this thing working, we will end Vietnam this year."[92] The White House attached so much importance to the China factor that now everything related to foreign policy in the region seemed to be falling into place.

Nixon was proud of these positive developments, and he was not about to let anyone steal his thunder.[93] He and his associates in the White House were most concerned that "we get credit for all the shifts in China policy, rather than letting it go to the State Department, who of course had nothing to do with it, in fact opposed every step the P[resident] took because they were afraid any moves toward China would offend Russia."[94] As Haldeman noted, in talking with Al Haig, Nixon himself made the point that "in describing Nixon you have to make the point that he's always like the iceberg, you see only the tip. You must never think that the surface is all that's going on. The real power is beneath the surface. He was discussing this in relation to Russia and China."[95]

Nixon was so certain of his China policy and so enjoyed the success that Mao's ping-pong move brought that he exploded when his vice president, Spiro Agnew, "inadvertently careened into this diplomatic china shop" by criticizing the favorable U.S. media coverage of the American visit.[96] Agnew had been kept in the dark about Nixon's China initiative, and only expressed his opinion in an off-the-record conversation with the press. But when Nixon learned of the vice president's critical comments, he was furious. As Haldeman wrote in his diary,

> The P wants him now to get off this wicket and say he has completely misunderstood. K[issinger] had recommended that [press secretary Ron] Ziegler say that the VP's expressing his personal view. But the P disagreed with that, and agreed with Ron's recommendation that he say that the VP authorized him to say that there is no difference on the part of the VP with the P's policy on China. The VP completely agrees with the initiatives the P has taken. He says it's clear that he doesn't understand the big picture in this whole Chinese operation, which is, of course, the Russian game. We're using the Chinese thaw to get the Russians shook. . . . The P got again to the point that Agnew shows qualities here that are very damaging.[97]

Nixon was so angry with the vice president's comments that he immediately asked Haldeman to look for a possible new vice presidential candidate.[98]

To keep the momentum going, Nixon wanted to have the American Ping-Pong team visit the White House immediately after it returned from China. John Scali, special consultant to the president, was the first person to get Nixon interested in the idea. As early as April 12, when the American team had just arrived in China, Scali wrote a long memo about how Nixon could "capitalize" on the visit.[99] Kissinger opposed the strategy, believing that Nixon should not "overplay the China thing until we get something more going."[100] But Nixon persisted. Although he did not manage to get the whole American team to the White House, he was determined to have Steenhoven meet with him as soon as possible. The team returned to the United States on Sunday night, and the White House called Steenhoven on Tuesday to inform him that he would meet with Nixon the next day. In his memo to Nixon regarding this meeting, Kissinger wrote, "Your meeting with Mr. Steenhoven will demonstrate to Americans and Chinese your personal interest in the successful opening of non-government contacts by Mr. Steenhoven's group." He pointed out that Premier Zhou Enlai had received Steenhoven and his team in China, and suggested these "talking points":

> You may wish to state to Mr. Steenhoven and the press your appreciation for the dignified and effective manner in which the U.S. table tennis team toured China. You understand the Chinese have accepted Mr. Steenhoven's invitation to send a team to the U.S. The Chinese visitors will be welcome. You hope that there will be a flow of interested Chinese and Americans between the two countries, which will bring about conditions allowing for progress toward your long-range goal of normal diplomatic relations with Peking.[101]

On April 21, 1971, Steenhoven arrived at the White House for his meeting with Nixon. Kissinger and Scali were also present, although as Steenhoven claimed later, he was not introduced to them and they "never said a word." By contrast, his conversation with Nixon was cordial, even humorous. Nixon asked Steenhoven how much a Ping-Pong ball cost, and Steenhoven replied that one could be purchased for a quarter. Steenhoven then told Nixon about the trip to China. After the meeting he also recounted this lighthearted exchange: "'I understand that you'd like to go to China.' And he said 'Yes, I very much would like to go.' And I said, 'Well, you have to be a member of the U.S. table tennis association to go there.' And he says, 'Well, I'll accept an honorary membership'—and right there we blew ten bucks."[102] Nixon spent nearly an hour with Steenhoven, and the White House even invited him to join a White House press conference to answer questions.[103]

Nixon was eager to move as quickly as possible after Beijing's initiative, and directed Kissinger and others to study possible diplomatic initiatives to further the improvement of relations and "explore the degree to which it is possible to build on recent progress."[104] On April 14 Nixon had announced many significant changes in U.S. policy toward China: the twenty-year-old embargo on trade with China was terminated, and the United States was now also prepared to expedite visas for visitors from the PRC. Currency controls were to be relaxed to permit the use of dollars by Beijing, restrictions on oil shipments to and from the PRC by American oil companies were to be ended, and other trade restrictions were also lifted. Nixon further promised that "after due consideration of the results of these changes in our trade and travel restrictions, I will consider what additional steps might be taken."[105] Two days later, on April 16, Nixon told the American Society of Newspaper Editors that he would love to visit China.[106] Nixon seemed to mean it with great urgency. Nixon was so encouraged by the Ping-Pong diplomacy development that, according to Kissinger, "he now wanted to skip the emissary stage lest it take the glow off his own journey" to China, even though Beijing had not yet officially invited him. Kissinger had to warn Nixon that "an unprepared presidential trip to China was much too dangerous."[107]

The Chinese side also began to move more decisively. On April 21, Zhou Enlai sent a response to Nixon's December 16, 1970, message via Pakistan, reaffirming Beijing's "willingness to receive publicly in Peking a special envoy of the president of the U.S.," "or even the president himself for a direct meeting and discussion."[108] After that, all signals became clear and direct, and important messages were exchanged more frequently. On April 29 Nixon declared at a press conference, "Now that we've broken the ice, we have to test the water."[109] Nixon did just that, with tremendous speed. Between April 28 and May 20, he asked Pakistani president Yahya Khan to convey three important messages to Zhou. In his April 28 message, Nixon conveyed to Beijing that he was personally handling negotiations with China and was encouraged by Zhou's "positive, constructive, and forthcoming" message. Nixon informed Zhou Enlai on May 10 that he was prepared to accept an invitation to Beijing due to the urgent importance of normalizing relations between the two countries. Kissinger would go first to arrange an agenda. And in his message to Beijing on May 20, Nixon promised that his government would "conclude no agreement" with the USSR that would be directed against the PRC.[110] On May 29, Zhou replied that Mao welcomed his visit and that he, Zhou, "warmly looks forward to the meeting with Kissinger" beforehand.[111] Kissinger called that message "the most important communication that has come to an American president since the end of World War II." Nixon was so excited that he dashed to the family kitchen to grab a bottle of brandy; he and Kissinger then toasted each other on their success at "a moment of historical significance."[112]

Kissinger's journey came together quickly. On June 4 Nixon told the Chinese, again through the Pakistan channel, that Kissinger would be on his way to China on July 9.[113] This message was transmitted to Beijing on June 9, and two days later, on June 11, Zhou responded that Kissinger's proposed day of arrival was fine and Beijing "would make all the necessary arrangements accordingly."[114] On June 19, President Yahya Khan instructed his ambassador in Washington, "Please assure our friend [Kissinger] that an absolutely fool-proof arrangement will be made by us and he need have no anxiety on this count."[115]

So Kissinger visited Beijing on July 9 as planned. During their first meeting, Zhou Enlai gave special credit to the after-effects of the Ping-Pong games. As Zhou reminded Kissinger, "Recently we invited the U.S. table tennis delegation to China . . . they can bear witness that the Chinese people welcomed this visit of the American people. We have also received many repeated invitations from the U.S. table tennis association to send a delegation to the U.S.; we feel this shows that the American people want to welcome the Chinese people."[116] When Nixon eventually arrived in Beijing himself on February 21, 1972, Mao explained why he had taken the ping-pong initiative:

> The situation between our two countries is strange because during the past twenty-two years our ideas have never met in talks, now the time is less than ten months since we began playing table tennis; if one counts the time since you put forward your suggestion at Warsaw, it is less than two years. Our side also is bureaucratic in dealing with matters. For example,

you wanted some exchange of persons on a personal level, things like that; but rather than deciding that we stuck with our stand that without settling major issues there is nothing to do with small issues. I myself persisted in that position. Later on I saw you were right, and we played table tennis.[117]

Mao clearly indicates that it was Ping-Pong that eventually allowed the two sides to meet. China's ping-pong diplomacy was one of the critical developments of the late twentieth century.

At this point, the White House was generally confident about the direction of the new approach toward China. In an off-the-record briefing given on August 12, 1971, after he had made significant concessions to Beijing on Taiwan, Kissinger said,

Necessity has brought us together with the Chinese, and necessity will dictate the future of our relationship. We are not hostages to the Chinese. They gave up something significant when they entered into this relationship with us. They gave up their revolutionary virginity. They will not cancel the visit [of Nixon] short of our destroying a Chinese city. The principle of revolutionary purity is gone for them now. It is like a situation where a girl will sleep with you for a million dollars but not for ten dollars. We have not paid anything in this China opening and I think we will pay nothing in the future.[118]

Here Kissinger tried to put a brave face on the whole issue. While it might be true that Mao lost a certain revolutionary purity by courting Nixon, the United States, in trying so hard to seduce China, gave up more than it admitted. Besides the crucial concessions on Taiwan, the United States handed to Beijing international legitimacy and credibility. The balance was tenuous. As the *Chicago Daily News* warned in an editorial, "This small beginning [the Ping-Pong invitation] does not and should not signal a grand rush to climb in bed with the rulers of the People's Republic."[119] Soon after this editorial was written, Beijing rather quickly realized significant returns on its ping-pong initiative when, to Nixon's dismay, it replaced Taiwan as the sole representative of China to the United Nations in October 1971.[120] Nonetheless, largely thanks to this diplomatic break-through, Nixon was fired up to pursue a surer footing in U.S. relations with Mao's China. One of the first steps toward this goal was to set up a reciprocal American event of sports diplomacy.

The Americans Return the Volley

Scholars have written extensively about Mao's ping-pong initiative in the spring of 1971, but this book is the first to use all available evidence from both China and the United States to shed new light on this complicated story—in particular, on events set in motion by the Americans before and during the Chinese team's visit to the United States in the spring of 1972. Events leading to this second act of ping-pong diplomacy were set in motion as act one was in progress. When the American team received the invitation to visit China, U.S. team leaders, the U.S. government, and private organizations realized that a natural development of the American visit would be a reciprocal Chinese experience in the United States. Consequently, when news of the Chinese invitation reached the United States, the State Department immediately commented, "We regard this invitation and its acceptance by the U.S. Team as a favorable development. It is clearly consistent with the hopes expressed by both the president and the secretary of state that there could be greater contact between the American and Chinese people. . . . We would view with favor a reciprocal visit of an athletic team or teams to this country. As a general proposition, we would envisage no difficulty with regard to visa."[121] The news that the U.S. government was interested in having a Chinese team come to the United States was immediately forwarded to the American team before its departure for Beijing. But any invitation to a Chinese team would have to be offered through the USTTA.[122] In other words, although the State Department thought it was important for a Chinese team to visit the United States, it realized that having the government fund the trip would make the event too politically charged.

But the USTTA, as noted earlier, had very little funding; sponsoring a visit by the Chinese team seemed out of the question. At this crucial moment, the National Committee on United States–China Relations, a private, nonprofit educational organization, stepped in to offer assistance to the USTTA; it would finance and organize the Chinese visit.

The timing was fortuitous for both the USTTA and the committee itself, which had been formed to encourage understanding and cooperation between China and the United States. Founded in 1966, the committee claimed among its nearly two hundred members many influential academics, business leaders, and former government officials—including John King Fairbank, William Bundy, and George Ball. Many of the members were scholars and specialists on Asia, and the chair in 1971–1972, Alexander Eckstein, was a leading authority on the Chinese economy and a professor of economics at the University of Michigan. In the several years since its founding, the committee, through briefings to Congress and lectures around the country, had quietly laid the groundwork for a reexamination of the China policy. Hosting the Chinese visit would create valuable opportunities for educating the general public about American relations with China and generate unprecedented publicity for the committee and its work.

The opportunity was nearly missed, however. On April 8, 1971, just one day before the American team was to leave Tokyo for China (via Hong Kong), Fay Willey of *Newsweek* learned from the magazine's Tokyo bureau that the USTTA was looking for private funding to set up a reciprocal invitation to the Chinese. She immediately contacted Douglas Murray, program director of the National Committee on United States–China Relations. The committee, acting on the tip from *Newsweek,* lost no time in contacting the team by cable through the U.S. consulate general in Hong Kong to express its willingness to provide support for a reciprocal Chinese visit.[123] That the committee managed to make all the necessary decisions and get word to the team that same day was just short of miraculous. The cable, sent under the name of B. Preston Schoyer, the committee's executive director, read: "Understanding your considering reciprocal invitation to Chinese sports group. If necessary and appropriate National Committee on U.S.-China Relations expects it could raise funds to support Chinese team U.S. visit if invitation is accepted." The committee confirmed its commitment through a second cable to the team on April 15.[124]

The significance of this intervention for the future trip by the Chinese cannot be overstated. In a confidential memo of April 29, 1971, to the committee's board members, Schoyer wrote, "Mr. Steenhoven has told us that without our cabled assurance, the invitation for the reciprocal visit—which has now been accepted—would not have been issued."[125] Harrison, deputy head of the American team, also admitted that USTTA would never have managed the trip on its own: "We didn't have any money. . . . We were completely reliant on the US-China committee."[126] As Steenhoven wrote to Eckstein on September 26, 1974, "without your approval and assistance the Chinese visit would never have happened and the changes it wrought in my life would have never been experienced."[127]

Now that financial support had been secured, Steenhoven was able to invite the Chinese team, and Beijing accepted. On June 25, 1971, Steenhoven, in his capacity as USTTA president, wrote to Song Zhong, acting president of the PRC's table tennis association:

> The response of the American people to the news of your coming visit to the United States has been overwhelming. We have received so many invitations for your group to visit all parts of the United States that no matter which area you select you will find friends waiting to meet you and pleased to be your hosts. We want you to know that we welcome anyone you would wish to add to your party, including officials and members of your press, radio, and television. If you think it advisable that we meet and discuss in more detail the places you wish to visit in the United States, I am available to travel to any place you think appropriate. It is our earnest wish that we can fully express our appreciation for the courtesy, kindness and consideration shown us during our memorable trip to China.[128]

Steenhoven's openness was not reciprocated; the Chinese would not commit to a specific time for the visit. The National Committee, in desperation, even suggested that the White House advance team for Nixon's visit to China raise the timing issue with Chinese leaders "in a suitable low-key way." But the White House seemed a bit uneasy about this role. As John Holdridge, a staffer in Kissinger's office, wrote to Kissinger, "My own feeling is that we should not involve ourselves in the role of postman. The Chinese are trying to keep contacts on a strictly non-governmental basis, and we would not want to complicate things by getting in the act." Holdridge also indicated, however, that "a low-level inquiry about the timing of the visit by someone on the next advance party (provided a suitable opportunity arose) might be acceptable."[129]

But the Chinese spoke up first. While meeting with the White House advance team on January 6, 1972, Zhou Enlai told Alexander Haig, then deputy assistant to the president for national security affairs, and others that "we would like to pay a return visit there next spring when the blossoms are in full bloom."[130] Unfortunately Zhou's message was so vague it was not much help. As Steenhoven later put it, "I didn't know when the flowers were going to bloom, whether that was in Maine or whether it was in California. So we still had no concept of when they were going to come here."[131] In fact, the Chinese did not inform the USTTA about their travel plans until March 15, 1972. In a cable to Steenhoven, Song Zhong informed his host that the Chinese would arrive on April 10 with twenty team members and six accompanying pressmen.[132] The Chinese team eventually arrived on April 12 and left on April 29. Zhou Enlai had personally selected which players would go to visit the United States and Canada.[133]

Another key concern of the USTTA and the National Committee was that the White House would restrict their independence and steal the spotlight during the Chinese visit. From their first meeting in New York on May 15, 1971, the joint committee of the two organizations stressed that "we are independent of the White House. The White House will be kept indirectly informed."[134]

To some, it seemed that the White House was only minimally involved. When asked what kind of role the American government played in the 1972 Chinese Ping-Pong tour of the United States, for example, Harrison recalled, "Virtually none." But either he intentionally played down the role of the White House or he did not know how deeply the White

House was involved, for it is clear that from the very beginning the White House played an extremely important role behind the scenes.[135] Nixon himself was involved in a substantial way. He not only invited Steenhoven to the White House to show his personal investment in ping-pong diplomacy, but he also, on that same day, appointed special consultant John Scali to be his own personal representative in handling the Chinese team's visit. Nixon even arranged to have William Gossett, a Detroit lawyer, serve as an unofficial adviser to Steenhoven, with Scali advising Gossett on all aspects of the proposed visit to make sure everything went smoothly.[136]

Although some in the State Department believed it was important that the United States not appear too eager about the Chinese visit, lest the Chinese conclude "they were in [the] driver's seat," Nixon wanted the visit to happen as soon as possible and worked hard toward that goal by writing to Steenhoven and meeting with the National Committee.[137] In a phone call with Scali on April 21, 1971, Nixon stated that he wanted the Chinese visit to take place "fairly soon" for "maximum impact . . . to capitalize on current news interest and because of a possibility that delay in some way might ruin prospects for a trip." To avoid both the criticism that Nixon was trying to politicize the Chinese visit and the impression that the White House was running the show, Nixon instructed that "all arrangements be handled very subtly"; Scali was to "coordinate everything from backstage, while someone else was out front, perhaps someone close to the president but outside the government." According to Scali's record of that phone call, Nixon then said, "Maybe I [Scali] should be out front, depending on what Kissinger and I decide is best." Nixon also indicated to Scali that the United States should offer "exactly the same" opportunities for travel throughout the country as the American table tennis team had experienced in China. He also told Scali that he himself "would be most pleased to meet with the Chinese." At the end of the conversation, Nixon even mentioned to Scali that Kissinger would be contacting him "to discuss first steps."[138] From this phone call, we can get a pretty clear idea of what was on Nixon's mind and how eager he was to have the visit happen sooner than later.

With Nixon's authorization, Scali became actively involved in coordinating the Chinese visit starting in the spring of 1971. Scali met several times with the National Committee and the USTTA to plan for the Chinese team's visit, and assumed control over communications with the Chinese. Upon discovering that Steenhoven had, on his own authority, sent a cable to the Chinese table tennis association, Scali told him bluntly, "it would be wise not to send any additional cables or letters without seeking unofficial advice from me." (Steenhoven promised to seek advance consultation in the future.)[139] As Scali assured Nixon in a memo on January 17, 1972:

> I am personally overseeing all arrangements, hoping to anticipate any problems, including those of security. In keeping with your instructions, the visit will be dignified, yet friendly, with time for some sightseeing and some contact with average Americans. I have suggested that a side trip to Williamsburg be added to the Washington stay, and that the San Francisco visit include a possible visit to the Stanford University campus. Further, I have suggested that Steenhoven indicate in his cable that it would be desirable that the Chinese team visit the United States in advance of a proposed similar tour of Canada, which tentatively has been set for sometime in April. I will continue to keep you abreast of all developments.[140]

Nixon in his own handwriting wrote on the Scali memo "OK—good plan," and the White House soon approved the overall strategy.[141]

Besides Scali, several other key members of the White House became deeply involved in the Chinese team's visit. Kissinger met with National Committee officials to make sure the financial support for the Chinese visit was in place.[142] Richard Solomon, one of Kissinger's aides and a former colleague of Eckstein's at the University of Michigan, joined Scali on March 20, 1972, to meet with the joint committee to discuss the itinerary and schedule issues. During the two-hour meeting, Solomon tried to convince Steenhoven of the need to persuade the Chinese that New York City might not be the best starting point for the tour because of security and other problems there. In his memo to Haig about the meeting, Scali wrote that "because of his unsophisticated bulldozer approach, he [Steenhoven] will need careful guidance and assistance."[143]

Another issue to be clarified was timing. Scali had once asked the joint committee to make sure the Chinese team wrapped up its visit on April 24 in order to shift the media's attention to Nixon's coming trip to the Soviet Union. But the next stop for the Chinese was Mexico, and their plans for visiting that country were so firm that they could not arrive there before April 29.[144]

The intense involvement of White House senior staff like Scali in planning the Chinese visit made the joint committee uneasy and upset. Dewey Clower, another White House staffer who had been setting up security around the country and checking on hotel accommodations and other arrangements for the Chinese, commented in his memo, "There is still considerable animosity between certain members of the USTTA, NCUS-CR and 'Government' as represented in this case by John Scali. The committee recognizes the need for government participation to assure coordination and security but refuses to include anyone of such stature that protocol would force recognition, i.e., John Scali. The committee recognizes my role and welcomes it, recognizing the fact I will operate at a low profile and not steal their show." But with John Scali in the tour as the "president's representative," they felt the situation would be different.[145] The joint committee sent a letter to Scali on April 5, 1972, urging him to make sure that "all parties concerned agree on the desirability of maintaining the integrity of this visit as a non-governmental, people-to-people exchange." As the joint committee saw it, this was a private visit and the U.S. government should maintain a low profile.[146]

Scali realized he had a major problem, and decided to fix it in a straightforward and forceful way. In an April 6 phone conversation with Eckstein, Scali told the National Committee chairman that as the president's representative, his task was to personally coordinate with the National Committee and USTTA, as well as convey "his [Nixon's] personal greetings to the Chinese. The reason this was done is because of the structure of government—only someone at my level could command the access to the resources that are necessary to carry out the practical security functions and the authority to exercise on-the-spot judgments which are always a part of that function. I don't know how much experience you have had with fast-moving trips that involve foreign delegations." Eckstein, by now thoroughly intimidated, mumbled something about having had no personal experience with this kind of situation, at which point Scali further pressed the security issue as a reason the joint committee should accept his ideas and his presence in the Chinese tour—after all, he was a senior White House adviser and "very conscious of the fact that I cannot demean the office of the President." The transcript shows that at this point the poor professor was left speechless.[147]

The White House used the same tactics to bring Steenhoven into line. Scali recommended that Steenhoven be approached with a phone call during which the White House representative would say, among other things:

> Mr. Scali is empowered by the president not only to extend official greetings, but also to be a liaison between your groups and the U.S. government. . . . The president will appreciate all the cooperation you can give Mr. Scali and his staff. . . . Frankly I have been disturbed at the continuing difficulties our people have experienced in developing a satisfactory liaison arrangement with your group and with the National Committee. While this visit, on the surface, is a 'people-to-people' exchange, I think you realize that the Chinese and the United States governments are directly involved and regard it as far more than an exhibition of table tennis. In order to enhance the prospects for further strengthening Sino-American relations, I trust that you as a patriotic citizen will listen very carefully to whatever suggestions Mr. Scali and his designated assistants may offer during the course of the tour. I also hope that in no way will your actions and arrangements during the tour reflect adversely on the office of the Presidency. The degree of cooperation and understanding which your people and the National Committee demonstrate will directly influence the degree of presidential involvement during the Washington phase of the visit. I would hope that both the Americans and the Chinese could be included in any events which might take place at the White House. But I must tell you frankly that it would be possible to recommend to the president that for foreign policy reasons and because of lack

of cooperation it would be preferable that he greet the Chinese delegation alone. I think you also understand that the role of the National Committee in sponsoring and assisting in future exchanges depends on the degree of cooperation that our liaison people receive during this tour.[148]

Scali's talking point clearly was designed for a senior White House person to use. To make sure the joint committee cooperated with Scali, Nixon himself wrote a letter to Steenhoven. In his letter, Nixon first expressed

appreciation for the arrangements that you and your organization are making, with the assistance of the National Committee for U.S.-China Relations, to facilitate the visit to our country of the table tennis team from the People's Republic of China. . . . As an expression of my personal interest in this important cultural exchange between the Chinese and American people, I have appointed Special Consultant John A. Scali as my personal representative to greet our guests from the People's Republic, and to assist you and the National Committee in contributing to their comfort and convenience.[149]

No matter how tense the relationship between the White House and the joint committee, true dissension was not an option. Each side needed the other, and Scali's high stature was especially important for taking care of the biggest concern surrounding the Chinese visit: security. Pro-Taiwan groups and right-wing organizations in the United States presented a major safety issue, and Beijing was obviously very worried. In his talk with Kissinger, Huang Hua, Beijing's representative in the United Nations, stated, "We appreciate very much the concern shown by the U.S. side over security and other matters with regard to the visit of our table tennis team. We hope, as our two sides have expressed, that this visit will help enhance understanding and friendship between our two peoples."[150]

The organization United States March for Victory presented one such security concern for the White House and the joint committee. Carl McIntyre, its leader, wrote a letter to Steenhoven on February 4, 1972, informing him that his organization had invited a team from Taiwan to tour the United States right when the PRC's team was supposed to come.[151] When the White House learned of the McIntyre plan, it instructed John

Holdridge, Kissinger's National Security Council aide, to contact the American embassy in Taipei and inform officials there not to grant visas for the Taiwan team's visit until after the PRC's team had come and gone. "If such visas have been issued, they should be revoked."[152] But such interventions behind the scenes did not stop the right-wing threats; McIntyre's followers openly threatened to harass the visiting Chinese at every stop. As McIntyre told the *Washington Post*, "We'll be at all those places with banners and pickets."[153]

McIntyre and his group eventually did make trouble during the Chinese visit. They organized picketers who dogged the Chinese delegation from city to city, carrying placards with such slogans as "No Mao," and "Mao killed more Christians than Hitler killed Jews." Another right-wing activist group, calling itself Breakthrough, also created headaches for the White House and the joint committee. As Scali reported to Nixon later, at one point this group greeted the Chinese with dead rats on parachutes thrown from a balcony and shouts of "red killers." The Nationalist Chinese flag also occasionally appeared when the PRC delegation showed up.[154]

Scali worked very hard on security concerns from the earliest planning stages, with support from Nixon. Initially he had planned to use the State Department's security forces. But the State Department did not command sufficient manpower, had no jurisdiction for such an assignment, and moreover could not carry weapons, make arrests, intercept assailants, or carry out other duties necessary to the task. Scali's next choice, the U.S. Marshals Service, was willing to take on the assignment but had no experience handling a cross-country tour. Scali then attempted to use the Secret Service, making it clear that "it was the President's wish" that the Secret Service be involved.[155] But it was questionable whether the Secret Service had the legal authority to undertake this assignment.

The situation became more urgent as the dates for the visit approached. Alex Butterfield, a White House staff member, recommended to Haldeman that to get around the legal limitations surrounding the Secret Service, a dissolved State Department security force should be reactivated and used as the mainstay of a protection detail. In Butterfield's (oddly chosen) words, "all things considered, there wasn't a Chinaman's chance that such an assignment of Secret Service agents would be approved."[156] Yet another possible solution was considered: having the secretary of state issue a directive to the Justice Department requiring use of the marshal service as a necessary extension of foreign policy. After all, it was clear by this point that to use the Secret Service to protect the visiting Chinese team, Nixon would have had to issue an executive order, which would have proven problematic.[157]

This bureaucratic infighting and lack of cooperation meant the security problem was an issue until early April, just before the Chinese were supposed to arrive. Scali became so frustrated by the mess that he dashed a memo to Alexander Haig declaring, "We are heading for a diplomatic disaster unless we resolve, in the next forty-eight hours, the matter of who is to protect the Chinese table tennis team when it visits the United States." In the same memo, Scali insisted, "If I am to be held responsible for this visit, I urge in the strongest terms that action be taken today so that we can have a decision. The alternative of relying on local police protection, in my view, will be totally unsatisfactory, inviting incidents instead of deflecting them."[158] The very next day, the State Department reluctantly agreed to take on the job of protecting the Chinese delegation. Although Scali complained that "State clearly is not enthusiastic about the task assigned to it," the protection issue was finally solved.[159] The State Department would provide protection for the Chinese with the support of the Secret Service, and security officials would report to Scali throughout the trip. Richard Solomon of the National Security Council and Dewey Clower of the White House staff would travel with the Chinese at all times during their visit, which was now scheduled from April 12 to 30, to make sure everything was fine.[160]

With the thorny security issue behind them, the White House and Nixon were eager to enjoy the glory of their own ping-pong diplomacy. But detailed plans were still coming together. On April 11, 1972, White House Chief of Staff Haldeman demanded, "What is the specific plan for Chinese ping pong team participation with the President? I need that as quickly as possible."[161]

Nixon was so excited about the Chinese visit that he toyed with the idea of staging a table tennis exhibition on the White House tennis court, as part of his meeting with the Chinese team.[162] To further publicize his own ping-pong diplomacy, Nixon considered inviting his Cabinet members, their wives, and perhaps others to watch the short exhibition.[163] But not everyone in his inner circle thought this would be a good idea. Kissinger, Haig, Ron Ziegler, and Chuck Colson did not favor it; as Scali noted, "They all tend to believe it would be undignified, something smacking of a publicity stunt." Scali himself also expressed serious reservations.[164] Nixon, however, seemed obsessed with the exhibition idea and of course got what he wanted. As a somewhat resigned Scali commented, "One point is certain, it would be an unusual news event that would be heavily covered by television and the written press."[165]

The final plan for Nixon's meeting with the Chinese in the White House was carefully orchestrated so that it would feature "the flowering of friendship." Premier Zhou Enlai had told the Americans in January 1972 that the Chinese team would visit the United States when the flowers were in bloom. The Rose Garden at the White House was now blooming, and the physical arrangements would be structured to show off the gorgeous flowers. The president's remarks would refer to "the opening of the buds of friendship." For a photo, a wide shot would be taken of the president flanked by the Chinese players standing with the roses as a backdrop, observing the table tennis exhibition directly in front of them. Nixon would deliver a brief greeting to the Chinese delegation, then invite the players to put on a brief exhibition on a table placed on the Rose Garden lawn. Afterward, the group would tour the White House.[166]

With the stage finally set, on April 12, 1972, when the Chinese finally arrived at Detroit after their Canadian tour, John Scali, as Nixon's personal representative, welcomed them to the United States. He said, "When Premier Chou En-lai advised us that you would be coming to our country when the blossoms are in bloom, he may not have had an appreciation of how late spring comes to Michigan. But I can assure you, you will see the flowers in bloom as a symbol of our improving relations, during your visit to many regions of our country."[167]

Nixon's decision on April 17, 1972, to renew bombing of Hanoi and Haiphong, however, sabotaged his Ping-Pong exhibition, scheduled for April 18. Before the ink had dried on the plans for the White House visit, staffers realized that they had to be revised given the new developments. As Scali wrote to Kissinger, "In view of the situation in Vietnam, Dick Solomon and I both would recommend that the table tennis exhibition phase of the visit be dropped. Such an event under the present circumstances could turn out to be embarrassing for the Chinese government. Photographs and stories about the Chinese playing ping pong at the White House at a time when North Vietnam is under attack might force the Chinese to explain why they were cozying up to the President at the moment he is ordering bombing of North Vietnam."[168]

Scali's reservations proved to be right. In fact, the Chinese nearly cancelled the White House visit altogether because of the bombing. Early in the morning of April 18 in China (late afternoon on April 17 in Washington, D.C.), Zhou Enlai gathered core members of the foreign ministry for an emergency meeting. They decided that the team should orally inform the American side that they would refuse to meet with Nixon in the White House. But when Zhou informed Mao of this decision, Mao disagreed. In Mao's view, the visit was supposed to be about people-to-people contact, and it might be considered rude to refuse to meet with Nixon given that the Chinese leaders had met with the American team during their visit. Both the team's meeting with Nixon and the plan to give pandas to the United States would go on as scheduled despite Nixon's bombing of North Vietnam.[169]

In his report to Nixon after the Chinese tour, Scali reported that the trip had gone well overall, with "the only sour notes [being] sounded by small right-wing groups demonstrating on the fringes of the tour." Scali told Nixon, "The Chinese appear to be directing most of their political pressure at Chinese-Americans encountered on the tour. One translator of Chinese origin was told that the University of Michigan was a 'bad institution' because its 'standpoint' was not clear—a reference to the presence there of Taiwan independence movement leader Peng Ming-min."[170] But in general Scali was pleased with the security provided by the State Depart-

ment and wrote a formal letter to Secretary of State William Rogers prais-
ing his department's security officers.[171]

After the tour, the three parties involved in the Chinese delegation's
visit continued to harbor some suspicion and hostility toward each other.
The National Committee felt that the American players and even the
USTTA officials had seemed "rather childish, ignorant of the real significance and importance of the Chinese visit and locked into their own little world of table tennis."[172] The USTTA group concluded that the Chinese
visit had been too much work and had involved too many people. And
among the government entities involved, the White House and the State
Department got into a dispute over how to cover the government officials'
expenses related to the Chinese visit. In his memo to Kissinger, Butterfield
wrote on April 17, 1972, that "responsibility for funding of U.S. Government activities undertaken in direct and indirect support of the tour of the
visiting Chinese table tennis delegates should be assumed by the Department of State."[173] The State Department, however, protested that "these
bills are not the responsibility of the Department of State" and refused to
pay them.[174] To make the situation more interesting, the White House got
into a dispute with the National Committee when the committee sent bills
to John Scali and Dewey Clower after the Chinese delegation had left. In
late July 1972, Scali received a bill of $826.76 from the National Commit-
tee for hotel expenses incurred during Scali's tour with the Chinese Ping-
Pong team. Dewey Clower also received a bill. In his memo to Butterfield,
Scali suggested the amount sounded about right and suggested that the
White House "pay the darn bill and write 'closed' to a unique, frustrating
experience, which, nevertheless, turned out to be indispensable to a successful visit."[175] Butterfield, however, asked Scali to negotiate.[176] Scali thus
wrote the National Committee to complain: "I recall a meeting with members of your committee in advance of the tour where there was a firm understanding that the National Committee would pay for hotel, meal and
incidental expenses incurred by me and members of my group during the
tour." He asked the committee to "reconsider its action in sending this bill
and meet the expenses as per our agreement."[177] Schoyer of the National
Committee responded by saying that no one "recalls any financial discus-

sion as regards your expenses and Dewey's." He continued, "Forgive me if I appear to be beating a dead horse, but we still have a considerable table tennis deficit to pay off; and so must try to leave no stone unturned in seeking funds."[178]

Yet no matter how distasteful such after-the-fact financial wrangling may appear, by and large, this second act of ping-pong diplomacy was a success. The Ping-Pong delegation was the first official PRC envoy to the United States since 1949, and its visit generated an enormous amount of interest in China among Americans. The Chinese Ping-Pong visit of 1972, sparked by Mao's initial breakthrough, kicked off a healthy and fast-developing trend toward expanded cultural exchange between the two countries.

A New Era Begins

The ping-pong diplomacy initiative of 1971–1972 was a pivotal development in Chinese diplomacy and internationalization, one that would serve as a model for future diplomatic maneuvers. In 1984, for instance, China and South Korea engaged in "tennis diplomacy" that symbolized rapprochement between the two nations. Their matches marked the first time Korean athletes had competed on Chinese soil, even though the two countries had met before at international sports meets.[179]

These matches became a part of China's effort to become a more fully integrated member of the international community. For many years, China and North Korea had been close allies, so when the Chinese invited South Korea to compete on Chinese soil, the symbolism was dramatic. As the *New York Times* reported, during the Davis Cup held in the southern Chinese city of Kunming in 1984, "the significance of eight South Koreans hitting tennis balls on the Chinese mainland was not lost in a country where virtually every action is weighed for its political effect." Even Japanese prime minister Yasuhiro Nakasone realized the importance of the match: he told a parliamentary committee that the Kunming tennis competition was a significant event in Asia and indicated that during his upcoming visit to Beijing he would encourage further exchanges between China and

South Korea. In Seoul, Lee Won Kyung, the South Korean foreign minister, predicted that further nonpolitical contacts between China and South Korea would be a natural trend after the tennis diplomacy. He was right. China and South Korea used the 1986 Asian Games and the 1988 Olympic Games, both of which took place in Seoul, to pave the way for establishing diplomatic relations, a goal realized in the early 1990s.[180]

Ping-pong diplomacy was a major achievement for Mao and Nixon, who both struggled with domestic scandals during their time in power. But the game of Ping-Pong not only saved the political legacies of these leaders; more importantly, it brought the two countries together during the 1970s, a critical time of uncertainty and conflict worldwide. The small Ping-Pong ball, worth only about twenty-five cents, played a unique and significant role not only in accelerating China's internationalization, but also in transforming Sino-U.S. relations and shaping world politics during the last part of the twentieth century.

THE MONTREAL GAMES
POLITICS CHALLENGE THE OLYMPIC IDEAL

We welcome the athletes from Taiwan. We hope they will compete. We
do not discriminate on the basis of sex, race or, indeed, national origin.
All we are saying, and it seems to me this is a policy that would have the
support of any member of this House regardless of his party, provided
he believes in a one China policy, is that we will not let athletes come
into Canada . . . to pretend that they represent a country, China, that
they do not represent.
     Prime Minister Pierre Trudeau to the House of Commons, 1976

BETWEEN JULY 17 AND AUGUST 1, 1976, the Olympic Summer
Games took place in Montreal. The occasion was supposed to be a joyful
moment for the Canadians, who were eager to show the best face of their
country to the world. But before the Games started, the Canadian government drew almost universal condemnation, including from such close
friends as Australia, the United Kingdom, Germany, and the United States.
The IOC talked about canceling the Games, and the Americans seriously
considered whether they should boycott Montreal. Canada, accustomed to
its good reputation and an unblemished image around the world, was sent
reeling from ferocious attacks in the media, not only from abroad but even
in its own newspapers. What was the issue that got the Canadian government into such trouble? Who should represent China at the 1976 Olympics?

The controversy that surrounded the Montreal Games illustrates the
important role that sports played in expanding China's international visibility and establishing China's national identity in the global setting. Although the PRC was not a member of the Olympic movement, Beijing was
determined to link sports events with its international status and legiti-

macy. Meanwhile Taiwan, which had been gradually marginalized diplomatically starting in the early 1970s, was using its membership in the
Olympic family both to attract world attention to its existence as a separate political entity and to force the world to consider the very identity of
China. These two perspectives clashed forcefully around the Montreal
Games, almost destroying the Olympic movement and sending diplomatic
shock waves around the world.

The Canadian Dilemma

When Montreal applied in 1969 for the honor to host the 1976 Olympic
Games, the Canadian government was supportive, promising the IOC that
Canada would welcome all member countries to compete. A letter to the
IOC from Secretary of State for External Affairs Mitchell Sharp, dated
September 29, 1969, stated, "I would like to assure you that all parties
representing the National Olympic Committees and international sports
federations recognized by the I.O.C. will be free to enter Canada pursuant
to the normal regulations."[1] The IOC accepted the Canadian promise and
on May 12, 1970, officially selected Montreal to be the host city.

About five months later, on October 13, 1970, Canada formally recognized the PRC (nearly nine years before the U.S. government did) and
severed relations with Taiwan. Canada was one of only a few Western
powers recognizing Beijing that time. Like every country that later established diplomatic ties with the PRC, Canada promised Beijing it would
honor the one-China policy and recognize the PRC as the sole legitimate
government of China and Taiwan as part of China. It is likely that no one
imagined in 1970 that hosting the Games in the context of Canada's new
relationship with the PRC would create so many problems. At that point,
Taiwan was a member in good standing of the Olympic family and the
PRC had not yet returned to the Olympic movement after having withdrawn from it in 1958.

But the incompatible promises Canada made to the IOC in 1969 and
to Beijing in 1970 would inevitably lead to conflict. In 1974, only two
years before the Montreal Games, the Canadian External Affairs Depart-

ment realized that Taiwan's participation in the Games might present an "important and potentially embarrassing issue."[2] It was not Taiwan's participation itself that was a problem; Taiwan was a duly recognized member of the Olympic movement. The problem was that Taiwan was recognized under the name of "Republic of China." If the Canadian government allowed Taiwan to compete under this name, it would certainly risk Beijing's wrath. And the PRC in fact conveyed to Canada in no uncertain terms that the name issue presented a serious difficulty.[3] A senior Chinese sports official told one Canadian diplomat in Beijing in November 1975, "It would be a very large problem for our bilateral relations if the Chiang clique was allowed to march into the stadium with their phony flag—surely the people of our two countries and participants from many countries would be outraged and relations between our two countries would be seriously damaged."[4]

The rhetoric from Beijing soon became more adversarial. On May 17, 1976, the PRC ambassador to Canada presented the External Affairs Department with an official note stating that Taiwan "has no right whatsoever to participate, under any name."[5] Thus the PRC's official position was that Taiwan should be denied entry into the Games "under any circumstances"; its participation would be "intolerable."[6]

The Canadian government hardly needed so pointed a reminder. The Canadian External Affairs Department was quite familiar with Beijing's stance long before these presentations. A secret memo prepared by the department in December 1974 for the prime minister predicted that Beijing "will be highly irritated, to say the least" if Taiwan were allowed to take part in the Games under its official name, and this irritation could "affect major bilateral issues" between the PRC and Canada. A. J. Beesley, the Canadian ambassador to Austria who was involved in discussions with the IOC on the Taiwan issue, wrote to Ottawa in February 1976 suggesting that "it might not be too early or inappropriate to consider smoking out PRC on whether they see it as a genuine bench-mark in our bilateral relations."[7] The External Affairs Department replied that there was no need to "smoke out" the PRC; it was clear that the Taiwan issue would affect bilateral relations.[8] In a restricted telegram to the External Affairs Department, the Canadian embassy in Beijing confirmed, "It seems clear that PRC has decided to put CDA-PRC bilateral relationship on the line if Taiwan is allowed to participate in Olympics."[9]

The Canadian government knew then that Beijing would respond harshly and retaliate seriously if Taiwan marched in the 1976 Games as a representative of China. Given the terrible economic problems and high inflation in Canada, trade with China was critically important to Prime Minister Trudeau, and the Canadian government could not afford to see its relations with Beijing destabilized. The *Wall Street Journal* claimed that these concerns shaped Canadian policy regarding Taiwan's participation in the Olympics. As the author of one editorial later explained, "Last year Canada posted a $144 million trade deficit with Taiwan and a $320 million trade surplus with Peking[;] had the situation been reversed, it's likely Taiwan would still be participating in the Olympic Games as the Republic of China."[10] The *New York Times* also reported that Canada's refusal to let Taiwan compete as the Republic of China "is linked to a major economic deal with mainland China's government in Peking. . . . In wheat alone, Canada had sales of $307 million to mainland China in 1975."[11] These observations were on the mark. A stable relationship with Beijing had been a major cornerstone and crucial mandate of the Trudeau administration's so-called new foreign policy.[12] It was too risky to allow the Montreal Games to interfere with this larger plan.

If allowing Taiwan to participate under its official name was unpalatable to Canada, one alternative was simply to bar Taiwan from competing. This choice, however, would draw serious criticism from the IOC and perhaps many others. Another choice, which the External Affairs Department called "the least desirable option," was to openly politicize the Games, thereby breaking its 1969 promise to the IOC.[13] In an effort to avoid being forced to choose between two bad alternatives, External Affairs, in a December 1974 memo, recommended that Canada help the PRC reach a deal with the IOC and become a member in the Olympic movement before the 1976 Games. In this way, Canada could deflect the two-China issue in advance of the Montreal Games; the PRC's membership would trump Taiwan's, at least for the purpose of representing China.[14]

Equipped with this preemptive strategy, External Affairs, through its embassies, tried very hard in 1975 and early 1976 to lobby for Beijing's membership in the Olympic movement. Canadian diplomats were instructed to approach other governments whose nationals were members of the IOC to try to initiate a movement to replace Taiwan with the PRC in the Olympic family. The Canadian government also maintained close contact with the IOC to stay on top of any developments; it even pushed hard for IOC president Lord Killanin to visit Beijing to patch up differences between the IOC and the PRC. To make sure the IOC understood Canada's dilemma, External Affairs requested a meeting with Killanin on April 23, 1975, in Toronto. A confidential memo prepared in advance of the meeting suggested: "You may wish to state at the outset that from the point of view of the Canadian government (and he will readily understand this) it would certainly be politically preferable to see the PRC, rather than Taiwan, participate in the Olympics."[15] At the meeting, Canadian External Affairs officials told Killanin that "Canada had divergent obligations, entered into in good faith with the I.O.C. and with Peking." Canada made it clear to the IOC that "as both Taiwan and the P.R.C. held the view that there was only one China, it was suggested that the I.O.C., in considering how to deal with both parties, might entertain a proposition involving an invitation to the P.R.C. to join the I.O.C. and to participate with the request that the P.R.C. assemble an all-China team, including representation from Taiwan."[16]

Killanin responded that he doubted the PRC would participate in the 1976 Games "because of the lack of time allowed for the I.O.C. to come to a decision on its formal application and supporting documentation." In other words, the IOC was dragging its feet. As Arthur Andrew, one External Affairs official who attended the meeting, reported, "There seems little disposition on the part of the I.O.C. to make any special effort to include the P.R.C. in the I.O.C., and thus make it eligible for the 1976 Games." The only thing Killanin promised on the Beijing membership issue was that he would take soundings at the IOC sessions and board meetings. "Until he had some readings from these he was unable to make any estimate of how the China questions would be handled."[17]

In these circumstances, Canadian officials realized that there was "little for us to do except to remain in close touch with Lord Killanin" and hope for the best.[18] Although the Canadians were obviously disappointed with the IOC president's pessimistic, passive approach, their hope that the PRC might join the Olympic movement did not completely evaporate.

In early 1976, Canadian External Affairs officials, armed with this hope and perhaps a sense of urgency and impatience, went to Austria to meet again with Killanin. The meeting took place on February 7, and included E. A. Skrabec from External Affairs; A. J. Beesley, Canadian ambassador to Austria; Killanin; and James Worrall, the Canadian IOC member. Their discussion largely focused on the two-China issue. This time the Canadians succeeded in making Killanin understand that the Canadian government's hands were tied regarding Taiwan's participation. Killanin retorted that he attached great importance to the assurances that had been offered by the Canadian government when it had bid for the Montreal Games. Canada could not forfeit its promises to the IOC just because it had chosen to recognize the PRC. To the further disappointment of the Canadians, Killanin now believed that the IOC would not resolve the Beijing/Taiwan issue anytime soon, perhaps not even in time for the 1980 Moscow Games.[19]

In hindsight, it seems obvious that the Canadians' strategy was bound to fail given Beijing's hard-line position on Taiwan and the IOC's general incompetence in handling the two-China issue; the Killanin meeting was not as significant as it seemed then. But at the time, the Canadian government felt an urgent need to try a new strategy for solving the two-China problem. As James Worrall wrote later, "The Canadian government was waiting for the IOC to make a decision regarding the People's Republic of China being admitted to the Olympic Movement, which would have relieved them of any obligation to admit the team from Taiwan under the name recognized by the IOC. When this did not occur and the IOC had not made a decision, the Canadian government found itself in an embarrassing situation."[20]

A clear change occurred in the Canadian government's approach to the Chinese representation issue after February 1976. The government moved from working with the IOC to solving the problem itself. In a confidential memo written on April 20, 1976, External Affairs concluded that "the last clear opportunity for the IOC to resolve this question before the Olympic Games in Montreal was at the IOC sessions during the winter Olympics at Innsbruck in February." But since the IOC and the PRC had been unable even to broach the issue then, "Canada is faced with the problem."[21]

Interestingly, the Canadian government's conclusion was confirmed by the IOC president himself. In a confidential letter dated April 30, 1976, to his confidant Masaji Kiyokawa, an IOC member in Japan, Killanin wrote,

> I had resigned myself to the fact that I do not think any move can be now made prior to Montreal, especially in view of the present political situation in China. . . . I would not dream of pushing in any way a change of name [for Taiwan]. Also I have not taken any positive action because I believe it would be negative in that the majority of the I.O.C., the majority of the NOCs [national Olympic committees], and the majority of the IFs [international federations] are only too anxious to recognize China, but have this predicament of what to do with Taiwan. . . . I put China very high on the priority list but I think we must keep things absolutely in balance.[22]

Clearly Killanin saw himself in the same dilemma as the Canadians; the IOC simply was not in a position to do anything regarding China prior to the Montreal Games. Killanin's strategy was to do nothing for the moment.

But the Canadian government could not afford to wait any longer—it had to make the call, and soon. The IOC expected Canada to keep its promise and allow Taiwan to participate in the Montreal Games under its official name. The PRC, of course, expected Canada to oppose the entry of participants from Taiwan under any circumstances and live up to its one-

China policy. In April 1976, after more than a year of vainly trying to bring Beijing and the IOC together, the Canadian government decided to strike a compromise.

The Compromise Formula

The compromise solution went like this: instead of barring Taiwan's participation, the Canadian government would allow Taiwan's team to compete on the strict condition that it would not use its officially designated name, flag, or anthem, all of which indicated that athletes from Taiwan represented the "Republic of China."[23] This compromise, from the Canadian government's perspective, "while not totally satisfactory, might at least be acceptable to the PRC and to Canadian sporting authorities."[24] On April 27, 1976, Alan MacEachen, Canadian secretary for the External Affairs Department (which had discussed a version of this plan as early as 1974), gave his official approval, and the compromise became the official policy of the Canadian government. In a memo to the prime minister the agency explained its rationale: if the government allowed Taiwan to compete at Montreal under the IOC's officially designated name "Republic of China," which would please the IOC, it "could lead to damage to Canadian commercial and political relations with the PRC." And if the government chose to prevent Taiwan from participating, relations between the PRC and Canada would be strengthened, but the IOC might cancel the Games. The prime minister should thus accept the compromise formula as potentially the least harmful; in any case, "it is the most defensible position whatever happens this summer."[25] Prime Minister Pierre Trudeau approved.

The Canadian government made this choice after it had ascertained that Beijing would accept the policy (though not entirely happily), given that this was the best the Canadian government could do under the circumstances. As a confidential memo from External Affairs makes clear, the government informed Beijing about every move it made regarding the Taiwan issue: "Notes outlining our position on Taiwanese entry have been provided to the PRC authorities in Ottawa and Peking." And although

Beijing's reply reasserted the PRC's position that Taiwan's entry into the Montreal Games should be denied under "all circumstances," according to the same secret External Affairs memo, "It is our impression, shared by our Ambassador in Peking, that the Chinese will be able to live with our compromise solution provided no unexpected problems are encountered in its execution."[26]

On May 28, 1976, the Canadian government officially informed the IOC in writing that under no circumstances would the national Olympic committee of the Republic of China (that is, Taiwan) be allowed entry into Canada under that name, nor could its members fly the flag or play the anthem they had chosen.[27] Later MacEachen declared that "the basic position of the Canadian Government on the issue in question involves our whole China policy and reflects the requirements of our national sovereignty. The position of the Canadian Government was set."[28] In early June, before it received the IOC's official response, External Affairs had already worked with the Ministry of Manpower and Immigration to make sure the Taiwanese team would not be allowed to enter the country until Canada and the IOC had reached an agreement.[29] The Canadian government invalidated for purposes of entry the Olympic identity cards held by the Taiwanese nationals. And on June 9, 1976, the Canadian government informed Taiwan of its decision through Taiwan's embassy in Washington.[30]

The Canadian government was determined to carry out its Taiwan policy, but it would be a challenge to sell this policy to the public and especially to the IOC. First of all, how could the Canadians claim that this policy did not violate its promise to the IOC? The Canadian government's tactic was to explain that its promise had been qualified in Sharp's 1969 letter, which had contained the proviso that participation would be allowed "pursuant to the normal regulations." The government had no intention of relinquishing its sovereignty to a private organization, no matter how venerated.[31]

It was clear from the discussion that followed the announcement, however, that Killanin and the IOC had not taken the qualification seriously and had never asked the Canadians to explain what they meant by the phrase. As Killanin explained later, he thought Sharp's qualification referred "to something like a cholera epidemic."[32] As early as 1974, however, the Canadian government had concluded that this language could "perhaps offer some element of qualification" to the broader commitment as needed.[33] Before the meeting between External Affairs officials and Killanin on April 23, 1975, a confidential memo from the Canadian side suggested that if Killanin asked whether the Canadian preference for including the PRC rather than Taiwan in the Olympic movement implied that Canada might not permit Taiwan's entry, "we suggest that you might wish simply to reply that we are, of course, examining this issue of entry very closely in the context of Mr. Sharp's earlier commitment that competitors could enter Canada to participate 'pursuant to the normal regulations.'"[34] Killanin did not think to ask the question, but the strategy stuck. This phrase, put there in 1969 with no China connection, now became a way for the Canadian government to justify the position that its Taiwan policy was not a violation of its promise to the IOC.

The second line of defense for this position was that since 1970, Canada had recognized only one China, the PRC. Canada welcomed Taiwan to participate in the Games, just not as the "Republic of China." The IOC, however, did not buy this argument at all. When it learned of the Canadian stance in late May of 1976, the IOC complained that the policy was "in complete conflict with Olympic rules and contrary to the conditions under which Montreal was allotted the Olympic Games." Killanin also claimed that the Canadians had never told him that Taiwan would be treated differently, and he "deplored" the "last minute" nature of Canada's advice to him on the Taiwan entry issue.[35] He even declared that if this had been known to him even as late as April 1975, he would have immediately begun to seek a new venue for the 1976 Games. From his perspective, Canadian officials had failed to tell him about the Taiwan stance when he met with them in April 1975 and February 1976.

Killanin was not really fighting for Taiwan; he was worried that the Canadian move could seriously damage the ongoing effort to keep the Olympic Games and international sports free from government interference.[36] For the IOC the Canadian move was serious because a "basic Olympic principle . . . is at stake."[37] At one point, Killanin complained to

Canadian officials that their Taiwan policy represented "direct govern-ment interference" in the Olympics, which was "intolerable." He added that under the circumstances, "there was a question of whether the Games would open." Canada, which Killanin blustered had been awarded the Games under "false pretences," seemed to be "driving a nail into the coffin of the Olympic movement."[38]

It had become obvious that the Canadian government and the IOC were on a collision course, but it was in both sides' interest to find a com-promise before the Taiwan issue destroyed the Games. On June 30, 1976, P. André Bissonnette and E. A. Skrabec of External Affairs met with Kil-lanin in Frankfurt at his request. During this meeting, Killanin reminded the Canadians of their promise under which Montreal had been awarded the Games: free access to Canada for all members of the Olympic move-ment. He told the Canadians that if he had known Canada would break its promise, Montreal would not have won the bid. Bissonnette retorted, say-ing that if the Canadian government had known the issue would develop as it had, "we might not have supported Montreal's bid." Responding to Killanin's attack on Canada's "last minute" move, the Canadian officials insisted their government had alerted him about the Taiwan problem sev-eral times in the past and as early as April 1975.[39]

The exchange stalled at this point, with Killanin insisting his story was correct and the Canadians claiming that their side of the story was reliable because there were meeting minutes to back it up. Since it is important for us to understand both sides' understanding and handling of the China rep-resentation issue, let us examine the accounts in detail.

The Perspective of the International Olympic Committee

Killanin genuinely believed that the Canadians had not on earlier occa-sions given him clear details on their Taiwan policy. On May 28, 1976, af-ter he had been officially informed about the Canadian government's deci-sion by James Worrall, Killanin wrote a confidential memo to the IOC executive board in which he reported that Worrall had phoned him on

May 27 to relay the Canadian government's decision on Taiwan, which Worrall had just learned on May 26, 1976. In this phone conversation, Killanin asked Worrall why Canada was raising the Taiwan issue "at this late date." The IOC president claimed that during his two previous meetings with Canadian External Affairs officials in April 1975 and February 1976 the Canadian government had not given him any indication that Canada would be going its own way on the Taiwan issue.[40]

Worrall made every effort to back up Killanin's account. In his confidential report about the issue of Taiwan, submitted to Killanin on October 1, 1976, Worrall laid out the essential issue: Canada had broken its promise and had failed to inform the IOC in a timely fashion. According to Worrall, "the words of 'qualification,' now so heavily relied upon by the Government of Canada, were assumed to be no more than matters of procedural detail." For Worrall, "If the wording reserved some kind of a right to change its mind on policy, the Government should have been forthright enough to declare it." Worrall recollected that at the April 23, 1975, meeting he had attended, the discussion had been "general," and only "touched on the possible involvement of South Africa, and of Taiwan in the Games in Montreal." This general discussion, according to Worrall, was in no way considered by the IOC to be any kind of formal policy declaration by the government of Canada regarding the status of Taiwan. In fact, both Killanin and Worrall himself had the impression that the two officials from External Affairs at that meeting were in no position to commit the government of Canada to a change in policy.[41]

As for the February 1976 meeting, which Worrall also attended, the question of Taiwan was again discussed. According to Worrall, however, it was clear that the representatives of the Canadian government did not have the authority to make a positive statement about the Taiwan policy (as subsequently stated in May 1976), and they did not in fact make such a statement. Based on his understanding, the two meetings between the Canadian government and the IOC could not be accepted as the Canadian government's "notifying" or "informing" the IOC of the position subsequently taken. In fact, if the government had wanted to give an official notice, "it would have been a very simple matter for the prime minister or the minister of External Affairs to write to the President of the I.O.C. and state their policy."[42]

Worrall, an attorney, used his skills to save the IOC and perhaps himself from embarrassment in this memo. After all, as the IOC member in Canada, his reputation was on the line: he shared the important responsibility of making sure communications between the host country and the IOC went smoothly and were effective. Since the situation did not develop well, he had a personal motivation to lay blame on the Canadian government. The same could be said about Killanin. In his letter to Worrall on October 14, 1976, Killanin thanked him for the report and "concurred with all the facts and opinions" about the Taiwan issue expressed by Worrall in the memo.[43] In a confidential memo to the IOC director dated October 12, 1976, Killanin wrote, "I now have a confidential report from James Worrall which confirms exactly the position regarding Taiwan and what I said at the time. I wish this to be kept in a sealed file at Vidy [the headquarters of the IOC] if at any future date this matter might arise again, when Canadian state papers can be released. I do not wish it generally distributed."[44] In his memoir, Killanin also claimed that he had no indication from the Canadians until the end of May 1976 that Taiwan would be excluded from the Games.[45]

The major problem with the IOC story is that neither Killanin nor Worrall took notes at the meetings and no minutes were compiled later. But the Canadian External Affairs Department kept very good records about what their people said at the meetings.

The Canadian Side of the Story

When External Affairs claimed that it had internal memos about the April 1975 meeting that contradicted Killanin's version, this was no fabrication, even though it may have looked suspiciously like one because at the time the agency refused to show the memos to anyone. In fact, a detailed memo was submitted to External Affairs on May 2, 1975, by Arthur Andrew, a senior External Affairs official who had attended the meeting. In this memo, Andrew indicated clearly that during that day's meeting, Canadian officials had discussed with Killanin the issue of Taiwan and Canadian recognition of the PRC. The memo states that Worrall bluntly asked what was meant by the phrase "pursuant to the normal regulations" in Sharp's 1969 letter regarding the admissibility of Olympic athletes. Andrew replied that "at its most obvious, it meant that we reserved the right to exclude persons with cholera, but that any decision on a less obvious issue would only be taken at the Ministerial level as a matter of national policy. No official could commit the Government on how this would be applied in advance."[46] Here the Canadian officials clearly implied that Canada might exclude Taiwan from participation if its ministries deemed that Canadian national policy was affected. Another confidential memo, from records also dated May 2, 1975, and concerning the same meeting with Killanin, reports that "Lord Killanin tried to press for an assurance that we would admit Taiwan but we advised him that this would be a ministerial decision and we were not able to say now what that would be. In giving this answer we reassured him of the Government's primary desire to do everything possible to ensure the success of the Games."[47]

It should be clear from these two memos that the Canadian government had warned Killanin in the spring of 1975 that Taiwan's participation posed serious problems and that nothing was certain about its participation in the Montreal Games. The IOC, however, missed the message— choosing instead to ignore the emerging problem until it was too late. Worrall, in his confidential memo of October 1976 to Killanin, claimed the IOC had no knowledge of the contents of the Canadian External Affairs memorandum on the April meeting, "but it should be pointed out at the very best it can only be regarded as a self-serving document which was made by one party as to their interpretation of what was said and for that reason, cannot be regarded as conclusive evidence of any formal advice of the Government of Canada to the I.O.C."[48] But there was no reason for the Canadian government to prepare biased memos in early May of 1975, when the dispute over what was discussed only erupted a year later. In his memo, Worrall admitted that the question of the qualified wording did come up in the meeting, but he claimed that it "was not accepted as invalidating the undertaking."[49]

As explored in previous chapters, the IOC had long been incapable of forthrightly managing complicated issues such as who represented China. Since the early 1950s, the IOC had closed its eyes to the emerging problems surrounding the two-China issue; no systematic or preemptive approaches had been formulated. Now that the Canadian government had taken the issue into its own hands and essentially forced the IOC to make a decision, the IOC still could not shake off its inertia and inability to take responsibility for its own role in the problem.

It would take time for the IOC to move beyond its usual passive way of dealing with tough issues. In its first important meeting after the Canadian government's announcement, on June 30, 1976 (when the Montreal Games were about two weeks away), the IOC continued its denunciation. Besides lambasting Canada for its "last minute" stance, Killanin at this meeting also charged that Canada was setting a dangerous precedent. Canadian officials responded that as a matter of fact, the IOC itself had created a precedent at the 1960 Rome Olympics by forcing Taiwan to use a different name if it wished to take part in the Games. In heated exchanges, the first vice president of the IOC, Willi Daume, stated that the alternative to acceptance of the ROC name would be cancellation of the Games. Bissonnette replied, "Abandonment of our policy vis-à-vis Taiwan would mean no policy, which was unthinkable."[50] It became clear that neither side would back down. Thus the first important meeting after the late May notification ended in a total impasse.

Since the Taiwan team was planning to arrive in Canada on the afternoon of July 9, the Canadian government, through its embassy in Washington, conveyed advance warning that their Olympic identification cards, which usually served as entry documents, had been rendered invalid. Canadian officials indicated that the Taiwan Olympic team was not welcome to enter Canada until an agreement had been reached with the IOC as to the appropriate conditions for their entry. Canada even bluntly warned of the potential for unfortunate circumstances should Taiwan try to circum-vent normal regulations and procedures.[51]

When the Canadian government took one step after another to block Taiwan from participating in the Games under its official name, the IOC realized that if it wanted the Games to take place it needed to focus on pos-sible solutions. In its next meeting with the Canadian officials on July 10, the IOC indicated that it was ready to discuss a compromise. Three senior members from External Affairs, Bissonnette, Skrabec, and Glenn Short-liffe, attended this meeting, while the IOC was represented by its presi-dent, Killanin, and some executive board members. The meeting was again tense. Killanin, "speaking with controlled emotion," asked the representa-tives of the Canadian government whether it had changed its position. The answer was "certainly not"; Canada was simply following its national one-China policy. At this point, Killanin asked whether the Rome formula would be acceptable to Canada, that is, use of the name Taiwan but allow-ing the ROC flag. Bissonnette replied that the key was the reference to "China" and asked what terminology had been used at Rome. Before Killanin could respond, the first vice president of the IOC, Willi Daume, stepped in to suggest a new option, namely, participation of an "ROC" team under the protection of the IOC. The team would carry the Olympic flag with the five rings and march under a placard with the initials "IOC" or "under the patronage of the IOC," and there would be no anthem. Killanin added that the Taiwan team would be, in effect, a "neutral" one. Canadian officials immediately jumped at the idea: they told Killanin that they preferred the neutral option and that the Canadian government could not accept the Rome formula, which allowed Taiwan to use its flag.[52]

It is interesting to note that the position on the Rome formula taken by the External Affairs officials at the meeting differed from what Allan MacEachen, secretary for External Affairs, had told the House of Com-mons on July 5, 1976. MacEachen had said, "Let us bear in mind that it is possible for the Taiwanese athletes to come to Canada to be admitted and to participate in the Games in precisely the same way they participated in the Olympic Games in 1960 in Rome, under conditions and regulations which were approved by the IOC. All we are asking is that they apply the same considerations to Canada which they applied to Italy in 1960."[53] In a press conference that same day, MacEachen again declared, "We are asking, in this case, that a formula be applied that was applied in the case of the Olympics in 1960 when, at the insistence of the International Olympic Committee, the athletes in question came to Italy as representatives of Taiwan."[54] It seems that the External Affairs Department officials decided to take advantage of the IOC's weakness at the meeting; they simply chose a better bargain when one was offered.

The "neutral" option was presented to Taiwan officials the same day by the IOC.[55] That same afternoon the IOC executive board passed a resolution to accept the Canadian suggestion that Taiwan take part in the Games without any reference to "China." Taiwan would participate under the IOC flag. It was a difficult decision and a challenging moment for the IOC's executive board, which briefly played with the idea of canceling the Games or removing the name "Olympic Games" from the competition. But eventually the board members concluded that they had no other good options and the Games must go on. In its statement issued on July 11, the executive board expressed its unanimous and strong protest of the decision taken by the government of Canada, explaining that "in view of the fact that athletes from over one hundred countries have, for several years, been preparing themselves to take part in this great gathering of the youth of the world, and that the city of Montreal, the Canadian Olympic Association and the Organizing Committee have fulfilled their commitments as far as the IOC is concerned," the executive board "has no other alternative but to recommend to the 78th Session that the Games must go on."[56]

But Taiwan balked. As Killanin reported when the IOC session started on July 13, Taiwan flatly refused to compete in any way but under its own name, flag, and anthem.[57] Killanin also informed the session that there were two principles involved—the Canadian government's breach of promises made when it had bid for the Games, and the violation of the basic principles of the IOC. He then asked the session to vote on the executive board's decision.

Many IOC members were truly angered at the Canadian government's interference and by its insistence on putting its China policy above the Games. One IOC member, Reginald Alexander, suggested that given the fact that the Canadian government had seriously embarrassed the IOC, the IOC should inform Trudeau that all members of his political party in parliament must excuse themselves from the Olympic sites and all social functions connected with the Games. Another member, Gunnar Ericsson, remarked that this was the first time the IOC had given in to political pressure. He felt that the executive board's decision should be accepted by the session, but under protest. Others argued that if the Republic of China team was asked to march under the Olympic flag, then other teams should be allowed to do the same as a vote of sympathy for Taiwan's national Olympic committee. Still others claimed that by accepting the Canadian government's policy, the IOC was signing its "own death warrant." Certain IOC members even suggested moving the Games to the United States or Mexico, or canceling them altogether.

Despite the group's anger and the many proposed responses, the IOC session realized it was quite powerless at that late date to call off the Games in Montreal. Eventually the session unanimously agreed that the Games had to continue and approved the executive board's decision that the Taiwan delegation "be offered the honor of marching under the Olympic flag, playing the Olympic anthem and using either a board with the Olympic rings, a blank board, or no board at all." But the IOC would not impose this formula on Taiwan. It was up to Taiwan to decide whether it would accept or reject the IOC decision.[58] It looked like the IOC had backed down and the Canadian government had won. But a major public-relations storm was brewing for the Canadian government.

Denunciations and the American Responses

The Canadian government's decision on Taiwan was unpopular even within Canada. The Canadian Olympic Association (COA) strongly disagreed with the Canadian government's policy. In a statement issued on July 7, 1976, it declared that recognition of the PRC in 1970 could not "alter the firm undertaking given by the Canadian Government in 1969. The undertaking was clear and binding to permit free access to Canada to representatives of all national Olympic committees recognized by the IOC, no political recognition or judgment is contained or implied in such obligation, which is entirely an Olympic matter." The statement further indicated that the Canadian government had not contacted the COA earlier to indicate that there was any problem, but rather had raised the matter at the last minute. The statement declared the government position "a serious and unacceptable breach of faith by the Canadian Government," one that "reflects badly on both the people of Canada and the COA as the organization which put forward Canada's bid for the Games to the IOC, in good faith and in reliance upon the word of the Government." Therefore, the COA "fully supports and endorses the position taken by the IOC in the matter."[59] Many Canadian newspaper columns also criticized the government for mishandling the Taiwan issue. Moreover, Canada was universally criticized by almost all Western powers. The *Economist* called the decision illegal, while Canada's own media lamented that it meant "shame and almost universal condemnation for Canada."[60]

But the most serious criticism came from the United States, Canada's powerful neighbor. The U.S. Olympic Committee (USOC) issued statements of strong protest and urged immediate reconsideration of the Canadian government's action. It even threatened that if the Games were declared by the IOC not to be "official," the United States might pull out.[61] Many Americans, including Senator Robert Taft, wrote letters to protest the Canadian decision. In his letter to Prime Minister Trudeau, Taft complained, "If we cannot set aside sports, art, science and other such activities to be the province of individuals, for the benefit of people, as individuals, everywhere, then I cannot believe that the word 'civilization' has much meaning left."[62] The American media were unanimously critical of the Canadian position. The *New York Times* wrote in one of its many editorials criticizing Canada that the IOC had been "duped" by the host country.[63] The Canadian embassy in Washington, shocked by the outrage, concluded that its government had been singled out in the American public mind as "the original and deepest sinner."[64]

When the controversy over Canada's Taiwan policy broke out, the

American government immediately began to devise a response. As early as July 2, 1976, a White House staff memo noted "a real possibility" that there would be no official Olympic Games at Montreal if the IOC withdrew the rights to the Games. If that happened, it was very likely that the USOC would decide not to send the American team to unsanctioned and unofficial games.[65] The State Department also issued its first major statement on the Montreal Games in early July. It declared that "the Olympics involve competition between individuals, not nations, and the question of who competes—which athletes compete— . . . is a matter for the International Olympic committee to decide. We do not believe that any political consideration should enter into the decision. So we hope that the matter will be resolved."[66] On July 6, 1976, the White House asked the State Department to provide an informational memo on the Taiwan issue at Montreal. In its report submitted the next day, the State Department claimed that the Canadian decision on Taiwan "was in part prompted by several strong approaches from the PRC over [the] past nine months." The memo also pointed out that U.S. influence over the IOC decision was limited since the United States did not have members on the IOC executive board and had only two votes in the IOC session.[67]

The State Department posed three options to the White House. The first was to maintain the current low-key position. As the State Department noted: "The department has taken the position that ROC participation is an issue to be settled by the IOC and Canada. In a low-key fashion we have expressed our regret about the politicization of the games. Such a position is consistent with our overall policy that participation in international sports should not be a political issue and should be decided by private sports groups themselves. This approach would also insulate our China policy from public controversy."[68]

The second option would involve the State Department or White House more actively supporting, with public statements, the principle that the Olympics should be insulated from politics. The memo related that the USOC had sought more positive U.S. government support for such a position, and advocated that a more active stance "would better position us to lend support to our athletes and those from other countries in the 1980

Games when we expect political problems to arise with the USSR as the host country." But the State Department memo reminded the White House that such public support also had two disadvantages: "creating the appearance that we are unnecessarily tangling with the PRC," and forcing the United States "to take issue, at least implicitly, with Canada."[69]

The third option was even more involved. The United States could actively lobby with Canada and other governments in support of the USOC and IOC positions. According to the State Department, this action had some drawbacks. It would mark "a significant shift from our policy of leaving these matters in private hands. The shift would prompt misleading and unhelpful speculation about changes in our China policy. Moreover, lobbying at this late date is not likely to be effective."[70]

Of the three options, the State Department recommended the first, that is, staying the course.

> We believe we should continue to take the first option and not go beyond what we have already stated publicly—[that] the question of participation is a matter for the IOC to decide and that we hope political considerations would not enter into the games. This position holds out the greatest promise for insulating our policy toward China from public controversy at a sensitive time. It is also consistent with the position the United States has taken on numerous occasions that participation in international sports events is purely a private matter.[71]

On July 8, this recommendation was revised a bit by suggesting the second option as a fallback position: "Depending on how the situation in Montreal evolves and if pressures on the USG build further, we might consider taking a look at the second option."[72]

In a confidential memo to the president, National Security Adviser Brent Scowcroft recommended a more confrontational approach than did the State Department. Scowcroft told President Ford, "I believe we should adopt option 2. The current case is the first in which a host government has attempted to interfere with the decision of the IOC and it will set a precedent for the 1980 Moscow Games. We should make it clear that the U.S. Government does not take a position as to whether the ROC should or should not be in the Olympics; this question is for the IOC to decide. We should, however, avoid lobbying the Canadian government."[73]

Some Americans even suggested to the White House that the United States should take over the Games if the IOC and Canada could not work out a solution and the Games would otherwise be canceled. If that happened, Mike Duval wrote in a memo to Dick Cheney on July 10, 1976, "I suggest that the President [after privately cutting a deal with the IOC] go on nationwide television and announce that he has offered to hold the Olympics in the United States. The President can make the point that America is the only country that could pull off such an event on short notice. . . . If Brent [Scowcroft] gives you any indication that Canadian-IOC negotiations may result in cancellation, please let me know so that we can go to work developing this idea."[74]

On the day that the IOC session was supposed to accept or reject the IOC executive board's decisions on the Taiwan issue, a memo by an unidentified White House aide recommended the following possible presidential actions: before the IOC's crucial meeting, the president could make a public appeal to the IOC members to reaffirm the IOC's principle of permitting all Olympic athletes to compete regardless of race, religion, or politics. After the IOC meeting, if the IOC executive board's decision was not reversed, the president could take the following actions: request that the USOC participate in the Games under a formal protest against the host country's exclusion of Taiwan, formally direct the U.S. ambassador to Canada not to attend the opening of the Games, or request that the USOC withdraw from the Games because of the Canadian government's violation of its contract as host country to the Olympics.[75]

The year 1976 was both the bicentennial celebration of American independence and a presidential election year. The Canadian government had become a favorite topic among the presidential candidates, with Jimmy Carter and Ronald Reagan both strongly criticizing Canada for playing politics with sports. Ford as a presidential candidate clearly wanted to gain more political points than his challengers from the Canadian Games dispute. As a former football star for the University of Michigan and once a football coach, Ford had remained interested in sports and used them to political advantage when he moved to the White House. Combining personal interest and political considerations, he had pushed hard to set up a presidential commission on the Olympics as soon as he moved to the White House in 1974, and one year later the commission was formed. In his executive order to create this commission, Ford informed Americans that "1976 is the bicentennial year of the United States. That same year amateur athletes from all over the world will be competing in the 1976 Olympic Games. It is vital that this nation be represented in those games and in future international competitions in the Olympic sports by the best team of amateur athletes we can field." The commission would evaluate the organization and activities of the United States Olympic Committee and its membership groups, in an effort to improve the performance and visibility of U.S. competitors. Ford personally met with commission members several times and reviewed their recommendations.[76]

In early July of 1976, the White House announced that President Ford would visit Plattsburg, New York, to attend a sendoff party for the United States Olympic team headed to the Montreal Games. He went there on July 10 and gave a speech encouraging the athletes to do well and win victories for the United States. Ford told them, "I am proud to join with 215 million Americans in wishing our Olympic team the greatest of success in the 1976 summer Games at Montreal. . . . there is no better or happier time to represent America than right now. . . . You will be representing your country in one of the most prestigious and renowned stages of international relations."[77]

Interestingly, before Ford headed to the sendoff, White House aides had discussed whether he should call Prime Minister Trudeau to address the problem of Taiwan's participation. They prepared detailed talking points, but the call was never made. Perhaps it was Scowcroft who vetoed the idea to avoid seeming to interfere in Canadian politics.[78]

Even though Ford was to see the American team compete in Montreal, he jumped into the Canadian-IOC dispute by claiming that "the games have now been totally corrupted by a politicization that reduces this international sports contest to a mocking of the Olympic Ideal and to a mere sideshow in the ideological wars."[79] As early as July 9, 1976, Ford openly criticized Canada: "I think it's tragic that international politics and foreign policy get involved in international sport competition."[80] Searching for positive ways to keep Ford in the spotlight for the presidential election, friends advised him to politicize the dispute over Taiwan by denouncing more actively the Canadian government's politicization of the Games. One such friend told him on July 12, 1976, "Your personal pressure against Canada's shopkeepers, as far as the Taiwan Olympic team is concerned, scored a one-column headline on the *New York Times'* sports page Sunday and 4 columns Monday, but now I urge you to move the story to front pages everywhere by using the blunt American language that translates clearly into every language. Remind Canada that the Munich Olympics were bloodied by the terrorist murder of 11 Israelis, and call on Trudeau to resist now the hijacking of the Montreal Olympics in our bicentennial year. Stay well. Carter is looking more like Dewey every day, so now you should start sounding like 'Give 'em hell' Harry Truman."[81]

Largely due to such political calculations, Ford was to become more deeply involved in the dispute. His White House staff followed the debate very closely from early July when the news of Canada's Taiwan policy first broke. On July 9 at a White House briefing, Ford's press secretary Ronald Nessen openly commented on the issue, saying that President Ford was hopeful the two-China dispute would be resolved.[82] When asked whether U.S. withdrawal was an option, Nessen replied, "It is too soon to progress to questions like that when the president hopes and expects the controversy to be resolved."[83]

On July 12 Ford personally phoned Philip Krumm, president of the USOC, to get a firsthand report. According to the White House press briefing afterward, Ford told Krumm that the IOC's executive committee's move to accept the Canadian government's Taiwan policy had been a "bad decision" and would set "a very bad precedent" if it were upheld. Ford also informed Krumm that he deplored the injection of politics into Olympic athletic competition. After asking Krumm to keep him fully posted on developments, Ford encouraged him to use his influence in the IOC to try to reverse the decision.[84]

Although no transcript was made of the call, rough handwritten notes jotted by James Cannon, the assistant for domestic affairs who was handling the Montreal Games dispute for Ford, give additional important hints as to where the conversation turned. Cannon scribbled "US will not participate if IOC allow" [the Canadian policy] and "US withdraw from the Games," suggesting that Ford and Krumm discussed a potential pullout of American athletes.[85] After the presidential phone call, the White House maintained direct contact with the USOC through Cannon. Based on Cannon's handwritten notes, we can assume that from July 12 to July 16, he talked with Krumm, as well as Donald Miller, executive director of the USOC, several times a day and reported anything significant to President Ford. On one piece of paper, Cannon wrote, "Trudeau thinks we are bluffing." This sentence might also indicate that the United States was considering not attending the Games.[86]

Trudeau in his memoir claimed that the Ford administration did nothing "that rubbed Canada the wrong way."[87] He would have been shocked if he had found out what Ford had intended to do with the Canadians' Taiwan policy. Although the White House claimed that President Ford never directly or indirectly pressured the Canadian government about the Taiwan dispute, the White House used press briefings to get its message out to the Canadian side. From July 9 till July 14, the White House spokesperson spent a lot of time explaining Ford's policy on the Games. For instance, Nessen declared on July 13 that "politics have no place in the Olympic Games . . . the host country should not stipulate political or other considerations for participation in the Games."

Such statements obviously were a direct criticism of Canada.[88] MacEachen, the Canadian secretary of External Affairs, bristled when asked about Ford's call for the USOC to reverse the IOC executive board's decision on Taiwan. He declared, "Certainly, when the head of a government suggests to the representatives of a national Olympic committee how they ought to vote, that really is bringing politics into the international Olympic committee."[89]

In the spirit of the more confrontational approach that Ford was interested in pursuing, presidential aides prepared detailed responses to anticipated questions. For instance, "Why did you put so much pressure on the

United States Olympic Committee and the International Olympic Committee to force Canada into allowing Taiwan to compete in the Olympics?" Answer: "My concern in this matter was not to champion Taiwan or to criticize Canada, but to see that the Olympic movement did not yield a fundamental principle that politics should not interfere in the participation of athletes in the games. I do not think that Canada, the host country, was right in denying entry to Taiwanese athletes unless they gave up their right to compete under the name 'Republic of China.'" Question: "If you feel so strongly about the maintenance of principle, why didn't you call for the withdrawal of U.S. athletes when Canada refused to withdraw all conditions on Taiwan's participation?" Answer: "The United States Olympic Committee, not the president, has the sole authority to order a withdrawal from the Games. While I felt it was proper for me to express my opinions in this matter to the USOC, I did not wish to further interject politics into this issue by exerting any influence on the USOC's decision. I am pleased that our athletes are participating and I am thrilled with their outstanding performance in the first day of competition."[90] These anticipated questions and responses suggest a course of action Ford would have preferred, but his chance to carry it out was soon blocked by advisers like Henry Kissinger, who kept a cooler head.

In an Oval Office meeting with his secretary of state and secretary of defense on the morning of July 13, Ford was eager to discuss the Montreal Games. He began the meeting by asking "How are we on the Olympics?" Henry Kissinger, the secretary of state, responded bluntly, "I think you should stay out of it. If Peking thinks we are trying to force Taiwan in, we could end up in a confrontation with Peking." Donald Rumsfeld, who was Ford's secretary of defense, commented, "This is a very touchy issue, with real down-side potential with the American people. We shouldn't get it turned into a one-China, two-China problem." Kissinger added, "That is why we must stay out of the substance and stick to the position that the host should not dictate the participation. Our position is that the Olympics are games, that participation is up to the IOC, and that the host's role is solely to provide facilities and it should not stipulate political conditions for attendance."[91] Kissinger's argument was powerful enough that Ford was forced to agree that the United States should "sit and wait until the U.S. Olympic Committee meets." On July 13 the IOC session officially accepted the Canadian position, and Ford realized that if Taiwan turned down the IOC decision, "I think the U.S. Olympic Committee will not withdraw from the Games. It is an outrage, but that's the way it is."[92]

Ford was obviously not happy with the situation and might have preferred a stronger policy. But Kissinger's argument that it was more important to protect the relationship with Beijing kept Ford from going too far in criticizing Canada. Like the Canadian government, the White House had no wish to offend Beijing. But Ford's frustration was apparent. At a July 14 morning meeting with Kissinger, Rumsfeld, and other top advisers, Ford exclaimed, "That Trudeau is being a real bastard."[93]

Indeed the relationship between Ford and Trudeau had soured considerably over the issue. Less than one month earlier, when Trudeau had visited Ford to present Canada's official congratulations to the United States on the celebration of its bicentennial, Ford had been friendly and even told Trudeau that the Montreal Olympics would be a great occasion to bring many Americans to Canada.[94]

Once Kissinger had advised Ford not to go too far, the White House immediately backed off from its earlier statements on the Montreal Games issue, at least in public. On July 14 Nessen softened the White House position by explaining that the president really couldn't order the U.S. team not to compete; it was not his role. Nessen said it was highly unlikely that the president would take any action in advising the team and would simply allow the situation to run its course. At this the media demanded to know, "Then why is he [Ford] meddling in it" in the first place? Nessen, defensive, could only answer, "I don't think he is meddling in it, I think it is a matter of principle."[95] But in fact we now know that James Cannon of the White House continued to strategize with the USOC about American options until July 16—one day before the Games' opening, and the very day Taiwan officially withdrew. On July 15, the Canadian government, under enormous public pressure, agreed that the Taiwanese athletes could enter the country and compete under their national flag, with their national anthem and with "Taiwan" written on their placard. But it would not agree to any mention of "China" in the Taiwan regalia.[96] The White House immediately announced that President Ford felt this new compromise upheld the principle he had been fighting for.[97] And so the saga of American involvement in the Taiwan dispute quietly ended.

Losers and Winners

The July 15 decision came about after Killanin met with Canadian prime minister Trudeau and told him the matter was still at an impasse because Taiwan had refused to accept the IOC decision of July 13. Trudeau, perhaps as a concession to world opinion, proposed that the IOC's Rome formula could be followed at the Montreal Games—namely, Taiwan could use its own flag and anthem but not its official name. The Canadian government described the concession as a demonstration of Canadian goodwill toward athletes and sports, and the IOC accepted the deal.[98] But Taiwan did not agree and chose to withdraw from the Games on July 16.[99]

The Canadian government immediately expressed regret that Taiwan had placed politics above sports. The Canadian government's shrewd move, agreeing to follow the Rome formula just one day before the opening of the Games, had not only provided the Americans with the pretense that the Olympic principle had been upheld, it had also allowed Canada to portray Taiwan as the party really politicizing the Games. Taiwan thus lost both the game of international politics and its shot at the Olympics. But why did Taiwan choose to withdraw?

Long before its altercation with the Canadian government, the Nationalist government in Taiwan realized it would have to fight a major battle to retain its China representation for the Montreal Games. To prepare for this battle, the Taiwan government established a powerful consortium to deal with international sports issues. Among the members of the group were cabinet councilor Zhou Shukai, education minister Jiang Yanshi, foreign minister Shen Changhuan, national Olympic committee president Shen Jiaming, and IOC member Xu Heng. This group was under the direct supervision of Premier Jiang Jingguo, the real leader of the government even then. When Jiang learned of the Canadian government's policy, he in turn insisted that Taiwan should use its own national flag, national anthem, and national name at the Games. Because neither Canada nor Taiwan would back down on the name issue, Taiwan had no choice in the end but to withdraw.[100]

Was this the right move for Taiwan? Tang Mingxin, a key member of Taiwan's delegation to the Montreal Games, commented that Jiang's decision was based on incomplete information and was not wise—it eventually led to the forced change of Taiwan's flag and anthem, as well as its official name in the IOC.[101] According to Xu Heng, the Nationalist government had trouble understanding the challenging and changing situation presented by Taiwan's representation issue. By insisting on an inflexible policy, the Taiwan government had bungled the Montreal Games.[102] Both Xu and Tang seem to suggest that the official policy should have reflected the changing times. They imply that Taiwan should have taken part in the Games after the Canadian government's concession.

The IOC also came out a loser in the China representation dispute. The IOC paid a huge price for missing the signs of trouble from the Canadian government and for not being prepared when the storm hit. Having its Taiwan policy effectively decided by the Canadian government was a terrible embarrassment. On principle, the IOC should have punished Canada for its breach of promise, but it lacked any means to do so. Its only powerful option would have been to cancel the Games, but with its overriding financial interest in the Olympic events, through having sold television rights, backing out was not an option.[103]

Moreover, the IOC knew that sooner or later it had to do something about the issue of who would represent China. From this perspective, the lost fight with the Canadian government can be seen as a blessing in disguise. After dawdling over the China issue for a quarter of a century, the IOC, given the light and heat of public debate and worldwide attention (courtesy of the Canadian government), had a powerful incentive to resolve the problem once and for all. The Canadian government understood this point well. As Skrabec of External Affairs wrote in 1975, "We believe that the I.O.C. would publicly deplore any indication that Canada might bar Taiwan from the 1976 Games but privately welcome it as a heaven-sent opportunity to avoid having to take a decision on their own problem with the PRC and Taiwan."[104] In this scenario, the IOC was not the real loser at all.

Was the United States, which became deeply involved in the dispute, a loser or a winner? As discussed earlier, the Ford administration wanted to take a stand for domestic political reasons. A 1995 book by Trudeau and his top aide pointed out that the American problem with Canada over the 1976 Montreal Olympics "was much more an American domestic political imperative than it was a reflection of bilateral differences."[105] Ford was so eager to engage in the dispute that he overreached and eventually had to back down, somewhat bruised, out of consideration for the standing U.S.-China policy.

In truth, the U.S. government might have liked to use the dispute to teach the Canadians a lesson, since the Trudeau administration had insisted on pursuing an independent foreign policy and had several other serious disagreements with the United States. In preparation for Ford's meeting on June 15, 1976, with Canadian opposition leader Joe Clark, Brent Scowcroft prepared talking points for Ford. The memo reminded Ford to make it clear to Clark that "excessive Canadian nationalism and anti-American Canadian policies" could be counterproductive, ultimately working against the best interests of both countries. It also pointed out that Canada "sees U.S. size and influence as a potential threat to Canadian independence and sovereignty. In recent months, Ottawa has taken a number of restrictive measures to preserve and enhance control over Canadian economic and cultural life." Scowcroft suggested that Ford indicate American concern that such programs frequently encroached on central U.S. interests. The United States, moreover, had problems with the new Canadian energy and security policies.[106]

In the end, the Ford administration was not able to win any points in its dispute over China. Still, the U.S. government did not really lose anything, at least not then. Its arguments with Canada in 1976 would, however, come to undermine American policy later, in 1980, when it took a stand regarding Taiwan's participation in the Winter Games and led a successful boycott of Moscow's team.

The main player in the Montreal Games dispute was of course the Canadian government. Its sole motive in creating this controversy was the protection of its one-China policy and its bilateral relations with the PRC. Since its establishment of diplomatic relations with Beijing, the Trudeau government had proceeded carefully in its China policy. As early as May 1975, the Canadian government had considered not allowing Taiwan into Canada for an international sporting event—in that case, to take part in judo championships.[107] In November 1975, the Canadian government denied entry to a Taiwan amateur boxing team competing under the name "Republic of China."[108] And in June 1976 the Canadian government even refused to fund its baseball team's participation in the World Baseball Championships, stating, "It would be inconsistent with our policy on relations with Taiwan for the Government to finance the participation of the team in competitions staged there."[109]

Indeed Canadian officials had considered sports to be a tool of international politics well before Trudeau became prime minister. In 1949 Lester Pearson, the Canadian secretary for External Affairs, had declared, "International sport is the means of attaining triumphs over another nation," and had urged Canada to try to excel in this area.[110] When Pierre Trudeau was elected in 1968, he carried on the same practice, only perhaps more effectively and forcefully. For instance, he used "hockey diplomacy" to facilitate Canadian-Russian relations just as the Chinese were using table tennis with the Americans.[111] Canadians and Russians, both hockey enthusiasts, used this common bond to strengthen their relations.[112] From this perspective, it is not surprising that in 1976 the Trudeau government used the Olympic Games as a forum for working out its China policy.

From the perspective of protecting its bilateral relations with the PRC, even after all the difficulties that arose from its Taiwan policy, the Canadian government felt it had achieved its goal. After all, as one confidential External Affairs memo concluded, Beijing seemed "highly pleased" in private with the Canadians' handling of the Taiwan issue.[113] It also can be argued that Beijing was a big winner, even though it was a largely silent party. It lost nothing and gained quite a lot of ground for its position on who represented China.

Still Canada did pay a price for taking on the Taiwan issue. According to a confidential report written after the Games by a senior External Affairs official, "What has the furor and the outcome of the application of our China policy gained us? It has certainly focused considerable public condemnation virtually internationally on the bases that we are 'renegers,' 'politicizers' of sport, and universal bad guys. It has affected our image, if not our relations with the U.S.A. to an undetermined extent, caused concern about our uncharacteristic stubbornness (critics would say 'pigheadedness') to policies and principles of our determination, like the French."[114]

According to the Canadian ambassador to the United States, there was "no doubt that Canada's image and reputation in the USA are suffering severe damage" as a result of the Olympic controversy. He even argued that given the importance of the Canadian relationship with the United States, "we are experiencing a setback of major proportions." While the United States and Canada had experienced problems before the Taiwan dispute, the ambassador pointed out, "The Olympic issue is adding fuel to a number of fires that were already burning and there is the serious possibility of a generalized anti-Canada sentiment developing. This is not without implications for our economic interest."[115] A Canadian scholar concluded in the 1990s that for the first time, Canada "had stood firm in the face of international condemnation and in the process had maintained the integrity of its foreign policy on China. For this action, it paid a heavy price in image, both at home and abroad."[116]

Postscript: The Diplomatic Games Continue

The Canadian government's stance on Taiwan was soon to be vindicated: in 1979 the IOC made a new decision on China's representation and in 1980, the United States refused to let Taiwan participate in the Winter Olympics, held in Lake Placid, New York.

When the Americans bid to host the 1980 Winter Olympics, President Ford, in his letter to Killanin on October 15, 1976, promised that the United States would not bring politics into Olympic Games: "I pledged that every team recognized by the International Olympic Committee will be welcomed at Lake Placid in 1980. I repeat that pledge to you."[117] He repeated this message to the American Olympic team when he hosted a White House reception for them on August 5, 1976, stating pointedly, "Attempts to use the Olympic Games for international power politics will ultimately backfire."[118]

When the Taiwan delegation arrived in the United States for the Winter Games, however, the American organizing committee, with the support of the IOC, refused to allow the athletes to participate under the "Republic of China" name, using arguments almost identical to those made by the Canadian government four years earlier. (The American government, which in 1979 had switched to recognizing Beijing as the diplomatic point of contact for China, now had no qualms about barring Taiwan because of the name issue.) Taiwan's team challenged the decision in the U.S. court system but failed; consequently, they withdrew from the 1980 U.S. Games.

After the Soviet invasion of Afghanistan in 1979, the Carter administration did not hesitate to use the Olympics as a political weapon. As Killanin wrote in his memoir, in early February 1980, Carter sent a presidential counsel, Lloyd Cutler, to visit Killanin in Dublin; his purpose was not to discuss the issue "but rather to instruct" the IOC in how it should respond to Washington's political position on the Moscow Games. Carter's message to Killanin: the IOC should either postpone or cancel the 1980 Moscow Games. Killanin rejected the American proposal and complained, "Here again was the American new world attitude of bringing out the bulldozer to save someone from an awful fate, or what America thought was an awful fate. It was this sense of arrogance, not personally shown by Cutler, but the high-handed nature of the approach of the White House, which raised my hackles."[119]

Killanin was indeed responding to a dramatic shift in tone. As a presidential candidate in 1976, Carter had strongly denounced the Canadian government's strategy of mixing politics and sports over the one-China issue. Four years later, however, President Carter went even further than the Canadians had by leading a successful—and purely politically motivated—campaign to boycott the 1980 Olympic Games held in Moscow.

CHINA AWAKENS
THE POST-MAO ERA

Citius, Altius, Fortius [faster, higher, stronger].
Olympic motto

WITH THE DEATH OF MAO in 1976 the disastrous decade-long Cultural Revolution came to an end. China's new leader, Deng Xiaoping, was determined to take the country in a new direction, opening up China to the world and liberalizing its economic and foreign policies.

As Deng Xiaoping's initiatives took hold in the early 1980s, the Chinese government decided to amp up its engagements internationally in a new quest for power and wealth. Sports once again came into play. No more "friendship first, competition second"—instead, winning in international sports became the Chinese obsession. In 1979 China's National Sports Commission came out with an "Olympic Model" and instructed each province to aim its sports programs at the collective goal of winning at the Olympic Games. In 1980 the commission coined a new slogan: "Break out of Asia, advance into the world" *(chong chu yazhou, zou xiang shijie),* which became the rallying cry for China's sports initiatives—and symbolized more broadly China's newfound self-confidence as an emerging member of the world economy.[1] For China, the days of self-inflicted isolation under Mao were over; China would march out to meet the world and demonstrate its prowess even in sports. According to one American journalist, "Gone are the days when China would artfully let visiting athletes win contests in order to strengthen international friendship."[2] In the new China, as Chen Zhili, a state councilor, declared in 2004, "Chinese victories in international sport competitions reflect the nation's good image and its rising international status."[3] Sports had once again become a key tool in Beijing's all-out campaign for international prestige, status, and legitimacy.

In Search of Power and Wealth: Chinese Sports in the 1980s

The 1980 Summer Olympic Games in Moscow would have been a wonderful opportunity for the PRC to reenter the realm of international competition after having rejoined the IOC in 1979. But Beijing had to contain its excitement until later because it followed the American-led boycott of Games to protest the Russian invasion of Afghanistan.

The Chinese decision made the IOC extremely unhappy. IOC president Lord Killanin wrote to the Chinese Olympic committee complaining, "Having worked for so long for the recognition of the Chinese Olympic Committee I must admit from a personal point of view I would have considerable reservations in proceeding with the candidature of a new member of the I.O.C. if the Chinese Olympic Committee does not participate in the [Moscow] Olympic Games."[4] Technically Beijing did return to the Olympic Games in 1980 by participating in the Lake Placid Winter Olympics, although few paid attention to that fact, and the Chinese performance there was not impressive.

The 1984 Olympic Games, however, provided an excellent opportunity for China to enhance its global visibility and national pride. Thanks to its timing and location, this Olympics could not have been better for Beijing. After all, it was in Los Angeles in 1932 that the Chinese had first taken part in the Olympics. Now China would once again, fifty-two years after its first appearance in the Games, have the opportunity to impress the world from the same stage. In addition, because Russia and other socialist countries were boycotting that year, the Chinese had a chance to claim more medals, garner more positive coverage, and better enjoy the interest and hospitality of Americans.

In March of 1982, Deng Xiaoping told the visiting IOC president Juan Samaranch that although Sino-American relations were not especially close, China would take part in the 1984 Los Angeles Games unless the United States treated Taiwan as an independent nation.[5] But the road to Los Angeles was not smooth for Beijing. According to the 1984 Games Organizing Committee chairman Peter Ueberroth, "Overall our relationship with the PRC was excellent, but there had been a few snags along the way."[6] One of these snags involved Hu Na, a Chinese tennis player. On July 20, 1982, she defected by slipping out of her hotel room on the eve of a key match in the federation cup tennis tournaments in Santa Clara, California, and applied for political asylum. This incident was so serious for Beijing that Deng Xiaoping personally spoke about it to the visiting U.S. secretary of state George Shultz in February 1983. Beijing was concerned that the incident might "set a dangerous precedent" that could crucially affect Sino-American relations.[7] When in April 1983 the United States granted Hu Na political asylum despite Deng's warning, Beijing immediately canceled all official cultural and athletic exchanges for the rest of 1983, including Chinese participation in pre-Olympic cycling, rowing, and canoeing events held in Los Angeles.

Although the Hu Na incident caused Olympic organizers grave concern about China's possible attendance, Beijing never seriously considered boycotting the Games. The Olympics were quite simply the best stage China could find for showing off its reinvigorated commitment to international sports, and it was the first time that Beijing and Taiwan would take part together in an international competition after having come to mutually agreeable terms.[8] In January 1984 in preparation for the Games, China sent a seven-person delegation to Los Angeles, led by Chen Xian, vice president of the Chinese Olympic Committee. In his statement, Chen Xian claimed that the visit by the Chinese delegation "has been crowned with success." He went on to promise that China would send a three-hundred-person delegation to the Games. He also said, "To further Sino-

Deng Xiaoping meets with IOC president Juan Antonio Samaranch on
March 30, 1982, in Beijing.

American relations in sports is our common desire. . . . Adhering to the
Olympic ideals, we will participate in the 23rd Olympiad with a view toward strengthening understanding and friendship among the peoples and
athletes of different countries, thus helping to safeguard world peace as
well as lending impetus to the improvement of sports, worldwide."[9] In its
official letter to the Los Angeles Olympic Committee dated May 12, 1984,
the Chinese Olympic Committee wrote in the name of its president, Zhong
Shitong, "I have the honor to inform you that the Chinese Olympic Committee has decided to send a sports delegation to the 23rd Los Angeles
Olympic Games" and wished the Games "every success."[10] The Americans
gave a big sigh of relief. According to Ueberroth, "The PRC announcement on May 12 gave us our first public victory over the Soviets."[11]

The timing could not have been better for China; the Los Angeles
Games had become a major political contest between the two superpow-

ers. In retaliation for the U.S. boycott of the 1980 Moscow Games, the USSR had chosen to boycott the Los Angeles Games (although the Soviets did not use the word boycott, preferring instead "non-participation").

When Russia announced its boycott in May, U.S. officials pretended not to care. Ueberroth declared, "We don't need them in Los Angeles to have one of the best Olympic competitions in history," and Los Angeles mayor Tom Bradley said, "To hell with them. They are our Games. Let's make them work."[12] Contrary to Herbert Hoover's less-than-enthusiastic attitude toward the last Los Angeles Games, President Ronald Reagan did his best to use the Games to score political points against the USSR and promote America's image. At the opening ceremony, Reagan wanted to give a longer speech than the prescribed sixteen words allowed by Olympic rules. According to U.S. officials, Reagan was anxious to "use the opportunity to welcome people there" and promised that his speech would not be political, would not mention the Soviet Union, and would not last even ten minutes.[13] But the rule was the rule, and the IOC did not give in. Eventually Reagan uttered the following formulaic proclamation (which included an extra word—"Olympic"): "I declare open the Olympic games of Los Angeles celebrating the twenty-third Olympiad of the modern era."[14]

With the heavy investment of U.S. political capital in the Games, China became a major beneficiary of the superpowers' struggle. China's participation gave the American government a powerful propaganda tool and created a special attraction for the Games. The Olympic organizers were determined to give China a special welcome. According to the Games' official report, "Everyone was smiling on 14 July when the villages at UCLA, USC and UC Santa Barbara opened. The first athlete to register at the UCLA village was Zou Zhenxian, a triple jumper from the People's Republic of China. His presence marked a return to the city where Chinese participation in the Olympics games had begun 52 years earlier."[15]

This seemingly simple description includes many symbolically important messages. At major games like this, the ceremonies opening the Olympic village were a very serious business, involving the formal pronouncement of the opening of the Games and a ribbon-cutting event with many dignitaries. When Chinese athlete Zou Zhenxian was given the honor of being the "first athlete to enter the Olympic village representing the official Olympic Family," China became the first nation to formally raise its flag at the UCLA village.[16] Wu Zhongyuan, director of the press and publicity commission of the Chinese Olympic Committee, was enormously pleased with the Americans' arrangement and said the ceremony was significant in marking "the friendship of the American and Chinese people."[17] When Zou received the symbolic key to the village, many doors were opened at once for China: the country gained access not simply to the Olympic Games, but also to new opportunities for impressing the world at large.

There were other nice gestures from the Americans, who went out of their way to make the Chinese feel comfortable and important. On July 24, 1984, the Los Angeles Olympic Committee organized a news conference for the Chinese delegation, an arrangement that is offered to only a few delegations at the Games. In his brief statement, the Chinese representative mentioned the historical connection, recounting how fifty-two years earlier China had managed to send only one athlete to Los Angeles, but this time 353 athletes had come to take part. The press wanted to know why the Chinese were excited about sports and the Games. The reply from their spokesman demonstrated the eagerness of the Chinese athletes to "win glory for the nation." He openly linked sports competition with national honor and prestige, and emphasized the importance of winning medals. When asked whether China would attend the 1988 Seoul Olympic Games since Beijing and Seoul did not recognize each other diplomatically, the Chinese representative promised to follow the Olympic Charter and thus indicated that China would take part.[18] The Chinese were also happy to be honored at a big reception hosted by the City of Los Angeles.[19]

At the opening ceremony, the Chinese delegation received an especially warm and enthusiastic welcome. Ueberroth wrote, "When the team from the People's Republic of China entered the stadium, the audience erupted in cheers. The entire crowd of 92,665 stood and applauded. It was a grand welcome."[20] Although the ideological and political differences between the United States and China had hardly disappeared overnight, for the Chinese it was largely a happy moment. The size of their team meant they were ready and determined to eradicate once and for all the old "sick man of East Asia" image and their reputation as a weak nation in sports.[21] They were pleased that a Chinese athlete had been honored to be the first villager, and they felt tremendous pride when the first Olympic gold medal was won by Chinese shooter Xu Haifeng in the opening event, the men's free pistol competition.

With this first gold medal of the Los Angeles Games, and the first gold ever won by a Chinese, Xu Haifeng became a national hero. People at home excitedly called his victory "just the beginning for we Chinese who have suffered so much to prove ourselves to the world."[22] With the Soviet Union and other strong sports countries out of the picture, the Chinese won fifteen gold medals and enjoyed a "cuddly reception from the rest of the world." Brook Larmer was right when he wrote that "nothing could have gratified the insecure nation more."[23]

The 1984 Olympic Games were indeed just the beginning. China's success as a world-class economic power has been paralleled in the realm of sports. In the 2004 Athens Olympics, China even competed with the United States, the sole superpower, for supremacy: the United States took thirty-five gold medals while China won thirty-two. China's sports minister, Yuan Weimin, told U.S. Olympic Committee Chairman Peter Ueberroth before the Athens Games, "Don't worry—we will not topple you. But we are making this effort."[24] It is no secret that China wants to do even better at the 2008 Games. After all, the Chinese government has long pursued winning at international games, especially Western sports, as a rite of passage into the top tier of world powers; it clearly understands the importance of sports to China's national fate and national honor.

China's internationalization through sports has sometimes produced positive diplomatic results not only for China, but for other countries as well. China's interactions with South Korea through sports is a good example. Beijing and Seoul did not establish diplomatic relations until the early 1990s because of the obstacles created by Beijing's close relations with North Korea. When the Chinese wanted to improve their ties with South Korea, sports provided a suitable medium for moving forward, despite the diplomatic obstacles.

Richard Pound, who served as the first vice president of the IOC and was intimately aware of the behind-the-scenes negotiations, noticed Beijing's friendly gestures to South Korea when South Korea was applying for and hosting the 1988 Olympic Games. "Regardless of its motivations, there can be no question that the quiet support of the Chinese was instrumental in the success of the Seoul Games. The Olympic conduct of China cannot be faulted in any way," Pound wrote. "And it sent the appropriate diplomatic signals to South Korea that it was ready to discuss a fuller series of trade and diplomatic ties when the time was ripe."[25] He Zhenliang, one of China's top sports officials, put it this way: "I think it became apparent that the Olympic Movement can bring people together, can be a universal bridge. Although we in China had no relationship with South Korea, we felt obliged to contribute to the success of the Olympic Games. Our participation in Seoul was an occasion to let our people know better the people of South Korea, and vice versa."[26]

Chinese foreign minister Qian Qichen confirmed the success of this approach, admitting that bilateral relations between South Korea and China had been improved through mutual participation in the Seoul Olympic Games in 1988.[27] Interestingly, when Qian attended the 1991 Asia-Pacific Economic Cooperation (APEC) meetings in South Korea before diplomatic relations had been established, a South Korean sports official paid him a surprise visit near midnight; he told Qian that he had visited China several times as a sports official and was willing to act as a secret channel to help establish diplomatic relations between the two countries. He even confided to Qian that this meeting had been approved by the South Korean president.[28]

Like ping-pong diplomacy with the Americans, sports diplomacy with the South Koreans proved very successful for the Chinese. After the Seoul Olympics, China and South Korea soon recognized each other diplomatically and their economic relations have since flourished. In fact, by cultivating good sports relations with the South Koreans, Beijing was able to realize its ambition to gain international stature through sports. Goodwill and help from the South Koreans certainly was a significant behind-the-scenes story to the successful hosting of the Asian Games by Beijing in 1990, the first major sporting event ever to take place in China.[29] Beijing's confidence after its hosting of the Asian Games became the foundation for its bid for hosting the Olympics.

China's enthusiasm for winning in sports sometimes went too far: the Chinese have been known to claim racial superiority. Communist China is not the only nation to have made such claims. As Ian Buruma has pointed out, Nazi Germany's obsession with racial virility "was exported and taken up by Hindu chauvinists in India, militarists in Japan, nationalists in China."[30] But the PRC went even further than the Nationalists and many other countries in using racial virility to disguise what some may call a sense of racial inferiority. From the time the Chinese began to embrace the ethos of modern sports in the late nineteenth century, they argued openly that Asian peoples generally were not suited to compete in games that demanded sudden and explosive physical power, such as the 100-meter dash or the hurdles.

In many countries, particularly the United States, this kind of racial stereotyping touched a raw nerve and was rarely embraced by official ideology. But among the Chinese, as a recent *New York Times* article has pointed out, the proposition that congenital shortcomings and genetic differences made Asian athletes slower at sprinting than their American, African, or European rivals was a widely accepted maxim, if an unproven one. Even the country's top Communist party newspaper, the *People's Daily,* openly cited this idea. In a corollary stereotype, it was widely believed that the Chinese were suited to sports like ping-pong, badminton, and gymnastics that require agility and technique, because the Chinese were deemed smart and disciplined.[31]

Recent competitions, then, have been in part about a new generation of Chinese overcoming stereotypes about their capabilities. As the *People's Daily* explained, "If the Chinese people want to make their mark in the major Olympic competitions, they have to break through the fatalism that race determines everything." Not surprisingly, then, the Chinese exploded with joy when Liu Xiang, a tall, handsome, and confident young man from Shanghai, won the 110-meter men's high hurdles at the 2004 Athens Games; they finally had evidence that the perceived racial handicap could be overcome. But Liu's victory could only partially erase the old

Can China compete against the best? Chinese athlete Liu Xiang wins the
110-meter hurdles at the 2004 Olympic Games in Athens. His victory, the
first ever for China in a sprinting event, thrilled the Chinese, many of
whom believed that he had overcome genetic physical limitations.

ingrained beliefs. Some high-level Chinese sports officials noted that hurdles also require technique, not just raw speed, to win. And Liu himself,
dubbed the "Yellow Bullet" by some commentators, openly talked about
his victory in the Olympic Games as "a kind of miracle." He told inter-
viewers, "It is unbelievable—a Chinese, an Asian, has won this event,"
adding, "It is a proud moment not only for China, but for Asia and all people who share the same yellow skin color."[32] As the *New York Times*
pointed out, "By becoming the first Chinese man to win a sprinting event
in modern Olympics history, Mr. Liu's victory has been particularly embraced by a younger generation of upwardly mobile, urban Chinese who
themselves are eager to shatter stereotypes."[33]

Internationalization, Chinese-style

Chinese participation and even interest in modern sports have been largely motivated by nationalism. But by importing modern sports from the West and taking part in world competitions, China has simultaneously used sports to express its worldview, promote its status in the world, and declare its national identity. When the world focuses on China during the 2008 Beijing Olympics, sports will offer possibly even greater opportunities for enhancing China's stature among other nations.

In the twentieth century, the world experienced many wars and political divisions. Fascism, capitalism, socialism, nationalism, and Communism created many divisions among people. Yet sports, especially the Olympic Games and the World Cup, have continued, by and large, to bring people together. Even as Communist China isolated itself from the world system during the Cold War era and with Mao's radical revolutionary fever, the country still tried to socialize with the world community through its so-called friendship games and Games of the Newly Emerging Forces. Since the 1980s, as China has surged forward economically and politically, and as the Chinese have gained confidence in themselves, nothing better symbolizes the drive to achieve greater prestige than sports. For the Chinese, embracing Western sports demonstrates their status and desire to keep abreast of world culture. Moreover, an appreciation of Western sports is politically safe.

Basketball perhaps best represents China's taste for this form of internationalization. From the beginning, when Canadian James Naismith invented it in 1891 at the YMCA's international training center in Springfield, Massachusetts, basketball was destined to become a global sport. As one observer has explained, "When YMCA missionaries arrived in the city of Tianjin in the 1890s carrying 'The Thirteen Rules of Basketball,' along with their Bibles, they believed that salvation would come through God and hoops, though not necessarily in that order."[34]

Although it hardly received salvation through basketball, China does try to stand out by choosing its tallest basketball players to be flag bearers at the opening ceremonies of the Olympic Games. Both the Nationalists and the Communists used the same trick in the 1948 and 1984 Games, respectively. At the 1988 Seoul Olympic Games, too, Wang Libin was initially chosen to serve as the flag carrier at the opening ceremony, but he was replaced by Song Tao, the former center of the Chinese basketball team, since Wang needed to concentrate on the game the team was going to play that day.[35] Not surprisingly, Yao Ming had that honor in the 2004 Athens Games: at seven feet, six inches, Yao towered over every other athlete, helping China's entire delegation of 226 officials and 407 athletes seem taller.

The transformation of Chinese society since the economic reforms of the late 1970s has finally made it possible for society and the government to begin working together to push China's internationalization even further through sports. According to a *Washington Post* article, in the 1990s Chinese schoolchildren ranked U.S. basketball star Michael Jordan and Zhou Enlai as the two greatest figures in twentieth-century history, and vendors in Beijing sold Michael Jordan posters and calendars alongside those of the late Chairman Mao.[36] When the NBA finals were broadcast live to China for the first time in 1994, according to one poll, Michael Jordan became China's premier pop-culture hero—more lionized than Mao. In 2006, an influential newspaper *Huanqiu shibao* (Global times) in Beijing decided to run a series of articles focusing on fifty foreigners who have had the greatest influence on modern China. The list, selected with the help of top Chinese scholars, includes not only Jean-Jacques Rousseau, Charles Darwin, Karl Marx, Lenin, and Richard Nixon—but also Michael Jordan.[37] According to Walter LaFeber, "The story of basketball, especially in the era of Michael Jordan, helps us understand this era known as 'the American Century.'"[38]

The Chinese have wholeheartedly embraced this facet of the American century without considering whether their obsession with the NBA is compatible with nationalism or even national pride. When on May 7, 1999, the American military bombed the Chinese embassy in Belgrade, many Chinese urban youths, obviously angry at the United States for this provocative anti-Chinese action, still called to complain when in June 1999 the China Central Television Station, in protest, canceled its scheduled broadcast of NBA games; the callers insisted that sports events "should have nothing to do with politics." According to one leader of the student demonstration in front of the American embassy, "I hate American hegemony, and [I] love the NBA games. But they are two different things. NBA games belong to the world, and everyone has the right to enjoy them."[39] In this way, sports have clearly brought about a convergence of Chinese and American popular cultures, when nationalism might well have kept them apart. Perhaps only sports can play such a subtle role in pushing China forward to continued internationalization.

World sports organizations have been working hard to cash in on Chinese interest. NBA commissioner David Stern, who is actively building the NBA into a global brand, considers China, with its 1.3 billion potential consumers of sports, basketball's "final frontier."[40] According to a recent statistic, 500 million Chinese were basketball fans, and they bought 400 million NBA "branded" products, from jerseys to basketballs, in 2005. These numbers, if reliable, put China at the very top of countries with NBA fans. The NBA also claims that more than one billion viewers sampled the 290-some games it televised in China during the 2005–2006 season.

Stern declared recently how pleased he is that the Chinese government has labeled his sport "important for fitness, exercise, and harmony."[41] From the NBA executives' perspective, the world doesn't have to take over the NBA, for the NBA to take over the world.[42] These days the official NBA web site has several language versions, including one in Chinese, and a significant portion of the NBA's income comes from international sales of its merchandise. The league itself is becoming more international; as of the 2005–2006 season, 18 percent of NBA players came from abroad and more are coming.[43] Yao Ming, a star foreign player, joined the Houston Rockets in 2002 as a first draft choice and has played for the team ever since. "Yao is a dream for David Stern and the NBA," says Rockets' president George Postolos. "He takes globalization to a new level."[44]

Although Yao was not the first Chinese NBA player and definitely will not be the last, he can still be described as emblematic of three trends taking place in China simultaneously: the rise of China as an economic power, the expansion of transnational capitalism, and the Chinese obsession with all things international, especially sports. In this sense, Yao has truly become the "poster child of globalization," as Brook Larmer observes.[45] For the Chinese, who have suffered from both a sense of inferiority and can-do bravado, Yao has become an icon of confidence for China; he can compete against the best in the world and stand taller than any, and has thereby helped to erase any doubt that Chinese players can succeed on the world stage.

Many Chinese follow Yao's games closely and watch his every step in the United States simply because he is one of them. Yao's first NBA game was seen by 287 million households in China, and during his first season, the NBA broadcast 170 games in China, including thirty featuring Yao's team, the Rockets.[46] Yao's regular-season NBA games draw about a million viewers in the United States, but they "regularly attract up to 30 million in China, making the Houston Rockets China's favorite team— and the world's most watched. When internet portal Sohu hosted a 90-minute online chat with Yao in December 2002, nearly 9 million fans logged on, crashing the system in six of China's largest cities."[47]

Chinese viewers have been happy to see Yao play well. In his rookie year in 2003, he averaged 13.5 points and 8.2 rebounds per game, a record that dispelled any doubt about his abilities. With so many well-educated, high-achieving Chinese in their audience, the NBA games have brought the Chinese people closer to American culture and allowed them to share their passion for basketball with the rest of the world. As one *New York Times* article noted, "Today, as China wades into the global market economy, as its children embrace Western culture, as a new urban professional set seeks self-expression at every turn, what better vehicle than basketball?"[48]

Yao Ming has also served as an effective ambassador, bringing the Chinese and American people together. When in his first year he repeatedly blocked shots by his hulking nemesis Shaquille O'Neal and sealed the outcome of one game with a dunk, the same *Times* article proclaimed that "he'd done more than win a game. . . . Around the world, he'd smashed the stereotype of the small, submissive Chinese."[49] A *Time* magazine article explained the Yao Ming phenomenon well:

There are 1.3 billion of them, but Westerners don't really know much about the citizens of the Middle Kingdom. For decades, China has existed in the international eye as either a megalomaniacal dictator (Chairman Mao) or a teeming mass of low-paid factory workers (everybody else). Maybe there's a hyperkinetic kung fu star or a nerdy computer whiz to round out the stereotype. But mostly, the Chinese have lived in Western minds as inscrutable, unknowable, [and] incalculable. Now comes Yao Ming—and all the ill-conceived clichés about those strange Chinese have been shattered like a glass backboard after a monstrous slam dunk. . . . Yao has single-handedly transformed his countrymen from nameless, faceless millions into mighty men who can jam with the very best. For Americans, Yao's affable demeanor and witty repartee are a welcome antidote to the antics of the NBA's bad boys. And for the Chinese, who are chronically obsessed with their overseas reputation, Yao's maturation from a meek athletic machine to a charismatic basketball personality is nothing less than proof that China finally measures up.[50]

These ideas from the American mainstream media might have exaggerated the role that Yao has played in affecting American perceptions of China, but clearly the obsession in China with the NBA and the Olympic Games are part of a larger trend. Yao Ming was the first high-profile, nonpolitical Chinese personality to come under the scrutiny of the Western media, and "basketball is his main mechanism for expression."[51] Yao represents both China's internationalization and the world's biggest multinationals: Pepsi, Reebok, Visa, and McDonald's all jumped at the opportunity to use Yao to gain access to the Chinese market. Yao has become so much a face of China that when President Hu Jintao visited the United States in April 2006, Yao was invited to attend the White House luncheon held in Hu's honor.

The Chinese are also obsessed with soccer, the "beautiful game" that has captivated billions of world fans. Here again China is participating in a global trend, joining in with most countries of the world in their devotion to the sport. The world may have changed enormously over the twentieth century, but people's obsession with soccer is still going strong. The final match of the 1986 World Cup drew a worldwide audience of 652 million, and the 2006 World Cup finals were viewed by an estimated three billion people worldwide. Roger Cohen of the *International Herald Tribune* has written that soccer "is as much the world's language as English and as close to the universal idiom of the planet's dreams as anything. Soccer is the 90-minute passion play of the everyman."[52] Franklin Foer recently asked, "What could be more global than soccer? The world's leading professional players and owners pay no mind to national borders, with major teams banking revenues in every currency available on the foreign exchange and billions of fans cheering for their champions in too many languages to count." Some people take soccer so seriously they go to wild extremes. During the 2002 World Cup held in Japan and South Korea, some Japanese professional women trimmed their pubic hair to express their obsession with the English player David Beckham. And a few years ago, a Swedish parliamentarian named Lars Gustafson nominated the game for a Nobel Peace Prize, unleashing a fury of ridicule.[53]

For many people in the world, soccer is a way of life.[54] As Bill Shankly, the acclaimed manager of the English club Liverpool, once said, "Some people believe football is a matter of life and death. I can assure you it's much, much more important than that."[55] According to the recent findings of three economists, people worldwide take soccer so seriously that "a loss in a significant international match can lead to a loss in a country's stock market the next day."[56]

The World Cup is perhaps the most successful forum by which to bring the world together and create a better and more exciting world order. In the World Cup, which Henry Kissinger has called a "world of wonder," everyone, rich or poor, from a strong country or from a small one, has an opportunity to achieve their potential.[57] More importantly, no country or regime, regardless of its wealth or power, can really manipulate a victory of championships given the nature of soccer games. In this sense, the beautiful game can do more to create a harmonious world than political forums or organizations. This is why even the United Nations uses the World Cup to convey its messages and ideals.

Like their counterparts in the rest of the world, many Chinese have caught World Cup fever, although China's men's teams have so far only

managed to enter the finals once in 2002 (and only then because the pow-
erhouses South Korea and Japan, which acted as co-hosts in 2002, allowed
China an easier entry). In the only Chinese men's appearance in the World
Cup, the team did not manage to score and so had to drop out in the group
stage.

Given their sheer numbers, the Chinese could have an extraordinary
influence on soccer. In 2006 the entire population of the thirty-two nations
entered in the World Cup was about 1.5 billion, while that of China was
1.34 billion.[58] And even when their men haven't made the World Cup
finals, Chinese fans have been no less crazy or excited than fans whose
teams were participating. Indeed, since the 1980s when China opened up
to the world, Chinese fans have become ever more obsessed with the
World Cup finals. More than five hundred Chinese journalists went to
Germany to cover the 2006 World Cup, and Chinese TV stations devoted
prime-time airtime to cover games live. The audience of the CCTV sports
channel increased fiftyfold during the 2006 World Cup. More than 700
million Chinese viewers watched the games over the course of the tournament, staying up all hours to watch the games played live in Germany.[59]

If the Chinese appreciation of basketball and soccer reflects a genuine
love of these games and points to the level of China's current internationalization, other forays into Western sports seem possibly less well considered. The European-style Formula 1 race track built in Shanghai in 2004 is
one example. The 5.45-kilometer track cost between $240 and $320 million to build and was designed by the German Herman Tilke, known for
his F1 circuits elsewhere in the world. Also in 2004, Shanghai staged a
Spanish bullfight, the first ever held there, in a stadium converted into a
bullfighting arena.

Even some of the stadiums and structures created to further China's
dreams of international sports success seem possibly disconnected from
the Chinese public. To prepare for the 2008 Beijing Olympics, for instance,
the city government hired world-famous architects like Ram Koolhass to
design stadiums that show off a level of international sophistication. The
famous "bird-nest" stadium is one of these.

To become a sports power, China has used its recent openness to draw coaching talent from around the world. Although as early as 1964 Premier Zhou Enlai invited the Japanese women's volleyball head coach, Damatsu Hirofumi, to Beijing to train Chinese players, very few Western coaches worked in China until the 1980s, when China determined to transform itself with the help of expertise from abroad.[60] Today many foreigners work in China as coaches or other leaders. The women's hockey team has been coached by Korean Kim Chang Buck since 1999; Germans and Canadians have coached rowing and canoeing teams; American Del Harris and then Lithuanian Jonas Kazlauskas took the helm of Chinese men's basketball; and Australian Tom Maher was chosen to coach women's basketball.[61] As Beijing prepares for the 2008 Games, more and more foreigners will be hired to help the Chinese compete successfully, a trend the *China Sports Journal* has dubbed the new "foreign affairs moment" *(yangwu yundong)*.[62]

Internationalization has also become a two-way street, with many Chinese going abroad to play or coach. Besides Yao Ming, many other Chinese have played important roles in this so-called reverse internationalization. For example, the former Chinese volleyball player Lang Ping is head coach of U.S. women's volleyball team, while her teammate Jiang Ying has become head coach of the Australian women's team. Many Chinese Ping-Pong players, too, work as coaches or players abroad.

In fact, people may be amazed by the speed with which products made in China have been reaching foreign markets, but few have really noted China's new type of export: expertise in sports. And unlike the usual manufactured goods, which often create trade friction, this new product promises to help China and the rest of the world live more harmoniously. It will be fascinating to see how this kind of internationalization will affect China's future national identity and what role it will play in further global developments.

Sports and the Rise of Nationalism

It is true that China has recently been asserting itself internationally in dramatic ways. But it is also true that sports still serve the Chinese cause of nationalism just as they have for a hundred years. Even for Chinese people who are not sports fans, the raising of the Chinese national flag and playing of the national anthem at international sports-award events like the Olympics is often a stirring moment. After all, the national anthem, "Yi yong jun jin xing qu," originally written for the Chinese military during the anti-Japanese war, is an expression of strident nationalism (as this rough translation demonstrates):

> Rise up, you people who do not want to be slaves! Let's use our blood and flesh to build up our new great wall. The Chinese nation has reached the most dangerous moment. Everyone is forced to utter their last roar. Rise up, rise up! Let's unite with one heart, facing the enemy's fire, and march on! Facing the enemy's gunfire, march on, march on, march on!

Since the 1980s the idea that winning is everything has entered the mindset of many Chinese, and the government has mobilized the nation's resources to achieve victories through administrative, legal, and political means. In 1995 the PRC passed its first sports-related law, *Zhong hua renmin gongheguo tiyu fa* (sports law of the PRC), which was clearly motivated by the nation's cry for more sports victories.[63] This law openly declares that sports activities should be under the direct control of the state council and serve the interests of national economic and social development and defense. It also insists that athletes should receive instructions on issues of patriotism, collectivism, and socialism.[64]

The Olympic Games and many other international sports competitions initially emphasized amateurism, and the most important principle was to take part, not to win. But since the creation of the People's Republic, China, like most other countries, has to a great extent violated this rule by emphasizing the winning of gold medals and by training athletes from the time they are children. The state takes care of all of the athletes' personal needs in order to make sure they will succeed in international competition. Sports thus becomes these athletes' vocation and their main goal becomes winning. In early 1979, even before Beijing officially returned to the Olympic movement, the National Sports Commission articulated an "important but pressing political task": China should focus on taking part in the 1980 Moscow Olympic Games and aim to be ranked among the top ten teams in the Games by winning about five gold medals (and fifteen medals overall).[65]

These same goals were restated in the National Sports Commission's report in early 1980. The 1980 report even suggested that China should aim to be among the top six teams in the 1984 Olympic Games to "win glory for the nation" *(wei guo zheng guang)*. To become a world sports power, a good strategy was key; the report suggested that China's sports policy should focus on important Olympic events.[66] Deng Xiaoping became personally involved in enacting this policy. In 1981 his office even called Li Menghua, the head of the sports commission, to ask why the national men's volleyball team was not eating enough high-quality food.[67]

The Chinese have called the winning of gold medals in the 1984 Los Angeles Games a "historic breakthrough," "a new page in China's involvement in the Olympic moment," "an encouraging great jump in the Chinese nation's revival," "a new chapter in China's emergence as a great sports power," and a "milestone."[68] With the gold medal in shooting, China had its first Olympic champion and the "label of the 'sick man of East Asia' was once and for all thrown away into the Pacific Ocean."[69] Deng Xiaoping was deeply impressed by the 1984 Los Angeles Games and told other Chinese leaders, "Now it looks like the impact and influence of sports are so great that they reflect a country's economy and civilization. They attract and inspire so many people. We need to improve our sports." Deng's instruction immediately became official policy.[70]

For the Chinese government, China's status and relative strength among nations became measured by the number of gold medals won at the Olympics. Consequently, all sports in China seemed to focus on winning the gold. In the name of winning, a principle of *"quan guo yi pan qi"* and *"guo nei lian bing, yi zhi dui wai"* has been established firmly. *"Quan guo yi pan qi"* means that individual provinces should concentrate on the sports in which they have a chance to win internationally. It also indicates that every athlete and every province should follow the overall plan of the central sports commission with a single purpose: to help the nation win a gold medal in an international arena. The principle of *"guo nei lian bing, yi zhi*

A big jump from "sick man of East Asia" to a sports powerhouse:
Chinese long jumper Guo Chunfang at the Sydney 2000 Olympic Games.

dui wai" suggests that competitions among Chinese teams should focus on the improvement of skills because the main objective is to win international championships. Under the guidance of these principles and in the name of winning national honor, results for games among Chinese players sometimes were decided even before they began.[71]

This unhealthy obsession with medals has been so intense that even some Chinese have complained that China needs to rethink its sports strategy. As early as the late 1980s, writers such as Zhao Yu questioned whether it was wise for China to link gold medals in sports to its *qiang guo meng,* or dream of becoming a superpower.[72] Zhao attacked the very premise behind the Chinese national sports policy by questioning whose interests the nation's sports strategy served. His pointed inquiry was especially relevant given that the emphasis on winning gold medals had been accompanied by a deterioration in the overall physical condition of the Chinese people.[73] Zhao asked the Chinese public to reconsider the meaning and usefulness of sports.[74] The Chinese sport authorities were extremely angry with Zhao for his criticisms, and Li Menghua, the head of the National Sports Commission, criticized the articles as politically detrimental.[75] Even so, another Chinese writer in the late 1980s observed that the policy of the day "sacrificed the whole nation's physical well-being for our Olympic strategy," since crucial resources were being used for winning medals instead of for mass physical education.[76]

Ironically, even elite athletes have paid a price for this strategy. In the late 1970s and 1980s in particular, these competitors did not have personal lives, a good education, or even healthy personalities. To make sure they concentrated on their sport, athletes were not allowed to fall in love or marry young (men were permitted to marry only after age twenty-eight and women after age twenty-six).[77] Their whole goal from childhood on was to win in major sports competitions.

If an athlete failed to win a medal, he or she sometimes suffered serious harassment from the Chinese public. For instance, when Zhu Jianhua, a high jumper and a favorite, was defeated at the 1984 Los Angeles Olympics, the windows of his house in Shanghai were broken and his family members were abused.[78] In 1994, after former Chinese Ping-Pong player

He Zhili, who had resigned from the China national team and later married a Japanese man, went on to represent Japan and defeat her former teammates to win a gold medal at the Twelfth Asian Games, many Chinese called her a traitor.[79] When the Chinese women's volleyball team lost in the 1988 Olympic Games, too, they were criticized so harshly that one of their star players, Yang Xilan, was completely heartbroken.[80] The same devastating criticism was inflicted on many others as well. As writers of the influential CCTV series *Heshang* observed then, China is a nation that cannot afford to lose anymore, even in sports. For these critics, athletes were to shoulder the burdens of the nation.[81]

For Zhao Yu and others, however, China could never really become a sports powerhouse without nurturing complete and robust individual rights and inculcating a healthy personality in its people.[82] By the late 1980s, then, some Chinese writers had declared that, in keeping with the true Olympic spirit, it was time for the Chinese to be strong enough to tolerate occasional losses in sports.[83]

Some Chinese have also expressed dismay at the financial cost of the gold medal strategy. Li Liyan, a researcher at the China National Sports Commission, recently concluded that for 1988 the annual budget for the sports commission was one billion yuan, or four billion over four years. For this huge investment, China had won five gold medals at the 1988 Seoul Olympics. Thus each medal had cost the country 800 million yuan. In 1992 China won sixteen gold medals at the Olympics but the National Sports Commission's annual budget had by then increased to three billion per year; in other words, China had spent 750 million yuan for each gold medal. In 2004 the sports budget increased to five billion yuan per year, a figure that does not include the financial bonuses awarded to winners. For medals won at the 2000 Sydney Games, the central government awarded 150,000 yuan for a gold medal, 80,000 for a silver, and 50,000 for bronze. Four years later, the amounts increased to 200,000, 120,000, and 80,000, respectively. Apparently, officials were unfazed by Li Liyan's analysis. According to one, China would chase the gold no matter the cost. The same official even claimed that a sport not focused on winning gold medals is a failed sport.[84]

Can you see my gold medal? Chinese badminton player Yang Zhang
(far left) wins gold at the 2004 Olympic Games in Athens, while Chinese
athlete Huang Gao (second from left) takes home the silver medal.

Even given the robust link between sports and nationalism, Chinese
responses to sports events sometimes have reached bizarre and even hys-
terical levels. When the news reached China that the Chinese men's soccer
team had prevailed over the Japanese in 1987, fans were so excited that
they marched out in groups and sang an old anti-Japanese song, "The
[Chinese] big swords are aiming at [Japanese] heads . . ." For these fans,
the Chinese soccer victory made them feel as if their country had defeated
Japan and won the war.[85]

Another incident was even more bound up with nationalistic feelings.
On the evening of May 19, 1985, a men's soccer match between Hong
Kong and China took place in Beijing. If China were to win, it might have
a chance to participate in the Mexico World Cup competition. Before the
game, China's was considered the stronger team. In fact, the Chinese team
had won second place in the Asia Cup of 1984 and had even defeated

Argentina in the India Cup of January 1984 (although some of the best Argentine players such as Maradona had not played). The Chinese, including the players, sport officials, and regular fans, all thought that the Chinese team would have no problem defeating Hong Kong. In its front-page article, the influential *Zuqiu bao* (Soccer journal) published in Beijing on May 14, 1985, predicted that China's team would defeat Hong Kong handily.

The day of May 19, 1985, proved to be a momentous one in Chinese sports history, and what happened after that game intensified to an extreme level both Chinese feelings of national inferiority and Chinese nationalism. Nearly eighty thousand fans went to the Workers' Stadium to watch the game, which kicked off at 7:30 PM. Eighteen minutes into the first half, Hong Kong scored first on a free kick. China tied the game with a score in the thirty-first minute. Fifteen minutes into the second half, the decisive moment arrived when Hong Kong scored again with another free kick. At this point the Chinese team came apart. They tried hard to regroup but were not able to score another goal. When the game was over at 9:30 PM, there was dead silence among the thousands of fans. No one had imagined that the weak Hong Kong team could defeat China.

As the Hong Kong players celebrated, the Chinese fans came to the realization that a British colony's team had defeated China's national team and humiliated the nation. Many remembered China's suffering at the hands of Great Britain and exploded. They threw glass bottles and broke chairs inside the stadium; burned cars and buses, including cars from foreign embassies; and damaged buildings. More than two thousand Beijing police were dispatched and at least 127 people were arrested that night. The Chinese soccer players had to be rescued by the police. And even after the players had safely returned to their residence compound, many fans surrounded their building, singing and shouting. The song they sang, with tears in their eyes, was the "International": "Rise up, you slaves who suffer from want of food and clothing. Rise up, you suffering folk of the world. Our blood has reached boiling level."

To quell the anger of the fans and of "the whole nation," the China national soccer team issued a public apology for the defeat on May 24, an apology that was published on the front page of the soccer journal that very day. On May 21, 1985, the *People's Daily* called the riot a dangerous unlawful event. Players did not dare to leave their compound for three days, and on May 31, head coach Zeng Xuelin was forced to resign.[86]

This was perhaps the first serious riot in PRC history, with the exception of unrest during the Cultural Revolution (which had been sponsored largely by Mao himself). China's National Sports Commission called the incident the "most serious" since the founding of the People's Republic of China and criticized it as "damaging to China's national dignity."[87] But that episode would not be the last. One week later, on May 26, soccer fans again rioted in China's northeastern city Shenyang after the Liaoning provincial team was defeated by the visiting Hong Kong team.

Of course, soccer fan riots were occurring everywhere, especially in England. In the same month, on May 29, 1985, more than thirty people died and hundreds were wounded in Belgium when English fans started a riot. But the Chinese riot on May 19 was different. This was the first time in the PRC's history that a sports event had triggered a large-scale disturbance. The riot's clearly political tone went beyond the match itself. The Chinese people wanted a victory, but they had been handed defeat by a European colony's team. They wanted to go to the World Cup, but their march toward that goal had been stopped by a supposedly weak Hong Kong squad. What should have been an easy win ended up a humiliating loss. The players, treated as national heroes two hours before the match, had become national traitors. They seemed to be part of, or even responsible for, the nation's past humiliations.

If the fan riot in 1985 caused concern among Chinese officials, Chinese behavior in a match between Japan and China in the 2004 Asia Cup soccer championship became international news and a diplomatic fiasco for the two countries. During the Asia Cup game, Chinese fans sang an old anti-Japanese song and yelled, "Kill! Kill! Kill!" and "little Japan, petty Japan" at television cameras.[88] When the Japanese soccer team defeated China and won the Asia Cup championship, Chinese fans exploded even though the Japanese team was generally considered stronger. They rioted after the game, burning Japanese flags and spitting at Japanese fans. These Chinese responses to the Japanese victory alarmed both the Chinese and the Japanese governments and stirred debate in both countries about sports and nationalism. The whole world watched with shocked fascination, wondering about the rise of Chinese nationalism. But if they had been at all familiar with the history of modern sports and its link to Chinese national sentiment, there would have been little surprise. In fact, the 2004 riots against the Japanese had its precursors. In the summer of 1987, when the Chinese men's soccer team defeated the Japanese in a qualifying match to enter the Seoul Olympics, Chinese fans became so excited that they marched out in groups and sang the by now familiar anti-Japanese song: "The [Chinese] big swords are aiming at [Japanese] heads. . . ."

The fan uprisings did have some positive effects. Concern about the riot in 1985 eventually helped China initiate sports reforms, starting with soccer. Moreover, Hong Kong, long blamed for China's loss in 1985, was now considered a model for improving the quality of Chinese men's soccer. As the diehard Chinese soccer fans after the 2006 World Cup debated why a nation of 1.3 billion people could not produce an eleven-member men's soccer team to play in the World Cup, some concluded that to make China a strong soccer nation, it should operate by the rule of law.

It does seem clear that without a transparent, lawful system, Chinese soccer teams will forever suffer from the effects of corruption, bad refereeing, and game fixing. Organizing its associations or clubs in Hong Kong, beyond the control of the corrupt and incompetent Chinese sports authorities, has been proposed as one solution to the problem. But how the "one country—two systems" arrangement will affect sports in China remains to be seen.[89]

If the goal is to make China a sports powerhouse, however, especially in men's soccer, the Chinese culture and political system have to be addressed. Teamwork and following orders, trademarks of the Chinese social system, may not be sufficient to develop great sports teams in general, and in particular, a soccer team that can compete internationally.[90] As the Chinese come to realize this incongruity, their obsession with winning at sports may become an impetus, however indirect, for political reform. If that is the case, sports may become much more than games or a locus of national pride; they may be an agent for social and political change.

How will China balance its longstanding passion for winning at all costs with its desire to host the 2008 Olympic Games with grace and confidence? The answer is unclear, but the stakes couldn't be higher: the Games offer an unprecedented opportunity for China to project an image of its social and political culture to a world audience, and thereby to enhance its standing among the international community.

BEIJING 2008

Winning isn't everything; it's the only thing.
                                    Vincent Lombardi

ON AUGUST 8, 2008, AT 8:00 PM, the opening ceremony of the Beijing Olympic Games will begin. For the Chinese, eight is a very lucky number. By starting on the eighth hour of the eighth day of the eighth year, the Communist regime clearly means to convey its high hopes that the Olympics will bring good fortune to China. But the Beijing Olympics is in fact a moment of crisis, in the Chinese sense of the word—a moment of mixed danger and opportunity. Will the Beijing Games end up like the 1936 Berlin Games, which strengthened a terrible regime, or the 1988 Seoul Games, which initiated democratic reform in South Korea and helped transform it into a dynamic democracy? Might Taiwan declare independence before or during the Olympics, a time when Beijing may not want to risk the Games by obvious countermeasures? The stakes are high for China: the 2008 Olympic Games offer a tremendous opportunity for Beijing to effectively communicate with the world about its vision of the future and the very course of its internationalization. The Chinese have waited for this moment for a century; if the Games are not a success, it will be difficult for China in general, and the Communist party in particular, to recover.

To understand the meaning, implication, and importance of the Beijing Olympic Games for China and the world, we must take a comparative and historical view. How has hosting the Olympics affected other countries throughout history, and what factors have guided China to this point in its own historical narrative?

Three Case Studies: Germany, Mexico, and South Korea

The Olympic Games have played a crucial role in shaping modern world history, influencing many aspiring nations' foreign policies and articulations of national identity. To illuminate the closest scenarios to Beijing's, I will focus on three countries that were in transition politically when they hosted the Summer Olympic Games: Germany, Mexico, and South Korea.

Berlin was chosen to host the 1936 Games in 1931, long before Hitler and the Nazi regime came to power. But Hitler ably exploited the opportunity provided by the Olympics to demonstrate the rise of Nazi Germany and legitimize his political system and policies.[1] Even though "sports were quite alien to Hitler's inner self," he managed to turn the 1936 Berlin Olympic Games into an aggressive instrument of German propaganda.[2] Indeed, during the Berlin Games, an editorial in the *International Herald Tribune* wondered whether the great festival "really belongs to the realm of sport or of diplomatic history."[3]

Although scholars have been debating the meaning of the Berlin Games since it took place, Willi Daume's interpretation, offered more than forty years ago, remains the most insightful. In 1962 Daume, a top sports official in Germany, delivered a "damning verdict" on the 1936 Berlin Games to foreign minister Gerhard Schröder. His goal in doing so was to persuade Schröder to support the idea of a Berlin Olympics in 1968 and to foil a potential bid by the Soviets: "Hitler's greatest hour and the greatest hour of the Third Reich, according to international opinion, was in 1936 during and after the Olympic Games in Berlin. Moscow would pursue the same goals with even more cunning propaganda and greater means."[4]

There were limits to Hitler's ability to make the Olympics a propaganda tool. Despite Hitler's skillful staging of the Games, he was forced into key compromises. According to a widespread and possibly true ac-count, IOC president Count Henri Baillet-Latour of Belgium told Hitler before the 1936 Games that he, Hitler, had nothing whatever to say about the conduct of the Games and he was not allowed to display anti-Semitic signs. "You are a spectator," the count told the dictator. "When the five-circled flag is raised over the stadium, it becomes sacred Olympian territory. For all practical purposes, the games are held in ancient Olym-pia. There we are the masters." Hitler, according to the account, "acqui-esced."[5]

Hitler was also instructed to follow the rules and traditions of the IOC when he opened the Games. Baillet-Latour told Hitler that his duty as host was to utter a single sentence, which Baillet-Latour had typed for him: "I declare the games of the Eleventh Olympiad of the modern era to be open." Hitler's response was, according to the story, "Count, I'll take the trouble to learn it by heart."[6] Avery Brundage later boasted that the IOC "was the only organization, not barring the League of Nations, which laid down the law to the Nazis before World War II and made it stick."[7]

The lessons of the 1936 Olympic Games are useful for Beijing.[8] Un-like Nazi Germany, which inherited the Games from the previous regime, Beijing applied for and won the honor to host the Olympic Games on its own account and therefore might feel more justified to use the Games to le-gitimize the Communist regime and its political system. Both the Nazi and the PRC regimes considered themselves masters of propaganda. But Beijing should perhaps think twice if this is its intention. If Hitler had to give in to external pressure exerted in the name of the Olympian move-ment, Beijing is in an even weaker position. When the Games begin, the world will focus on China. Media, tourists, and politicians will pay careful attention to the government's behavior. The PRC, which has been obsessed with internationalizing its economy and international acceptance, must make sure its propaganda machine will not overdo its spin. Will the Games strengthen the Chinese party-state as the Berlin Games invigorated the Hit-ler government? The answer to this question is subtle, involving both party and nation. The Communist party's possible success—measured by its ability to adhere to international standards and hold a splendid Olympics—may in fact sow the seeds of its destruction, not strengthen it. But for the Chinese nation, such a success could stimulate renewal.

Now let's turn to the Mexico City Games. Until 1968 the Olympics had never been hosted by a developing country. Like the hosts of all Olympic Games, Mexico wanted to use the Games to present itself in very positive ways. Pedro Ramírez Vázquez, president of the Mexico Olympic Organizing Committee, once told an interviewer that what the committee wanted most from the Games was for the world audience to remember Mexico.[9]

But there were certain events and images the organizing committee simply could not control. For example, as many as five hundred Mexican students were massacred just ten days before the opening of the Games, an incident that made headlines and caused great concern during the Olympics.

Even without this violence, the Mexico City Games presented confused, often contradictory, representations of Mexico to the world, due to the complexity of its emerging social, economic, and political systems. As Claire and Keith Brewster have argued, major differences emerged between the Mexican elite's vision for their country's place in the world and that of the vast majority of the Mexican people.[10]

This dissonance had deep historical roots. Mexico had endured repeated national identity crises and had been unable to develop a truly representative national image. The country and its people were never sure about themselves and they suffered from a sense of inferiority and a lack of self-respect, all of which made it difficult for Olympic organizers to present a consistent, positive image of Mexico to the world. For Claire and Keith Brewster, "The interplay between Mexico's lack of self-assuredness and tension between the different Mexicos that comprised the nation continued into the planning of the 1968 Games."[11] The rest of the world, too, seemed to be concerned about Mexico City's attitude and the ability of Mexicans to host a successful Olympics.

Despite international doubts and domestic problems, organizers of the 1968 Games wished to present Mexico as a modern, forward-looking nation with a proud ancient civilization. They had reason to feel encouraged about their prospects in the new world order: like the Chinese, Mexicans were enjoying their own economic miracle years as the city prepared for the Games.[12] To make sure everyone would do his or her share in the collective effort to polish and promote the Mexican image during the Games, the organizing committee launched a huge media campaign to teach the people of Mexico City "to establish a sense of national responsibility" and "to awaken the national hospitality of Mexicans toward foreign athletes and visitors." The campaign included a series of messages "given in an official paternalistic tone, informing Mexicans of the right and wrong ways to behave in front of foreigners." The messages from the officials were very clear: "Mexicans needed to modify their behavior to create a good impression, to present Mexico in the best possible light, and to lend dignity to the Mexican nation."[13]

The Beijing Olympic Games and the Mexico City Games, despite the forty-year gap between them, have a lot in common. In both cases, the hosts are developing countries that have enjoyed years of astounding economic growth. Both suffer from serious national identity crises as well as self-doubt and a certain inferiority complex. Both are worried about their citizens' behavior and have tried to teach their people how to behave for an international audience. Mexico envisioned its Games as a cultured, high-minded experience and had grand expectations that the Games would allow it to project a better image and enhance its status in the world—hopes that China holds for its upcoming Olympics. Yet in the end the 1968 Olympic Games did not do very much for Mexico politically. No major democratic reforms occurred before or after the Games, and Mexico seemed not to benefit much internationally from its experience as host. Will Beijing similarly fail to live up to its aspirations regarding the 2008 Games?

The 1988 Summer Games held in South Korea were perhaps the most controversial and problematic of the three examples. One problem was diplomatic: South Korea did not have official relations with many socialist countries when Seoul won its bid to host the Games, and socialist bloc nations threatened a boycott—a threat that seemed very real after the boycotts of the Moscow and Los Angeles Games. But there was also a political problem: South Korea was itself politically unstable and undemocratic in the early 1980s; at that point, the country remained under military dictatorship. More importantly, the peninsula, already dangerous, had been made more so by North Korea's demand that it co-host the Games. During 1985 and 1986, the IOC president organized many meetings to discuss possible solutions, but when the impasse proved difficult to overcome, the IOC executive board allowed North Korea to co-host some of the matches of events such as table tennis and archery. Even with these concessions, things did not work out well; there were no fully co-hosted events, and North Korea eventually boycotted the Games.[14]

Many influential organizations thought the IOC had made a mistake in choosing Seoul. The *New York Times* published several editorials denouncing the choice of Seoul as host. In one published August 26, 1984, the paper's editor argued, "Another boycott in 1988, when the Games are scheduled for South Korea, would surely risk the survival of the modern Olympics." The article suggested that the Games take place at a permanent, neutral site. Later, IOC president Juan Antonio Samaranch acknowledged that when the Games were awarded to Seoul in 1981, "many political observers and international specialists throughout the world raised their eyebrows in concern and expressed doubts regarding the decision taken."[15]

Yet despite all the problems and predicted troubles, the 1988 Seoul Olympic Games were a great success and marked a crucial turning point in South Korean history. The Games served as a bridge to better relations with countries with which South Korea had not before enjoyed diplomatic relations, such as China. (As mentioned earlier, the PRC did not have diplomatic relations with Seoul before the Games, but afterward, the two countries quickly found common ground and patched up their relationship.)[16] For the South Koreans, the 1988 Seoul Games were significant in several ways. Most basically, the Games were their ticket to international recognition and membership in the family of nations.[17] The official slogan of the Seoul games was "Seoul to the world, the world to Seoul."[18] In his official speech to the IOC session on September 13, 1988, Park Seh Jik, president of the Seoul Olympic Organizing Committee, expressed South

Koreans' feeling about the Games: "This fall season is a very, very special one for all Koreans. It is a time of excitement and renewal, a time of progress and harmony, and a time of peace and prosperity. . . . As we welcome our friends from the four corners of this globe to our peninsula we realize now that we have history in our hands."[19]

Park Seh Jik was right. The Games provided an unparalleled chance to show South Korea to the world and to demonstrate what Koreans had accomplished since the end of the Korean War. They also offered "international recognition, acceptance, and membership in the family of nations."[20] As David Miller explains, by offering the Games to Seoul, "Samaranch had brought to South Korea the most valuable gift that anyone can bring to a nation: status. With status comes respect and recognition. And with the staging of the Olympic Games began an accelerating trend of the trade and diplomatic relations with the communist world which had pretended since 1953 that South Korea did not exist."[21]

The most important legacy of the Seoul Games was that it helped to initiate a populist democratic movement in South Korea—a movement that eventually turned the country into one of the most dynamic democracies in East Asia. As IOC President Samaranch declared, "Apart from being a tremendous success for the entire Olympic family, one could perhaps even say that the Olympic Games in Seoul were a major factor behind the rapid democratization of the Republic of Korea and the development of an element of international goodwill, cooperation and fraternity, a new hope for Peace."[22]

Which among these Games from the past is likely to hold the most pertinent lessons for Beijing? The answer is both none and all. From the Chinese Communist party's point of view, the legacy of the Berlin Games is likely the most attractive since Nazi Germany used the Games to promote the legitimacy of its regime. The Mexico City games, by contrast, did not advance the cause of Mexico in the world, and so would not be an appealing example. And the political legacy of the Seoul Games must certainly seem the least favorable to the Communist regime because the democratization that followed in South Korea, if replicated in China, would threaten the very existence of the party.

What effect will the 2008 Beijing Olympic Games have on China and on the world? Will it make China more belligerently nationalistic or a more responsible player in the international system? Will the embrace of world sport help China become a friendly country or make it more assertive? The Olympic Games will draw the world's eye to China, and this intense international attention will itself influence China's political system and social stability. Even now, as Beijing prepares for the Games, the Chinese are reassessing their self-image while they craft the view of China they will show the rest of the world. Whether the Games become a "coming-out party" that brings political legitimacy to the Chinese Communist regime, spark political reform and a new identity, or even bring down the existing political order, remains to be seen. What is certain is that the 2008 Beijing Games will shape both China's relationships with other countries and its national development—and that the outlines of this transformation can be understood from the recent history of China's association with the IOC and the Olympic movement.

China's Lost Bid for the 2000 Olympic Games

As previous chapters have shown, Chinese relations with the IOC and the Olympic movement have had their share of twists and turns. Between 1947 and 1955, China had three IOC members, an unusual situation for a nation with a weak sports program since it put China on a par with the world's most powerful nations in sports. Moreover, even as China's society and political system changed dramatically—from a dynasty system, to the Nationalist regime, to Communist control—Chinese interest in the Olympic movement remained remarkably consistent. As mentioned earlier, as early as 1907 when China was under the rule of the Qing dynasty, some Chinese elites had dreamed of one day hosting the Olympic Games in China. In 1945 Wang Zhengting proposed that China apply to host the 1952 Games, and along with Zhang Boling and others even discussed with certain government agencies the possibility of a Chinese bid.[23] Dong Shouyi visited IOC member Kong Xiangxi, who was serving as minister of the treasury, to discuss this matter in late 1945; Kong promised his support, and more importantly, financial backing.[24] But even with the advocacy of powerful individuals, China was in fact not in a position to pull off this plan, due to the civil war that began immediately after the Japanese surrender. Consequently, the official bid never was extended to the IOC.[25]

In fact, it would be more than half a century before China was able to host the Olympics. After Mao's death, once the government had decided to engage the world and actively pursue internationalization through pragmatic diplomatic, cultural, and economic policies, Chinese leaders thought the time was right for China to host the Games; like their predecessors, the Communist leadership wanted to use the Olympics as a platform from which to enter the family of nations as an equal and respected member. The obsession with the Olympics, then as now, was really an obsession with attaining international prestige, expressing Chinese national pride, and overcoming historical frustrations.

The most recent impetus to host an Olympic Games in the PRC came directly from Deng Xiaoping in an interview with Japanese journalist Takeji Watanabe on February 26, 1979. When Takeji Watanabe asked Deng, "The 1980 Olympic Games will take place in Moscow. Is China interested in attending these Games and hosting the Olympic Games in the future?" Deng's response, though typically pragmatic, reinvigorated a movement to host the Games. He replied, "China is preparing to take part in the Moscow Olympic Games. The Olympic Games happen every four years; this means the Games will take place in 1984 and then 1988. It may not be possible for China to host one of those. But we may be able to host the Games" later.[26]

After Deng Xiaoping's published expression of interest, starting in 1981, sports authorities in China seriously pursued the possibility of hosting the Asian Games as an early step toward hosting the Olympics. In 1983, China officially applied to host the 1990 Asian Games and one year later, Beijing was awarded the honor. In a press conference held during the Los Angeles Games in 1984, the Chinese delegation also announced that China was preparing to apply to host the Games before the end of the century; specifically, it was hoping for a shot at the 2000 Games.[27]

From the mid-1980s, then, top Chinese leaders began preparing in earnest to host the Olympics. On February 28, 1991, Premier Li Peng approved the joint report of the China Sports Commission, the Foreign Ministry, the Ministry of the Treasury, and the Beijing municipal government in support of Beijing's bid. On December 3, 1992, the deputy mayor of Beijing, Zhang Baifa, personally delivered the application package to IOC headquarters in Lausanne, Switzerland. Thus began Beijing's official quest to host the Games.

In its proposal, the Beijing bidding committee wrote, "The hosting of the XXVIIth Olympiad would represent more than a great honor. It would give China the opportunity to show the world that our dream for the new millennium is the Olympic dream."[28] A new journal in Beijing, *China Today*, offered its own plea: "As for Beijing 2000—we all know that while man proposes, heaven disposes. Let's hope heaven decides in our favor."[29]

If the official bid proposal emphasized the Chinese dream, Chen Xitong, then president of the bidding committee and mayor of Beijing, stressed Chinese internationalization. He told the IOC, "We in China need understanding from the rest of the world, and we need a peaceful environment so that we can develop our production, expand our economy, and improve the quality of life for our people. This is in perfect harmony with the Olympic spirit, which calls for building a better and peaceful world." Like many others who had bid, Chen tried to establish a link between the Beijing Games and culture: "Beijing is a famous cultural city . . . more than three thousand years old. The ancient oriental civilization gives her an enchanting charm. I believe that if Beijing has the honor to host the Olympic Games, it will surely become an unprecedented cultural exchange when east meets the west, which will give full expression to the Olympic Movement characterized by sports plus culture."[30] In a booklet titled "Beijing 2000: Barcelona Olympics Special," distributed by the Beijing 2000 committee in support of its bid, Beijing's hosting of the Games is termed "a chance for China, an honor for Beijing." The slogan of the Beijing 2000 bid was "A more open China awaits the Olympic Games in the year 2000."[31]

As part of its effort to win the 2000 bid, the entire city of Beijing underwent a face-lift prior to the IOC inspection team's visit in the spring of

1993. Many buildings around the city were freshly painted, and the government even closed factories so black fumes wouldn't mar the skies. Electricity was shut off in neighborhoods that the IOC inspection team would not visit—even traffic lights were cut there—to ensure an adequate supply at sports facilities. Every taxi in the city was ordered to bear a "Beijing 2000" bumper sticker. Homeless people were shipped out of town.[32] And famously, in September 1993 Wei Jingsheng, a famous political dissident who fought for democracy, was released from jail early to polish China's human rights record.

Beijing was not alone in making such gestures to show the IOC its best face. Sydney, also a competitor for the 2000 Olympics, did its share of manipulation, though perhaps with greater subtlety. According to Rod McGoech, chief executive of the Sydney 2000 Olympic bid, when the IOC members visited Sydney the bid committee, with the cooperation of the police and traffic control departments, turned every light green as they approached an intersection; consequently, there were never any traffic delays for the IOC. As a matter of fact, McGoech later revealed that whenever any IOC member visited Sydney, the traffic lights were so adjusted whenever he reached an intersection.[33]

Besides traffic control, IOC members in Sydney received other perks. Take the opera. Usually if one is late for the opera in Sydney, no entry is allowed until the end of the first act. But when IOC members were in town and happened to show up late, the performance was not allowed to begin until they were seated. This special treatment was also extended to IOC members' wives. McGoech recalled that when one member's wife was caught in the powder room line at intermission, the opera was not allowed to resume until she had returned to her seat.[34]

But for all Beijing's efforts, heaven was not on China's side and the world was not ready for China to host the 2000 Games. Western governments, politicians, and major media outlets strongly opposed Beijing's bid. An article in the *Los Angeles Times* argued that China's human rights record should disqualify it. The *Daily News of Los Angeles* ran a piece that chided, "Olympics in China is a human wrong, not a human right"; and the *New York Times* wrote, "The city in question is Beijing in the year

2000, but the answer is Berlin 1936. The history of the modern Olympics is too short and the world is too small to forget murder." The same article argued that "denying Beijing [is] in the best interests of humanity."[35]

Politicians were eager to join the media protest. Once Beijing's application became public, American politicians openly lobbied against China hosting the games. U.S. senator Bill Bradley, a former athlete, played an active role in the opposition campaign. He wrote for newspaper opinion pages and to IOC members claiming that the IOC "would undermine the spirit of the Games if it selected the Chinese capital. The Olympic Games should not be awarded to a country that tortures and imprisons political dissidents."[36] The U.S. House of Representatives passed resolutions opposing Beijing's bid and urging IOC members to do the same. Sixty senators, too, signed a letter prepared by Bradley that called on all IOC members to reject Beijing as a site for the Olympic Games. The letter claimed that if Beijing won its bid, the regime would gain "enormous . . . propaganda value" in spite of its terrible human rights abuses. The letter continued, "The Olympic Games represent the best ideals and aspirations of the world community. They seek to bestow honor and recognition on those who have earned it through fair play and a commitment to high ideals." In these senators' view, it was not yet time for a Beijing Olympic Games.[37]

Officially the Clinton administration seemed to be neutral, but as Secretary of State Warren Christopher acknowledged, "We have provided information [to the International Olympic Committee] on the human rights performance of all possible candidates."[38] Indeed, the White House openly argued that "the administration strongly believes that a country's human rights performance should be an important factor in the selection of a site for the 2000 Olympics."[39]

Nongovernmental entities joined the clamor. James D. Ross of the U.S. Lawyers Committee for Human Rights wrote on behalf of that organization to U.S. IOC member Anita DeFrantz on August 19, 1993, expressing opposition to the PRC bid. He argued that Article 3 of the Olympic Charter stated, "The goal of Olympism" is to promote sport "with a view to encouraging the establishment of a peaceful society concerned with the pres-

ervation of human dignity." "To hold the Olympic Games in China," the
letter continued,

> is contrary to that spirit and will detract from the high esteem in which
> the Olympics are held. . . . The Olympics are first and foremost about
> sports. But for the Chinese government, having Beijing chosen as the site
> for the 2000 Summer Olympics would be an important political victory.
> It would send a message that the world no longer is concerned about the
> very serious human rights violations occurring in China. We urge you and
> the other delegates to the International Olympic Committee to reject
> China's bid to host the 2000 Summer Games.[40]

Despite the strong criticism from the West, Beijing did quite well in the
first three rounds of voting. The morning of the vote, September 23, 1993,
Berlin went first and presented its case at 9:00, followed by Sydney at
10:15, then Manchester at 11:30. Beijing made its presentation at 2:30 the
same day, followed by Istanbul at 3:45. At 5:00, the IOC Enquiry Commission (which later came to be called the evaluation commission) reported to the session its final evaluation of the bidding cities, and at 5:45
PM, September 23, 1993, the vote started. For the first two rounds, 89
votes were distributed and 89 received. Whoever received 45 would win.
In round one, Beijing received 32 votes, Berlin 9, Istanbul 7, Manchester
11, and Sydney 30. The city of Istanbul was eliminated. In round two, the
votes were Beijing 37, Berlin 9, Manchester 13, and Sydney 30—which
eliminated Berlin. In rounds three and four, 88 voting slips were distributed and 88 received. The results of round 3 were Beijing 40, Manchester
11, and Sydney 37, causing Manchester to drop out. From the first three
rounds, Beijing was clearly favored. But in round four, something dramatic
happened. In this final round, the result was Beijing 43, Sydney 45. Sydney
was elected to host the Games of the Twenty-seventh Olympiad in 2000.[41]

R. Kevan Gosper, a member of the Sydney bid committee and the first
vice president of the IOC, made a speech after Sydney's victory. In his
speech, "he felt that there were probably people who had voted for Sydney
with Beijing in their hearts."[42] He Zhenliang, the Chinese IOC member,

followed with his own speech, in which he promised "that China would continue to play an active role in the Olympic Movement and promote the Olympic ideal which admitted no discrimination and promoted friendship between all peoples." IOC president Juan Antonio Samaranch said "he was aware that Mr. He might have been feeling sad" after Beijing's loss and reminded He Zhenliang that "his country knew the relative value of time."[43]

Samaranch soon found out that a great many Chinese people were unhappy and upset with the IOC's decision.[44] In fact, many Chinese believed the United States was against the rise of China and its internationalization and saw Beijing's lost bid for the Olympics as part of a Western plot to contain China. Chinese urban youth and intellectuals especially felt that the West treated China as a third-rate country and was conspiring to keep it from taking its rightful place on the world stage.

Some Chinese even linked the loss to a clash of civilizations, an idea promoted in Harvard professor Samuel P. Huntington's influential article in the journal *Foreign Affairs*. In his article, Huntington openly argued that China posed a danger and should be contained.[45] Beijing's loss seemed to fit with the clash of civilizations notion. After all, although the Olympics promote an image of internationalization, its controlling body has been decidedly European. When the current IOC president, Belgium's Jacques Rogge, reaches the end of his first presidential term in 2009, it "will mark 95 years of European presidential leadership in the IOC's 115-year history." Europe also enjoys a striking concentration of political power and decision-making authority in the IOC. European countries hold approximately 45 percent of all IOC seats, and two-thirds of the committee's executive board are European.[46] This structure did not sit well with the Chinese in the excruciating aftermath of Beijing's loss to Sydney.

Beijing's outrage was exacerbated by the double standards employed, especially regarding the public outcry against China in the United States. The inconsistency of the American government was especially obvious in its handling of the 1980 and 1984 Olympic Games. To protest the Soviet invasion of Afghanistan, Americans had argued that politics was more important than a single Olympics and had led the boycott campaign. For the

1984 Los Angeles Games, the American argument had been reversed, with the emphasis that politics should have no part in Olympic events. And when Beijing bid for the 2000 Games, it was politics again.

Americans are not famous for their consistent policies or long memories and opposing Beijing's bid not only failed to serve American long-term national interests, but also offended most Chinese elites. David M. Lampton, a noted China scholar in the United States, made a fair point when he wrote,

> Beijing has had many motivations for joining international organizations, among which is global standing. When Beijing is a full partner in the global community, it frequently has sought to live up to what is expected of it. . . . Rather than pushing to have the Olympic Games awarded to another nation [in retaliation for Chinese human rights infractions], Washington should not have opposed Beijing's bid. Decision makers might have realized, instead, that China would do all within its power to make the event a success. By following the path of stigmatization, Washington lost an opportunity to support positive change and fostered resentment throughout the broader Chinese populace.[47]

But Washington's shortsighted policy was not the only reason for Beijing's loss in 1993; the corrupt IOC system was responsible as well.[48] In late January of 1999, in the wake of the Salt Lake City bribery scandal, Sydney Olympic officials were called on to defend their Olympic bidding practices. Sydney officials acknowledged that they had made offers of $35,000 apiece to the two African delegates—Charles Mukora of Kenya and Major General Nyangweso of Uganda—the night before the vote.[49] John Coates, president of the Australian Olympic Committee, admitted that he himself had made the offer.[50] Coates also acknowledged that he had arranged accommodations in a luxury London hotel for the two IOC members while they were en route to casting their deciding votes. Coates defended his actions by claiming that Sydney would not have won the Games solely on the basis of its world-renowned geographic features and the quality of its facilities.[51]

According to an authoritative account about the Sydney bid, the bid committee even secretly assisted with the immigration to Australia of a daughter of Romanian IOC member Alexandru Siperco, presumably in exchange for a favorable vote.[52] Although these offers might differ from Salt Lake's "scholarship" scandal, Sydney obviously violated the IOC's bidding rules in making them. Even Australia's own IOC member Kevan Gosper openly criticized the practice and called it a "very serious revelation . . . I can't rule out that some [IOC members] may call for the Games not to proceed in Sydney."[53] To be fair to Sydney, other bidding cities engaged in the same sorts of practices. Bob Scott, Manchester's bid committee chair for the 1996 and 2000 Games, claimed that he even knew the shoe size of the second daughter of one particular IOC member.[54]

Although the IOC later declared it found nothing wrong with the Sydney bid, some of Sydney's practices clearly went well beyond the IOC rules. After Sydney had won, Sydney mayor Frank Sartor was reported to have told the *London Times* something to the effect that he had felt like a prostitute going each day to the Hotel Paris, where the members were staying, to look for votes. The *Sydney Morning Herald* ran similar comments on its front page. In response, the IOC's Samaranch declared, "I've never heard of anything like this. I can understand the mayor of a losing city saying something like this, but for the mayor of the winning city to say something like this is unbelievable."[55]

Clearly, the IOC was not in a position to police itself; bribery had become part of the bidding culture. But after the serious charges of corruption that emerged from the Salt Lake City and Sydney bidding scandals, the IOC realized it had to do something dramatic to save itself. In 1999 it decided to create a special session, an ethics commission, and an IOC reform commission to deal with the most serious crisis in its history. In its 108th session, held in Lausanne on March 17–18, 1999, the IOC expelled six members because of the scandals.[56] Not surprisingly the image of IOC president Samaranch was tarnished, too. Despite a long speech Samaranch gave describing accomplishments under his watch, in which he asked for the support of the membership, the session decided to hold a vote of confidence to decide whether he still held a mandate to lead. He survived.

The Sydney bidding committee had used other tactics to ensure a suc-

Liu Qi (mayor of Beijing, fourth from left) and Wu Shaozu
(chairman of the Chinese National Olympic Committee, second from
right) meet with IOC president Juan Samaranch (third from left)
in Lausanne, Switzerland, on April 7, 1999, and inform the IOC of
Beijing's intention to bid for the 2008 Games.

cessful bid for the 2000 Olympic Games. Realizing that Beijing presented a
major threat, the Sydney committee, through its chairman McGoech, had
secretly commissioned and funded a London-based public relations firm
led by Tim Bell to badmouth Beijing by finding embarrassing information
on the Chinese human rights record. McGoech met Bell in London in late
1992 and arranged then for Bell to handle the smear campaign in such a
way that it could not be traced back to Australia. The Sydney committee
would send one of its members, Gabrielle Melville, who was already working to dig up dirt on China, to London to work secretly in the office of Tim
Bell, who was also close to former prime minister Margaret Thatcher. Melville and Bell then worked out a strategy that included, among other ele-

ments, helping to fund a London-based human rights group to speak out on China issues and arranging for publication of a booklet about China entitled "The So-Called Suitable Candidate," which would be published ahead of the decision in Monte Carlo.[57] Since the Sydney bidding committee knew this behavior was illegal, it made sure that the booklet and the other actions critical of Beijing "have been produced by the London-based organization but we would mastermind it with Tim in London. It would have nothing to do with Australia," wrote McGoech.[58] When Australia's IOC member Kevan Gosper found out about the bid committee's activities, he was so concerned that he tried to convince Premier John Fahey to put a stop to the plan since it was "too risky—if it ever came out it would destroy the Sydney bid."[59]

And of course, Beijing soon got a second chance. When Deng Xiaoping was told the result of the Beijing's first bid, he said simply that it did not matter; China needed to learn its lesson and try again.[60] Beijing did just that.

Beijing's Second Bid: Victory at Last

When Sydney was chosen to host the 2000 Olympic Games, Samaranch was asked whether he had supported Beijing as a candidate. Samaranch replied, "This is untrue. There is not a single member of the IOC who could say that I wanted to favour Beijing or to lobby in favour of China. I respect the IOC's decision . . . and I believe that this choice [of Sydney] is the best possible one. I would also like to say that the IOC and myself personally are extremely concerned by the human rights issue." In addressing the journalist's question "Would you like China to resubmit its candidature for 2004?" he replied, "I hope that China will be represented. Let us not forget that Australia was chosen at its third attempt. Mr. He [Zhenliang], China's NOC [national Olympic committee] President, assured us after the vote that a Chinese city would soon be chosen as a candidate for 2004."[61]

Samaranch might have wanted to cast himself as neutral and the outcome of the bidding as fair, but as it turned out, Beijing was so upset about the 1993 loss that it decided not even to bid for the 2004 Games.[62]

Beijing's decision was a disappointment to many in the IOC. As Kevan Gosper, who had played a crucial role in Sydney's bid, wrote, "Beijing was an important bid and the Chinese would deliver good Games. Having the Games in Beijing would strengthen the Olympic movement in a part of the world that had never had Games before—we would be bringing 1.2 billion people more firmly into the Olympic circle."[63]

Because of the link between sports events and national pride, between international prestige and worldview, another Olympic bid by Beijing seemed inevitable. As the *New York Times* reported, "Winning the Olympic bid is much more than a matter of civic or even national pride." As host to the Games, "China believes it will stand as a respected member of the world community, a position it has long felt the West has denied it."[64] After everyone had cooled down from the loss of its first bid, Beijing officially declared on November 25, 1998, that it would bid to be the host city for the 2008 Olympics—and on April 4, 1999, Chinese officials delivered the official application package to IOC headquarters. This official decision was backed by overwhelming popular support. According to Susan Brownell, in 2001 the IOC commissioned a Gallup poll that showed a 94 percent approval rating for the Games among Beijing residents.[65] This time Beijing appeared more confident and the world more accommodating.

In its official application, Beijing promised to the world and to the IOC that the Games slogan would be "New Beijing, Great Olympics." Interestingly, the Chinese version of the slogan was *Xin Beijing, Xin Aoyun* (New Beijing, New Olympics). Why the difference? One China sport official told a foreign journalist that if China had proclaimed that it wanted a "new Olympics," "it would seem as if China wanted to change the Games," and "the I.O.C. wouldn't like that. They'd think here's this Communist country that's trying to take over the Olympics."[66] This careful play of language indicated one lesson China had learned from its first bidding experience: the importance of considering what others might think of China and making adjustments to be sure that nothing offended. Beijing also promised that it would host a "green" and "high-tech" Olympics.[67] But the essence of the Beijing Olympic Games, according to its organizers, will be to present a "people's and cultural Olympics" *(renwen aoyun)*. The goal is to promote cultural exchange and understanding among nations through the Games.[68] In its official proposal package for 2008, the Beijing bid committee wrote that "history has presented a unique opportunity for the IOC to create an unparalleled legacy for Olympianism through its 2008 decision. China is ready to welcome the world."[69] Beijing also argued that "the Olympic Games in Beijing will be a bridge of harmony between cultures and embody the Olympianism's unique integration of sport and culture."[70] It was an idea whose time had come. As Larmer commented, "The meeting of East and West—China and the world—will likely be the defining encounter of the twenty-first century."[71]

The emblem Beijing chose for its 2008 bid was a five-pointed star, in the same five colors as the Olympic rings, and in the shape of a person doing traditional *tai ji*, a traditional Chinese exercise. The choice was clearly intended to highlight the country's traditional sports culture.[72] The emblem also resembles the Chinese knot, a traditional handicraft, and symbolizes unity and cooperation among people from all over the world. Chinese president and Communist party boss Jiang Zemin, in his official letter to the IOC supporting Beijing's bid, wrote, "It will be of extremely great significance to promoting and carrying forward the Olympic spirit in China and across the world, and to facilitating cultural exchanges and convergence between East and West, if the Games of the XXXIX Olympiad are held in China."[73]

The idea of the Olympics as a meeting place for East and West was not a Chinese invention; the IOC itself had been a major promoter of it. IOC president Samaranch once said, "Olympic principles and ideals have universal value and importance. We must cherish them because Olympianism is the bridge, the meeting point uniting very different worlds."[74] The South Koreans used the concept brilliantly in their Seoul 1988 Games. As the South Koreans told the IOC, "Most importantly these Games will provide a rare opportunity for the basically different peoples and cultures of East and West to meet in dramatic fashion . . . at a moment when East and West need to share the strengths of their cultures to foster a more harmonious international atmosphere."[75] The organization committee for the 1988 Seoul Olympic Games informed the IOC 92nd session that the arrangement of its programs aimed to "achieve a dramatic blend between the cultural tradition of East and West."[76] By playing cards successfully cast by many others in the past, China was trying to convey to the world that it was a normal and more mainstream nation, not the isolated, ideologically determined country it had been earlier.

Some Western powers and politicians, however, greeted Beijing's new bid with suspicion and still did not want to see Beijing succeed. Both the European Parliament and some members of the U.S. Congress called for the Games to be hosted by non-Chinese cities. But world opinion, as well as Beijing's attitude and bidding strategy, had changed substantially after its lost bid in 1993. For the 2008 Olympic Games, Beijing was competing with Osaka, Paris, Toronto, and Istanbul. Among these five cities, Istanbul, according to the IOC's evaluation report, was the weakest prospect. As Hein Verbruggen, the evaluation commission chairman, told his colleagues on July 13, 2001 (the date of the IOC vote), Istanbul had not fully addressed some problems with its planning strategy for the Games. Osaka, too, seemed to have financial problems, according to the IOC Evaluation Commission's May 15 report.[77]

Paris and Toronto, by contrast, were strong contenders. Paris had modified its original Olympic Village plan, causing the commission to maintain "its conclusion that Paris would stage excellent Olympic Games." And Toronto had erased initial concerns by the IOC about funding with a "letter from the Premier of Ontario guaranteeing the necessary resources for the OGOC to meet its commitments."

Especially warm praise was evident in the IOC's evaluation report on Beijing's bid. The commission concluded,

> This is a Government-driven bid with considerable assistance of the NOC. The combination of a good sports concept with complete Government support results in a high quality bid. The Commission noted the process and pace of change taking place in China and Beijing, and the possible challenges caused by population and economic growth in the period leading up to 2008, but was confident that these challenges could be met. There is an environmental challenge, but the strong Government actions

and investment in this area should resolve this and improve the city. It is the Commission's belief that a Beijing Games would leave a unique legacy to China and to sport, and the Commission is confident that Beijing could organise excellent Games.[78]

On the day of the vote, July 13, Verbruggen confirmed that "the conclusion stated in the report remained unchanged."[79] The IOC seemed to understand that although Beijing faced certain challenges, its bid had the wholehearted support of the central government; in addition, an Olympic Games in China would have an unprecedented influence on both the Olympics and the country. In other words, the IOC members' judgment was clearly colored by political considerations.

In the IOC's Moscow session, on July 13, 2001, IOC members voted to choose a winner. In the first round, of 102 valid votes, the results were Beijing 44, Toronto 20, Istanbul 17, Paris 15, and Osaka 6. Osaka was eliminated. In the second round of voting, Beijing won 56 votes (four votes above a simple majority), Toronto had 22, Paris won 18, and Istanbul netted 9. Beijing therefore won immediately. The IOC members had delivered the Games to Beijing.

After the vote was in, Chinese IOC member He Zhenliang read a prepared letter from Chinese president Jiang Zemin to the IOC president, thanking him for his support in Beijing's successful bid to host the Games in 2008. He added his sincere thanks for the trust placed in his country; said that July 13, 2001, would remain engraved forever in the memories of the people of Beijing; and assured the IOC members that they would be proud of their decision.[80]

When news spread that Beijing had been chosen to host the 2008 Olympics, the Chinese press was exuberant. One *Xinhua* editorial exclaimed,

> Today, the world chooses Beijing! Today, the world admires Beijing! That the IOC members tonight voted for Beijing indicates the world has confidence in Beijing and high expectations for China. . . . Beijing's victory in bidding for the 2008 Olympic Games is another milestone in China's efforts to enhance its international status. It is another major achievement

for the Chinese nation's great revival . . . the competition for hosting the Olympic Games is a test of a country's comprehensive national power, economic potential, scientific strength, and cultural attraction; it marks the achievement of a country's international presence and status. Whoever wins the bid has won the respect, trust and love of the world community. Today, Beijing wins such trust. It's a victory for Beijing, it is a victory for China, and it is also a victory of Olympic spirit! . . . Tonight will be a sleepless one for the 1.3 billion [celebrating Chinese] people.[81]

The *People's Daily* crowed, "The Chinese 'Olympic dream' has come true! [Tonight] is a sleepless night, a sleepless night for the 1.3 billion [Chinese] people! . . . We have waited for this moment for a long time. . . . The Olympics choose Beijing, the world has confidence in China. . . . The 2008 Olympic Games are an opportunity for China and the world. . . . [China's] victory in bidding for the Olympic Games will play an important role in its reforms and its modernization; it will also make the world understand China better and speed up China's internationalization." In short, when Beijing won, the Chinese people were victorious as well.[82]

It is true that many other countries before China had linked the hosting of major games with national pride, prestige, and honor. When Sydney was chosen to host the 2000 Olympics, Australian prime minister Paul Keating announced that the decision had put Australia "in the swim with the big boys."[83] When in the spring of 2004 South Africa was chosen to host the 2010 World Cup, Irvin Khoza, chairman of South Africa's bidding committee, commented, "This is for Africa. This is the people of the world voting for Africa's renewal." Nelson Mandela, the former president of South Africa who was an ambassador for the bid, said that hosting the 2010 World Cup finals would be a perfect gift for the country as it celebrates ten years of democracy.[84] For the Japanese, whose exclusion from the London Olympics of 1948 was painful, the choice of Tokyo to host the 1964 Olympics "was celebrated as [a] symbol of Japan's acceptance within the community of nations."[85] And when South Korea was chosen to cohost the 2002 World Cup finals, Jere Longman wrote in the *New York Times*, "The image that will linger from this World Cup is not the soccer, but the people of South Korea. As its national team kept winning, the country became united and self-confident in ways that people could not have imagined. . . . This is a good chance for Korea to move out of that historical inferiority complex."[86]

Let the Games Begin: Dangers Posed by the 2008 Olympics

The Chinese people's exuberance at hosting the Olympics clearly demonstrates the depth and significance of their passion for achieving international status and asserting national pride, as well as the importance of sports in China's internationalization. As one Chinese journal noted, "In 2008 Beijing has an appointment with the world, and China has an appointment with the new millennium."[87] But after all the excitement and joy, major challenges lay ahead for the regime and the Chinese people. The Chinese term *weiji* (crisis) nicely characterizes the situation: as the two characters *wei* (danger) and *ji* (opportunity) are combined, dangers and opportunities coexist and one can be turned into the other.

Significantly, China remains a party-state rather than a regular nation-state. When the interests of the party clash with the national interest, the regime will no doubt serve itself first. Additionally, the danger and opportunity inherent in this situation do not apply to the party and the nation in the same way or to the same degree; the dangers and challenges the Games present to the party may be wonderful opportunities for the nation and the people. As former U.S. president Jimmy Carter's national security adviser Zbigniew Brzezinski commented, "The Olympics may be a triumph for China, but by intensifying the pressures for change, the Games are quite unlikely to be a triumph for China's waning Communism. In fact, the Games may accelerate its fading."[88]

Indeed, as Juan Antonio Samaranch, the president of the IOC, noted, the awarding of the Games to Beijing could mark the start of "a new era for China." Henry Kissinger also weighed in, "I think this is a very important step in the evolution of China's relation with the world. . . . I think it will have a major impact in China, and on the whole, a positive impact, in the sense of giving them a high incentive with the Games."[89]

Certainly the whole world will be watching China during the Olympics, if past Games are any indication. A record 202 national Olympic committees took part in the 2004 Athens Games, which comprised a total of 10,500 competitors and 5,500 team officials. By the time of the closing ceremony, organizers had sold 3,589,000 tickets, in a country of only 10 million people. More than twenty thousand accredited members of the media flocked to Athens, sixteen thousand of whom were with broadcasting companies. About 3.9 billion viewers had access to programs featuring the Athens Olympics, compared to 3.6 billion who had watched the Sydney Games in 2000. Some 35,000 hours were dedicated to coverage in 2004, compared to 20,000 for Barcelona, 25,000 for Atlanta, and 29,600 for Sydney. More people watched the 2004 Games on TV than ever before. In Spain, for instance, each individual, on average, watched more than eight hours of the Games; in the United Kingdom, each viewer watched more than thirteen hours of the Olympic coverage, with several peak audiences of over ten million. In the United States, NBC's coverage ranked among the most watched programs aired every night during the Games. The Chinese, meanwhile, were able to watch more than fifty-three hours of prime-time coverage, attracting an average audience of 85 million viewers.[90] We can presume that at least this level of viewership—in person and via TV—will be reached for the 2008 Games.

Because of this remarkable visibility, the Olympics are obviously the best time to show off the new China and its people. It is also an excellent opportunity for outsiders to see the complex reality of China. This exposure, however, will likely create huge problems for the regime. The Chinese Communist party dictatorship has consistently, and as a matter of policy, constrained the free flow of information. Part of Beijing's bid was a promise to allow visiting reporters to work freely in China as they covered the Games. Thanks to the 2008 Games, Beijing announced temporary regulations on December 1, 2006, that loosened restrictions on foreign journalists. Later the same regulations were extended to journalists from Taiwan, Hong Kong, and Macao. The new regulations take effect on January 1, 2007, and end October 17, 2008, one month after the Paralympics concludes. Under existing rules, foreign reporters need government permission to report outside their home base, usually Beijing or Shanghai. Under the new rules, a foreign journalist will only need to obtain the permission of the person being interviewed. The new regulations will also allow a foreign journalist to hire Chinese assistants more easily.

Yet there are limitations. It is unclear, for example, how the new regulations will be implemented by local governments. Moreover, the new rules do not apply to far western Xinjiang and Tibet; foreign journalists will still need state permission to visit these regions. One other possible issue is whether the foreign journalists will have to use the Chinese television satellite service, through which the government has been able to censor news items in the past. But although the new regulations are temporary and will be implemented as a public relations gesture, they do underscore China's desire to use the Games to demonstrate that it follows international practices and norms. That is, the new rules at least set a good precedent and the positive gesture itself is progress.[91]

Of course, this kind of gesture may prove to be a double-edged sword for the regime. The presence of more than twenty thousand foreign journalists will force the regime to polish its rough image, but it will also undermine the control of information that is an important part of the regime's power. In other words, as the Games present China to the world, they pose the risk to the regime of bringing to light the country's problems.

Another major challenge for the nation and regime is the potential for overly zealous expressions of Chinese nationalism. Communism in China may be dead, but the Communist party is still alive and well. And since the collapse of socialism in the 1980s, the legitimacy of the party and the party-state regime has rested on three pillars: nationalism, economic growth, and social stability. These three elements are a potentially volatile mixture, however, without the rule of law. During the Olympic Games, the contradiction between nationalism and social stability, for instance, could become a major issue. On the one hand, the regime will celebrate every Chinese victory as an occasion for national pride; on the other hand, every effort will be made to ensure that any nationalist fervor does not rise to an irrational level.

The situation is especially delicate in China for a few reasons. As discussed earlier, either the celebration of victory or the disappointment of a loss can spark social unrest. Similarly, since the 1980s, as China has grown economically, both the Chinese people and the Communist party have embraced a can-do optimism even as they have continued to suffer from a painful inferiority complex. In the area of sports, especially the Olympic Games, this dissonance—if combined with an episode of irrational nationalism—could ignite outbursts of violent behavior that, ironically, the regime itself cultivated as properly revolutionary during the Maoist era.

China promised the world that its Olympic Games would be *Renwen Aoyun,* or "the people's Olympics."[92] As early as 2003, to achieve Beijing's goal, the central government and the Beijing Organizing Committee for the Olympic Games established a Beijing Olympic action plan, under which more than one million people would learn foreign languages. Like the Mexicans forty years ago, the Chinese regime realized that the Chinese themselves might become a problem and an embarrassment. The Humanistic Olympics Studies Center, a city-government-sponsored institute in Beijing, declared, "In 2008, what kind of Beijing shall we present to the globe?" Its answer: "a Beijing both ancient and modern, a Beijing friendly and smiling." To the Communist leaders in Beijing, hosting a successful Olympics did not require broad avenues, lush parks, high-rise buildings, or elegant hotels; instead "common courtesy" was the most important factor. To show its best face during the Olympics, then, several years prior to the start of the Games the Chinese government launched a full-blown campaign against bad manners such as spitting, littering, and being noisy. Foul-mouthed taxi drivers have been called on to clean up their acts, and rowdy soccer fans have been asked to show more sportsmanship toward opposing teams.

But the government has faced an uphill battle. To take just one example, the custom elsewhere of standing in line does not have an equivalent in Chinese public culture. According to a *Wall Street Journal* article, "Patiently awaiting one's turn isn't a big feature of life in Beijing." Chinese traditional codes of politeness, like those in other Asian nations such as Japan, were shattered during the Communist revolution and subsequent campaigns as a way of stamping out "feudal thinking." As noted in the same *Wall Street Journal* article, "China's pell-mell transformation to a market economy has brought out even ruder behavior, as people elbow others aside in pursuit of every advantage, whether in competing for school admission, jobs or business deals. But now a growing number of Chinese feel that something important may have been left behind in today's increasingly fierce struggle to get ahead."

The Communist regime realized it had to do something quickly to deal with Chinese behavior problems before the Olympic Games began. A local government body in Beijing, dubbed the Capital Civilization Office, was set up to oversee educational projects and contests to discourage spitting, littering, foul language, aggressive driving, and catcalls directed at the opposing team during sports events. As the author of the *Wall Street Journal* article observed, "Few Beijingers these days are given to parroting such party propaganda campaigns. But the incessant talk of the Olympics does mean that they increasingly feel the world's eyes upon them. The lining-up campaign is striking a chord with some people who feel that contemporary Chinese [*sic*] has gotten a bit too rough and rude."[93] According to a *New York Times* report, 4.3 million copies of a new booklet on manners have been delivered to households around Beijing. The booklet includes advice such as "Look straight ahead when walking. Do not look left and right." "Watch games and matches in a civilized way, and be reasonable and sane whether facing victory or defeat." "The host audience should show grace and fairness. Applaud and cheer the other team." The booklet reminds every Chinese that "the fundamental principle is not to disturb others unnecessarily."[94]

So that Beijing will be a smiling host for the 2008 Olympic Games, the city has also been conducting a "smile campaign" that was organized by local television stations, newspapers, and other organizations in 2006. This campaign encourages citizens to literally smile and to be less angry and rude. But the initiative has not been successful. Although Chinese living standards have improved enormously, widespread social injustice and a weak legal system have made China a very unhappy society that simply cannot make its population smile no matter how much pressure or encouragement the government exerts. Beijing will need to rise to the challenge of being a good host without forcing its own people to suffer and without

Can the nation be as confident as she is? Chinese swimmer
Luo Xuejuan wins the 100-meter breaststroke gold medal at the
2004 Olympic Games in Athens.

having to lie to its own people and foreign guests. A confident country will
be happy by just being itself.

If the 2008 Olympics are also meant to show off traditional Chinese
culture, the government will have a tough sell there, too. As authorities

prepared for the Games, they largely destroyed the city's historic neighborhoods, demolishing courtyard houses and old buildings, and forcing many residents to move without providing sufficient compensation or alternative arrangements.[95] In place of these historically significant structures, the city has put up high-tech modern buildings designed by foreigners. Perhaps most notorious among these is the National Stadium in Beijing, nicknamed "the bird's nest." It is the brainchild of the Swiss architect Jacques Herzog, who once said, "You couldn't do such an avant-garde structure anywhere else. . . . But Chinese are so fresh in their mind. . . . Everyone is encouraged to do their most stupid and extravagant designs there. They don't have as much of a barrier between good taste and bad taste, between the minimal and expressive. The Beijing stadium tells me that nothing will shock them." The Chinese are so determined to become an internationalized nation that they will try everything and anything. As Arthur Lubow writes, "The Olympics have galvanized China's imperial impulse to impress the world, by whatever means necessary. . . . By taking on the Olympics, China committed itself to demonstrating that it is [a] world-class power."[96] But does building modern Westernized architecture around the city make the Beijing Games a cultural event? And can the same regime that came to power by declaring war on Chinese traditions now plausibly use the Games to celebrate Chinese traditional culture? No matter how skillful the party has been at domestically oriented propaganda, it will be difficult for Beijing to realize its "cultural Games" idea in a way that is convincing to the world or perhaps even to the Chinese people themselves.

But Beijing obviously will use its propaganda machine to the utmost, in an attempt to promote and spin the greatest sports event in the world. The Communist party has long had propaganda in its blood; it could not have survived without it. During the Cultural Revolution, when China was totally isolated and even friendly countries such as Cambodia pondered whether to break off relations with Beijing, the Chinese people were told by the party that China had friends all over the world. And as millions of Chinese starved to death, the propaganda journals and papers were full of rosy pictures, telling the world that China had no internal or external debt and everything was perfect. Now, even as the Communist party tries very hard to project an image of itself as a responsible power to be reckoned with, it still remains responsible only to itself. Although China has changed tremendously since Mao's death, the party still refuses to allow independent expression by the media, free thinking, or universal application of the rule of law.

For many years, the official Chinese view of sports followed the old Soviet ideology: "[Sport] is another sphere, another criterion for evaluating the advantages of the Soviet political system. . . . Competitions are not just sports events. They carry a tremendous ideological and political charge; they demonstrate the aspirations of the Soviet People."[97] But over-playing politics in a muscular propaganda campaign can backfire. Although this concept may lie beyond the Communist party's understanding, the best propaganda of all may be not to overplay politics. IOC president Avery Brundage once told a story about the Bolivar Games in Caracas, Venezuela. Brundage, who was president of the U.S. Olympic Committee when he attended the Games, was pleased that the event was carried out according to the best amateur tradition, and without political interference. When he congratulated the president of Venezuela on this point, the dictator smiled. "Ah," he said, "but that is the best politics."[98] Whether the Chinese regime will grasp the wisdom of this lesson remains to be seen, but surely overpoliticizing the Games would be counterproductive for Beijing.

Cross-strait relations may pose another serious challenge to the success of the 2008 Games. Will Taiwan boycott the Beijing Games? Will Taiwan use the opportunity to declare independence or create de jure independence? Will the mainland then use its military to stop Taiwan? The outcome does not have to be dire; in fact, sports have occasionally proved successful in bringing political rivals together. The two Koreas, for example, have moved quite a bit closer in connection with major sports events. During 1962–1963, the suggestion from the IOC that the two Koreas organize a united Korean team to participate in the 1964 Tokyo Olympic Games brought two deadly political rivals face to face. Although negotiations failed to produce a united Korean team in 1964, the sheer power of sports to bring the two Koreas together to talk is significant.[99] Some in South Korea like Kim Seong Ho, a professor of political science at Kyunghee University in Seoul, even argue that sports may bring the two Koreas to reunification.[100]

There is some evidence to support this claim. In November of 2005, North and South Korea agreed to compete as a single team for the first time at the 2006 Asian Games in Doha, and then to field a single Korean team at the 2008 Olympic Games in Beijing. In this agreement, the two Koreas agreed to march under the name Korea and a "Korea-is-one" flag that shows a blue and undivided Korean peninsula against a white ground. The anthem for the team is to be a traditional Korean love song popular in both Koreas. "The significance of this is we will be going onto the world stage as a unified team, and this will serve as a symbol of reconciliation and cooperation," a South Korean unification ministry official said.[101]

Plans for a united team at the Fifteenth Asian Games held in December 2006 were put aside when North Korea conducted a missile test in the fall of 2006. It may prove quite difficult for the two Koreas to work out a mutually acceptable way to compete as a single team in the 2008 Beijing Games, given the instability that has again beset the region. Nevertheless, a unified Korean team marched under the Unification Flag in the opening ceremonies of the 2000 Olympics in Sydney, the 2002 Asian Games in Busan, the 2004 Olympics in Athens, and the 2006 Winter Olympics in Turin—with athletes from the North and South later competing for their own countries. Even the plan to field a single team was remarkable, considering that the two Koreas are technically still at war. It may be a stretch to link this unified team to political and economic reunification, but the appeal of a single Olympic team for the two Koreas may indeed help bring the Koreas closer together.[102]

If two Koreas can compete together, might mainland China and Taiwan do the same? Can sport serve as a matchmaker, bringing Beijing and Taiwan into peaceful unification? No one knows for sure. In fact, some politicians and scholars have suggested that the 2008 Olympic Games pose the possibility of a decidedly unfriendly outcome: war between Beijing and Taiwan. American scholar Jennifer Lind, for example, recently argued that

Taiwanese leaders may gamble that the 2008 Olympics will provide them with their best chance to declare formal independence from the mainland. With the world's spotlight trained on Beijing, they may reason, China might not attack, as it has vowed to do in the event of such a declaration. After all, military conflict would jeopardize the games and create an international embarrassment for China. Moreover, it would drive investors away and possibly lead to economic sanctions that would damage China's flourishing economy.[103]

It seems improbable to many that the Olympics will provide Taiwan any cover should it provoke Beijing during the Games. But even the possibility of this scenario excites anxiety for leaders on both sides of the strait and around the world, since nobody wins if there is war.

"One World, One Dream": Opportunities Brought by the Beijing Games

The Communist regime's realization that it will be under intense foreign scrutiny during the 2008 Olympic Games has engendered some—albeit small or officially temporary—changes in its behavior. Even the challenges of the Games, then, may well bear seeds of opportunity for the nation as a whole.

One obvious opportunity for China provided by the Beijing Olympics is that it might really become a great sports power in terms of winning gold medals in 2008. China won the second-highest number of gold medals of all teams competing in Athens. For the 2008 Games, China enjoys a home court advantage, and it is very possible that it will, by its state-centric sports system, surpass the United States as the recipient of the most medals. Historically host countries have generally done well, with a few exceptions. The Germans came out on top in their capture of Olympic medals in 1936, reflecting the Nazi regime's growing power. Both the Japanese and Koreans, too, did marvelously well when they served as hosts.

For the Chinese, any victories in Olympic Games will reflect the rise of its national power overall *(zonghe guoli)*. Even the journal *Economist* pointed out in a recent article, "Over its long history, success at the Olympics has usually been a fairly accurate measure of global political power."

Chinese skater Chen Xiaolei (front) competes against Canadian
Tania Vicent in short-track speed skating during the 2006 Winter
Olympics held in Turin, Italy.

During the Cold War, the United States and the Soviet Union repeatedly
struggled to gain a symbolic victory by winning the most medals at the
Olympics. In 2008, if Beijing surpasses the United States in sports victories, it will give both the Chinese people and the Communist regime an
enormous boost in the already politically charged battle with the United
States for international prestige.[104]

Another opportunity lies in the simple fact that Beijing feels driven to
host a great Olympics, or to use Samaranch's frequent phrase, "the best
Games ever." In fact, Beijing's zeal is one of the major reasons that the IOC
awarded it the honor of hosting the Olympic Games. In its recent sessions,
the IOC noted, "In Beijing, the city and national governments' involvement and dedication to the Games were beyond all doubt."[105] To host a
great Olympics, the central government and city were committed to spending as much as it took and never imposed any financial constraints. By con-

trast, when the 1976 Montreal Games were over, Quebec and the city of
Montreal were stuck with a big bill (this even though after Montreal had
won the bid for the 1976 Games, Mayor Jean Drapeau had exclaimed—in
response to a question about whether Montreal would end up with a
financial deficit—"Deficit? That would be as impossible as for me to give
birth to a baby"[106]). The province of Quebec and the city of Montreal had
to absorb a billion-dollar deficit, shared 80–20 between the province and
the city—a debt that will not be paid off until 2012.[107]

The citizens of Beijing will not face this kind of burden since the whole
of China is paying for the Games. In fact, so eager was Beijing to host an
extravagant Games, and so earnest was the city about planning lavish facilities, that some became uneasy. Worried about the cost of the 2008
Games—the budget is officially $2 billion, with another estimated $40 billion or more spent on improving Beijing's infrastructure—several members
of the Chinese People's Congress in their 2006 session suggested that the
country could not afford to spend so much on the Games while many people in the countryside lived below the poverty line. One of the delegates
said the Games should be about entertainment, not "peacockery." Cost
concerns expressed by the Chinese themselves and the IOC eventually
caused organizers to revise their initial plans for projects such as the national stadium and to cut back generally.[108] According to a report to the
IOC prepared by Richard Pound, "Many of the venue capacities in Beijing
had been reviewed since the bid had been accepted, and reduced."[109]

Globalization has long been one of the major themes of international
sports. The slogan of the 1964 Tokyo Games was "The World Is One." Japan's successful hosting of those Games marked its formal emergence as a
dominant economic power in the postwar world and as a full participant
in the international community; it also symbolized the arrival of the New
Japan. China as a nation will definitely benefit from the Beijing Olympic
Games in terms of its internationalization. According to Pound, the Olympic Games "provide an unequaled opportunity for promotion of the host
country and a showcase for its people, culture, industry, tourism, and virtually everything about it."[110]

Explicitly using culture as a key theme of these games is itself an exciting development in China's internationalization. To reflect their determination to bring China to the world and indicate a sense of inclusiveness, on June 26, 2005, Beijing announced its slogan for the 2008 Games, "One World, One Dream." Like slogans for other Games, this one will be forever associated with this event. All of the Olympic slogans reflect the host countries' understanding of their national identity and self-presentation in the world. The slogan for the 2004 Games in Athens, "Welcome Home," reminded the world of the origins of the Games and the historical glory of Greece. Sydney 2000, with its "Share the Spirit," made a point of global participation. And South Korea's "Bring the World to Seoul, Bring Seoul to the World" conveyed the strong desire of Koreans to be recognized as a respected member of the world community.

To indicate the importance of Beijing's slogan, it was first announced at a ceremony attended by six thousand guests and broadcast live on national television. The ceremony was also relayed by text message to all the cellular phone service subscribers, about 230 million, of China Mobile, one of Beijing 2008's official partners. Liu Qi, chairman of the Beijing Organizing Committee for the Olympic Games and Beijing city's Communist party boss, claimed that the slogan "voices the aspirations of 1.3 billion Chinese people to contribute to the establishment of a peaceful and bright world. . . . It conveys the lofty ideal of the people in Beijing as well as in China . . . to create a bright future, hand-in-hand, with people from the rest of the world." According to George Hirthler, in research conducted by the IOC since 1998 to measure the public perception of the Games, "The Chinese people always rank near the top of the 11 nations surveyed in their esteem of—and appreciation for—the Olympic ideals." This research showed that Chinese people exceeded the rest of the world in their association of key words such as "unity," "global," "peace," and "friendship" with the Olympic Games. In this regard, writes Hirthler, "'One World, One Dream' is an accurate expression of the sentiments of a nation that views the Beijing 2008 Olympic Games as a milestone of hope on its long journey to a better future—in a country that is clearly opening its doors to the world."[111]

Symbols of the 2008 Olympics

The symbols China has chosen to use for the Olympics hint at Beijing's promotional strategy. The official game emblem, unveiled in the summer of 2003, clearly indicates China's welcoming face to the world. It shows a traditional red chop (or seal) depicting a figure with arms outstretched as in victory or greeting; it also looks like a running figure or someone practicing *tai ji,* whose posture resembles the Chinese character for "capital" *(jing).* In a lavish ceremony at Beijing's Temple of Heaven, the emblem was dubbed "Dancing Beijing." IOC president Jacques Rogge told the 2,008 guests gathered for the ceremony in a taped video statement, "Your new emblem immediately conveys the awesome beauty and power of China which are embodied in your heritage and your people. . . . In this emblem, I saw the promise of a new Beijing and a great Olympics."[112]

Beijing's choice of logos, emblems, and slogans for the Olympics all reflect the deep Chinese commitment to internationalization. In November 2005, in a live nationwide broadcast only a thousand days before the opening ceremony on August 8, 2008, Beijing announced its choice of mascots for the 2008 Games. These consist of five stylized dolls representing a fish, a panda, the "spirit of the Olympic flame," a Tibetan antelope, and a swallow. The design of the five dolls was clearly influenced by Chinese traditional culture: they represent the five elements—water, wood, fire, iron, and earth. But their colors match those of the Olympic rings. The number five also coincides with the five rings of the IOC and the five continents. Each doll has a name consisting of two characters, one character repeated twice, in the traditional affectionate way of naming children. Beibei is the fish, Jingjing is the panda, Huanhuan represents the Olympic flame, Yingying is the Tibetan antelope, and Nini is the swallow. When the names are put together—Bei Jing Huan Ying Ni—they form the message "Welcome to Beijing." According to Liu Qi, the Communist head of Beijing and chair of the organizing committee, these mascots "reflect the cultural diversity of China as a multi-ethnic country; they represent the enthusiasm and aspirations of our people."[113]

The choices of the five mascots were brilliant, but the organizing committee got carried away with its show of Western fluency and friendship by referring to their mascots collectively as "Friendlies." Why choose an English name when each of them had a beautiful Chinese name? Moreover, as some Chinese scholars pointed out, the sound of the name was not appropriate since people might mistakenly interpret it as "friendless," or worse, "friend lies." In October 2006, the organizing committee, without any fanfare, changed the collective name to "Fuwa." Fuwa certainly sounds more Chinese, and it is more in tune with the mascots' individual names and the images they present. "Fu" means "happy" or "lucky," while "wa" means "children" or "babies." The switch demonstrates that the Chinese have discovered that not everything sounds better in English; the Chinese language (and indeed Chinese traditional culture) has its own charms. Equally important, the name change indicated that the officials realized they had made a poor judgment and were determined to correct it in time.

Beijing is not the only country to have chosen multiple mascots; the 2000 Sydney Games featured three native Australian animals, and for Salt Lake City, a hare, coyote, and bear were selected to represent the event. Moreover, Beijing is not the first to use the slogan, the emblem, and its mascots to promote both itself and the Games. In fact, the IOC expects the host country to engage in this sort of promotion. In its 113th session, the IOC coordination commission reported that as soon as Beijing was selected, it "had advised BOCOG [the Beijing organizing committee] to take steps to promote China and the Olympic Games." The chairman of this commission, Hein Verbruggen, told the session that "as far as he could see, this statement had been a very serious one." In the same session, the IOC president noted "that the chairman of the coordination commission had promised to learn Mandarin, but it appeared that the Mayor [of Beijing] was learning English faster than Mr. Verbruggen was learning Mandarin!"[114]

The West has for many years criticized China for violating intellectual property rights. But with Beijing's successful bid for the 2008 Olympics, China has been learning first-hand about the value of those rights. Although China is still awash in pirated goods, the Olympic Games may provide a starting point for rethinking the problem, since in this case China's own interest is at stake.[115] In 2003 Yu Zaiqing, one Chinese IOC member, informed the IOC session that "the national and city governments had issued laws protecting the Olympic symbols and Olympic property rights. In March [2003], the central government had approved preferential taxation policies for BOCOG and Games stakeholders."[116] The organizers of the 2008 Olympic Games are determined to protect the valuable Beijing Olympic symbol and ban any fake versions of products bearing it. According to a recent article in the *Wall Street Journal,* "Beijing's motivation to protect the red running man, which doubles as a stamp of the Chinese character meaning 'capital city,' is clear: The real thing has massive economic value." "We have no fixed assets," says Liu Yan, deputy director of legal affairs for the Beijing organizing committee, which operates under the Beijing city government and various national government agencies. "So the Olympic logo is the most valuable thing we own."[117]

In fact, the Beijing organizing committee hopes that through merchandising, sponsorships, and other commercial applications, China's logo will by and large pay for the Games.[118] The Chinese government made the logo an official priority in 2002, passing a national law exclusively to defend the intellectual property rights attending Olympic symbols. That law technically collects existing laws in one place, applying them to Olympic logos for all levels of government. "Regulations tend to be more general, so these [2002] details make it easier to enforce the law for the administrative authorities," notes Liu Yan. China isn't the first to jealously guard its Olympic icons; other countries, including Australia, also passed special laws to protect their logos. In this case, then, the Chinese are not only learning a lesson about the importance of protecting intellectual property rights; they are also beginning to align themselves with world trends.[119]

How will the 2008 Olympic Games affect China's future? IOC president Pierre de Coubertin attached great importance to the link between sport and culture, and Juan Antonio Samaranch, a recent successor to the post, once declared that "the Olympic Movement is one of the greatest social forces of our era."[120] Both of these IOC leaders, and others, saw the Games as a force for social good, and there are high hopes that sports will initiate a positive social movement in Beijing.

The Chinese, who have lived in an ideological and religious vacuum and are searching for moral values after the collapse of Communism, may well find international competition on the playing field the best valve for their frustrations. After all, the value of sports in a closed society is greater than in an open one, since open societies already provide many channels for self-expression. Take Iran, for example, where the national team's victory against Australia in the 1997 World Cup qualifying game led to a soccer revolution: Iranian women demanded the right to celebrate in Tehran's Stadium Azadi. They shouted, "Aren't we part of this nation? We want to celebrate too—we aren't ants!" Eventually the police had to overlook the women's entry into the stadium despite a decree issued in 1987 by the county's spiritual and political head Ayatollah Ruhollah Khomeini that women could watch soccer on television but not watch it or celebrate outside. As one American author recently wrote, "The football revolution holds the key to the future of the Middle East."[121]

Although the elite sports are, by and large, under state control in China, there is now an exciting new trend in Chinese sports. In early April 2007, China took part in a world yachting event called the America's Cup. It was the first time in the event's 156-year-old history that China had participated. Given their inexperience, there was no real chance that the Chinese team would win; the best they could do was to stay afloat. But the Chinese were not focusing on any present victory; rather, they were in the game for the promise of future success. To make the leap into this new sport, the team, financed by a private fund, was managed by a French national and had a majority of French sailors aboard.[122] This shift toward involving foreigners in Chinese sports is a new and healthy one for China. Foreign players, coaches, and managers bring with them international norms and the genuine spirit of competition through sports. And when more Chinese or international entrepreneurs sponsor, own, or otherwise finance sports teams or events, they are creating a new type of sports separate from the state-controlled sports system in China. It seems this trend will only grow stronger, and if it does, perhaps sports in China will, over the long run, foster developments that spark dramatic and lasting political change.

CONCLUSION

Wars break out because nations misunderstand each other. We shall not
have peace until the prejudices which now separate the different races
shall have been outlived. To attain this end, what better means than to
bring the youth of all countries periodically together for amicable trials
of muscular strength and agility?

Pierre de Coubertin

Visitors to the International Olympic Committee headquarters at Château de Vidy, Lausanne, Switzerland, will find two sculptures
given by the two Chinese national Olympic committees. One is a nude female athlete by artist Tian Jinduo called *Walking onto the World,* a present
from Beijing.[1] Another sculpture, from Taipei's national Olympic committee and by artist Zhu Ming, is of a man dressed in traditional clothes practicing *tai ji.*[2] If the first sculpture clearly conveys the Chinese quest for internationalization, then the *Tai ji Man* statue portrays the beautiful and
dynamic nature of traditional Chinese culture. These two sculptures can be
understood as symbolizing, in part, both the century-long Chinese obsession with internationalization through modern sports and the struggle to
blend modernity and tradition within a single culture.

During the late nineteenth century, many Chinese elites declared a total break from their traditional culture and values and started to embrace
Western sports. Just like the statue of the female athlete running unencum-
bered by clothing, these Chinese wanted China to join the world without
the burden of its many centuries-old traditions.

But the Chinese attitude toward both traditional and modern sports

Walking onto the World, a sculpture by Chinese artist Tian Jinduo
located in front of the International Olympic Committee headquarters
building in Lausanne, Switzerland.

was then, and is now, complicated by multiple layers of contradictions. Until the second half of the twentieth century, the Chinese seemed to impress the West more with their skills in martial arts and other traditional types of exercises than with their performances in international sports competitions. Even around the start of the twenty-first century, when China was emerging as a major sports power and preparing for the 2008 Olympic Games, the Chinese tried very hard to link their still-evolving national identity with their traditional values. The many carefully chosen symbols of Beijing's 2008 Games, too, clearly reflect a renewed appreciation for ancient Chinese traditions.

★

For the last one hundred years, the Chinese interest in Western sports has been largely motivated by a collective desire to establish a modern national identity: that is, to save the nation, to rid China of the "sick man of East Asia" label, and to make China strong and secure.

Even given this shared goal, however, differences can be detected in the approaches of the late Qing dynasty, the Nationalist regime, and the PRC. Between 1895 and 1912, when China was still under Qing rule, foreigners were allowed to play a crucial role in the introduction and development of modern sports. From 1912 to 1928, when China made the transition from an imperial system to republicanism, from the warlord era to the founding of Chiang Kai-shek's Nationalist regime, two changes emerged. First, the leadership role within modern sports shifted from foreigners to Chinese elites with the rising tide of nationalism in the 1920s. Second, sports became a coherent part of China's nation-building program and national policy. From 1928 to 1945, modern sports were debated and discussed largely within the framework of Chinese national salvation and the war effort against the Japanese.

With the Communist rise to power in 1949, two political entities claimed to be the legitimate governments of China; consequently, membership in international sports federations and especially the Olympic movement became major battlefields on which Beijing and Taiwan fought for their rights to represent China and so claim international legitimacy. For the PRC, perhaps more than for previous regimes, sports emerged as an important political tool, both domestically and internationally. This was especially true in the Maoist era, from the 1950s to the 1970s. Moreover, from the late 1970s, after Deng Xiaoping initiated his "Reform and Opening" policies, sports were deployed both as a vehicle for China's return to the international community and as a symbol of the new China.

Ever since the Maoist era, sports have been an elite domain, financed and controlled by the state. Under Mao, the regime was interested in using elite athlete activities to score political points in international politics, even if it often meant intentionally throwing a game. In the post-Mao era, by contrast, China has been obsessed with winning gold medals in major international competitions to demonstrate China's new status as an economic and political powerhouse. If in Mao's time Chinese athletes deliberately lost to opponents in order to score political points under the guiding principle "friendship first, competition second," post-Mao China has cultivated a striking "championship mentality," with victory becoming the sole motivation. With its total devotion to winning gold medals and the regime's mobilization of national resources to achieve that goal, China has emerged as a major competitor in sports, and Olympic gold has become an important measure of China's strength.

Although China's pursuit of Olympic gold medals clearly coincides with the nation's journey toward internationalization and achieving new status in the world, the state-driven championship mentality still reflects a combination of Chinese can-do confidence and the country's lingering inferiority complex. A nation that obsesses over gold medals is not a self-assured nation. A government that needs gold medals to bolster nationalist sentiment and its domestic legitimacy is not a confident government. And a population that cannot gracefully accept losses in sports is not a composed and secure population.

Beijing has used its so-called gold medal strategy to demonstrate China's rise in power and wealth, but the political system that the Communist party has tried to legitimize through sports and other means cannot produce a healthy and strong nation when its citizens have been forced to give up their independence and even personal dignity. A dictatorship that keeps its citizens mentally weak and living without a sense of self-worth cannot create a truly strong nation. The Communist one-party dictatorship might want its citizens to be physically strong, but it has discouraged the healthy development of free thinking among its people. A vigorous, powerful nation requires both strong bodies and free and healthy minds.

Since its founding, Communist China has remained a giant propaganda machine, through which everything is examined and controlled. Independent thinking and political initiative from citizens have systematically been undermined by the party. Although both the party and the country have changed a great deal over the last fifty years, today's China is still not a true nation-state; instead, it is a party-state in which the Communist party's interest is considered more important than the national interest. Consequently, it is still unclear whether the Communist regime's ultimate goal is to build a strong nation or simply use the idea of a strong nation as a means to keep the party in power.

★

Even as the Communist party has mobilized every resource to boost the country's image as a sports power through its elite sports program, the health of the general population has been declining. In particular, according to a recent survey, the physical condition of Chinese youth has been deteriorating since 1985. Young Chinese have become fatter, less active, and overall less healthy, mainly due to a lack of exercise. This situation has arisen for several reasons. First is a dearth of funding for sports programs in the schools, which has led to inadequate physical education facilities and little encouragement from schools and teachers for children to engage in sports.[3] China also fails to fund sports for the general population, even as it spends heavily on the training of elite athletes in pursuit of gold medals.[4]

Second, both parents and schools emphasize book learning and preparation for examinations and actually discourage young people from spending time being physically active. In the late nineteenth century, members of the Chinese elite blamed the old civil service examinations for China's weakness; now it appears that a new examination culture has emerged as the Chinese middle class tries to improve its livelihood by focusing on college entrance examinations, graduate student placement tests, and many different career development tests. China has, in a sense, again become an examination country, in which sports and exercise have little place in people's lives.

It is true that China has become a sports power if the number of gold medals won is used as a yardstick. Nevertheless, when most of its people become less healthy, China may actually become a new "sick man of East Asia," even though foreigners may not notice and the Chinese themselves are not paying much attention. The paradox is that the "sick man" label of long ago spawned the worship of gold medals, a mentality that may lead China back to that old hated condition.

★

More than any other sports event, the 2008 Olympic Games promise to accentuate the significance of sports as a political endeavor rather than a personal leisure pursuit—at least in the minds of recent Chinese leaders. Elsewhere I have argued that for the Chinese the twentieth century started with World War I.[5] The century ended, it seems, in the late 1970s with Deng Xiaoping's reforms. China has entered the twenty-first century with a new campaign to determine its new national identity and advance its position in the international arena. The first campaign in the twentieth century seemed to fail miserably with the founding of a Communist China that was isolated and poor by the time Mao died. How successful the new campaign in the twenty-first century will be largely depends on the country's ability to undo some of its political choices of the previous century. Political radicalism is not the answer: it played a crucial part in the failure of China's twentieth-century efforts at internationalization, and today's China, which is more diversified and open, is much less likely to engage in another mass political revolution.

CONCLUSION

★ ★ ★ ★

A sports revolution, however, seems very possible. Sports seem to bring people together regardless of their economic class, political ideas, or social rank. Given the widespread anger, anxiety, and frustration regarding social injustice in today's China, sports, as a focus of popular interest, may bring about major social changes. If such a transformation occurs, it could cause serious problems for the Communist regime.

We have observed that sports events such as soccer's World Cup have the capacity to move markets, start wars, make peace, and shift national moods.[6] But how will such events affect China's efforts to carve out a new national identity? One answer is suggested by developments in China's professional soccer establishment. The Chinese have long been deeply obsessed with soccer, but the Chinese team has often brought national humiliation because of its poor performances. As an article in the *Economist* recently pointed out, Chinese sports, like the country at large, are riddled with corruption, abuse of power, and injustice, and the problem is especially acute in Chinese soccer.[7] For several years, illegal gambling has fueled rampant match-fixing by corrupt players and referees—problems that have devastated the country's favorite sport and repeatedly disappointed its diehard fans. Chinese soccer fans have recently not been shy to demand reforms that would rid the sport of these systematic abuses. And largely under the pressure exerted by fans, Chinese sports authorities recently launched crackdown campaigns to stop the match-fixing (as well as the online gambling that encourages the fixers). But the root of the problem is the political system that controls sports.

As the previous chapters show, although the IOC and Beijing are close allies in the 2008 Games, the PRC regime's attitude toward sports has been fundamentally contrary to Olympic principles. According to the Olympic charter, "The practice of sport is a human right. Every individual must have the possibility of practicing sport, without discrimination of any kind and in the Olympic spirit, which requires mutual understanding with a spirit of friendship, solidarity and fair play. The organization, administration and management of sport must be controlled by independent sports organizations."[8] In China, however, sports at the national level have been closely controlled by the state and subject to political consideration and manipulation. Like many Chinese government agencies, the national and local sport commissions are subject to little public scrutiny.

The real solution to the corruption and other problems that plague Chinese sports is to create governing bodies for sports that are free from government control. To achieve that goal, China needs political reforms— and an overwhelming cry for cleaner, better sports might lead to such reforms. As the same *Economist* article pointed out, "Few dare to suggest that what the party needs are independent checks and balances. But that is precisely what anyone reading the sports pages might think."[9] More importantly, if we look at the eighteen World Cups held so far, no Communist countries have won a championship. Beijing may have a can-do attitude, but the curse of political control can be difficult to break. Can a soccer revolution lead to a political transformation?

Coubertin, the founder of the modern Olympic movement, once wrote, "Days in history are long; it is not yet midday. Let us be patient."[10] As we enter the new millennium, China has become an ever more impatient society. The Chinese want to get rich quickly, they want to be powerful soon, and nowhere can this impatience be seen as plainly as in their attitude toward sports. Here there is great hope for China, but perhaps also an element of danger.

Five years after completing his *Olympic Memoirs,* Coubertin began his final add-on chapter, which he carefully titled "La symphonie inachevée" (The unfinished symphony)—a coda that would remain incomplete and unpublished.[11] The history of sports in China, like Coubertin's lifework, is unfinished, with the most important movements still to be written. Try as we might, we simply cannot know what lies ahead for China as it transforms itself as a competitor on the field and on the international stage. We may, however, get a preview of the nation's global destiny when the 2008 Olympic Games open at 8:00 PM on August 8, 2008.

Notes

Abbreviations

ABC   Avery Brundage Collection, University of Illinois
Archives, Urbana

Bentley Library   National Archives on Sino-American Relations,
Bentley Historical Library, University of Michigan,
Ann Arbor, Michigan

Canada Archives Library and Archives Canada: Department of
External Affairs files, Ottawa, Ontario, Canada

Ford Library   Gerald Ford Presidential Library, Ann Arbor, Michigan

FRUS   *Foreign Relations of the United States,* published by
the U.S. State Department

IJHS   *International Journal of the History of Sport*

IOC Archives   International Olympic Committee Historical
Archives, Lausanne, Switzerland

LA Sports   Paul Ziffren Sports Resources Library, Los Angeles,
Library   California

LAT   *Los Angeles Times*

National   National Archives, College Park, Maryland
Archives

Nixon Project   Nixon Presidential Materials Project, National
Archives, College Park, Maryland

NSA   National Security Archives, George Washington
University

NYT   *New York Times*

PRC Sport   Zhonghua renmin gongheguo tiyu yundong weiyuan
Commission   hui yundong jishu weiyuan hui

UCLA   Special collections, Los Angeles Olympic Organizing
Committee records, Library of University of California,
Los Angeles

USTTA   U.S. Table Tennis Association

WSJ   *Wall Street Journal*

INTRODUCTION

Epigraph: Mao Zedong, "Tiyu zhi yanjiu" (On physical culture), *Xin Qingnian* (New youth), April 1, 1917.

1. Eric Hobsbawm, *Nations and Nationalism since 1780: Programme, Myth, Reality* (Cambridge, Eng.: Cambridge University Press, 1990), 143.
2. Adrian Smith and Dilwyn Porter, eds., *Sport and National Identity in the Post-war World* (London: Routledge, 2004), 2.
3. Jacques Barzun, *God's Country and Mine* (Boston: Little, Brown, 1954), 159.
4. Xu Guoqi, *China and the Great War*, 19.
5. Quoted in Joseph Maguire, *Global Sport: Identities, Societies, Civilizations* (Cambridge, Eng.: Polity Press, 2001), 2.
6. For details see Benedict Anderson, *Imagined Communities: Reflections on the Origin and Spread of Nationalism* (London: Verso, 1991).
7. So far there are only two books that cover well the topic of sports in China. They are Susan Brownell, *Training the Body for China: Sports in the Moral Order of the People's Republic* (Chicago: University of Chicago Press, 1995), and Andrew D. Morris, *Marrow of the Nation: A History of Sport and Physical Culture in the Republican China* (Berkeley: University of California Press, 2004). Both books are very different from this one in scope, focus, and even methodology. Brownell, an anthropologist, largely focuses on the relationship between morality and the culture of the body in 1980s China. Morris's book concentrates on the connections between Chinese ideas and practices of physical culture and notions of the nation, modernity, and modern citizenry in the 1920s and 1930s.
8. For details, see Maguire, *Global Sport*, 35.
9. Ommo Grupe, "The Sport Culture and the Sportization of Culture: Identity, Legitimacy, Sense, and Nonsense of Modern Sport as a Cultural Phenomenon," in Fernand Landry, et al., eds., *Sport . . . the Third Millennium, Proceedings of the International Symposium, Quebec City, Canada, May 1990* (Sainte-Foy, Quebec City: Les Presses de L'Université Laval, 1991) 141.
10. For details on this point, see Xu, *China and the Great War*, 1–77.
11. From 1959 to 1990, 383 Chinese athletes became world champions. Among them were 194 women. During the same period, China won a total of 490 world championships while Chinese women won 258.5 of them. In 1998, Chinese athletes broke world records 68 times. Only 4 of them were created

by Chinese men. Among 30 Chinese athletes who were world-record holders that year, 26 of them were Chinese women. In the 2004 Athens Olympic Games, Chinese athletes won 35 gold, 17 silver, and 9 bronze medals. Once again, more than 60 percent of these medals were won by Chinese women who brought home 19.5 gold, 11 silver, and 9 bronze medals. For details see China National Sport Commission, ed., *Zhong guo tiyu nianjian, 1949–1991* (Year book of China sports, 1949–1991), vol. 2 (Beijing: Ren min tiyu chubanshe, 1993), 414–415; China Sport Commission, ed., *Zhong guo tiyu nianjian, 1999* (Beijing: Zhong guo tiyu nianjian chubanshe, 1999), 347, 352–354; and China National Sport Commission, ed., *Zhong guo tiyu nianjian, 2005* (Beijing: Zhong guo tiyu nianjian chubanshe, 2006), 456.

12. For details on this point, see James Riordan and Dong Jinxia, "Chinese Women and Sport: Success, Sexuality, and Suspicion," *China Quarterly* 145 (March 1996).

1. Strengthening the Nation with Warlike Spirit

Epigraphs: Chiang Kai-shek's inscription for *Shishiyuebao*'s special issue on Republican China's Fifth National Games—see *Shishiyuebao* (Current events monthly) 9, no. 4 (October 1933); Coubertin quoted in Young, *Modern Olympics*, 112.

1. For instance, even a recent book published in China asserts without reservation that China did not have the phrase *tiyu* until the nineteenth century, when it imported it from abroad. See Liu Bingguo, *Zhong guo tiyu shi*, 1–3. Technically the term *tiyu* did exist in premodern China. A search of the *Siku Quanshu* database hosted by Academia Sinica in Taiwan—a gigantic collection of premodern Chinese texts—yields at least nine matches for the word. Of course, almost all of these referred to something other than physical education or exercise. In some cases, *ti* and *yu* do not even occur as a single phrase. For this reason, it is valid to argue that the traditional use of *tiyu* was fundamentally different than its modern, imported meaning.
2. Xu Yixiong, "Zhong guo jindai minzu zhuyi tiyu si xiang zhi tezhi" (The nature of nationalistic thinking about sports in modern China), in Xu Yixiong, *Zhong guo jindai tiyu si xiang*, 12.
3. Bender, "Wholes and Parts," 126.
4. See *Beijing 2000 Bulletin*, no. 7. All of the bidding materials from Beijing can be found in the LA Sports Library.
5. See Jiang Xiongfei, "Kongzi de tiyu si xiang."
6. For many outstanding pictures of ancient sports in China, see Chinese Olympic Committee, ed., *Zhong guo tiyu wen hua wu qian nian.*

7. Gu Shiquan, *Zhong guo tiyu shi,* 52. See also Cui Lequan, *Tu shuo zhong guo gu dai you yi,* 142.

8. For details, see Zhou Linyi, "Han dai tiyu xian xiang kao."

9. For a good study of ancient polo in China, see Su Jingcun, "Zhong guo gu dai ma qiu yun dong de yan jiu," 3:17–47. See also Tang Hao, "Shi kao wo guo Sui Tang yi qian de ma qiu," 2:1–9.

10. For excellent studies on *chui wan* (golf) in ancient China, see Tang Hao, "Wo guo gu dai mou xie qiu lei yun dong de guo ji ying xiang," 3:48–52; Fan Sheng, "Wo guo gu dai chui wan yun dong," 2:10–20; and Hoh, *Physical Education in China,* 27–28.

11. The civil service examination was open only to men and was in use until 1905, when it was abolished. There were also some irregular and different types of civil service examinations for selecting military officials, which were called *wu ju,* but this kind of military service examination was rarely employed and not at all influential. For details, see Xu Baoyin, "Tang dai tiyu huo dong zhi yan jiu."

12. For the most recent study on foot-binding, see Ko, *Cinderella's Sisters.*

13. For recent studies of the Boxer Rebellion, see Preston, *Boxer Rebellion;* Esherick, *Origins of the Boxer Uprising;* Cohen, *History in Three Keys;* Elliott, *Some Did It for Civilization;* and Xiang, *Origins of the Boxer War.*

14. For details on the effect of the Sino-Japanese war of 1894–1895 on the Chinese mindset, see Xu, *China and the Great War,* 19–49.

15. Wang Shi, *Yan Fu ji,* 1:13–18.

16. Ibid., 40–54.

17. Xu Yuanmin, "Yan Fu de tiyu si xiang," 13–24.

18. Schwartz, *In Search of Wealth and Power,* 86.

19. "Tianxia si bing ren" (Four sick men in the world), translated from *North-China Daily News* (Shanghai), November 30, 1896, in *Shiwubao,* December 15, 1896. See also Gao Cui, *Cong dong ya bing fu dao tiyu qiang guo,* 9.

20. Liu Qingbo and Peng Guoxing, eds., *Chen Tianhua ji* (Collections of Chen Tianhua's writings) (Changsha: Hunan renmin chubanshe, 1958), 69.

21. Xu Yixiong, "Wan Qing tiyu si xiang zhi xing cheng," 1–17; see also Xu Yixiong, "Jin dai Zhong guo min zu zhu yi tiyu si xiang zhi xing cheng," 1–8.

22. Liang Qichao, "Xin min shuo" (Theories of new citizenship), in Liang Qichao, *Liang Qichao quan ji,* 2:709.

23. Ibid., 2:713.

24. Zhang Luya and Zhou Qing, *Shi ji qing,* 11.

25. Gu Shiquan, *Zhong guo tiyu shi,* 204.

26. For an excellent study of this issue, see Cheng Ruifu, "Qing mo nü zi tiyu si xiang de xing cheng."

27. Quoted in Chen Shien, "Qing mo min chu jun guomin jiao yu zhi tiyu si xiang," 27.

28. Cai Yuanpei, "Dui yu jiao yu fang zhen zhi yi jian."

29. Chen Shien, "Qing mo min chu jun guomin jiao yu zhi tiyu si xiang," 28.

30. Gu Shiquan, *Zhong guo tiyu shi*, 23.

31. Avery Brundage, who held a large collection of Chinese artifacts, considered himself an expert on Chinese culture. For the quotation, see Brundage, "Civilization May Be Saved by Athletes," n.d. The article may have been written sometime around 1938. ABC, box 249, reel 144.

32. Quan guo yun dong da hui xuan chuan zu, *Quan guo yundong da hui yao lan, 1930*, 1.

33. Ibid., 6.

34. Wang Zhengya, *Jiu zhong guo tiyu jian wen*, 20.

35. Ibid., 140.

36. Chen Shien, "Qing mo min chu jun guomin jiao yu zhi tiyu si xiang," 32.

37. Quoted in ibid., 36.

38. Morris, *Marrow of the Nation*, 96.

39. Gunsun Hoh, *Physical Education in China*, v.

40. Chen Shien, "Qing mo min chu jun guomin jiao yu zhi tiyu si xiang," 40.

41. Remarks by Coubertin in the foreign correspondence press club files, Tokyo, June 29, 1968, ABC, box 246.

42. Coubertin and Muller, *Olympism*, 288.

43. Ibid., 292.

44. Ibid., 38.

45. MacAloon, *This Great Symbol*, 528, 472. See also Young, *Modern Olympics*, 68; and Espy, *Politics of the Olympic Games*, 12–18.

46. Coubertin, *Olympism*, 532.

47. Quoted in Young, *Modern Olympics*, 112.

48. Lucas, *Modern Olympic Games*, 236.

49. Ali Mazrui, *A World Federation of Cultures: An African Perspective* (New York: Free Press, 1976), 41, quoted in Barbara Keys, "The Internationalization of Sport, 1890–1939," in Ninkovich and Liping Bu, *The Cultural Turn*, 201.

50. Lucas, *Modern Olympic Games*, 31.

51. Coubertin, *Olympism*, 697.

52. For details on this point, see Richard Hofstadter, *The Paranoid Style in American Politics, and Other Essays* (New York: Knopf, 1965).

53. For details, see Wu, "The Influence of the YMCA on the Development of Physical Education in China," 71–72.

54. Little, "Charles Harold McCloy," 76.

55. For a complete study on McCloy's contribution to physical education, see ibid. and Gerber, "Three Interpretations of the Role of Physical Education, 1930–1960."

56. Little, *Charles Harold McCloy*, 53.

57. Ibid., 90.

58. Mai Kele (McCloy), "Di liu jie yuan dong yun dong hui de jiao xun," 4.

59. Little, *Charles Harold McCloy,* 96.

60. Kolatch, *Sports, Politics, and Ideology in China,* 3.

61. Allen Guttmann and Lee Thompson, "Educators, Imitators, Modernizers: The Arrival and Spread of Modern Sport in Japan," in J. A. Mangan, ed., *Europe, Sport, World: Shaping Global Societies* (London: Frank Cass, 2001), 26. For a recent study on Japanese sports from the Christian point of view—and with a focus on how Japanese modern sports were influenced by the hybridizations of *Bushido* and Christianity—see Abe, "Muscular Christianity in Japan," 714–738.

62. Morris, *Marrow of the Nation,* 3.

63. *Tiantsin Young Men* 19 (October 26, 1907), quoted in Chih-Kang Wu, "Influence of the YMCA," 103–104; see also Xu Yixiong, *Zhong guo jindai tiyu si xiang,* 153. For many years, Chinese scholars repeated a widespread but never verified story that Coubertin had invited the Qing to attend the first Olympic Games. I have searched for evidence in the IOC Archives, Chinese First Historical Archives, French Foreign Ministry Archives, and other places, but have failed to find documents showing that the IOC or Coubertin contacted China regarding the first two Olympic Games. Luo Shimin in his recent book has offered the best argument so far from Chinese scholars about this issue. He convincingly argued that the Chinese might have first heard about the Olympic Games in 1900. For details, see Luo Shimin, *Ao yun lai dao Zhong guo,* 12–22.

64. *Tiantsin Young Men* (May 23, 1908), quoted in Chih-Kang Wu, "Influence of the YMCA," 106–107.

65. Chih-Kang Wu, "Influence of the YMCA," 108.

66. One YMCA report from China in 1910 claimed, "The Young Men's Christian Association of China and Korea have been for some years pushing an athletic campaign, which has had as its slogan these three questions." See *Annual Reports of the Foreign Secretaries of the International Committee* (New York: YMCA, 1909–1910), 192.

67. For an excellent study of the relationship between China and the Far Eastern Championship Games, see Dong Shouyi, "Zhongguo yu yuan dong yun dong hui," 2:81–92.

68. The Far Eastern Championship Games had previously been called the Far Eastern Olympic Games. After 1927, the games took place in 1930 and 1934.

69. For details, see Hao Gengsheng, *Hao Gengsheng hui yi lu,* 35–38.

70. Coubertin, *Olympic Memoirs,* 171.

71. Ibid., 232.

72. Wolf Lyberg, *The IOC Sessions, 1894–1955* (unpublished volume at the IOC Archives), 84.

73. Ibid., 91.
74. The IOC records clearly indicate that it recognized the Chinese Olympic Committee in 1922. See "Recognition of the National Olympic Committee for China," in IOC Archives, République Populaire de Chine, correspondence, January–June 1975; see also Tang Mingxin, *Wo guo can jia ao yun hui cang sang shi,* 1:45.
75. Crowther, "Sports, Nationalism and Peace in Ancient Greece," 588–589.
76. Spivey, *The Ancient Olympics,* 2; Dale Russakoff, "Team Rice, Playing Away," *Washington Post,* February 6, 2005, D1.
77. For details, see Mewett, "Fragments of a Composite Identity."
78. Xu Yixiong, "Zhong guo jindai min zu zhu yi tiyu si xiang zhi te zhi," 12.
79. Quoted in Hoganson, *Fighting for American Manhood,* 36.
80. Ibid., 37.
81. Roosevelt was familiar with the Olympic ideas. In his capacity as the IOC president, Coubertin once asked Roosevelt, then president of the United States, to be president of the 1904 Chicago Olympic Games. Roosevelt replied that he would take the keenest interest in the undertaking and would do his utmost to make the meeting at Chicago successful. Roosevelt's letter "is couched in the warmest terms. He referred to Baron Coubertin's works on sports, with which the President showed acquaintance." Chicago eventually abandoned the Games in 1904 to Saint Louis, which served as the host city instead. The next year Roosevelt was awarded the Nobel Peace Prize for his role in the Russo-Japanese War. But few noticed that in the same year he received, along with Norwegian explorer Fridtjof Nansen, an Olympic diploma from the IOC. For details, see Lyberg, *IOC Sessions,* 35; and *NYT,* December 28, 1901, 5.
82. Quoted in Hoganson, *Fighting for American Manhood,* 144–145.
83. Quoted in Pope, *Patriotic Games,* 123.
84. Quoted in Hoganson, *Fighting for American Manhood,* 146.
85. Pope, *Patriotic Games,* 126, 121.
86. Pope, "Army of Athletes," 435–456.
87. Guttmann and Thompson, *Japanese Sports,* 154.
88. Ibid., 156–158.

2. Reimagining China through International Sports

Epigraph: Coubertin, "An Expression," 4.

1. Coubertin, "An Expression," 4.
2. Foer, *How Soccer Explains the World,* 3.
3. Morris, *Marrow of the Nation,* 96.

4. Buruma, "The Great Black Hope."

5. Kempe, "Fevered Pitch."

6. For details on these points, see Magdalinski, "Sports History and East German National Identity."

7. Margolick, *Beyond Glory*, 127–128.

8. Kempe, "Fevered Pitch"; Landler and Longman, "Germans' Main Objective Is a Good Time for All."

9. Christopher Young, "Munich 1972: Re-Presenting the Nation," in Tomlinson and Young, *National Identity and Global Sports Events*, 118.

10. For an excellent study on this fight, see Margolick, *Beyond Glory*.

11. Coubertin, *Olympic Memoirs*, 103.

12. Bairner, *Sport, Nationalism, and Globalization*, 92–93, 103.

13. Pope, *Patriotic Games*, 85.

14. Although the Olympics may seem international, its controlling body has been definitely European. The end of current IOC president Jacques Rogge's first presidential term in 2009 will mark ninety-five years of European presidential leadership in the IOC's 115-year history; Rogge is from Belgium. Europe also enjoys a striking centralization of political power and decision-making authority in the IOC. Europeans hold approximately 45 percent of all seats on the IOC, and two-thirds of the members of the IOC's powerful executive board are European.

15. LaFeber, *Michael Jordan and the New Global Capitalism*.

16. Quoted in Bairner, *Sport, Nationalism, and Globalization*, 11.

17. Sugden and Tomlinson, *FIFA and the Contest for World Football*, 228.

18. Xing Junji and Zu Xianhai, *Bai nian chen fu*, 20.

19. Jiang Huaiqing, *Liu Changchun duan pao cheng gong shi*, 3–5.

20. Tang Mingxin, *Wo guo can jia ao yun cang sang shi*, 1:212.

21. Hao was former chairman of the physical education department at Northeastern University. He became a professor of physical education in Shandong University after the Northern Eastern region was occupied by the Japanese in 1931. For Liu's own explanation of his participation in the Games, see Jiang Huaiqing, *Liu Changchun duan pao cheng gong shi*, 26–27.

22. Ibid., 5.

23. Ibid., 7. See also Xing Junji and Zu Xianhai, *Bai nian chen fu*, 7.

24. Jiang Huaiqing, *Liu Changchun duan pao cheng gong shi*, 7.

25. Department of Special Collections, UCLA, Los Angeles Olympic Organizing Committee (LAOOC), collection 2025, *The Xth Olympiad*, Los Angeles, 1932, box 4, 397.

26. *Los Angeles Times*, July 31, 1932, part 6A, 3.

27. Ibid., 4.

28. Jiang Huaiqing, *Liu Changchun duan pao cheng gong shi*, 11.

29. LAOOC, collection 2025, *The Xth Olympiad.*

30. Jiang Huaiqing, *Liu Changchun duan pao cheng gong shi,* 7.

31. Liu Changchun, "Can jia shi jie yun dong hui gan yan," 18.

32. Shen Siliang, "Wo guo can jia di shi jie shi jie yun dong hui sheng kuang" (China's participation in the 1932 Olympic Games), in Zhong guo di er li shi dang an guan, *Zhong hua min guo shi dang an zi liao hui bian,* di wu ji, di yi bian, Wen hua (2) (Nanjing: Jiangsu gu ji chubanshe, 1994), 994–995.

33. *Dagongbao* (Tianjin), editorial, "Jin hou zhi guo min tiyu wen ti" (Questions regarding the future of Chinese sports), August 7, 1932, in Chengdu tiyu xueyuan tiyu shi yan jiu suo, ed., *Zhong guo jindai tiyu shi zi liao,* 406–409.

34. The statement can be found in LAOOC, collection 2025, *The Xth Olympiad.*

35. M. K. Lo, "Progress of Sport among Chinese in Hong Kong."

36. Zheng Zhilin and Zhao Shanxing, "Zhong hua tiyu kao cha tuan fu ou kao cha ping shu," 36–38.

37. Hua Zhi, *Su yuan—Dong Shouyi zhuan,* 63–68.

38. Quoted in Wu Wenzhong, *Zhong guo jin bai nian tiyu shi,* 265.

39. Quoted in Morris, *Marrow of the Nation,* 176.

40. Zhong guo di er li shi dang an guan, *Zhong hua min guo shi dang an zi liao hui bian,* di wu ji, di yi bian, Wen hua (2), 1005–1007.

41. The total budget of the delegation should have been 150,000 U.S. dollars. But the government provided only $25,000, or about 16.6 percent of the budget. For details on this point, see Hua Zhi, *Su yuan—Dong Shouyi zhuan,* 100; and Jin Yuliang, "Di 14 jie Ao yun hui yu Zhong guo dai biao tuan."

42. Hua Zhi, *Su yuan—Dong Shouyi zhuan,* 101–102.

43. China National Sport Commission, "Zhong yang ti wei dang zhou guang yu jia qiang renmin tiyu yundong gongzuo de bao gao, November 17, 1953" (National sport commission's party authority report on how to strengthen its work on citizens' sports, November 17, 1953), in Guo jia ti wei zheng ce yan jiu shi, *Tiyu yun dong wen jian xuan bian (1949–1981),* 5.

44. He Long's Report to Party Central Committee's Conference on Sports, January 16, 1954, in Guo jia ti wei zheng ce yan jiu shi, *Tiyu yun dong wen jian xuan bian (1949–1981),* 13.

45. For details on how sports are used for political propaganda in other countries, see Hazan, *Olympic Sports and Propaganda Games.*

46. For details, see Zhou's letter to Mao, March 15, 1971, in Lu Guang, *Zhong guo titan da ju jiao,* 139–141.

47. Zhong gong zhong yang wen xian yan jiu shi, *Zhou Enlai nianpu, 1949–1976,* 3:463.

48. Lu Guan, *Zhong guo ti tan da ju jiao,* 156–157; and Zhao Zhenghong, "Ping pang wai jiao shi mo" (The inside story of ping-pong diplomacy), in An Jianshe, *Zhou Enlai de zui hou sui yue, 1966–1976,* 308–309.

49. Xing Junji and Zu Xianhai, *Bai nian chen fu,* 346.
50. Liang Lijuan, *He Zhenliang,* 55.
51. Indonesia, as a Muslim country, also kept Israel out of the Games. See Brundage's draft memoir in ABC, box 250, reel 244.
52. For details on China's relationship with GANEFO, see Dang dai zhong guo zhuan ji cong shu, *He Long zhuan,* 517–520.
53. China National Sport Commission, *Zhong guo tiyu nian jian,* 39.
54. Liang Lijuan, *He Zhenliang,* 57.
55. Ibid., 57–58; see also Li Lingxiu and Zhou Minggong, *Tiyu zhi zi Rong Gaotang,* 312–313.
56. Zhong gong zhong yang wen xian yan jiu shi, *Zhou Enlai nianpu,* 2:574.
57. Quoted in *Zhong guo tiyu* (China's sports) 11–12 (1965): 31.

3. Modern Sports and Nationalism in China

Epigraph: George Orwell, *Shooting an Elephant and Other Essays* (New York: Harcourt, Brace, 1950), 153.

1. Coubertin, *Olympism,* 541.
2. Quoted in Guttmann, *The Games Must Go On,* 12.
3. Quoted in John Hoberman, "Toward a Theory of Olympic Internationalism," 15.
4. Weiland and Wiley, *Thinking Fan's Guide to the World Cup,* 53.
5. Quoted in Kellas, *Politics of Nationalism and Ethnicity,* 28.
6. Jarvie, "Sport, Nationalism and Cultural Identity," 74–75.
7. John Hoberman, "Sport and Ideology in the Post-Communist Age," in Allison, *Changing Politics of Sport,* 18.
8. Hobsbawm, *Nations and Nationalism since 1780,* 143.
9. Senn, *Power, Politics, and the Olympic Games,* 154.
10. Buruma, "The Great Black Hope."
11. Tony Mason, "England 1966," in Tomlinson and Young, *National Identity and Global Sports Events,* 94.
12. Ibid., 97.
13. Pope, *Patriotic Games,* 5.
14. Shaikin, *Sport and Politics,* 62.
15. Belbin and Agosto won a silver medal in the 2006 Winter Olympic Games.
16. For the best study on the Russian use of sport in international relations, see Keys, *Globalizing Sport,* 158–180.
17. Senn, *Power, Politics, and the Olympic Games,* 90.
18. Hazan, *Olympic Sports and Propaganda Games,* 36.

19. Morrow and Wamsley, *Sport in Canada*, 240.
20. For details on Ben Johnson and the Canadian national identity, see Jackson, "A Twist of Race," 21–40.
21. For recent studies on the connections between sports and Japanese international politics, see Collins, "'Samurai' Politics" and "Conflicts of 1930s Japanese Olympic Diplomacy in Universalizing the Olympic Movement."
22. In 1988, the IOC officially recognized Sohn Kee-chung's record in the 1936 Berlin Olympic Games as a Korean, not Japanese, honor.
23. Rob Hughes, "Winners and Losers, On and Off the Field," *International Herald Tribune*, June 24, 2006, 20.
24. Shao Rugan, "Jian she min zu ben wei de tiyu," 5.
25. Quoted in Lu Mu, *Tiyu jie de yi mian qi zhi Ma Yuehan jiao shou*, 52.
26. *Shishiyuebao* 9, no. 3 (October 1933): 1.
27. Zhang Boling, "Tiyu cong shu xu yan" (Preface to a series of sport books), in Jiang Huanqing, ed., *Liu Changchun duan pao cheng gong shi*, 1933.
28. Chengdu tiyu xueyuan tiyu shi yan jiu suo, *Zhong guo jindai tiyu shi zi liao*, 418–419.
29. Liu Shencheng, "Tiyu jiu guo lun," 519, 713–719.
30. For details on this point, see Dai Weiqian, "Kang zhan shi qi min zu jiao yu tiyu si xiang zhi ren shi," 33–49; and Gu Shiquan, *Zhong guo tiyu shi*, 255.
31. Quoted in Morris, *Marrow of the Nation*, 167.
32. Chen Dengke, "Wo men ying fou ti chang Zhong guo de min zu tiyu," 2.
33. Zhong guo di er li shi dang an guan, *Zhong hua min guo shi dang an zi liao hui bian*, di wu ji, di yi bian, Wen hua (2), 929.
34. "Zeng xiu tiyu fa an" (November 28, 1936) (Bill for revising the sport law), in Zhong guo di er li shi dang an guan, *Zhong hua min guo shi dang an zi liao hui bian di wu ji*, di yi bian, Wen hua (2), 959.
35. Huang Renyi, "Wo guo tiyu zheng ce zhi ding guo cheng zhi yan jiu," 24.
36. Wu Chih-Kang (Wu Zhigang), "The Influence of the YMCA on the Development of Physical Education in China," 17.
37. Zhong guo di er li shi dang an guan, *Zhong hua min guo shi dang an zi liao hui bian*, di wu ji, di yi bian, Wen hua (2), 934.
38. The bylaw was revised in June 1934 to make it more practical. See Zhong guo di er li shi dang an guan, *Zhong hua min guo shi dang an zi liao hui bian*, di wu ji, di yi bian, Wen hua (2), 913–920.
39. Quoted in Huang Renyi, "Wo guo tiyu zheng ce zhi ding guo cheng zhi yan jiu," 21–22.
40. Er shi er nian quan guo yundong dahui choubei weiyuan hui, *Er shi er nian quan guo yundong dahui zong bao gao shu*, pt. 1, p. 72.
41. Ibid., pt. 2, p. 3.

42. Zhong guo di er li shi dang an guan, *Zhong hua min guo shi dang an zi liao hui bian,* di wu ji, di yi bian, Wen hua (2), 947–948.

43. For details on the proposal and the government's responses, see "Xing zheng yuan jiao jiao yu bu ban li guomin can zheng hui guan yu ti chang shangwu jing shen yi gu guo ji er li kang zhan an de tong zhi dan" (The executive Yuan's notice to the education ministry regarding the Association of Citizens' Participation in Politics' bill on promoting a warlike spirit for the sake of strengthening the nation's foundation and to aid in the anti-Japanese War) (January 19, 1939), in Zhong guo di er li shi dang an guan, *Zhong hua min guo shi dang an zi liao hui bian,* di wu ji, di yi bian, Wen hua (2), 701–705.

44. For details on his speeches, see Chiang Kai-shek, "Di si jie quan guo yundong dahui xun ci (1–2), April 1930" (Two instructional speeches to the Fourth National Games, April 1930); "Huanying di si jie quan guo yundong dahui xuanshou yanshuo ci, April 1930" (Welcome address to the Fourth National Games); and "Di wu ci quan guo yundong dahui banci, October 10, 1933" (Congratulation address to the Fifth National Games, October 10, 1933), all in Zhang Qiyun, ed., *Xian zongtong Jiang gong quanji,* 3:3120–3122, 3:3126–3127. See also Tang Mingxin, *Wo guo can jia ao yun cang sang shi,* 1:92, 247.

45. Chiang Kai-shek, "Tichang dang, zheng, jun, xue ge ji guan ren yuan tiyu tong dian, March 2, 1935" (Telegram on encouraging officials in the offices of the party, national and local governments, military, and education to do physical training), in Zhang Qiyun, *Xian zongtong Jiang gong quanji,* 3:3147–3148. See also Chengdu tiyu xueyuan tiyu shi yan jiu suo, *Zhong guo jindai tiyu shi zi liao,* 419–420; and Zhong guo di er li shi dang an guan, *Zhong hua min guo shi dang an zi liao hui bian,* di wu ji, di yi bian, Wen hua (2), 1009–1010.

46. Quoted in Zhong guo di er li shi dang an guan, *Zhong hua min guo shi dang an zi liao hui bian,* di wu ji, di yi bian, Wen hua (2), 1010–1011.

47. Chiang Kai-shek, "Zai san min zhu yi qing nian tuan quan guo gan bu gong zuo hui yi xun ci" (Speech at the national conference of San min zhu yi youth league cadres), in Chengdu tiyu xueyuan tiyu shi yan jiu suo, *Zhong guo jindai tiyu shi zi liao,* 420–421.

48. Zhong guo di er li shi dang an guan, *Zhong hua min guo shi dang an zi liao hui bian,* di wu ji, di yi bian, Wen hua (2), 712–722.

49. Robert Culp, "Rethinking Governmentality," 533.

50. For details, see Huang Jinlin, "Jindai zhong guo de jun shi sheng ti jian gou, 1895–1949."

51. Chiang Kai-shek, "Di yi jie tiyu jie xun ci, September 9, 1942" (Instructional address given to the first national sport festival), in Zhang Qiyun, *Xian zongtong Jiang gong quanji,* 3:3226–3227.

52. The name of Far Eastern Olympiad, under the IOC's new regulation, was changed in 1915 to Far Eastern Athletic Association and its games were renamed Far Eastern Championships. In 1934 it ceased to exist for political reasons and was later replaced by the Asian Games.

53. *Jiao yu za zhi* 6, no. 10 (1914): 31–32, quoted in Mao Anjun [Andrew Morris], "1909–1919 [Jiao yu za zhi] Tiyu wen zhang fen xi de chu bu," 50.

54. Morris, *Marrow of the Nation*, 34.

55. Chinese Historical Association, ed., *Xin hai ge ming* (Historical materials on the 1911 revolution) (Shanghai: Shanghai renmin chubanshe, 1957), 27.

56. Xing Junji and Zu Xianhai, *Bai nian chen fu*, 6.

57. Quoted in Mao Anjun, "1909–1919 [Jiao yu za zhi] Tiyu wen zhang fen xi de chu bu," 45.

58. For details, see Xu, *China and the Great War*, chap. 3.

59. Quoted in Mao Anjun, "1909–1919 [Jiao yu za zhi] Tiyu wen zhang fen xi de chu bu," 53.

60. Song Ruhai, *Wo neng bi ya*, Song's note.

61. Ibid., Wang's preface.

62. Ibid., Yu's preface.

63. Morris, *Marrow of the Nation*, 99.

64. For details, see Jun Xing, "The American Social Gospel and the Chinese YMCA," 284.

65. LaFeber, *Michael Jordan and the New Global Capitalism*, 141.

66. Lu Mu, *Tiyu jie de yi mian qi zhi Ma Yuehan jiao shou*, 52–53.

67. Ibid., 58, 147.

68. Morris, *Marrow of the Nation*, 60.

69. Rong Gaotang, *Dang dai zhong guo tiyu*, 13.

70. Xing Junji and Zu Xianhai, *Bai nian chen fu*, 6.

71. Ibid., 138; Zhuang Zedong and Sasaki Atsuko, *Zhuang Zedong yu zuo zuo mu dun zi*, 222.

72. Quoted in Rong Gaotang, *Dang dai zhong guo tiyu*, 198; see also Xing Junji and Zu Xianhai, *Bai nian chen fu*, 319.

73. Peng Yongjie, Zhang Zhiwei, and Han Donghui, *Ren wen Ao yun*, 258.

74. The interview with Nie Weiping was broadcast on Beijing TV's *Wang shi* (Past) program on February 20 and 27, 2006.

75. "Zhongyang pizhuan guo jia ti wei dangwei guan yu 1966 nian quan guo tiyu gong zuo huiyi de bao gao, May 2, 1966" (Comments of CCP's central committee on the national sport commission's party committee report to the 1966 national conference on sports, May 2, 1966), in Guo jia ti wei zheng ce yan jiu shi, *Tiyu yundong wen jian xuan bian (1949–1981)*, 107–111.

76. Zhong gong zhong yang wen xian yan jiu shi, *Zhou Enlai nianpu*, 1:352.

77. Li Lie, *He Long nianpu*, 564–565.

4. The Two-China Question

Epigraph: The Analects of Confucius, trans. Simon Leys (New York: W. W. Norton, 1997), 60–61.

1. Coubertin, *Olympic Memoirs,* 126.
2. Ibid., 138.
3. *NYT,* July 21, 1920, 23.
4. For an excellent study of Puerto Rico's case, see MacAloon, "*La Pitada Olympica,*" 315–355. For the most recent examination of the Koreans' case, see Bridges, "Reluctant Mediator."
5. Guttmann, *The Games Must Go On,* 145.
6. The other two, Wang Zhengting and Kong Xiangxi, decided to leave. Kong lived in the United States after 1949 while Wang resided in Hong Kong.
7. Beijing's national Olympic committee was not established until November 1952. For details on the impact of the Helsinki Games on Beijing's thinking, see the report to the party's central committee from China's delegation to the 1952 Olympic Games, August 21, 1952, which can be found in Rong Gaotang, *Rong Gaotang tiyu wen lun xuan,* 5–8. See also Li Lie, *He Long nianpu,* 519–520.
8. Brundage draft memoir, chapter 11, ABC, box 250, reel 244.
9. Ibid., 7–8.
10. Edström to Otto Mayer, March 24, 1952, IOC Archives, République Populaire de Chine, correspondence, 1924–1958.
11. For details on the internal discussion about this issue, see Fan Hong and Xiong Xiaozheng, "Communist China," 320–327.
12. "Dui zhong guo shifou canjia di shi wu jie guo ji ao lin pi ke yun dong hui wenti de piyu" (Comments on the report regarding whether China should take part in the Fifteenth Olympic Games), February 1952, in Zhong gong zhong yang wen xian yan jiu shi and Zhong yang dang an guan, *Jian guo yi lai Liu Shaoqi wen gao,* 4:4–5. See also Zhong gong zhong yang wen xian yan jiu shi, *Zhou Enlai nianpu,* 1:214.
13. Edström to R. M. Ritter [honorary secretary of FINA], June 6, 1952, IOC Archives, République Populaire de Chine, correspondence, 1924–1958.
14. For details, see IOC Archives, Minutes of the Forty-sixth IOC Session, Oslo, February 12–13, 1952.
15. For details on this point, see Hua Zhi, *Su yuan—Dong Shouyi zhuan,* 114.
16. Ibid., 111–113.
17. IOC Archives, Minutes of the Forty-sixth IOC Session.
18. IOC Archives, République Populaire de Chine, juridique, 1947–1975, folder Peking: 1952–1958.
19. R. M. Ritter [honorary secretary of FINA] to Edström, June 9, 1952, and

Ritter to the All-China Athletic Federation, April 25, 1952, IOC Archives, République Populaire de Chine, correspondence, 1924–1958.

20. IOC Archives, République Populaire de Chine, juridique, 1947–1975, folder Peking: 1952–1958.

21. Ibid.

22. The new rule, however, allowed present members who were not familiar with those languages to be assisted by an interpreter. In other words, the IOC used a pretext to reprimand Beijing during their first official contact, which did not improve the organization's own credibility.

23. IOC Archives, Minutes of the Forty-seventh IOC Session, Helsinki, July 16–27, 1952.

24. Hua Zhi, *Su yuan—Dong Shouyi zhuan*, 118–119.

25. "Dui zhongguo shifou canjia di shi wu jie guo ji ao lin pi ke yundong hui wenti de piyu," 4:4–5. See also Zhong gong zhong yang wen xian yan jiu shi, *Zhou Enlai nianpu*, 1:214.

26. Zhong gong zhong yang wen xian yan jiu shi, *Zhou Enlai nianpu*, 1:250.

27. Liang Lijuan, *He Zhenliang*, 19, 27.

28. Rong Gaotang to Otto Mayer, August 3, 1952, IOC Archives, République Populaire de Chine, correspondence, 1924–1958.

29. IOC Archives, Minutes of the IOC Session, Athens, 1954.

30. IOC Archives, République Populaire de Chine, correspondence, 1924–1958.

31. Liang Lijuan, *He Zhenliang*, 32; Brundage to T. J. Mathews, *Harvard Crimson*, November 16, 1966, IOC Archives, République Populaire de Chine, juridique, 1947–1975, folder Peking: 1952–1958, protestations/soutiens, 1956–1966.

32. Brundage to Dong, June 1, 1958, in IOC Archives, République Populaire de Chine, juridique, 1947–1975, folder Peking: 1952–1958.

33. Zhong gong zhong yang wen xian yan jiu shi, *Zhou Enlai nianpu*, 2:149.

34. IOC Archives, République Populaire de Chine, juridique, 1947–1975, folder Peking: 1952–1958.

35. Ibid. See also Chi-wen Shih, *Sports Go Forward in China*, 52–53.

36. Liang Lijuan, *He Zhenliang*, 34.

37. Guo jia ti wei zheng ce yan jiu shi, *Tiyu yun dong wen jian xuan bian (1949–1981)*, 175.

38. IOC Archives, République Populaire de Chine, correspondence, 1924–1958.

39. "Red China Blasts Olympic Games," *Chicago Daily News*, May 25, 1964. See also N.a., "Firmly Support Indonesian and Korean Boycott of the Tokyo Olympics," [Beijing] *China's Sport* 6 (1964): 1.

40. For details on Taiwan's relations with the IOC during the early 1950s, see Hao Gengsheng, *Hao Gengsheng hui yi lu*, 40–54, 72–95.

41. Tang Mingxin, an important sports scholar and official in Taiwan, later claimed that Taiwan's withdrawal from the 1952 Olympic Games and late

march under the "UNDER PROTEST" banner in the 1960 Rome Olympics were not good strategies since neither helped Taiwan stay in the Olympic movement under the name of Republic of China. See Tang Mingxin, *Tang Mingxin xiansheng fangwen jilu*, 176–177.

42. Announcement of Withdrawal from Participation in the XVth Olympiad Helsinki 1952 by Chinese National Olympic Committee, July 17, 1952, in Hao Gengsheng to Edström, July 19, 1952, IOC Archives, République Populaire de Chine, histoire, 1952–1986.

43. ABC, box 201, reel 116.

44. Hao officially informed Edström on July 19, 1952, about Taiwan's withdrawal from the Games. See IOC Archives, République Populaire de Chine, juridique, 1947–1975, folder Taiwan: 1951–1964. Hao Gengsheng in his memoir did not mention this tactical error. For details, see *Hao Gengsheng hui yi lu*, 40–54.

45. On July 31, 1952, after Taiwan's withdrawal to protest Beijing's participation, Hao Gengsheng wrote an angry letter to Edström stating that he did not have the authority to cable Taiwan on June 16, 1952, "the following abrupt and insolent message: 'you may not participate.'" IOC Archives, République Populaire de Chine, juridique, 1947–1975, folder Taiwan: 1951–1964. See also "Hao to Brundage, personal and confidential," ABC, box 120, reel 66.

46. Brundage to Hao Gengsheng, June 17, 1952, ABC, box 120, reel 66.

47. ABC, box 120, reel 66.

48. Ibid.

49. Ibid.

50. IOC to Brundage, May 3, 1954. ABC, box 120, reel 66.

51. Lyberg, *Fabulous One Hundred Years of the IOC*, 113–114.

52. "China and the Olympics," editorial, *NYT*, May 30, 1959.

53. Wm. de Bary to Brundage, June 8, 1959, ABC, box 121, reel 67.

54. 86th Cong., 1st sess., H. Cong. Res. 191, June 2, 1959.

55. Guttmann, *The Games Must Go On*, 149.

56. See his letter dated July 31, 1959, in IOC Archives, République Populaire de Chine, juridique, 1947–1975, folder protestations/soutiens: 1956–1966.

57. IOC Archives, Minutes of the Fifty-seventh IOC Session, 7.

58. For details, see Zhang Qixiong, "1960 nian qianhou zhong hua min guo dui guo ji ao wei hui de hui ji ming cheng zhi zheng," 140–141.

59. Brundage and Mayer to the president of Taiwan's Olympic Committee, August 29, 1960, IOC Archives, République Populaire de Chine, juridique, 1947–1975, folder Taiwan: 1951–1964.

60. For a detailed study of Taiwan's official discussions and responses to the name issue around the Rome Olympic Games, see Zhang Qixiong, "1960 nian qianhou zhong hua min guo dui guo ji ao wui hui de hui ji ming cheng zhi zheng," 103–153.

61. Guoshi guan, Waijiaobu files, cases of Tokyo Olympic Games, 172-4/0135-4.
62. Ibid.
63. Brundage informed Taiwan on October 24, 1968, that per a decision made at the IOC's Mexico City session, "your Olympic committee will be named 'Republic of China Olympic' committee, and will be listed under China, R.O." effective November 1, 1968. This letter was dated and signed by Brundage. It is rather strange that Brundage's successor in 1978 "spoke of the document in Mr. Brundage's papers about how the IOC had recognized Taiwan as the Republic of China, however it had no date and was not signed, therefore, of questionable legality." (See IOC Archives, Minutes of the IOC executive board meeting in Athens, May 13, 14, 16, and 18, 1978, 28.) Perhaps Killanin was only trying to cover up the embarrassing mess that his predecessor had left behind at the IOC. For details on Taiwan's name issue, see Guoshi guan, ed., *Xu heng xian sheng fang tan lu* (The reminiscences of Xu Heng) (Taipei: Guoshi guan, 1998), 49–87. See also Brundage to Yang Sen, October 24, 1968, IOC Archives, République Populaire de Chine, reconnaissance, 1968–1979, demande de reconnaissance, 1968.
64. Even Hong Kong complained to the IOC about Taiwan. In a letter to Taiwan's Olympic committee dated September 9, 1966, Brundage wrote that the IOC had received many serious complaints from the Amateur Sports Federation and Olympic Committee of Hong Kong "against the practice of your national federations in enlisting by one method or another Chinese living in Hong Kong on their athletic teams." One of the complaints from Hong Kong was that Taiwan, which had more than twice the population of Hong Kong, should be able to put up teams of their own. "If they are not able to stand on their own two feet, they should have the courage to withdraw from international competitions. The situation is most unsatisfactory. . . . I think this policy makes a mockery of the International Olympic Committee and its rules." Brundage agreed, warning that this practice was counter to both the spirit and letter of the Olympic movement and "we think that you should take steps immediately to prevent such violations of Olympic rules by your constituent federations." See IOC Archives, République Populaire de Chine, reconnaissance, 1968–1979, demande de reconnaissance, 1968.
65. For an inside account of Xu Heng's election as an IOC member, see Killanin and Rodda, *My Olympic Years*, 112.
66. Guoshi guan, special group for international sports question cases, 172-3/4141.
67. IOC Archives, Minutes of the Seventy-sixth IOC Session, Lausanne, May 21–23, 1975, 54–56.
68. Xu Heng, an IOC member in Taiwan from 1970 to 1987, had intimate knowledge about Taiwan's negotiations with the IOC regarding its name

and status in the organization. See *Xu heng xian sheng fang tan lu,* 49–87, 183–249.

69. Brundage draft memoir.

70. J. Sigfrid Edström letter (no recipient's name, presumed to be addressed to the IOC members in China), May 30, 1951, IOC Archives, République Populaire de Chine, correspondence, 1924–1958.

71. Kong Xiangxi to Otto Mayer, May 16, 1952, IOC Archives, République Populaire de Chine, histoire, 1952–1986. Both Wang and Kong were high officials of the Nationalist government and had political reasons to support Taiwan's claims. Moreover, although both were IOC members, they had not been actively involved in IOC business for a long time.

72. J. Sigfrid Edström to Otto Mayer, March 24, 1952, IOC Archives, République Populaire de Chine, correspondence, 1924–1958.

73. Frenckell to Edström, June 19, 1952, IOC Archives, République Populaire de Chine, juridique 1947–1975, Helsinki 1952, Rome 1960.

74. Brundage to Edström, June 2, 1952, IOC Archives, République Populaire de Chine, correspondence, 1924–1958.

75. Ibid.

76. "Account of Exchange of Telegram between the President of the International Olympic Committee, J. Edström, and the All China Athletic Federation, Peking," IOC Archives, République Populaire de Chine, histoire, 1952–1986.

77. Brundage to Edström, July 3, 1952, IOC Archives, République Populaire de Chine, correspondence, 1924–1958.

78. Edström to Mayer, June 16, 1952, IOC Archives, République Populaire de Chine, juridique, 1947–1975/Helsinki 1952, Rome 1960.

79. Frenckell to Edström, June 19, 1952.

80. IOC Archives, Minutes of the Forty-seventh IOC Session, Helsinki, July 16–27, 1952.

81. Guttmann, *The Games Must Go On,* 208.

82. Japan eventually gave up its 1940 Tokyo Games. For details on this point, see Sandra Collins, "'Samurai' Politics" and "Conflicts of 1930s Japanese Olympic Diplomacy in Universalizing the Olympic Movement."

83. N.a., "Civilization May Be Saved by Athletes, by Brundage, American Olympic Committee," n.d. (possibly around 1938), ABC, box 249, reel 144.

84. Avery Brundage, "The Future of the Olympic Games," ABC, box 249, reel 144.

85. Christopher Young, "Munich 1972, Representing the Nation," in Tomlinson and Young, *National Identity and Global Sports Events,* 120–121.

86. Brundage draft memoir.

87. Minutes of the IOC executive board meeting, October 23–25, 1979, Nagoya, Japan.

88. Killanin to R. S. Alexander, June 13, 1979, IOC Archives, République Populaire de Chine, correspondence, June–July 1979.
89. IOC Archives, République Populaire de Chine, juridique, 1947–1975, folder Peking: 1952–1958.
90. IOC executive board, press file, The China Question, March 10–11, 1979, IOC Archives, Chinese Taipei, correspondence, 1979. Killanin used the wrong name even in his memoir; see Killanin and Rodda, *My Olympic Years,* 110.
91. In his memoir, Killanin still called him "Shou Yi-Tung." See Killanin and Rodda, *My Olympic Years,* 108–110.
92. The IOC was hardly alone in its ignorance. Many American politicians made even worse mistakes. One example suffices here. When Congressman Silvio O. Conte, a Republican from Massachusetts, introduced a Congressional resolution expressing U.S. support and encouragement for the goals and ideals of international Olympic competition, he made several factual mistakes in his references to China. He mentioned that the People's Republic of China did not participate in the 1952 Olympic Games although it did, and he further claimed that "in 1976, Taiwan did not participate in the Games because the Republic of China participated." This assertion pulls together two serious misunderstandings: First, Taiwan's official name *was* the Republic of China; second, it was Beijing that did not take part in the 1976 Games and Taiwan by its own initiative chose to withdraw from the Games. (98th Cong., 1st sess., H. Res. 366, in LA Sports Library, Amateur Athletic Association, Paul Ziffren collection, roll 3.) These errors of fact suggested not only that members of Congress did not know what they were talking about, but also that they were too lazy or arrogant to check their facts. For some background on the issue, see Killanin and Rodda, *My Olympic Years,* 134.
93. See Samaranch's letter dated November 12, 1981, to Zhong Shitong, IOC Archives, République Populaire de Chine, correspondence, 1981.
94. See Monique Berlioux to He Zhenliang, November 12, 1981, IOC Archives, République Populaire de Chine, correspondence, 1981.
95. In his memoir, Wu reiterated the story and included the copy of his pledge card with Samaranch's corrections. On the pledge card, the country's name is listed as "Chinese Taipei." At the last minute, Samaranch deleted the name and allowed him not to mention his country's name during the pledge ceremony. See Wu Jingguo, *Ao lin pi ke zhong hua qing,* 50–54; Wu Jingguo, *Ao yun chang wai de jing ji,* 33–35.
96. "Address by Avery Brundage," Mexico City, October 1968, ABC, box 249, reel 144.
97. Alex Frere, "China, in a Quiet Way, Makes Olympic Gains," *International Herald Tribune,* May 8, 1974.

98. Miller, *Olympic Revolution,* 174.

99. Killanin, *My Olympic Years,* 108–111.

100. Liang Lijuan, *He Zhenliang,* 71.

101. ABC, box 58, reel 34.

102. Liang Lijuan, *He Zhenliang,* 71–79.

103. Zhao Zhenghong to Killanin, April 9, 1975. IOC Archives, République Populaire de Chine, correspondence, January–June, 1975.

104. Report by M. Kiyokawa at the IOC sessions at Athens on May 20, 1978, in IOC Archives, République Populaire de Chine, correspondence, 1978. Killanin later visited Taiwan as well. See the memo on the meeting between the IOC president and the prime minister of Taipei, October 19, 1979, in IOC Archives, République Populaire de Chine, juridique, Comités Nationaux Olympiques, 1979–1980.

105. For the transcript of Lu's talks with Killanin, see Confidential report on visit of Killanin to the PRC, IOC Archives, République Populaire de Chine, correspondence, 1977.

106. IOC Archives, Minutes of the Eightieth Session of the IOC, Athens, May 17–20, 1978, 41.

107. Ibid., 112–113.

108. Ibid.

109. Ibid., 52.

110. Ibid., 42.

111. IOC Archives, Minutes of the Eighty-first IOC Session, Montevideo, April 5–7, 1979.

112. Confidential letter to Killanin from Siperco, October 24, 1978, IOC Archives, Chinese Taipei, correspondence, 1978.

113. IOC Archives, Minutes of the IOC executive board, Lausanne, March 9–10, 1979.

114. IOC Archives, Minutes of the Eighty-first IOC session.

115. Ibid.

116. IOC Archives, Minutes of the IOC executive board meeting, Nagoya, Japan, October 23–25, 1979.

117. Even the name issue was not quite solved legally for the IOC since Xu Heng filed a lawsuit against the IOC; see Guoshi guan, *Xu heng xian sheng fang tan lu,* 69–85.

118. For details, see Henry Hsu to Killanin, December 11, 1979, IOC Archives, République Populaire de Chine, correspondence, September–December 1979; Henry Hsu to the IOC members, 1980, IOC Archives, Chinese Taipei, correspondence, 1980.

119. Gosper with Korporaal, *An Olympic Life,* 191.

120. Zhong gong zhong yang wen xian yan jiu shi, *Deng Xiaoping nianpu,* 1:167.

121. He zhenliang, "Quanmian zouxiang shijie," in Guo jia tiyu zheng ce fa gui shi, *Zhonghua titan si shi chun*, 32–33.
122. Liang Lijuan, *He Zhenliang*, 226–229. See also Wu Shaozu, *Zhong hua renmin gong he guo tiyu shi*, 253.
123. Wu Jingguo, *Ao lin pi ke zhong hua qing*, 65, 205–206; Wu Jingguo, *Ao yun chang wai de jing ji*, 97–105. Although it allowed Taiwan to use "Zhong hua Tai Bei," Beijing itself uses "Zhong guo tai bei" in its own media. Song Shixiong remembered that he always marked Zhong guo Tai Bei clearly to make sure he got it right. As he explained, although the difference between "Zhong hua Tai Bei" and "Zhong guo Tai Bei" was only one character, it involved a "major principal question" and "cannot be confused." See *Song Shixiong zi shu*, 208.
124. Pound, *Five Rings over Korea*, 42.
125. IOC Archives, Minutes of the IOC executive board meeting, Lausanne, September 3–6, 1997.

5. The Sport of Ping-Pong Diplomacy

Epigraph: Wu Shaozu, *Zhong hua ren min gong he guo tiyu shi*, 243.

1. Xu Tao, "Mao Zedong de bao jian yang sheng zhi dao" (Mao's way of being healthy), in Lin Ke, Xu Tao, and Wu Xujun, *Li shi de zhen shi*, 256–276.
2. Zhuang Zedong, *Zhuang Zedong yu zuo zuo mu dun zi*, 258.
3. Liu Shufa, *Chen Yi nianpu*, 2:695.
4. Zhong gong zhong yang wen xian yan jiu shi, *Zhou Enlai nianpu, 1949–1976*, 2:584.
5. Ibid., 2:541.
6. Song Shixiong, *Song Shixiong zi shu*, 216.
7. Ibid., 217. See also Zhong gong zhong yang wen xian yan jiu shi, *Zhou Enlai nianpu, 1949–1976*, 3:386.
8. Song Shixiong, *Song Shixiong zi shu*, 218.
9. Ibid., 206–207.
10. Nixon, "Asia after Vietnam," *Foreign Affairs* 46, no. 1 (October 1967).
11. "Memorandum from President Nixon to his assistant for national security affairs, February 1, 1969," in *FRUS, 1969–1976: China, 1969–1972*, vol. 17 (2006) (hereafter *FRUS*, vol. 17), 7; see also Nixon, *RN: The Memoirs of Richard Nixon*, 545.
12. Mann, *About Face*, 14.
13. Kissinger, *White House Years*, 176–177.
14. Mann, *About Face*, 25

15. Memorandum from Kissinger to Nixon, February 5, 1970, *FRUS,* vol. 17, 176–178.

16. Kissinger memo to the president, subject: contact with the Chinese, September 12, 1970, National Security Archives, "China and the United States: From Hostility to Engagement, 1960–1998" (hereafter NSA: China and the U.S.).

17. Memorandum of conversation on meeting between the president and Pakistan President Yahya, October 25, 1970, the Oval Office, NSA: China and the U.S.

18. Memorandum of conversation between Kissinger and Ceaușescu, October 27, 1970, NSA: China and the U.S.

19. Nixon, *Memoirs,* 546.

20. Stoessel, memorandum of conversation with Nixon concerning China and U.S.-China contacts, September 9, 1969, *FRUS,* vol. 17, 80–81.

21. Minutes of meeting no. 135, January 20, 1970, National Archives, RG 59, box 2189.

22. State Department confidential telegram, subject: dropping passport restriction on travel to communist China, National Archives, RG 59: general records of the Department of State, subject: numeric files, 1970–1973/entry 1613, box 2188.

23. For a recent study on Sino-American rapprochement from Chinese domestic political perspectives, see Yafeng Xia, "China's Elite Politics and Sino-American Rapprochement, January 1969–February 1972," *Journal of Cold War Studies* 8, no. 4 (Fall 2006): 3–28.

24. Kissinger, *White House Years,* 178–186.

25. Joseph Y. S. Cheng, "Mao Zedong's Perception of the World in 1968–1972: Rationale for the Sino-American Rapprochement," *Journal of American–East Asian Relations* 7, nos. 3–4 (Fall–Winter 1998): 251.

26. Mann, *About Face,* 16.

27. For example, the book on ping-pong diplomacy by Qian Jiang opened with the story of border clashes between China and Russia. See Qian Jiang, *Xiao qiu zhuan dong da qiu.* Western scholars seem to agree with this idea, but I believe it is only partially correct. Mao's realization that it might be time to cut a deal with Nixon on Taiwan was also a major motivation for pursuing Sino-American rapprochement, and may have been an even more important factor. Although Kissinger wrote in his *White House Memoir* (749) and other places that Taiwan was mentioned only briefly during his first meeting with Zhou on his historical July 1971 trip to China, this characterization doesn't fit with transcriptions of what was happening in the meeting. Indeed, Taiwan played an extremely important role in Beijing's negotiations with the United States during the early 1970s. In every message to the White House, Beijing

conveyed the importance of the Taiwan issue for improving overall Sino-American relations.

28. See Kissinger, *White House Years*, 167–194.

29. Wu Xujun, "Mao Zedong de wu bu gao qi," 249. Gao Wenqian mentioned the Russia factor in Mao's thinking as well. See his *Wan nian Zhou Enlai*, 413.

30. Gong Li, *Mao Zedong yu Meiguo*, 195.

31. The best piece on the four marshals' study of Sino-American relations is Xiong Xianghui, *Wo de qing bao yu wai jiao sheng ya*, 170–201. See also Du Yi, *Da xue ya qing song*, 208–212; and Zhong gong zhong yang wen xian yan jiu shi, *Zhou Enlai nianpu, 1949–1976*, 3:301–302, 305.

32. Zhong gong zhong yang wen xian yan jiu shi, *Zhou Enlai nianpu, 1949–1976*, 3:341.

33. For some inside information on Snow's visit, see Xiong Xianghui, *Wo de qing bao yu wai jiao sheng ya*, 202–235.

34. Wu Xujun, "Mao Zedong de wu bu gao qi," 231.

35. Ibid., 238.

36. See Kissinger, *Diplomacy*, 725–726; and Kissinger, *White House Years*, 698. During the White House background briefing, Kissinger said: "Edgar Snow played no role, except that he conveyed in his article in life [*sic*] which is the only thing we saw, a general attitude which we had received already in other ways and it simply confirmed a general attitude which we had already become aware of." See Nixon Project, Haldeman, box 82: Kissinger background briefing at the White House, July 16, 1971.

37. Kissinger, *White House Years*, 699.

38. The story was true and is confirmed in several places. See Tian Zengpei and Wang Taiping, *Lao waijiao guan huiyi Zhou Enlai*, 298; Gao Wenqian, *Wan nian Zhou Enlai*, 403; and Kong Dongmei, *Gai bian shi jie de ri zi*, 48–49.

39. Kissinger memo to Nixon on Mao's statement on U.S. action in Cambodia, May 23, 1970, *FRUS*, vol. 17, 212–213.

40. Kissinger, *White House Years*, 695.

41. Mann, *About Face*, 19.

42. Kissinger, *Diplomacy*, 725.

43. Kissinger, *White House Years*, 685.

44. Dale Russakoff, "Team Rice, Playing Away," *Washington Post*, February 6, 2005, D1; Mandell, *Sport*, 233.

45. Haldeman, *Haldeman Diaries*, 110.

46. Mandell, *Sport*, 233.

47. Zhong gong zhong yang wen xian yan jiu shi, *Zhou Enlai nianpu, 1949–1976*, 3:431.

48. Ibid., 3:435, 442; Lu Guang, *Zhong guo ti tan da ju jiao*, 136–137.

49. Qian Jiang, *Xiao qiu zhuan dong da qiu,* 127–128.

50. Jenkins memo, National Archives, RG 59: general records of the Department of State, subject numeric files, 1970–1973, entry 1613, box 2187.

51. Zhou's complete letter to Mao and Mao's comment can be found in Lu Guang, *Zhong guo ti tan da ju jiao,* 139–141. See also Zhong gong zhong yang wen xian yan jiu shi, *Zhou Enlai nianpu, 1949–1976,* 3:443–444.

52. Lu Guang, *Zhong guo ti tan da ju jiao,* 142–143.

53. Ibid., 146.

54. Bentley Library, J. Rufford Harrison files, box 19/original.

55. Bentley Library, Steenhoven materials, box 19.

56. Transcript of CCTV interview with Zhuang Zedong: "Zhuang Zedong: Qin li ping pang wai jiao," April 18, 2006, *Xinwen huike ting* program.

57. Kissinger, *White House Years,* 709. Kissinger's account was based on a UPI story by Arnold Dibble published on July 16, 1971.

58. Mao had serious vision problems then and relied on his assistants to read materials for him. See Wu Xujun, "Mao Zedong de wu bu gao qi," 240.

59. National sport commission and foreign ministry, "Report on the Requests of Ping-Pong Teams from Columbia, Jamaica, and the United States to visit China and Request of American Journalists to Interview our Ping-Pong team," April 3, 1971, secret, PRC Foreign Ministry archives.

60. The story of Mao's invitation via Wu can be found in Wu Xujun, "Mao Zedong de wu bu gao qi," 245–247. See also Zhong gong zhong yang wen xian yan jiu shi, *Zhou Enlai nianpu, 1949–1976,* 3:449.

61. For details on Mao's role, see Zhou Yihuang, "Mao Zedong behind the Sino-American Ping Pong Diplomacy," *Renmin Ribao,* December 19, 2003, 15.

62. Fifteen-year-old team player Judy Bochenski, for example, had to borrow nine hundred dollars from a bank to finance her trip to Japan.

63. Bentley Library, J. Rufford Harrison files, box 19/original.

64. Official report, n.d., PRC Foreign Ministry archives.

65. Kissinger, *White House Years,* 709–710.

66. Department of State memorandum for Henry Kissinger, December 22, 1971, Nixon Project, White House special files, staff member and office files, Dwight Chapin, box 31, folder China—general information.

67. Zhou Enlai office phone record on the issue of whether to show Americans the Red detachment of women, 8:30 PM, April 10, 1971 (the original record was mistakenly dated March 10; April 10 is correct), PRC Foreign Ministry archives.

68. Department of State memorandum for Henry Kissinger, December 22, 1971, Nixon Project, White House special files, staff member and office files, Dwight Chapin, box 31, folder China—general information.

69. See the official schedule for the American Ping-Pong team's visit, which can be found in the PRC Foreign Ministry archives.

70. Song Shixiong, *Song Shixiong zi shu,* 223.

71. Bentley Library, Tim Boggan files, box 1: "Ping-Pong Oddity by Tim Boggan," unpublished manuscript, 76. Boggan was an assistant professor of English at Long Island University, vice president of the USTTA, and a member of the famed American Ping-Pong team that visited China in 1971.

72. Bruce Weber, "Ping-Pong Diplomacy Revisited," *NYT,* July 26, 1997.

73. Kissinger, *White House Years,* 710. See also "Tong meiguo pingpang qiu daibiaotuan de tanhua" (Conversations with the American Ping-Pong team), in PRC Foreign Ministry archives; and Zhong gong zhong yang wen xian yan jiu shi, *Zhou Enlai waijiao wenxian,* 469–475.

74. "Foreign Ministry's Note to Friendly Countries' Embassies in China about the Visit of the American Table Tennis Team to China," n.d., PRC Foreign Ministry archives.

75. "Foreign Ministry's Report about Cowan's Mother's Plan to Send Premier Zhou Flowers and Message," April 23, 1971, PRC Foreign Ministry archives.

76. Bentley Library, Boggan files, box 1: "Ping-Pong Oddity," 63.

77. See Judy Bochenski's account after her return from the 1971 trip to China in Bentley Library, USTTA-Kaminsky, 1972, box 3.

78. Bentley Library, Boggan files, box 1: "Ping-Pong Oddity," 239–240.

79. Ibid., 251.

80. Memorandum from Holdridge to Kissinger, on possible significance of PRC invitation to U.S. table tennis team to visit China, April 9, 1971, *FRUS,* vol. 17, 289–290.

81. For the most recent materials from China about the era of ping-pong diplomacy, see Xiong Xianghui, *Wo de qing bao yu wai jiao sheng ya,* 236–259.

82. Nixon Project, Haldeman files, box 77: Statement of Senator Edward W. Brooke on the floor of the Senate, April 15, 1971.

83. Confidential telegram from American embassy in Canberra to Department of State, April 1971, National Archives, RG 59: general records of the Department of State, subject numeric files, 1970–1973, entry 1613, box 2188.

84. Department of State, memorandum of conversation, April 20, 1971, National Archives, RG 59: general records of the Department of State, subject numeric files, 1970–1973, entry 1613, box 2678.

85. Kissinger, *White House Years,* 709–710.

86. Nixon, *Memoirs,* 548.

87. Kissinger, *White House Years,* 711.

88. Ibid., 710.

89. Ibid.

90. Haldeman, *Haldeman Diaries,* 271.

91. Nixon Project, Haldeman files, box 43, Haldeman handwritten notes, April–June 1971.

92. Phone conversations between Nixon and Kissinger, April 27, 1971, NSA: China and the U.S. See also *FRUS*, vol. 17, 303–308.

93. Nixon Project, Haldeman files, box 43, Haldeman handwritten notes, April–June 1971.

94. Haldeman, *Haldeman Diaries*, 271.

95. Ibid., 283.

96. Nixon, *Memoirs*, 549.

97. Haldeman, *Haldeman Diaries*, 275.

98. Ibid.

99. John Scali to Dwight Chapin, April 12, 1971, Nixon Project, White House central files, subject files: P.R. China, box 19, PRC 1/1/71–5/31/71.

100. Haldeman, *Haldeman Diaries*, 273–274.

101. Nixon Project, Haldeman files, box 77, file Kissinger, April 1971: Kissinger memo to the president April 20, 1971, subject: meeting with Graham Barclay Steenhoven, head of the U.S. table tennis team recently in China, April 21, 1971.

102. At the time, membership dues were ten dollars a year. Later, when the U.S. table tennis officials wanted to attempt a version of ping-pong diplomacy with other countries, they tried to solicit Nixon's help by reminding him that he was an honorary member of the USTTA. In his telegram to Nixon (no date can be seen on the document), Tim Boggan asked the president to support a plan for the American Ping-Pong team to visit the USSR, reminding Nixon that he was "the only honorary lifetime member of the United States table tennis association." See Bentley Library, USTTA-Kaminsky, 1972 files [Yaroslav Kaminsky was the Washington, D.C., coordinator for the Chinese Ping-Pong visit in 1972], box 3.

103. The White House press conference of Graham Steenhoven, April 21, 1971, transcript, Nixon Project, Scali files, box 3.

104. National security study memorandum 124, April 19, 1971, NSA: China and the U.S.

105. Statement by the president, the White House, April 14, 1971, NSA: China and the U.S.

106. The president's remarks at a question and answer session with a panel of six editors and reporters at the society's annual convention, April 16, 1971, NSA: China and the U.S.

107. Kissinger, *White House Years*, 711.

108. Zhou's message did not reach the White House until April 27, 1971; see "Message from Premier Chou En Lai dated April 21, 1971," NSA: China and the U.S.; and Nixon, *RN: The Memoirs of Richard Nixon*, 549.

109. Haldeman, *Haldeman Diaries*, 283.

110. The complete message from Nixon to Zhou, which Kissinger handed to Hilaly

on May 10, 1971, can be found in the National Security Archives and *FRUS,* vol. 17, 300–301, 312–313, 318–320.

111. Handwritten message from Premier Zhou Enlai to President Nixon, May 29, 1971, NSA: China and the U.S.

112. Nixon, *RN: The Memoirs of Richard Nixon,* 552.

113. Message for the government of the People's Republic of China, June 4, 1971 (there was a handwritten note on it indicating the message was the fifth draft and that it was handed to Hilaly at 5:30 on that date), NSA. See also *FRUS,* vol. 17, 340.

114. Zhou Enlai to Nixon, June 11, 1971, NSA: China and the U.S.

115. Handwritten letter to Kissinger from ambassador of Pakistan, June 19, 1971, NSA: China and the U.S.

116. Memorandum of conversation between Kissinger and Zhou, July 9, 1971, *FRUS,* vol. 17, 364.

117. Minutes of Mao's meeting with Nixon, February 21, 1971, NSA: China and U.S. See also *FRUS,* vol. 17, 681–682.

118. Nixon Project, White House special files staff member and office files, Alexander Haig files, 1970–1973, box 49.

119. Proceedings and Debates (June 9, 1971), "The So-Called New Era of Ping-Pong Diplomacy," 92d Cong., 1st sess., *Congressional Record* 1, vol. 117, pt. 14, 18994.

120. Nixon did not want to be criticized for betraying Taiwan. See Nixon Project, White House special files, staff member and office files, Haldeman files, box 85: memo from Pat Buchanan to Haldeman, October 11, 1971. In the memo, Buchanan quoted a leading Republican conservative who had said in private, "I can swallow the Peking visit," "but expulsion of Taiwan would be my Rubicon."

121. Bentley Library, Steenhoven files, box 20, State Department press briefing.

122. Bentley Library, Boggan files, box 1: "Ping-Pong Oddity," 65–66.

123. The cable can found in Bentley Library, Steenhoven files, box 20.

124. Bentley Library, Eckstein papers, box 4.

125. Bentley Library, Eckstein papers, box 3: exchange with the PRC, athletic exchanges, table tennis.

126. Bentley Library, Harrison files, box 19.

127. Bentley Library, Eckstein papers, box 3: exchange with the PRC, athletic exchanges, table tennis.

128. Bentley Library, USTTA, Kaminsky 1972 files, box 3.

129. John Holdridge to Kissinger, November 19, 1971, Nixon Project, Scali files, box 3.

130. Nixon Project, Chapin box 32, minutes of China meetings.

131. Bentley Library, Steenhoven files, box 20.

132. Ibid.

133. Zhou Enlai seemed to be delighted about the visit. After the Ping-Pong team returned from touring the United States and other countries in the spring of 1972, he invited the team members to his house for dinner. See Zhong gong zhong yang wen xian yan jiu shi, *Zhou Enlai nianpu, 1949–1976*, 3:515–516; and Li Lingxiu and Zhou Minggong, *Tiyu zhi zi Rong Gaotang*, 326–328.

134. Bentley Library, USTTA Kaminsky 1972 files, box 3, meeting minutes.

135. Bentley Library, J. Rufford Harrison files, box 19, original interview transcript.

136. John Scali to John Dean, May 19, 1971, Nixon Project, Scali files, box 3.

137. Memo for China file, April 22, 1971, Nixon Project, Scali files, box 3.

138. Scali, telephone conversation with the president, 3:00 PM, April 21, 1971, Nixon Project, Scali files, box 3.

139. John Scali to John Holdridge, July 23, 1971, Nixon Project, Scali files, box 3.

140. Memo for the President from John Scali, subject: Chinese table tennis visit, January 17, 1972, Nixon Project, White House special files, staff member and office files, Ronald Ziegler, box 35: trip story material—China.

141. Memo to Scali from Bruce Kehrli, January 24, 1972, in ibid.

142. Scali to Kissinger, March 14, 1972, Nixon Project, Scali files, box 3.

143. Scali to Haig, March 20, 1972, Nixon Project, Scali files, box 3.

144. White House memo, March 27, 1972, subject: table tennis visit, Nixon Project, Scali files, box 3.

145. W. Dewey Clower memo to Dwight L. Chapin, April 8, 1972, Nixon Project, White House central files, subject files, P.R. China, box 19.

146. The letter pointed out that the government liaison person "should not be so highly placed as to require a protocol position in ceremonial functions or command high public visibility." See Robert W. Gilmore (chairman of joint committee) to Scali, April 5, 1972, Nixon Project, Scali files, box 3.

147. Transcript of Scali conversation with Professor Eckstein, April 6, 1972, Nixon Project, Scali files, box 3.

148. Nixon Project, Scali files, box 3.

149. Nixon to Steenhoven, April 11, 1972, in ibid.

150. Memorandum of conversation between Huang Hua [PRC Ambassador to the UN] and Kissinger, New York, April 12, 1972, *FRUS*, vol. 17, 884.

151. Bentley Library, Steenhoven files, box 20: McIntyre files.

152. White House memo, February 14, 1972, Nixon Project, Scali files, box 3.

153. Stanley Karnow, "China Ping-Pong Team Starts U.S. Tour Soon," *Washington Post*, April 4, 1972, A2.

154. John Scali, memorandum for the president, April 17, 1972: subject: progress report on the U.S. tour of the Chinese table tennis team, Nixon Project, Scali files, box 3.

155. Memo from Butterfield to Haldeman, March 28, 1972, Nixon Project, Haldeman files, box 93, Alex Butterfield, March 1972.

156. Ibid.

157. Butterfield to Kissinger, March 31, 1972, Nixon Project, Scali files, box 3.

158. Scali to Haig, April 3, 1972, Nixon Project, Scali files, box 3.

159. Scali to General Haig, April 4, 1972, subject: protection for Chinese ping pong team, Nixon Project, Scali files, box 3.

160. Scali to Bruce Kehrli, April 10, 1972 subject: Chinese table tennis team. Nixon Project, Scali files, box 3.

161. Haldeman to David Parker, April 11, 1972, Nixon Project, White House central files, subject files, P.R. China, box 19.

162. In an interview with the University of Michigan's oral history project, Steenhoven said when the U.S. team was in China, he asked if the team could see Zhou Enlai, but "to my knowledge, and, I'm pretty sure, no Chinese asked to see President Nixon. In my discussions with Nixon, he had indicated that if possible he would like to meet them." Bentley Library, Steenhoven files, box 19.

163. Dwight Chapin to Stephen Bull, David Parker, and Ronald Walker, subject: PRC ping pong visit, March 20, 1972, Nixon Project, Scali files, box 3.

164. John Scali to Dave Parker, April 3, 1972, subject: Chinese table tennis visit to the White House, Nixon Project, Scali files, box 3.

165. Scali to David Parker, April 10, 1972, subject: president's meeting with Chinese table tennis delegation, Nixon Project, Scali files, box 3.

166. Memo from Stephen Bull to Haldeman, re: greeting PRC table tennis team, April 17, 1972, Nixon Project, Haldeman files, box 94: Ronald Ziegler, March 1972.

167. Bentley Library, Eckstein files, box 4: National Committee, ping-pong, miscellanies.

168. Scali to Kissinger, April 17, 1972, subject: Chinese ping pong tours, Nixon Project, Scali files, box 3.

169. Zhong gong zhong yang wen xian yan jiu shi, *Zhou Enlai nianpu, 1949–1976*, 3:520.

170. John Scali, memorandum for the president, April 17, 1972, subject: progress report on the U.S. tour of the Chinese table tennis team, Nixon Project, Scali files, box 3.

171. Scali to William Rogers, May 2, 1972, Nixon Project, Scali files, box 3.

172. Anthony J. Shaheen to Harrison, August 13, 1979, Bentley Library, Harrison files, box 19.

173. Butterfield to Kissinger, April 17, 1972, Nixon Project, Scali files, box 3.

174. Memo from Jeanne Davis of the president's office to Theodore Eliot, Department of State, June 10, 1972, Nixon Project, Scali files, box 3.

175. Scali to Butterfield, August 1, 1972. Nixon Project, Scali files, box 3.

176. Bruce Kehrli to Scali, August 4, 1972, Nixon Project, Scali files, box 3.

177. Scali to Schoyer, August 7, 1972, Nixon Project, Scali files, box 3.

178. B. Preston Schoyer [executive director of the national committee] to Scali, September 11, 1972, Nixon Project, Scali files, box 3.

179. "Tennis Diplomacy between China and South Korea," *Christian Science Monitor*, March 5, 1984.

180. Christopher Wren, "China's Quiet Courtship of South Korea," *NYT*, March 11, 1984, A5.

6. THE MONTREAL GAMES

Epigraph: "Olympics and Taiwan," Canada Archives, RG 25, vol. 3062, file 103.

1. Sharp letter to Brundage, November 28, 1969, IOC Archives, Affaires politiques aux jeux Olympique d'Eté de Montreal 1976: correspondence, rapports, etc., SD5 rapport de James Worrall.

2. Draft memo from Allan MacEachen to prime minister, "Taiwanese Participation in the Montreal Olympic Games," December 12, 1974, Canada Archives, RG 25, vol. 3056, file 36, pt. 2.

3. In February 1969, when Canada and the PRC met in Stockholm to begin negotiating for diplomatic relations, Arthur Andrew, then Canadian ambassador to Sweden, was the chief Canadian negotiator. He commented later that from the very beginning, the Chinese conditions for diplomatic relations with Canada were completely focused on the one-China issue; the Chinese insisted that Canada break off its diplomatic relations with Taiwan and recognize Beijing as the sole legal government of China. For many months, Andrew was lectured on these conditions from his Beijing counterparts and Canada kept reiterating its position. Eventually Andrew suggested that the negotiations be adjourned until both sides had something new to discuss. Before the Chinese demurred, they asked him one more time whether he now understood Beijing's Taiwan position. Andrew's reply: "I would be deaf if I didn't." Canada eventually accepted Beijing's position on Taiwan. For details on the negotiations, see Mitchell Sharp, *Which Reminds Me . . . A Memoir* (Toronto: University of Toronto Press, 1994), 203–207.

4. Confidential memo for minister, "The Problem of Participation of the 'Republic of China' and the People's Republic of China in the 1976 Olympic Games," April 20, 1976, Canada Archives, RG 25, vol. 3056, file 36, pt. 2.

5. Chinese Canadian embassy to External Affairs Department, May 17, 1976, Canada Archives, RG 25, vol. 3056, file 36, pt. 3.

6. External Affairs to Canadian Beijing embassy, June 14, 1976, Canada Archives, RG 25, vol. 3056, file 36, pt. 3.

7. Beesley confidential telegram to External Affairs, February 9, 1976, Canada Archives, RG 25, vol. 3056, file 36, pt. 1.

8. External Affairs department, confidential telegram to Beesley, February 16, 1976, Canada Archives, RG 25, vol. 3056, file 36, pt. 2.

9. Telegram to External Affairs, November 26, 1975, Canada Archives, RG 25, vol. 3059, file 53.

10. "The Tarnished Olympic Games," *Wall Street Journal,* July 13, 1976, A16.

11. Steve Cady, "Taiwan Seems Loser in Olympics Dispute," *NYT,* July 12, 1976.

12. For details, see Donald Macintosh and Michael Haws, *Sport and Canadian Diplomacy* (Montreal: McGill-Queen's University Press, 1994).

13. Draft memo from Allan MacEachen to prime minister, "Taiwanese Participation in the Montreal Olympic Games."

14. Ibid.

15. D. Molgat confidential memo, "Your Meeting with Lord Killanin: The China/Taiwan question," July 16, 1975, Canada Archives, RG 25, vol. 3056, file 36, pt. 2.

16. Arthur Andrew confidential memo, "Olympic Games 1976: Meeting in Toronto, April 23, 1975 with Lord Killanin," May 2, 1975, Canada Archives, RG 25, vol. 3062, file 105.

17. Ibid.

18. Ibid.

19. Beesley, confidential telegram to External Affairs, February 9, 1976.

20. James Worrall, confidential report to Killanin, "Olympic Games, Montreal 1976."

21. Confidential memo for minister, "The Problem of Participation of the 'Republic of China' and the People's Republic of China in the 1976 Olympic Games."

22. Kallanin to Masaji Kiyokawa, April 30, 1976, confidential, IOC Archives, République Populaire de Chine, correspondence, 1976.

23. Confidential memo for minister, "The Problem of Participation of the 'Republic of China' and the People's Republic of China in the 1976 Olympic Games."

24. Draft memo from Allan MacEachen to prime minister, "Taiwanese Participation in the Montreal Olympic Games."

25. Draft memo from M. Sharp to prime minister, May 21, 1976, Canada Archives, RG 25, vol. 3056, file 36, pt. 3.

26. External Affairs confidential memo, June 24, 1976, "Taiwan and Olympics," Canada Archives, RG 25, vol. 3056, file 36, pt. 1.

27. Mitchell Sharp to the IOC, May 28, 1976, Canada Archives, RG 25, box 3056, file 36, pt. 1.

28. Telex from Allan MacEachen to the IOC president, June 27, 1976, Canada Archives, RG 25, box 3056, file 36, pt. 1.

29. Draft letter to minister of manpower and immigration from Allan MacEachen, June 1976, Canada Archives, RG 25, box 3056, file 36, pt. 1.

30. External Affairs Department, confidential memo, June 24, 1976, "Taiwan and Olympics."

31. Background materials for secretary of state for External Affairs, Canada Archives, RG 25, box 3056, file 36, pt. 1.

32. Mary Janigan, "How the Taiwan Issue Erupted," *Toronto Star,* July 17, 1976.

33. Draft memo from Allan MacEachen to prime minister, "Taiwanese Participation in the Montreal Olympic Games."

34. D. Molgat confidential memo, "Your Meeting with Lord Killanin: the China/Taiwan question," July 16, 1975, Canada Archives, RG 25, vol. 3056, file 36, pt. 2.

35. External Affairs draft minute of the meeting with Killanin, June 30, 1976, confidential, July 2, 1976, Canada Archives, RG 25, vol. 3056, file 36, pt. 1.

36. IOC President to Sharp, June 8, 1976, and IOC: Affaires politiques aux jeux Olympique d'Eté de Montreal 1976, both in Canada Archives, RG 25, vol. 3056, file 36, pt. 1.

37. IOC to members of the IOC international federations, July 1, 1976, Canada Archives, RG 25, box 3056, file 36, pt. 1.

38. External Affairs draft minute of the meeting with Killanin, June 30, 1976, confidential, July 2, 1976, Canada Archives, RG 25, vol. 3056, file 36, pt. 1.

39. Ibid.

40. Killanin confidential memo to the IOC executive board, May 28, 1976, IOC Archives, Affaires politiques aux jeux Olympique d'Eté de Montreal 1976: correspondence, rapports, etc., SD5 rapport de James Worrall.

41. James Worrall, confidential report to Killanin, "Olympic Games, Montreal 1976: Commentary on Status of Republic of China Olympic Committee," Toronto, October 1, 1976. IOC Archives, Affaires politiques aux jeux Olympique d'Eté de Montreal 1976: correspondence, rapports, etc., SD5 rapport de James Worrall.

42. Ibid.

43. Killanin to Worrall, October 14, 1976, IOC Archives, Affaires politiques aux jeux Olympique d'Eté de Montreal 1976: correspondence, rapports, etc., SD5 rapport de James Worrall.

44. Killanin to IOC director, confidential, October 12, 1976, IOC Archives, République Populaire de Chine, histoire, 1952–1986.

45. Killanin, *My Olympic Years,* 133.

46. Arthur Andrew confidential memo, "Olympic Games 1976: Meeting in Toronto, April 23, 1975, with Lord Killanin," May 2, 1975, Canada Archives, RG 25, vol. 3062, file 105.

47. External Affairs department, confidential memo for the minister, "1976 Olympics: Meeting with Lord Killanin," May 2, 1975, Canada Archives, RG 25, vol. 3062, file 105.

48. Worrall, confidential report to Killanin, "Olympic Games, Montreal 1976."

49. Ibid.

50. External Affairs department, draft minute of the meeting with Killanin, June 30, 1976, confidential, July 2, 1976, Canada Archives, RG 25, vol. 3056, file 36, pt. 1.

51. Canadian embassy in Washington to Ottawa, confidential and Canadian eyes only, July 9, 1976, Canada Archives, RG 25, vol. 3056, file 36, pt. 3.

52. Minutes of meeting with Killanin, July 10, 1976, Canada Archives, RG 25, vol. 3056, file 36, pt. 3.

53. Canadian External Affairs department memo, "Olympics and Taiwan," Canada Archives, RG 25, vol. 3062, file 103.

54. Press conference of the secretary of state for External Affairs, July 5, 1976, Canada Archives, RG 25, box 3056, file 36, pt. 1.

55. Confidential minute of meeting with Killanin, July 10, 1976, Canada Archives, RG 25, vol. 3056, file 36, pt. 3.

56. IOC Archives, Minutes of the Seventy-eighth IOC Session, Montreal, July 13–17, 19, 1976.

57. Killanin reported that he had met the IOC member in Taiwan, Xu Heng, and the vice president of the Republic of China Olympic Committee in Munich on June 27, 1976, and informed them about the Canadian government's stance.

58. Ibid.

59. IOC Archives, Affaires politiques aux jeux Olympique d'Eté de Montreal 1976: correspondence, rapports, etc., SD4/communiqué de press et response, 2–7 July 1976.

60. Donald Macintosh and Michael Hawes, *Sport and Canadian Diplomacy* (Montreal: McGill-Queen's University Press, 1994), 37.

61. IOC Archives, Minutes of the Seventy-eighth IOC Session.

62. Taft to Trudeau, July 15, 1976, IOC Archives, Letters de protestation concernant la question des dux Chine aus jeux Olympiques d'Eté de Montreal, 1976.

63. "The Flickering Flame," *NYT* editorial, July 19, 1976.

64. McKinney confidential telegram to Ottawa, July 13, 1976, Canada Archives, RG 25, vol. 3056, file 36, pt. 3.

65. Ford Library: White House office of editorial staff Robert Orben, box 64/7/4/76, memo from Lynn May to Kim Cannon, July 2, 1976, subject: Summer Olympic Games in Montreal.

66. Ford Library: National security adviser, NSC Press and congressional liaison staff, files 1973–1976, box 5: press guidance, July 1–16, 1976.

67. Ford Library: State Department memo to the White House, "The Olympics: Chinese Representation Issue," White House central files, subject file box 5, 6/1/76–7/26/76.
68. Ibid.
69. Ibid.
70. Ibid.
71. Ibid.
72. See the second memo on the same topic, July 8, "Memorandum for Mr. Brent Scowcroft from George S. Springsteen," July 8, 1976, subject: Issue concerning the Olympics: participation by republic of China athletes, Ford Library: White House central files, subject file, box 5, 6/1/76–7/26/76.
73. Ford Library: Ron Nessen papers, 1974–1977, general subject files, box 17: Olympics.
74. Memo from Mike Duval to Dick Cheney, July 10, 1976, subject: Olympics. Ford Library: White House central files, subject file, box 5, 6/1/76–7/26/76.
75. Ford Library: National security adviser, NSC Press and congressional liaison staff, files 1973–1976, box 5: press guidance, July 1–16, 1976.
76. Ford Library: O'Donnell and Jenckes files 1974–1976, box 7: Olympic sport commission, 1974 (1), and Olympic sport commission 1975, statement by the President, June 19, 1975.
77. Ford Library: office of the editorial staff, reading copies of presidential speeches and statements, box 36.
78. Ford Library: White House central files, box 11: Canada 7/1/76–1/20/77, Dennis Cliff memo to Brent Scowcroft, subject: telephone call to Trudeau on Olympics, July 9, 1976. For the recommended talking point, see White House central files, subject file, presidential telephone calls, box 67: recommended telephone call to Trudeau on Olympics, July 9, 1976.
79. "Olympics Betrayal," NYT editorial, July 13, 1976.
80. Public Papers of the Presidents of the United States: Gerald R. Ford, 1976–1977 (Washington, D.C.: Office of the Federal Register, 1979), vol. 2: April 9–July 9, 1976, 657/9.
81. Ford Library: Richard Cheney files, 1974–1977, box 9: Olympics.
82. Ford Library: Ronald Nessen files, box 20: White House briefs, July 12, 1976.
83. Ibid.
84. No transcript of the phone call can be found in the Ford presidential library. For the White House's explanation of the call, see Ford Library: Ronald Nessen files, box 20: White House briefs, July 13, 1976.
85. Ford Library: James Cannon files, box 25: Olympic sports, July 1–31, 1976.
86. Ford Library: Ronald Nessen files, box 20, White House brief, July 15, 1976. Ford later wrote thank-you letters to both Krumm and Miller for helping the administration. In a letter to Donald Miller, Ford wrote, "Thank you for the

fine efforts of yourself and your colleagues to resolve the issue of the Republic of China's participation in the 1976 summer games. The time you took to periodically brief my staff on developments at Montreal, during a period when there were many demands on your time is much appreciated. . . . I have asked Phil Krumm to use his good offices with the United States Olympic committee and the international Olympic committee to eliminate political interference with the Olympics." The letter can be found in Ford Library: White House central files, subject file, box 13: CO-34-1, Republic of China, 1/1/76–1/20/77.

87. Pierre Trudeau, *Memoirs* (Toronto: McClelland & Stewart, 1993), 219.

88. Ford Library: Ronald Nessen files, box 20, White House brief, July 13, 1976.

89. Press conference of the Secretary of State for External Affairs Allan J. MacEachen, July 12, 1976, Canada Archives, RG 25, vol. 3056, file 36, pt. 3.

90. Ford Library: Office of the press secretary, David Gergen files, 1974–77/Olympics.

91. Ford Library: National security adviser, memoranda of conversations, 1973–1977, box 20: July 13, 1976, Ford, Kissinger, Rumsfield, 9:16–10:23 A.M.

92. Ford Library: National security adviser, memoranda of conversations, 1973–1977, box 20: meeting with Kissinger, Donald Rumsfeld, Richard Cheney, and Brent Scowcroft, July 14, 1976.

93. Ibid.

94. *Public Papers of the Presidents of the United States: Gerald R. Ford, 1976–77* (Washington, D.C.: Office of the Federal Register, 1979), 2:600.

95. Ford Library: Ronald Nessen files, box 20, White House brief, July 14, 1976.

96. IOC Archives, Minutes of the Seventy-eighth IOC Session.

97. Ford Library: Ronald Nessen files, box 20, White House brief, July 15, 1976.

98. IOC Archives, République Populaire de Chine, correspondence, 1976.

99. Canadian External Affairs department memo, "Olympics and Taiwan."

100. Tang Mingxin, *Wo guo can jia ao yun hui cang sang shi,* 2:361–362.

101. Tang Mingxin claimed that it would have been in Taiwan's long-term interest not to have withdrawn from the Montreal Games. Taiwan might have been able to keep its national Olympic committee under the name of "Republic of China" and Beijing might have had more trouble promoting its "one country, two systems" policy within the Olympic movement. See ibid., 2:362; and Tang Mingxin, *Tang Mingxin xiansheng fangwen jilu,* 182, 184–185.

102. For details, see Guo shi guan, *Xu Heng xian sheng fang tan lu,* 49–87, 183–249.

103. IOC president Lord Killanin was even advised to threaten to cancel the Games if the Canadian government still refused to change its policy regarding Taiwan's participation. See Pound, *Five Rings over Korea,* 30.

104. Canadian External Affairs, Skrabec confidential memo, October 22, 1975, Canada Archives, RG 25, vol. 3059, file 53.

105. Head and Trudeau, *The Canadian Way,* 193.
106. Ford Library: Brent Scowcroft memo, "Meeting with Canadian Opposition Leader Joe Clark," White House central files, box 11: Canada, 7/1/76–1/20/77.
107. The Canadian government eventually decided to issue visas. See External Affairs Confidential memo: "Question of Taiwanese Participation at the Canadian International Judo Championships, July 1975," May 29, 1975, Canada Archives, RG 25, vol. 3059, file 65.
108. Canadian External Affairs, Skrabec confidential memo, October 22, 1975; Confidential memo, anticipated question, House of Commons, Taiwanese boxers, November 24, 1975, Canada Archives, RG 25, vol. 3060, file 68.
109. Canadian External Affairs draft memo, June 14, 1976, Canada Archives, RG 25, vol. 3060, file 68.
110. Donald Macintosh and Donna Greenhorn, "Hockey Diplomacy and Canadian Foreign Policy," *Journal of Canadian Studies* 28, no. 2 (Summer 1993): 98.
111. For details, see ibid., 96–112.
112. Donald Macintosh, "Sport and Government in Canada," in Chalip, Johnson, and Stachura, *National Sports Politics,* 50.
113. Canadian External Affairs Department confidential memo, "Canadian Position on Taiwan at the Olympics," July 28, 1976, Canada Archives, RG 25, vol. 3059, file 103.
114. E. A. Skrabec, Confidential memo, "Taiwan in Retrospect," August 6, 1976, Canada Archives, RG 25, vol. 3061, file 97.
115. McKinney confidential telegram to Ottawa, July 13, 1976, Canada Archives, RG 25, vol. 3056, file 36, pt. 3.
116. Macintosh and Hawes, *Sport and Canadian Diplomacy,* 58.
117. Ford Library: White House central files, name file, box 1723: Killanin file.
118. *Public Papers of the Presidents of the United States: Gerald R. Ford,* 3:716.
119. Killanin, *My Olympic Years,* 172–173.

7. CHINA AWAKENS

1. "Guowu yuan pizhuan guojia ti wei guang yu sheng, shi, zizhiqu ti wei zhuren huiyi de ji ge wenti de baogao de tongzhi, April 22, 1981" (Notices and comments of the state council on the National Sport Commission's report about the provincial-level sport officials conference), in Guojia ti wei zheng ce yan jiu shi, *Tiyu yun dong wen jian xuan bian (1949–1981),* 154–160; Zhong guo tiyu fa zhan zhan lüe yan jiu hui, *1987 nian quan guo tiyu fa zhan zhan lüe lun wen xuan,* 4.

2. Julian Baum, "Friendship No Longer Ranks Ahead of Winning for Chinese Olympians," *Christian Science Monitor,* July 26, 1984.

3. China National Sports Commission, *Zhong guo tiyu nian jian, 2005,* 3.

4. Killanin to Zhong Shitong, March 28, 1980, IOC Archives, République Populaire de Chine, correspondence, 1980.

5. Zhong gong zhong yang wen xian yan jiu shi, *Deng Xiaoping nianpu,* 2:808–809.

6. Ueberroth, *Made in America,* 278.

7. Zhong gong zhong yang wen xian yan jiu shi, *Dong Xiaoping nianpu,* 2:885–886.

8. China's entrance-of-athletes order is no. 28 in the 1984 Games; the United States, as the host, is last, no. 141. UCLA, 1403, box 352, folder 2, press operation department files: ceremonies. For the Los Angeles Games, Taiwan used the anthem, flag, emblem, and a constitution that were designed for its national Olympic committee in conformity with post-1979 IOC rules dealing with Taiwan's membership in the Olympic family. See UCLA, LAOOC 1403, box 352, press operation department files, folder 3: China.

9. Chinese delegation statement, UCLA, LAOOC 1403, box 352, folder 3, press operation department files: China.

10. The statement can be found in LA Sports Library, Paul Ziffren Collection, roll 3. See also UCLA, LAOOC 1403, box 437, folder 7: press releases, vol. 5: Chinese; UCLA, LAOOC 1403, box 437, folder 12: press releases, vol. 5, folder 19: NOC's participation.

11. Ueberroth, *Made in America,* 279–280.

12. Ueberroth quoted in "LAOOC Names Delegation for Lausanne meeting," UCLA, LAOOC 1403, box 437, folder 12: press releases—vol. 5; LA Sports Library, LACOC–Ken Reich interviews, Reich interview with Tom Bradley, May 9, 1985.

13. Kenneth Reich and James Gerstenzang, "Reagan Hoping to Expand His Talk at Games," *LAT,* June 29, 1984.

14. UCLA, LAOOC 1403, box 352, folder 2: press operation department files: ceremonies.

15. LA Sports Library: "Official Report of the Games of the XXXIII Olympiad, Los Angeles," 1984, 3.

16. UCLA, LAOOC 1403, box 426, folder 26: Olympic village at UCLA final report: executive summary.

17. David Holley, "China Raises Flag over New Era of Competition," *LAT,* July 18, 1984.

18. For details, see the interview tapes, in UCLA, LAOOC 1403, box 476, interview tapes: Chinese Olympians.

19. Ueberroth, *Made in America,* 335.

20. Ibid., 351.

21. UCLA, Los Angeles Olympic Organizing Committee 1403, box 426, folder 32: Olympic village at UCLA final report, government relations.

22. Xing Junji and Zu Xianhai, *Bai nian chen fu*, 2.

23. Brook Larmer, "The Center of the World," *Foreign Policy* (September/October 2005): 69.

24. Jennifer Lind, "Dangerous Games," *Atlantic Monthly* (March 2006): 38.

25. Pound, *Five Rings over Korea*, 333.

26. Miller, *Olympic Revolution*, 135.

27. Qian Qichen, *Wai jiao shi ji*, 145.

28. Ibid., 148.

29. Kim Un-Yong, *The Greatest Olympics*, 131. Kim served as a longtime IOC member and later was expelled from the IOC and even imprisoned in South Korea for embezzlement and other wrongdoings.

30. Buruma, "Great Black Hope."

31. Jim Yardley, "Racial 'Handicaps' and a Great Sprint Forward," *NYT*, September 8, 2004, A4.

32. Quoted in ibid.; Liu Xiang, "Zhong guo you wo, Yazhou you wo" (I belong to China and Asia), in China National Sport Commission, *Zhong guo tiyu nian jian, 2005*, 445–446.

33. Yardley, "Racial 'Handicaps' and a Great Sprint Forward."

34. Larmer, "Center of the World," 66.

35. Liao Hui and Xia Li, *Yin ying xia de fan si*, 178.

36. Quoted in LaFeber, *Michael Jordan and the New Global Capitalism*, 27, 135.

37. "Fifty Foreigners Who Have Influenced Modern China," *Huanqiu shibao* (Global times), July 28, 2006.

38. LaFeber, *Michael Jordan and the New Global Capitalism*, 22.

39. Yan, "Managed Globalization," 19–20.

40. Larmer, "Center of the World," 70–71.

41. Adam Thompson and Mei Fong, "Can Half a Billion Chinese Be Wrong? The NBA Hopes Not," *WSJ*, August 25, 2006, A9, A11.

42. Daniel Eisenberg, "The NBA's Global Game Plan," *Time*, March 9, 2003.

43. Greg Boek, "Team-First, Back-to-Basics Foreigners Changing NBA," *USA Today*, April 20, 2006, 1A, 2A.

44. Quoted in Larmer, "Center of the World," 73.

45. Ibid., 68.

46. Phil Schaaf, *Sports, Inc.*, 307.

47. Larmer, "Center of the World," 73.

48. Jeff Coplon, "The People's Game," *NYT Sunday Magazine*, November 23, 2003.

49. Ibid.

50. *Time*, April 28, 2003.
51. Schaaf, *Sports, Inc.*, 305–307.
52. Roger Cohen, "Playing Field as Symbol for Global Conversation," *International Herald Tribune*, May 31, 2006.
53. Franklin Foer, "Soccer vs. McWorld," *Foreign Policy* (January/February 2004): 32–40.
54. For the best study on this point, see Alex Bellos, *Futebol: The Brazilian Way of Life* (New York: Bloomsbury, 2002).
55. Cohen, "Playing Field as Symbol."
56. Dennis K. Berman, "Losing at World Cup Can Hit a Nation's Stocks," *WSJ*, June 3–4, 2006, B3.
57. Henry Kissinger, "World of Wonder," *Newsweek*, June 12, 2006, 37–39.
58. In modern times, Chinese women have generally performed much better than Chinese men in sports competitions. This is especially true in women's volleyball and soccer, where the Chinese teams have enjoyed extraordinary success.
59. For details on these points, see Qiu Liben and Jiang Xun, "Zhengjiu Zhong guo zu qiu, tipo zu xie longduan" (To save Chinese soccer, we have to break the official soccer association's control), *Yazhou zhoukan* (July 23, 2006): 32–35.
60. Lu Guang, "Zhong guo gu niang" (Chinese girls), in Zhong guo zuo jia xue hui, *Quan guo you xiu bao gao wen xue ping xuan huo jiang zuo pin ji*, 54–61.
61. In the 2004 Athens Olympic Games, seven foreign coaches were members of the Chinese delegation. See China National Sport Commission, *Zhong guo tiyu nian jian, 2005*, 437–441.
62. Xin Jiang, "Zhong guo tiyu yang wu yun dong" (Foreign coaches call the shots), *Zhong guo tiyu* (Beijing) 431, no. 5 (May 2005): 90–93.
63. Zhang Caizhen, *Ao yun zhan lue si kao*, 14–15.
64. *Zhong hua ren min gong he guo tiyu fa quan min jian shen ji hua gang yao.*
65. "1979 nian quan guo tiyu gongzuo huiyi jiyao, March 9, 1979" (Summary of the national conference on sports in 1979) in Guo jia ti wei zheng ce yan jiu shi, *Tiyu yun dong wen jian xuan bian (1949–1981)*, 133.
66. For many years, the first article in the athletes' handbook issued by the sport authorities has been *"Yong pan gao feng, wei guo zheng guang"* or "strive for the best and win glory for the nation." See "Guo jia ti wei guan yu jia qiang ti gao tiyu yun dong ji shu shui ping de ji ge wen ti de qing shi bao gao, March 28, 1980" (National sport commission's report on how to strengthen and improve Chinese sports competitions, March 28, 1980), in Guojia ti wei zhengce yanjiu shi, *Tiyu yun dong wen jian xuan bian (1949–1981)*, 140–144, 486; Rong Gaotang, *Dang dai Zhong guo tiyu*, 167.
67. Zhong gong zhong yang wen xian yan jiu shi, *Deng Xiaoping nianpu, 1975–1997*, 2:779.

68. Xin hua she tiyu bu, ed., *Cong ling dao shi wu* ([China's gold medals] from zero to fifteen) (Beijing: Xinhua chubanshe, 1985), 1–2, 4.

69. Xin hua she tiyu bu, *Cong ling dao shi wu,* 13.

70. Guo jia tiyu zheng ce fa gui shi, ed., *Zhonghua titan si shi chun,* 15, 23.

71. For details on these principles, see China National Sport Commission, *Zhong guo tiyu nian jian, 1999,* 199, and *Zhong guo tiyu nian jian, 1998,* 167. For an excellent study of the fixed games and their effects, see Ye Yonglie, *Zhong guo ping pang nei mu.*

72. Zhao Yu, *Bing bai han cheng,* 53–183.

73. Ibid., 8.

74. For details, see ibid., 55–183.

75. Li Dan and Yang Kuangman, *Wu huan qi xia de zhui hui,* 63.

76. Zhao Yu, *Bing bai han cheng,* 187.

77. Guo jia ti wei zheng ce yan jiu shi, *Tiyu yun dong wen jian xuan bian (1949–1981),* 454.

78. Liao Hui and Xia Li, *Yin ying xia de fan si,* 36.

79. He Zhili was the women's singles champion at the 1987 world table tennis championships. Her victory did not bring her glory in China, however, since she had refused to lose to a fellow Chinese player in order to make sure China would win when it faced a foreign player. As punishment, she was not selected to be a member of the 1988 Olympic team and was forced to criticize publicly her decision. She later chose to leave the Chinese team. For her story, see Wang Chongli, *Zhong guo ti tan re dian xie zhen,* 106–145. See also Ye Yonglie, "He Zhili dui wo shuo," 125–142.

80. Li Dan and Yang Kuangman, *Wu huan qi xia de zhui hui,* 52.

81. Liao Hui and Xia Li, *Yin ying xia de fan si,* 156–157.

82. Zhao Yu, *Bing bai han cheng,* 51.

83. Li Dan and Yang Kuangman, *Wu huan qi xia de zhui hui,* 65.

84. *Da jia wen zhai bao* (Shanghai), August 10, 2004, 3.

85. Xing Junji and Zu Xianhai, *Bai nian chen fu,* 10.

86. The head coach of the Chinese team was Zeng Xuelin, who was born in Thailand and had been appointed to that position just two years earlier, in April of 1983. See Liu Xinwu, "5.19 chang jintou," 5:311–333; and Li You, "Qing xie de zu qiu chang," 1:188–210.

87. Yu Zhuli and Zhang Yihui, *Mu ji er shi nian Zhong guo shijian ji,* 167–168.

88. The song "Da dao jin xing qu" was written during the war with Japan. Its lyrics, translated here, are quite violent: "Let a big knife chop off the enemy's head! All of our patriotic fellow Chinese, the day when we fight against the Japanese has arrived, the day for fighting the Japanese has arrived. At our front, we have the brave righteous soldiers, at our back we have the whole nation. Let's unite like one man and march on bravely. Aiming at the enemy, exterminate them. Let's dash and chop off the enemy's head with a big knife."

89. For details on these points, see Qiu Liben and Jiang Xun, "Zhengjiu Zhong guo zu qiu, tipo zu xie longduan"; Mao Shanglong, "Xiang jiang jihuo Zhongguo zuqiu sishui" (Hong Kong may help revitalize Chinese soccer); and Xie Zhiheng and He Xueying, "Fa zhi shi Xiang Gang zuqiu qianfeng" (The rule of law is key to Hong Kong's soccer's success), all in *Yazhou Zhoukan* (Asia weekly), July 23, 2006, 32–35, 36–38, 39.

90. For the best argument on this point, see Franklin Foer, "How to Win the World Cup," in Weiland and Wilsey, *Thinking Fan's Guide to the World Cup,* 385–390.

8. BEIJING 2008

1. The IOC officially awarded the Olympic Games of 1936 to Berlin on May 13, 1931.

2. Guttmann, *The Games Must Go On,* 63.

3. Lucas, *Modern Olympic Games,* 125.

4. Alan Young, "Munich 1972: Re-Presenting the Nation," in Tomlinson and Young, *National Identity and Global Sports Events,* 123.

5. *NYT,* May 31, 1942, S3. See also ABC, box 2499, reel 144.

6. Allen Guttmann, "Berlin 1936: The Most Controversial Olympics," in Tomlinson and Young, *National Identity and Global Sports Events,* 71.

7. ABC, box 2499, reel 144.

8. There are several parallels between the Beijing Games and the 1936 Berlin Games. Like the Chinese Communist regime today, the Nazi regime saw the Games as a giant image-making machine; exhorted its citizens to smile more and behave better for the sake of creating more positive images of the regimes; and tried to polish its image by keeping unwanted people out of sight—in the Nazi case by arresting gypsies and prostitutes and trying to clean up the city. For a recent study on this point, see Large, *Nazi Games.*

9. Claire Brewster and Keith Brewster, "Mexico City, 1968: Sombreros and Skyscrapers," in Tomlinson and Young, *National Identity and Global Sports Events,* 99.

10. Ibid., 100.

11. Ibid., 100–102.

12. Ibid., 103–104.

13. Ibid., 110.

14. IOC Archives, Minutes of the Ninety-first IOC Session, Lausanne, Oct. 12–17, 1986, "Games of the XXIVth Olympiad: Negotiations between the Two Korean NOCs."

15. Samaranch preface, in Kim, *Greatest Olympics,* 13.

16. Quoted in Miller, *Olympic Revolution,* 135.

17. Pound, *Five Rings over Korea,* 322.

18. Kim, *Greatest Olympics,* 292.

19. IOC Archives, Minutes of the Ninety-fourth IOC Session, Seoul, September 13–16, 1988.

20. Pound, *Five Rings over Korea,* 322.

21. Miller, *Olympic Revolution,* 142.

22. Kim, *The Greatest Olympics,* 14.

23. Tong Le, *Meng xiang yu hui huang,* 74.

24. Hua Zhi, *Su yuan—Dong Shouyi zhuan,* 93.

25. Hua Chenxi, "Jiu Zhong guo shen ban ao yun hui de yi chang feng bo," 67.

26. Quoted in Liang Lijuan, *He Zhenliang,* 113.

27. With the successful bid for the Asian Games, Deng Xiaoping in early 1985 told a foreign leader that Beijing was prepared to host the 2000 Olympic Games. Subsequently, on September 22, 1990, then-Chinese president Yang Shangkun told IOC president Samaranch that China hoped "to host the 2000 Olympic Games." For details, see the interview tapes in UCLA, LAOOC 1403, box 476, interview tapes: Chinese Olympians.

28. LA Sports Library: "Beijing 2000, the Year of the Games—a Summary," Beijing 2000 Olympic Games bid committee, box Beijing 2000.

29. *China Today* (North American edition), no. 69 (June 1993), 13.

30. LA Sports Library, "The Olympic Games at Beijing."

31. LA Sports Library, Beijing 2000 Olympic Games bid committee (in an envelope titled Beijing for 2000 bulletin).

32. See Kristof and Wudunn, *China Wakes,* 94–110.

33. McGeoch, *Bid,* 196, 208.

34. Ibid., 203.

35. Tom Lantos, "Scratch Beijing from the Olympics Wish List," *Los Angeles Times,* May 20, 1993, B7; Ron Rapoport, "Olympics in China Is a Human Wrong Not a Human Right," *Daily News of Los Angeles,* June 30, 1993, S1; Robert Lipsyte, "Tug of War Emerging over the 2000 Games," *NYT,* August 1, 1993, S2.

36. *USA Today,* July 20, 1993, 11A.

37. LA Sports Library, Proposal materials for the Olympic Games at Beijing.

38. Mann, *About Face,* 289.

39. Robert Greenberger, "U.S., Unhappy with Beijing's Abuse of Human Rights, Focuses on Olympics," *WSJ,* August 23, 1993.

40. LA Sports Library, OLY Col, GV 722 2000, A1 B422g, 1993.

41. IOC Archives, Minutes of the 101st IOC Session, Monaco, September 21–24, 1993.

42. Ibid.

43. Ibid.

44. On November 27, 1998, Wu Shaozu, head of the China National Sports Commission, acknowledged that Beijing lost to Sydney because it lacked bid-

ding experience and was overconfident. Beijing's strategy of relying on a mass campaign did not work well either. See China National Sport Commission, Zhong *guo tiyu nianjian, 1999,* 226.

45. Huntington, "Clash of Civilizations?"

46. Barney, Wenn, and Martyn, *Selling the Five Rings,* 286.

47. Lampton, "A Growing China in a Shrinking World," 139–140.

48. Gosper, *An Olympic Life,* 328–348.

49. *NYT,* July 14, 2001, D7.

50. According to Wu Jingguo, the IOC member from Taiwan, those two votes would have been Beijing's if Coates had not offered them the money. See Wu Jingguo, *Ao lin pi ke zhong hua qin,* 88.

51. Jobling, "Bidding for the Olympics," 270–271.

52. McGeoch, *Bid,* 268–269.

53. Jobling, "Bidding for the Olympics," 270–271.

54. Simon and Jennings, *Lords of the Rings,* 241.

55. Quoted in Gosper, *An Olympic Life,* 267.

56. IOC Archives, Minutes of the IOC 108th Session, March 17–18, 1999, Lausanne, Switzerland.

57. Gosper, *An Olympic Life,* 257.

58. McGeoch, *Bid,* 225–228.

59. McGeoch, *Bid,* 233. Other bids have also been subject to corruption and just bad luck. According to one report from the Associated Press dated December 23, 2005, "a misplaced vote might have helped London win the bid" for the 2012 Olympics. According to this article, one IOC member mistakenly voted for Paris rather than Madrid in July 2005, when another vote for Madrid might have stopped London from winning.

60. Zhong gong zhong yang wen xian yan jiu shi, *Deng Xiaoping nianpu,* 2:1365.

61. Samaranch, *Samaranch Years,* 104.

62. The corruption case of Beijing Mayor Chen Xitong and its aftermath might have played a role in Beijing's decision not to bid for the 2004 Games; what happened to Chen Xitong created distrust among the top leaders, the Beijing municipal government, and the sports commission. In fact, this earlier incident may explain why in late 1998, when China decided to bid again for hosting the 2008 Olympic Games, the state council at first did not support Beijing as the bidding city. For details, see China National Sports Commission, *Zhong guo tiyu nian jian, 1999,* 226.

63. Gosper, *An Olympic Life,* 260.

64. Craig S. Smith, "Joyous Vindication and a Sleepless Night," *NYT,* July 14, 2001.

65. Susan Brownell, "China and Olympism," 60.

66. Hessler, *Oracle Bones,* 261.

67. IOC Archives, the official Beijing bid proposal, Beijing 2008, 1:3.

68. Peng Yongjie, Zhang Zhiwei, and Han Donghui, *Ren wen ao yun,* 7.

69. LA Sports Library, *New Beijing, Great Olympics: Highlights of Beijing's Olympic Candidacy,* official publication of the bid committee, OLY Col, GV 722 2008, A1 B42N, 2000 (hereafter Beijing 2008 official proposal).

70. Ibid., 1:5.

71. Larmer, "Center of the World," *Foreign Policy* (September/October 2005): 68.

72. The explanation comes from a booklet titled *2008, See You in Beijing,* a special journal designed to help Beijing win the 2008 bid, February 2001 issue, by Beijing 2008 Olympic games bid committee, 17, LA Sports Library, OLY Col, GV 722, 2008, A1 B42S.

73. LA Sports Library, Letter of support by President Jiang Zemin, November 21, 2000, Beijing 2008 official proposal, 1:7.

74. IOC Archives, Minutes of the Ninety-fourth IOC Session, 149.

75. Ibid., 148.

76. IOC Archives, Minutes of the Ninety-second IOC Session, Istanbul, May 9–12, 1987, 27.

77. IOC Archives, Minutes of the 112th IOC Session, Moscow, July 13–16, 2001, 231.

78. Ibid., 240.

79. Ibid., 38.

80. Ibid., 40.

81. Editorial, *Xinhua News,* July 14, 2001.

82. Tong Le, *Meng xiang yu hui huang,* 1–2.

83. Schaffer and Smith, *Olympics at the Millennium,* 2.

84. Reuters, "Joyful South Africa Celebrates World Cup Award," May 15, 2004.

85. Guttmann and Thompson, *Japanese Sports,* 166.

86. Jere Longman, "How a Sport Galvanized South Korea," *NYT,* June 30, 2002, A5, A8.

87. China's Olympic Dream, in *2008, See You in Beijing,* 15.

88. Quoted in Barney, Wenn, and Martyn, *Selling the Five Rings,* 285.

89. Jere Longman, "Beijing Wins Bid for 2008 Olympic Games," *NYT,* July 14, 2001, D7.

90. "The Number Game," in *Olympic Review* 53 (October–November–December 2004): 32–34.

91. Jim Yardley, "China Plans Temporary Easing of Curbs on Foreign Journalists," *NYT,* December 2, 2006, A6.

92. Peng Yongjie, Zhang Zhiwei, and Han Donghui, *Ren wen Ao yun,* 7.

93. Andrew Batson, "China Officials Train Crowds to Be More Polite, Orderly as 2008 Olympics Approach," *WSJ,* December 27, 2005, A13, A18.

94. Howard W. French, "Minding Their Manners, Looking to the Olympics," *International Herald Tribune,* June 29, 2006, 2.

95. For details, see Jim Yardley, "Olympics Imperil Historic Beijing Neighborhood," *NYT,* July 12, 2006.

96. Both quotations are from Arthur Lubow, "The China Syndrome," *NYT Sunday Magazine,* May 21, 2006, 70.

97. Hazan, *Olympic Sports and Propaganda Games,* 36.

98. ABC, box 2499, reel 144.

99. For an excellent study on the Korea situation, see Bridges, "Reluctant Mediator," 375–391.

100. Longman, "How a Sport Galvanized South Korea."

101. Reuters, "Hurdles Ahead for Two Koreas' Single Olympic Team," November 2, 2005.

102. Ibid.

103. Lind, "Dangerous Games," 38.

104. "Let the Games Begin," *Economist,* June 10, 2006.

105. IOC Archives, Minutes of the 116th IOC Session, Athens, August 10–12, 29, 2004, 42.

106. Lyberg, *Fabulous One Hundred Years of the IOC,* 226.

107. Morrow and Wamsley, *Sport in Canada,* 238.

108. Reuters, "China Can't Afford Extravagant Games, Congress Delegate," March 3, 2006.

109. IOC Archives, Minutes of the 115th IOC Session, Prague, November 2–4, 2003, 21.

110. Pound, *Five Rings over Korea,* 4.

111. Hirthler, "One World, One Dream," 38.

112. Reuters, "Beijing Puts Chinese Stamp on 2008 Olympic Emblem," August 2, 2003.

113. Reuters, "Beijing Chooses Five Dolls for Olympic Mascot," November 11, 2005.

114. IOC Archives, Minutes of the 113th IOC Session, Salt Lake City, February 4–6 and 23, 2002.

115. In February 2002, Beijing passed a law to protect the Olympic symbols for its 2008 Games. The text of the law can be found in China National Sport Commission, *Zhong guo tiyu nian jian 2003,* 155–156.

116. Minutes of the 115th IOC Session, 38.

117. Geoffrey A. Fowler, "China's Logo Crackdown," *WSJ,* November 4, 2005, B1, B5.

118. Organizers of the 2004 Olympic Games in Athens raised $796 million from selling the rights to use its logo to domestic sponsors, and an additional $87 million from licensing its logo on products.

119. Fowler, "China's Logo Crackdown," B1, B5.

120. IOC Archives, Minutes of the Eighty-eighth IOC Session, Los Angeles, July 25–26, 1984, 40.

121. Foer, *How Soccer Explains the World*, 222.

122. Christopher Clarey, "China Plants Seed to Contend for America's Cup," *NYT*, April 16, 2007, D5.

Conclusion

Epigraph: Coubertin, *Olympic Games of 1896*, 53.

1. The sculpture was presented to the IOC as a gift in April 1986.

2. The sculpture *Tai ji Man* was presented to the IOC in 1986.

3. The party and the central government have acknowledged the declining health of Chinese youth. In May 2007 the party and state council collectively issued a document titled "Zhong gong zhong yang guowuyuan guanyu jia qiang qing shao nian tiyu zeng qiang qing shao nian tizhi de yi jian" (The central party committee and state council's opinion on strengthening youth's physical exercises and improving their physical quality). The document pointed out that due to a one-sided emphasis on book learning and examination results, society as a whole and schools in particular were not paying enough attention to students' physical exercises; in addition, physical education was suffering due to a lack of funding and equipment. Since the report was released, the physical condition of China's youth has continued to decline.

4. For recent reports, see Shi Jia, "Ren jun tiyu jing fei bu zu san yuan, xue sheng ti zhi zen neng bu xia jiang" (No wonder the students' health deteriorates when the budget for physical education per capita is less than three yuan), *Zhong guo qingnian bao*, September 9, 2006; Zhou Shijun, "Shao nian ti zhi xia jiang yu ao yun jin pai biao sheng" (While the physical fitness of China's youth is declining, Chinese athletes are winning more and more gold medals in the Olympic Games), *Zhong guo qingnian bao*, August 22, 2006.

5. Xu, *China and the Great War*, 282.

6. Kempe, "Fevered Pitch."

7. "Football Code," *Economist*, October 7, 2006, 52.

8. IOC Archives, *Olympic Charter* (1994), 9.

9. "Football Code."

10. Samaranch, *Samaranch Years*, 31.

11. Coubertin, *Olympic Memoirs*, 11.

SELECTED GLOSSARY

Ao yun mo shi　奥运模式

Aoyun zhanlue　奥运战略

Ban Gu　班固

Baxian guo hai, ge xian shentong
　八仙过海，各显神通

Cai E　蔡锷

Cai Yuanpei　蔡元培

Chen Dengke　陈登科

Chen Tianhua　陈天华

Chen Xian　陈先

Chen Xitong　陈希同

Chen Yi　陈毅

Chen Zhili　陈至立

Chiang Kai-shek　蒋介石

Chong chu yazhou, zou xiang shijie
　冲出亚洲，走向世界

Chui wan　捶丸

Civil service examinations
　科举考试

Cuju　蹴鞠

Dagongbao　大公报

Deng Xiaoping　邓小平

Ding Shanli　丁善理

Dong fang za zhi　东方杂志

Dong Shouyi　董守义

Dong ya bing fu　东亚病夫

Feng Wenbin　冯文彬

Fuwa　福娃

Geng Biao　耿飙

"Guo nei lian bing, yi zhi dui wai"
　国内练兵，一致对外

Guo shu　国术

Guo zhi da shi, wei si yu rong　国之
　大事，唯祀与戎

Guomin canzheng hui　国民参政会

Guomin tiyu fa　国民体育法

Han Nianlong　韩念龙

Han Shu　汉书

Han zei bu liang li　汉贼不两立

Hao Gengsheng　郝更生

Hao nan bu dang bing, hao tie bu da
　ding　好男不当兵，
　好铁不打钉

He Long　贺龙

He wei gui　和为贵

He Yingqin　何应钦

He Zhenliang　何振梁

He Zhili　何智丽

Heshang　河殇

Hong deng ji　红灯记

Hong qi　红旗

Hong sao　红嫂

Hong se niang zi jun　红色娘子军

Hu Na　胡娜

Huang Hua　黄华

Huang Wuxi　黄无锡

Huanqiu shibao　环球时报

Internationalization　国际化

Ji qi xian e　极其险恶

Jiajin tichang quanguo tiyu, yi shuli
　fuxing minzu zhi jichu an　加紧
　提倡全国体育，以树立复兴民族之
　基础案

Jiang Jingguo　蒋经国

Jiang Yanshi　蒋彦士

Jiang Ying　姜英

Jiang Zemin　江泽民

Jiaoyu jiuguo　教育救国

Jiaoyubu tiyu weiyuanhui guicheng
　教育部体育委员会规程

Jingshizhong　警世钟

Jiuguo qiangzhong　救国强种

Jun guomin　军国民

Jun guomin zhuyi　军国民主义

Junzi dong kou bu dong shou　　君子
　　动手不动口
Kong Xiangxi　　孔祥熙
Kong zi　　孔子
Lang Ping　　郎平
Lao qi jin gu　　劳其筋骨
Lao xin zhe zhi ren, lao li zhe zhi yu
　　ren　　劳心者治人，劳力者治于人
Lei Yang　　雷阳
Li Liyan　　李力研
Li Menghua　　李梦华
Li Peng　　李鹏
Liang Qichao　　梁启超
Liang Shuming　　梁漱溟
Lin Sen　　林森
Liu Bang　　刘邦
Liu Changchun　　刘长春
Liu Qi　　刘淇
Liu Shaoqi　　刘少奇
Liu Shencheng　　刘慎称
Liu Shuya　　刘叔雅
Liu Xiang　　刘翔
Liu yi　　六艺
Lou Dapeng　　楼大鹏
Lu Jindong　　路金栋
Ma Yuehan　　马约翰
Mao Zedong　　毛泽东
Meng zi　　孟子
Minzu tiyu　　民族体育
National identity　　国家认同
Neiyou wai huan　　内忧外患
Nie hai hua　　孽海花
Nie Rongzhen　　聂荣臻
Nie Weiping　　聂卫平
Ning Encheng　　宁恩承
Ping pong waijiao　　乒乓外交
Qian Qichen　　钱其琛
Qiang guo meng　　强国梦
Qiang guo shang xu wu gong　　强国
　　尚须武功
Qiangzhong jiuguo　　强种救国
Qiu Jin　　秋瑾

Quan guo yi pan qi　　全国一盘棋
Quan min tiyu hua　　全民体育化
Quan xue pian　　劝学篇
Renwen aoyun　　人文奥运
Rong Gaotang　　荣高棠
Rong Guotuan　　荣国团
Shangwu　　尚武
Shenbao　　申报
Shen Changhuan　　沈昌焕
Shen Jiaming　　沈家铭
Shen Junru　　沈钧儒
Shen Siliang　　沈嗣良
Sheng shi wei yan　　盛世危言
Sheng Zhibai　　盛之白
Shishiyuebao　　时事月报
Shiwubao　　时务报
Siku quanshu　　四库全书
Song Junfu　　宋君复
Song Ruhai　　宋如海
Song Shixiong　　宋世雄
Song Tao　　宋涛
Song Zhong　　宋中
Tai ji　　太极
Tang Mingxin　　汤铭新
Tiyu　　体育
Tiyu jiu guo lun　　体育救国论
Tiyu jiuguo　　体育救国
Tiyu jun shi hua　　体育军事化
Tiyu zhi yanjiu　　体育之研究
Tian Jinduo　　田金铎
Tichang shangwu jingshen yi gu guo ji
　　er li kang zhan an　　提倡尚武精
　　神以固国基而利抗战案
Tu tiyu　　土体育
Wan ban jie xia pin, wei you du shu
　　gao　　万般皆下品，唯有读书高
Wang Jingwei　　汪精卫
Wang Libin　　王立彬
Wang Zhengting　　王正廷
Wei guo zheng guang　　为国争光
Wei Jingsheng　　魏京生
Weiqi　　围棋

Wo neng bi ya   我能比呀

Wu gong   武功

Wu Jingguo   吴经国

Wu ju   武举

Wu shu   武术

Wu Tingfang   伍廷芳

Wu Xujun   吴旭君

Wu yue jiu ri xin qi cao   五月九日新旗操

Wuzu gonghe   五族共和

Xi Enting   郗恩庭

Xie Qimei   谢其美

Xin Beijing, Xin Aoyun   新北京，新奥运

Xin min shuo   新民说

Xin Qingnian   新青年

Xin sheng huo yun dong   新生活运动

Xu Haifeng   徐海峰

Xu Heng   徐亨

Xu Xiangqian   徐向前

Xu Yibing   徐一冰

Yan Fu   严复

Yang Sen   杨森

Yang Shangkun   杨尚昆

Yangwu yundong   洋务运动

Yang Xilan   杨锡兰

Yao Ming   姚明

Ye Jianying   叶剑英

Yi yong jun jin xing qu   义勇军进行曲

Yihequan   义和拳

Yong pan gao feng, wei guo zheng guang   勇攀高峰，为国争光

You yi di yi, bi sai di er   友谊第一，比赛第二

Yu Rizhang   余日章

Yu Xiwei   于希渭

Yu Zaiqing   于再清

Yuan qiang   原强

Yuan Weimin   袁伟民

Zeng Pu   曾朴

Zeng qiang zhong hua minzu tizhi, xi shua dong ya bing fu chi ru   增强中华民族体质，洗刷东亚病夫耻辱

Zeng xiu ti yu fa an   增修体育法案

Zeng Xuelin   曾雪麟

Zhang Baifa   张百发

Zhang Boling   张伯苓

Zhang Jian   张謇

Zhang Lianhua   张联华

Zhang Xueliang   张学良

Zhang Xueming   张学铭

Zhang Zhidong   张之洞

Zhang Zhijiang   张之江

Zhao Yu   赵瑜

Zhao Zhenghong   赵正洪

Zheng Guanying   郑观应

Zheng Minzhi   郑敏之

Zhi qu Weihu Shan   智取威虎山

Zhibao   直报

Zhong guo ti yu nian jian   中国体育年鉴

Zhong hua renmin gongheguo tiyu fa   中华人民共和国体育法

Zhong hua tiyu zong hui (All China Athletic Federation)   中华全国体育总会

Zhong Shitong   钟师统

Zhong yang guo shu guan   中央国术馆

Zhonghua Taibei   中华台北

Zhongguo Taibei   中国台北

Zhonghua tiyu xiehui   中华体育协会

Zhou Enlai   周恩来

Zhou Shukai   周书楷

Zhu Jianhua   朱建华

Zhu Ming   朱铭

Zhuang Zedong   庄则栋

Zonghe guoli   综合国力

Zou Zhenxian   邹振先

Zuqiu bao   足球报

SELECTED BIBLIOGRAPHY

ARCHIVES

Bentley Historical Library, University of Michigan, Ann Arbor

National Archives on Sino-American Relations

Tim Boggan files
Alexander Eckstein papers
J. Rufford Harrison files
Graham Barclay Steenhoven files
USTTA—Kaminsky, 1972 files

The University of Illinois Archives, Urbana

Avery Brundage Collection, 1908–1975

Guo Shi Guan (National Historical Archives), Taipei

Caizhengbu files
Can jia shi jie yun dong hui bu zu fei an
Jiaoyubu files
Tiyu lei: Zhong hua tiyu xue hui file
Zhong hua quan guo tiyu xie jing hui qing bu zhu an
Zhong yang guo shu tiyu yanjiu hui qing bu zhu an (1938)
Waijiaobu files
Di er shi jie ao yun an
Dong jing shi yun an
Fei ping pong wai jiao an
Guo ji tiyu jing sai an
Guoji tiyuwenti zhuan an xiao zu an (1972)
Tiyu, ao yun an
Tiyu huo dong juan
Tiyu tong zhan an
Xinwen, wenhua, tiyu jiao liu an

SELECTED BIBLIOGRAPHY

★ ★ ★ ★

Gerald Ford Presidential Library, Ann Arbor, Michigan

James M. Cannon files, Olympic sports
John Carlson files
Richard Cheney files, Olympics
James E. Connor files
Gerald Ford vice presidential papers, Olympics
David Gergen files, Olympics
F. Lynn May files, Olympic Games
National security adviser, memoranda of conversations
Ron Nessen papers, Olympics
Patrick O'Donnell and Joseph Jenckes files, Olympic Sports Committee
Presidential handwriting files, Olympics
Presidential speeches, Olympics
White House central files name file, Killanin files
White House central files subject file, box 5

IOC Archives, Lausanne, Switzerland

Affaires Politiques aux Jeux Olympiques d'Eté de Montreal, 1976
China Taipei correspondence, 1976–1978, 1980, 1981–1982
Lettres de Protestation concernant la question des deux Chine aux Jeux
     Olypiques d'Eté de Montreal, 1976
Minutes of the International Olympic Committee
Moscow boycotts, countries A–C
République Populaire de Chine, contrats, 1979–1981
République Populaire de Chine, correspondence, 1924–1958, 1976, 1977,
     1978, 1979, 1980
République Populaire de Chine, histoire, 1976, 1952–1986
République Populaire de Chine, juridique, 1947–1975, 1979–1980
République Populaire de Chine, process—verbaux, 1921–1976
République Populaire de Chine, rapports, 1952–1959

National Archives, College Park, Maryland

Nixon Presidential Materials Project, White House special files, staff member
     and office files
Dwight Chapin files
Alexander Haig files
H. R. Haldeman files
President's office files

President's personal files
Ronald Ziegler files
Nixon Presidential Materials Project, White House central files, subject files
Country files (CO 34–2), People's Republic of China, boxes 18–21
Federal government (FG 11), State Department, box 5
Foreign affairs (FO), boxes 51–53, 55–58
General record of the State Department, RG 59, entry 1613, boxes 2188,
    2189, 2190, 2678

Public Archives Canada, Ottawa

RG 25 (External Affairs), series E9 "Olympic Games Montreal," boxes
    3054–3062

Department of Special Collections, University of California, Los Angeles

LAOOC (Los Angeles Olympic Organizing Committee), collection 2025,
    the Xth Olympiad, Los Angeles, 1932
LAOOC records, 1403
Special collection, Olympic Games, 10:1932

National Security Archives, George Washington University

China and the United States: From Hostility to Engagement, 1960–1998

PRC Foreign Ministry Archives, Beijing

Ping-pong waijiao files

Paul Ziffren Sports Research Library, Los Angeles

2000 and 2008 Beijing bid materials
Minutes of the International Olympic Committee
LAOOC–Ken Reich interviews
Paul Ziffren collections

SELECTED READINGS

Abe, Ikuo. "Muscular Christianity in Japan: The Growth of a Hybrid," *International Journal of the History of Sport* 23, no. 5 (August 2006).

Allison, Lincoln. *The Changing Politics of Sport*. Manchester, Eng.: Manchester University Press, 1993.

———. *The Politics of Sport*. Manchester, Eng.: Manchester University Press, 1986.

An Jianshe, ed., *Zhou Enlai de zui hou sui yue, 1966–1976 (The later years of Zhou Enlai)*. Beijing: Zhong yang wen xian chubanshe, 2002.

Anderson, Benedict R. *Imagined Communities: Reflections on the Origin and Spread of Nationalism*. London: Verso, 1991.

Ao yun hui yu zhong guo (Olympics and China). Beijing: Wen shi ziliao chubanshe, 1985.

Arnaud, Pierre, and James Riordan, eds. *Sport and International Politics*. London: E & FN Spon, 1998.

Bairner, Alan. *Sport, Nationalism, and Globalization: European and North American Perspectives*. Albany: State University of New York Press, 2001.

Bale, John, and Mette Krogh Christensen, eds. *Post-Olympism? Questioning Sport in the Twenty-first Century*. New York: Berg, 2004.

Barney, Robert Knight, Stephen R. Wenn, and Scott G. Martyn. *Selling the Five Rings: The International Olympic Committee and the Rise of Olympic Commercialism*. Salt Lake City: University of Utah Press, 2002.

Barry, James P. *The Berlin Olympics, 1936: Black American Athletes Counter Nazi Propaganda*. New York: F. Watts, 1975.

Barzun, Jacques. *God's Country and Mine: A Declaration of Love Spiced with a Few Harsh Words*. Boston: Little, Brown, 1954.

Beacon, A. "Sport in International Relations: A Case for Cross-Disciplinary Investigation." *Sports Historian* 20, no. 2 (2000).

Beck, Peter J. *Scoring for Britain: International Football and International Politics*. London: Frank Cass, 1999.

Bender, Thomas. "Wholes and Parts: The Need for Synthesis in American History." *Journal of American History* 73, no. 1 (June 1986).

Berger, Peter L., and Samuel P. Huntington, eds. *Many Globalizations: Cultural Diversity in the Contemporary World*. New York: Oxford University Press, 2002.

Blain, N. "Current Developments in Media Sport, and the Politics of Local Identities: A 'Postmodern' Debate?" *Culture, Sport, Society* 3, no. 2 (2000).

Booker, Christopher. *The Games War: A Moscow Journal*. Boston: Faber and Faber, 1981.

Booth, D. *The Race Games: Sport and Politics in South Africa*. London: Frank Cass, 1998.

Bridges, Brian. "Reluctant Mediator: Hong Kong, the Two Koreas, and the

Tokyo Olympics," *International Journal of the History of Sport* 24, no. 3 (March 2007).

Brownell, Susan. "China and Olympism." In John Bale and Mette Krogh Christensen, eds., *Post-Olympism? Questioning Sport in the Twenty-first Century*. Oxford: Berg, 2004.

———. *Training the Body for China: Sports in the Moral Order of the People's Republic*. Chicago: University of Chicago Press, 1995.

Burstyn, Varda. *The Rites of Men: Manhood, Politics, and the Culture of Sport*. Toronto: University of Toronto Press, 1999.

Buruma, Ian. "The Great Black Hope." *New York Review of Books*. January 12, 2006.

Cai Yuanpei, "Dui yu jiao yu fang zhen zhi yi jian" (Preliminary ideas on education policies), in *Dong fang za zhi* 8, no. 10 (April 1912).

Cai Zhengjie. "Ji du jiao qing nian hui yu zhong guo jindai tiyu zhi fa zhan, 1895–1928" (The YMCA and the development of sports in China). Master's thesis, National Taiwan Normal University, 1992.

Cashman, Richard I. *The Bitter-Sweet Awakening: The Legacy of the Sydney 2000 Olympic Games*. Sydney: Walla Walla Press, 2006.

Cashman, Richard I., and Anthony Hughes. *Staging the Olympics: The Event and Its Impact*. Sydney: University of New South Wales Press, 1999.

Chalip, Laurence, Arthur Johnson, and Lisa Stachura, eds. *National Sports Politics: An International Handbook*. Westport, Conn.: Greenwood, 1996.

Chan, Gerald. "The 'Two-China' Problem and the Olympic Formula." *Pacific Affairs* 58, no. 3 (Autumn 1985).

Chen Dengke. "Wo men ying fou ti chang Zhong guo de min zu tiyu?" (Should we encourage nationalist sports in China?). *Qin fen tiyu yue bao* 4, no. 1 (1937).

Chen Shien. "Qing mo min chu jun guomin jiao yu zhi tiyu si Xiang" (Ideas for militarizing citizens in the late Qing and early republican China). Master's thesis, National Taiwan Normal University, 1989.

Cheng, Joseph Y. S. "Mao Zedong's Perception of the World in 1968–1972: Rationale for the Sino-American Rapprochement." *Journal of American–East Asian Relations* 7, nos. 3–4 (1998).

Cheng Ruifu. "Qing mo nü zi tiyu si xiang de xing cheng" (Theories regarding women and sports in the late Qing dynasty). Master's thesis, National Taiwan Normal University, 1994.

Chengdu tiyu xueyuan tiyu shi yan jiu suo, ed., *Zhong guo jindai tiyu shi zi liao* (The history of sports in modern China: documentary collection). Chendu: Sichuan jiaoyu chubanshe, 1988.

China National Sport Commission, ed. *Zhong guo tiyu nian jian* (Yearbook of Chinese sports). Beijing: Ren min tiyu chubanshe, 1965, 1973–1974, 1975–2005.

Chinese Olympic Committee, ed. *Zhong guo tiyu wen hua wu qian nian* (A five-thousand-year history of Chinese physical culture). Beijing: Beijing tiyu daxue chubanshe, 1996.

Chinese Society for the History of Physical Education and Sport, ed. *Zhong guo jindai tiyu shi* (The history of sports in modern China). Beijing: Beijing tiyu xueyuan chubanshe, 1989.

Chongqing shi tiyu yundong weiyuan hui and Chongqing shi zhi zong bian shi, eds. *Kangzhan shiqi peidu tiyu shiliao* (Archival materials on sports in Chongqing during the anti-Japanese war era). Chongqing: Chongqing chubanshe, 1989.

Close, Paul, David Askew, and Xu Xin. *The Beijing Olympiad: The Political Economy of a Sporting Mega-Event.* London: Routledge, 2007.

Cohen, Paul A. *History in Three Keys: The Boxers as Event, Experience, and Myth.* New York: Columbia University Press, 1997.

Cohen, Richard. *By the Sword: A History of Gladiators, Musketeers, Samurai, Swashbucklers, and Olympic Champions.* New York: Random House, 2002.

Collins, Sandra. "Conflicts of 1930s Japanese Olympic Diplomacy in Universalizing the Olympic Movement," *International Journal of the History of Sport* 23, no. 7 (November 2006).

———. "'Samurai' Politics: Japanese Cultural Identity in Global Sport—The Olympic Games as a Representational Strategy." *International Journal of the History of Sport* 24, no. 3 (March 2007).

Coubertin, Pierre de. "An Expression." In *Official Program: Xth Olympiad, Los Angeles.* Special collections, Los Angeles Olympic Organizing Committee records, Library of University of California, Los Angeles, 10: 1932, box 2, folder 1: official programs, Tenth Olympiad, July 30–31, 1932.

———. *The Olympic Games of 1896.* Lausanne: International Olympic Committee, 1983.

———. *Olympic Memoirs.* Lausanne: International Olympic Committee, 1997.

Coubertin, Pierre de, and Norbert Muller. *Olympism: Selected Writings.* Lausanne: International Olympic Committee, 2000.

Cronin, Mike. *Sport and Nationalism in Ireland: Gaelic Games, Soccer, and Irish Identity since 1884.* Dublin: Four Courts Press, 1999.

Crowther, Nigel. "Sports, Nationalism, and Peace in Ancient Greece." *Peace Review* 11, no. 4 (1999).

Cui Lequan. *Tu shuo Zhong Guo gu dai you yi* (An illustrated history of ancient Chinese games). Taipei: Wen jin chubanshe, 2002.

————. *Zhong jin dai tiyu shi hua* (A history of sports in modern China). Beijing: Zhong hua shuju, 1998.

Culp, Robert. "Rethinking Governmentality: Training, Cultivation, and Cultural Citizenship in Nationalist China." *Journal of Asian Studies* 65, no. 3 (2006).

Dai Weiqian. "Kang zhan shi qi min zu jiao yu tiyu si xiang zhi ren shi" (Sports under the nationalist education during the anti-Japanese war period). Zhong hua tiyu xue hui, ed., *Tiyu xue bao* (Taiwan) 14 (December 1992).

Dang dai zhong guo zhuan ji cong shu, ed., *He Long zhuan* (Biography of He Long). Beijing: Dang dai zhong guo chubanshe, 1993.

Di liu jie quan guo yun dong da hui bao gao chou bei zu, ed. *Di Liu Jie Quan Guo Yun Dong Da Hui Bao Gao* (Report of the Sixth National Games). Shanghai: Di liu jie quan guo yun dong da hui bao gao chou bei zu, 1935.

Donald, Macintosh, and Michael Hawes. *Sport and Canadian Diplomacy.* Montreal: McGill-Queen's University Press, 1994.

Dong, Jianxia. "The Female Dragons Awake: Women, Sport, and Society in the Early Years of the New China." *International Journal of the History of Sport* 18, no. 2 (2001).

Dong, Jie. *Ao yun hui dui ju ban cheng shi jing ji de ying xiang* (The economic impact of the Olympic Games on the host cities). Beijing: Jing ji ke xue chubanshe, 2004.

Dong Shouyi. "Ao lin pi ke jiu shi" (Story of the Olympics). In *Wen Shi Zi Liao Xuan Ji* 53, ed. Zhong guo ren min zheng zhi xie shang hui yi quan guo weiyuan hui wen shi zi liao yan jiu wei yuan hui. Beijing: Wen shi zi liao chubanshe, 1964.

————. "Ao lin pi ke jiu shi xu pian" (The continued story of the Olympics). In *Wen Shi Zi Liao Xuan Ji* 70, ed. Zhong guo ren min zheng zhi xie shang hui yi quan guo weiyuan hui wen shi zi liao yan jiu wei yuan hui. Beijing: Wen shi zi liao chubanshe, 1980.

————. "Zhong guo yu yuan dong yun dong hui" (China and the Far Eastern Championship Games). In *Zhong guo tiyu shi cankao ziliao,* ed. Zhonghua renmin gongheguo tiyu yun dong weiyuan hui yun dong jishu weiyuan hui. Beijing: Renmin tiyu chubanshe, 1957.

————. "Zhong guo yu yuan dong yun dong hui" (China and the Far Eastern Championship Games). In *Zhong hua ren min gongheguo tiyu yundong wei yuan hui yun dong jishu wei yuan hui,* ed. Zhong guo tiyu shi chankao ziliao, no. 2. Beijing: Renmin tiyu chubanshe, 1957.

Du Yi. *Da xue ya qing song: Wen ge zhong de Chen Yi* (Chen Yi during the Cultural Revolution). Beijing: Shijie zhishi chubanshe, 1997.

Dyreson, Mark. "Globalizing the Nation-Making Process: Modern Sport in

World History." *International Journal of the History of Sport* 20, no. 1 (2003): 91–106.

Ecker, Tom. *Olympic Facts and Fables: The Best Stories from the First Century of the Modern Olympics*. Mountain View, Calif.: Tafnews Press, 1996.

Elliott, Jane E. *Some Did It for Civilization, Some Did It for Their Country: A Revised View of the Boxer War*. Hong Kong: Chinese University Press, 2002.

Er shi er nian quan guo yundong dahui choubei weiyuan hui, ed. *Er shi er nian quan guo yundong dahui zong bao gao shu* (Complete report of the 1933 National Games). Shanghai: Zhonghua shuju, 1934.

Esherick, Joseph. *The Origins of the Boxer Uprising*. Berkeley: University of California Press, 1987.

Espy, Richard. *The Politics of the Olympic Games*. Berkeley: University of California Press, 1979.

Fan Sheng. "Wo guo gu dai chui wan yun dong" (Golf in ancient China). In *Zhong Guo tiyu cankao ziliao* (Reference materials on the history of sports in China). Beijing: Renmin tiyu chubanshe, 1957.

Fan Yisi and Ding Zhongyuan. *Gu dai Aolinpike yun dong hui* (Ancient Olympic Games). Jinan: Shandong jiao yu chubanshe, 1982.

Findling, John E., and Kimberly D. Pelle. *Encyclopedia of the Modern Olympic Movement*. Westport, Conn.: Greenwood, 2004.

Finn, Gerry P. T., and Richard Giulianotti. *Football Culture: Local Contests, Global Visions*. London: Frank Cass, 2000.

Foer, Franklin. *How Soccer Explains the World: An Unlikely Theory of Globalization*. New York: HarperCollins, 2004.

———. "Soccer vs. Mcworld." *Foreign Policy* (January/February 2004).

Ford, Gerald. *Public Papers of the United States: Gerald Ford*. Washington, D.C.: Office of the Federal Register, 1979.

Franks, Joel. "Chinese Americans and American Sports, 1880–1940." *Chinese America: History and Perspectives* (1996).

Frey, James, and D. Stanley Eitzen. "Sport and Society." *Annual Review of Sociology* 17 (1991).

Gao Cui. *Cong dong ya bing fu dao tiyu qiang guo* (From the sick man of East Asia to a strong sport power). Chengdu: Sichuan renmin chubanshe, 2003.

Gao Lao. "Yuandong Yun Dong Hui" (Far Eastern Championships). *Dong fang za zhi* 12, no. 6 (1915).

Gao Wenqian. *Wan nian Zhou Enlai* (Zhou Enlai's later years). Hong Kong: Mingjing chubanshe, 2003.

Gerber, Ellen W. "Three Interpretations of the Role of Physical Education,

1930–1960: Charles H. McCloy, Jay Bryan Nash, and Jesse Feiring Williams." Ph.D. diss., University of Southern California, 1966.

Gong Li. *Mao Zedong yu Meiguo* (Mao Zedong and the United States). Beijing: Shijie zhishi chubanshe, 1999.

Gordon, Harry. *The Time of Our Lives: Inside the Sydney Olympics; Australia and the Olympic Games, 1994–2002.* St. Lucia: University of Queensland Press, 2003.

Gosper, Kevan, with Glenda Korporaal. *An Olympic Life: Melbourne 1956 to Sydney 2000.* St. Leonards, New South Wales: Allen & Unwin, 2000.

Grupe, Ommo. "The Sport Culture and the Sportization of Culture: Identity, Legitimacy, Sense, and Nonsense of Modern Sport as a Cultural Phenomenon." In Fernand Landry et al., eds., *Sport . . . the Third Millennium, Proceedings of the International Symposium, Quebec City, Canada, May 1990.* Sainte-Foy, Quebec City: Les Presses de L'Université Laval, 1991.

Gu Shiquan. *Zhong guo tiyu shi* (The history of sport in China). Beijing: Beijing tiyu daxue chubanshe, 2002.

Guan Wenmin et al., eds. *Tiyu shi* (History of sports). Beijing: Beijing gaodeng jiaoyu chubanshe, 1996.

Guo jia ti wei zheng ce yan jiu shi, ed. *Tiyu yun dong wen jian xuan bian (1949–1981)* (Collection of selected official documents on sports, 1949–1981). Beijing: Renmin tiyu chubanshe, 1982.

———. *Zhong guo tiyu nian kan* (Annual journal of Chinese sports). Beijing: Renmin tiyu chubanshe, 1985.

———. *Zhonghua titan si shi chun* (Forty years of Chinese sports). Beijing: Renmin tiyu chubanshe, 1990.

Guo Jianhui et al. *Bai nian ti tan lue ying* (A glimpse of sports in China over the last one hundred years). Beijing: Zhong guo jing ji chubanshe, 2000.

Guo Xifen, ed. *Zhong guo tiyu shi* (A history of sports in China). Shanghai: Shangwu yinshu guan, 1919.

Guojia tiyu wenshi gongzuo weiyuan hui, ed. *Zhongguo jindai tiyu wenxuan* (Selected materials on sports in modern China). Beijing: Renmin tiyu chubanshe, 1992.

Guoshi guan, ed. *Xu Heng xian sheng fang tan lu* (The reminiscences of Xu Heng). Taipei: Guoshi guan, 1998.

Guttmann, Allen. *Games and Empires: Modern Sports and Cultural Imperialism.* New York: Columbia University Press, 1994.

———. *The Games Must Go On: Avery Brundage and the Olympic Movement.* New York: Columbia University Press, 1984.

———. *The Olympics: A History of the Modern Games.* Urbana: University of Illinois Press, 2002.

Guttmann, Allen, and Lee Thompson. *Japanese Sports: A History.* Honolulu: University of Hawai'i Press, 2001.

Haldeman, H. R. *The Haldeman Diaries: Inside the Nixon White House.* New York: G. P. Putnam's Sons, 1994.

Hao Gengsheng. *Hao Gengsheng hui yi lu* (Memoirs of Hao Gengsheng). Taipei: Zhuan ji wen xue chubanshe, 1969.

Hart-Davis, Duff. *Hitler's Games: The 1936 Olympics.* New York: Harper & Row, 1986.

Hazan, Barukh. *Olympic Sports and Propaganda Games: Moscow, 1980.* New Brunswick, N.J.: Transaction Books, 1982.

He Huixian and Li Renchen. *San lian guan* (Three championships in a row). Wuhan: Hubei renmin chubanshe, 1984.

Head, Ivan, and Pierre Trudeau. *The Canadian Way: Shaping Canada's Foreign Policy, 1968–1985.* Toronto: McClelland & Stewart, 1995.

Hessler, Peter. *Oracle Bones: A Journey between China's Past and Present.* New York: HarperCollins, 2006.

Hirthler, George. "One World, One Dream." In *Olympic Review* 56 (July–August–September 2005).

Hoberman, John. "Purism and the Flight from the Superman: The Rise and Fall of Maoist Sport." In *Sport and Political Ideology,* ed. John Hoberman. Austin: University of Texas Press, 1984.

———. "Toward a Theory of Olympic Internationalism." *Journal of Sport History* 22, no. 1 (1995).

Hobsbawm, Eric J. *Nations and Nationalism since 1780: Programme, Myth, Reality.* Cambridge, Eng.: Cambridge University Press, 1990.

Hoganson, Kristin. *Fighting for American Manhood: How Gender Politics Provoked the Spanish-American and Philippine-American Wars.* New Haven: Yale University Press, 1998.

Hoh, Gunsun (Hao Gengsheng). *Physical Education in China.* Shanghai: Commercial Press, 1926.

Hong, Fan. *Footbinding, Feminism, and Freedom: The Liberation of Women's Bodies in Modern China.* London: Frank Cass, 1997.

———. "Not All Bad! Communism, Society and Sport in the Great Proletarian Cultural Revolution." *International Journal of the History of Sport* 16, no. 3 (1999).

———. "The Significance of the Cultural Revolution for the Evolution of Sport in Modern China." In *Sports and Social Changes,* ed. J. Buschmann and G. Pfister. Sankt Augustin, Germany: Academia Verlag Richarz, 2001.

———. "Which Road to China? An Evaluation of Two Different Approaches: The Inadequate and the Adequate." *International Journal of the History of Sport* 18, no. 2 (2001).

Hong, Fan, and Tan Hua. "Sport in China: Conflict between Tradition and Modernity, 1840s–1930s." *International Journal of the History of Sport* 19, nos. 2, 3 (2002).

Hong, Fan, and Xiong Xiaozheng. "Communist China: Sport, Politics and Diplomacy." *International Journal of the History of Sport* 19, nos. 2, 3 (2002).

Hong, Fan, and J. A. Mangan, eds. *Soccer, Women, Sexual Liberation: Kicking Off a New Era.* London: Frank Cass, 2004.

Hong, Zhaohui, and Sun Yi. "The Butterfly Effect and the Making of 'Ping Pong Diplomacy.'" *Journal of Contemporary China* 9, no. 25 (2000).

Hong Kong World News Service, ed., *The Hong Kong Centenary Commemorative Talks, 1841–1941.* Hong Kong: Hong Kong World News Service, 1941.

Hong Kong you yi chuban gong si, ed., *You yi zhi hua bian di kai: Zhong Guo Ping Pong dai biao tuan can jia di san shi yi jie shi jie Ping Pong qiu jin biao sai she ying ji* (Friendship flowers are everywhere: Official photos of the Chinese table tennis delegation's participation in the Thirty-first World Table Tennis Championships). Hong Kong: You yi chuban gong si, 1971.

Houlihan, Barrie. *Sport and International Politics.* New York: Harvester Wheatsheaf, 1994.

Howell, Collin. *Blood, Sweat and Cheers: Sport and the Making of Modern Canada.* Toronto: University of Toronto Press, 2001.

Hua Chenxi. "Jiu Zhong guo shen ban ao yun hui de yi chang feng bo" (Dispute over China's bid for hosting the Olympic Games during the pre-1949 era). *Tiyu Wen Shi* 3 (1992).

Hua Zhi. *Su yuan—Dong Shouyi zhuan* (Biography of Dong Shouyi). Beijing: Renmin tiyu chubanshe, 1993.

Huang Jinlin. "Jindai Zhong guo de jun shi shen ti jian gou, 1895–1949" (Production of the militarized body in China, 1895–1949). *Zhong yang yan jiu yuan jindai shi yanjiu suo ji kan* 43 (March 2004).

Huang Renyi. "Wo guo tiyu zheng ce zhi ding guo cheng zhi yan jiu: Yi guomin tiyu fa di er ci xiu ding guo cheng wei fen xi dui xiang" (The process of making sport policy in our country). Master's thesis, National Taiwan Normal University, 1992.

Huntington, Samuel P. "The Clash of Civilizations?" *Foreign Affairs* 72, no. 3 (Summer 1993).

Hwang, T. "Sport, Nationalism and the Early Chinese Republic, 1912–1927." *Sports Historian* 20, no. 2 (2001).

Iriye, Akira. *Global Community: The Role of International Organizations in the Making of the Contemporary World.* Berkeley: University of California Press, 2002.

Jackson, Steven J. "A Twist of Race: Ben Johnson and the Canadian Crisis of Racial and National Identity." *Sociology of Sport Journal* 15, no. 1 (1998).

Jarvie, Grant. "Sport, Nationalism and Cultural Identity." In Lincoln Allison, ed., *The Changing Politics of Sport*. Manchester, Eng.: Manchester University Press, 1993.

Jiang Huaiqing, ed. *Liu Changchun duan pao cheng gong shi* (The story of Liu Changchun's success as a runner). Shanghai: Shanghai qin fen shu ju, 1933.

Jiang Xiongfei. "Kongzi de tiyu si xiang" (Confucius's thoughts on physical education). Master's thesis, National Taiwan Normal University, 1972.

Jin Shan. *Bei zhuang man chang de chong ji: zhong guo zu qiu qi ci chong ji shi jie bei ji shi* (Long and heroic effort: The story of China's seven attempts to enter the soccer World Cup). Beijing: Hua yi chubanshe, 2002.

Jin Yuliang. "Di 14 jie Ao yun hui yu Zhong guo dai biao tuan" (The Fourteenth Olympiad and the Chinese delegation). *Tiyu wen shi* 1 (1994).

Jobling, Ian. "Bidding for the Olympics: Site Selection and Sidney 2000." In *The Olympics in the Millennium: Power, Politics, and the Games*, ed. Kay Schaffer and Sidonie Smith. New Brunswick, N.J.: Rutgers University Press, 2000.

Jones, Robin. "Ten Years of China Watching: Present Trends and Future Directions of Sport in the People's Republic." In *Old Borders, New Borders, No Borders: Sport and Physical Education in a Period of Change*, ed. J. Tolleneer. Oxford, Eng.: Meyer and Meyer Sport, 1998.

Kanin, David B. "Ideology and Diplomacy: The Dimensions of Chinese Political Sport." In *Sport and International Relations*, ed. B. Lowe et al. Champaign, Ill.: Stipes, 1978.

———. *A Political History of the Olympic Games*. Boulder, Colo.: Westview, 1981.

Ke Ling, ed. *1976–1999: You si yu xi wang* (Anxiety and hope). Shanghai: Wen Hui chubanshe, 1999.

Kellas, James G. *The Politics of Nationalism and Ethnicity*. New York: St. Martin's, 1998.

Kempe, Frederick. "Fevered Pitch." *Wall Street Journal*, June 13, 2006, A4.

Keys, Barbara J. *Globalizing Sport: National Rivalry and International Community in the 1930s*. Cambridge: Harvard University Press, 2006.

———. "The Internationalization of Sport, 1890–1939." In Frank Ninkovich and Liping Bu, *The Cultural Turn: Essays in the History of U.S. Foreign Relations*. Chicago: Imprint Publications, 2001.

Killanin, Michael Morris. *My Olympic Years*. London: Secker and Warburg, 1983.

Killanin, Michael Morris, and John Rodda, ed. *The Olympic Games, 1980: Moscow and Lake Placid*. New York: Collier, 1980.

———. *The Olympic Games, 1984: Los Angeles and Sarajevo*. New York: M. Joseph, 1983.

Kim, Un-Yong. *The Greatest Olympics: From Baden-Baden to Seoul*. Seoul: Si-sa-yong-o-sa, 1990.

Kissinger, Henry. *Diplomacy*. New York: Simon & Schuster, 1994.

———. *White House Years*. Boston: Little, Brown, 1979.

———. "World of Wonder." *Newsweek*, June 12, 2006.

Knuttgen, H. G., Qiwei Ma, and Zhongyuan Wu, eds. *Sport in China*, Champaign, Ill.: Human Kinetics Books, 1990.

Ko, Dorothy. *Cinderella's Sisters: A Revisionist History of Footbinding*. Berkeley: University of California Press, 2005.

Kolatch, Jonathan. *Sports, Politics, and Ideology in China*. New York: Jonathan David, 1972.

Kong Dongmei. *Gai bian shi jie de ri zi: Yu Wang Hairong tan Mao Zedong wai jiao wang shi* (Discussions with Wang Hairong about Mao's foreign policy). Beijing: Zhong yang wen xian chubanshe, 2006.

Kreuger, Arnd, and W. J. Murray. *The Nazi Olympics: Sport, Politics and Appeasement in the 1930s*. Urbana: University of Illinois Press, 2003.

Kristof, Nicholas, and Sheryl WuDunn. *China Wakes: The Struggle for the Soul of a Rising Power*. New York: Vintage, 1994.

LaFeber, Walter. *Michael Jordan and the New Global Capitalism*. New York: W. W. Norton, 1999.

Lampton, David. "A Growing China in a Shrinking World; Beijing and the Global Order." In *Living with China: U.S.-China Relations in the Twenty-first Century*, ed. Ezra Vogel. New York: W. W. Norton, 1997.

Landler, Mark, and Jere Longman. "Germans' Main Objective Is a Good Time for All," *New York Times*, June 9, 2006.

Landry, Fernand, Marc Landry, Magdeleine Yerlès, and International Olympic Committee. *Sport, the Third Millennium: Proceedings of the International Symposium, Quebec City, Canada, May 21–25, 1990*. Sainte-Foy, Quebec City: Les Presses de L'Université Laval, 1991.

Large, David C. *Nazi Games: The Olympics of 1936*. New York: W. W. Norton, 2007.

Larmer, Brook. "The Center of the World." *Foreign Policy* (September–October 2005).

———. *Operation Yao Ming: The Chinese Sports Empire, American Big Business, and the Making of an NBA Superstar*. New York: Gotham Books, 2005.

Larson, James F., and Heung-Soo Park. *Global Television and the Politics of* the Seoul Olympics, Politics in Asia and the Pacific. Boulder, Colo.: Westview, 1993.

Lee, Jae-won. Seoul Olympics and the Global Community. Seoul: Seoul Olympics Memorial Association, 1992.

Li Dan and Yang Kuangman, eds. Wu huan qi xia de zhui hui (Sorrow and regret under the five-ring Olympic flag). Beijing: Zhong guo wenlian chuban gongsi, 1990.

Li Lie, ed. He Long nianpu (Chronological biography of He Long). Beijing: Ren min chubanshe, 1996.

Li Lingxiu and Zhou Minggong. Tiyu zhi zi Rong Gaotang (Son of sports: Rong Gaotang). Beijing: Xinhua chubanshe, 2002.

Li Xing. "Guo chi de wu yue yu tiyu" (May's national shame and sports). In Zhejiang Provincial Library, ed., Tu shu zhan wang yue kan 2, no. 7 (May 10, 1936).

Li Xiumei. Zhong hua ren min gong he guo tiyu shi jian bian (A concise history of sports in the PRC). Beijing: Beijing tiyu da xue chubanshe, 2002.

Li You. "Qing xie de zu qiu chang" (Unbalanced soccer stadium), in Quan guo you xiu baogao wen xue huo jiang zuo pin ji, 1985–1986 (Collections of a national-award-winning journalism, 1985–1986), ed. Zhong guo zuo jia xie hui. Beijing: Zuojia chubanshe, 1988.

Liang Jisheng. Nankai da xue xiao zhang Zhang Boling (President Zhang Boling of Nankai University). Jinan: Shandong jiaoyu chubanshe, 2003.

Liang Lijuan. He Zhenliang: Wu huan zhi lu (He Zhenliang and the Olympics). Beijing: Shijie zhishi chubanshe, 2005.

Liang Qichao. Liang Qichao quan ji (Complete collections of Liang Qichao's Writings). Beijing: Beijing chubanshe, 1999.

Liao Hui and Xia Li, eds. Yin ying xia de fan si: Er shi si jie Ao yun hui ji shi (Reflections in the shadow: The true story of China's participation in the Thirty-fourth Olympic Games). Wuhan: Hubei renmin chubanshe, 1988.

Lin Ke, Xu Tao, and Wu Xujun, eds. Li shi de zhen shi (Return truth to history). Beijing: Zhong yang wen xian chubanshe, 1998.

Lind, Jennifer. "Dangerous Games." Atlantic Monthly (March 2006).

Link, E. Perry, Richard Madsen, and Paul Pickowicz. Popular China: Unofficial Culture in a Globalizing Society. Lanham, Md.: Rowman & Littlefield, 2002.

Little, James Robert. "Charles Harold McCloy: His Contributions to Physical Education," Ph.D. diss., University of Iowa, 1968.

Liu Bingguo. Zhong guo tiyu shi (The history of Chinese sports). Shanghai: Shanghai gu ji chubanshe, 2003.

Liu Changchun. "Can jia shi jie yun dong hui gan yan" (Reflections on my participation in the Olympic Games). *Tiyu zhou bao* (Tianjin) 38 (October 1932).

———. "Liu Changchun de ri ji" (Diary of Liu Changchun), *Tiyu zhou bao* (Tianjin) 32 (1932).

———. "Wo guo shou ci zheng shi can jia ao yun hui shi mo" (The true story behind China's first official participation in the Olympics), in *Wen shi zi liao xuan ji* 70, ed. Zhong guo ren min zheng zhi xie shang hui yi quan guo weiyuan hui wen shi zi liao yan jiu wei yuan hui. Beijing: Wen shi zi liao chubanshe, 1980.

Liu Qi. *Beijing Ao yun jing ji yanjiu* (A study of Beijing's Olympic economy). Beijing: Beijing chubanshe, 2003.

Liu Qingli, ed. *Tiyu wu qian nian* (Five thousand years of sports). Changchun: Jilin ren min chubanshe, 200.

Liu Shencheng, "Tiyu jiu guo lun" (On using sports to save the nation) (1–2). In *Qin fen tiyu yue bao* (Shanghai) 2, no. 8 (May 1935), and 2, no. 10 (July 1935).

Liu Shufa, ed. *Chen Yi nianpu* (Chronological biography of Chen Yi). Beijing: Renmin chubanshe, 1995.

Liu, Xinwu. "5.19 Chang Jing Tou" (Report on the May 19th incident). In *Liu Xinwu wen ji* (Collections of Liu Xinwu's writings). Beijing: Hua yi chubanshe, 1993.

Liu, Xiuwu. *Aolinpike yun dong hui cheng ji* (Records of the Olympic Games). Beijing: Ren min tiyu chubanshe, 1984.

Liu Yangdong, and Meng Chao, eds. *Zhongguo chong ji bo: Dang dai she hui wen ti bao gao wen xue xuan* (Shock waves of China). Beijing: Zhongguo renmin daxue chubanshe, 1988.

Lo, M. K. "Progress of Sport among Chinese in Hong Kong." In Hong Kong World News Service, ed., *The Hong Kong Centenary Commemorative Talks, 1841–1941* (Hong Kong: World News Service, 1941).

Long teng hu yue (Dragons fly and tigers jump). Nanning: Guangxi ren min chubanshe, 1978.

Los Angeles Olympic Organizing Committee, ed., *Tenth Olympiad, 1932*. Los Angeles: Los Angeles Olympic Organizing Committee, 1932.

Lu Guang. *Zhong guo ti tan da ju jiao* (Focus on Chinese sports). Jinan: Shandong chubanshe, 1999.

Lu Guang. "Zhongguo guniang" (Chinese girls). In Zhongguo zuojia xuehui ed., *Quan guo you xiu baogao wen xue pingxuan huo jiang zuo pin ji* (Collections of national-award-winning journalism). Beijing: Renmin wenxue chubanshe, 1984.

Lu Guang and Zhang Xiaolan. *Jinpai Cong Ling Dao Shiwu* (Gold medals from nothing to fifteen). Changsha: Hunan shao nian er tong chubanshe, 1985.

Lu Mu, ed. *Tiyu jie de yi mian qi zhi Ma Yuehan jiao shou* (Ma Yuehan as a flag bearer in Chinese sports). Beijing: Beijing tiyu daxue chubanshe, 1999.

Lu Yunting. *Jing ji Zhong guo: Jing ji wen hua yu Zhong guo de guomin xing* (Competitive games and the Chinese national character). Beijing: Zhong hua gong shang lian he chubanshe, 1997.

Lubow, Arthur. "The China Syndrome." *New York Times Sunday Magazine,* May 21, 2006.

Lucas, John. *The Modern Olympic Games.* South Brunswick, N.J.: A. S. Barnes, 1980.

Luo Dacheng. *Zhong guo de xuan feng* (Big storm from China). Chengdu: Sichuan renmin chubanshe, 1983.

Luo Shimin. *Ao yun lai dao Zhong guo* (The Olympics arrive in China). Beijing: Qinghua daxue chubanshe, 2005.

Lyberg, Wolf. *Fabulous One Hundred Years of the IOC: Facts, Figures, and Much, Much More.* Lausanne: International Olympic Committee, 1996.

———, ed. *The IOC Sessions, 1894–1988.* Lausanne: International Olympic Committee, n.d.

Ma Lan and Li Wen. *Qi ji zai Zhong guo* (Miracles have happened in China). Beijing: Zuojia chubanshe, 1991.

Ma Tongbing and Qing Yuanyuan, eds. *Beijing 2008: Shen ao de tai qian mu hou* (Beijing 2008: The inside story of Beijing's bid). Beijing: Beijing tiyu daxue chubanshe, 2001.

MacAloon, John. "*La Pitada Olympica:* Puerto Rico, International Sport, and the Constitution of Politics." In Edward M. Bruner, ed., *Text, Play, and Story: The Construction and Reconstruction of Self and Society* (Prospect Heights, Ill.: Waveland, 1988).

———. *This Great Symbol: Pierre de Coubertin and the Origins of the Modern Olympic Games.* Chicago: University of Chicago Press, 1981. The second edition was published in a special issue of *International Journal of the History of Sport* 23, nos. 3–4 (May–June 2006).

———. "The Turn of Two Centuries: Sport and the Politics of Intercultural Relations," in Fernand Landry et al., eds., *Sport . . . The Third Millennium, Proceedings of the International Symposium, Quebec City, Canada, May 1990.* Sainte-Foy, Quebec City: Les Presses de L'Université Laval, 1991.

MacClancy, Jeremy, ed. *Sport, Identity and Ethnicity.* Oxford, Eng.: Berg, 1996.

MacFarlane, Neil, and Michael Herd. *Sport and Politics: A World Divided.* London: Collins, 1986.

MacFarquhar, Roderick, and Michael Schoenhals. *Mao's Last Revolution.* Cambridge: Belknap Press of Harvard University Press, 2006.

Macintosh, Donald. "Sport and Government in Canada." In *National Sports Policies,* ed. Laurence Chalip et al. Westport, Conn.: Greenwood, 1996.

———. "Trudeau, Taiwan, and the 1976 Montreal Olympics." *American Review of Canadian Studies* 21, no. 4 (1992).

Macintosh, Donald, and Thomas Bedecki. *Sport and Politics in Canada: Federal Government Involvement since 1961.* Kingston, Ont.: McGill-Queen's University Press, 1987.

Macintosh, Donald, and Donna Greenhorn. "Hockey Diplomacy and Canadian Foreign Policy." *Journal of Canadian Studies* 28, no. 2 (Summer 1993).

Macintosh, Donald, and Michael Haws. *Sport and Canadian Diplomacy.* Montreal: McGill-Queen's University Press, 1994.

Magdaliński, Tara. "Sports History and East German National Identity," *Peace Review* 11, no. 4 (December 1999).

Maguire, Joseph A. *Global Sport: Identities, Societies, Civilizations.* Cambridge, Eng.: Polity Press, 1999.

———. *Power and Global Sport: Zones of Prestige, Emulation, and Resistance.* London: Routledge, 2005.

Mai Kele (McCloy). "Di liu jie yuan dong yun dong hui de jiao xun" (Lessons from the Sixth Far Eastern Championship Games). Zhong hua quan guo tiyu yan jiu hui, ed., *Tiyu ji kan* (Chinese journal of physical education) 2, no. 2 (1923).

Mallon, Bill, and Ture Widlund. *The 1896 Olympic Games: Results for All Competitors in All Events, with Commentary.* Jefferson, N.C.: McFarland, 1998.

Mandell, Richard D. *The First Modern Olympics.* Berkeley: University of California Press, 1976.

———. *The Nazi Olympics.* Urbana: University of Illinois Press, 1987.

———. *The Olympics of 1972: A Munich Diary.* Chapel Hill: University of North Carolina Press, 1991.

———. *Sport: A Cultural History.* New York: Columbia University Press, 1984.

Mangan, J. A. *The European Sports History Review,* vol. 3: *Europe, Sport, World: Shaping Global Societies.* London: Frank Cass, 2001.

———, ed. *The Cultural Bond: Sport, Empire, and Society.* London: Frank Cass, 1992.

———, ed. *Superman Supreme: Fascist Body as Political Icon—Global Fascism.* London: Frank Cass, 2000.

———, ed. *Tribal Identities: Nationalism, Europe, Sport.* London: Frank Cass, 1996.

Mangan, J. A., and Fan Hong, eds. *Sport in Asian Society*. London: Frank Cass, 2003.

Manheim, Jarol. "Rites of Passage: The 1988 Seoul Olympics as Public Diplomacy." *Western Political Quarterly* 43, no. 2 (June 1990).

Mann, James. *About Face: A History of America's Curious Relationship with China, from Nixon to Clinton*. New York: Vintage, 2000.

Manzenreiter, Wolfram, and John Horne, eds. *Football Goes East: Business, Culture and the People's Game in China, Japan, and South Korea*. New York: Routledge, 2004.

Mao Anjun (Andrew Morris). "1909–1919 [jiao yu za zhi] tiyu wen zhang fen xi de chu bu" (A preliminary study of sport articles in the journal of education, 1909–1919). Zhong hua min guo tiyu xue hui, ed., *Tiyu xue bao* (Taiwan) 21 (June 1996).

Mao Zedong. "Tiyu zhi yanjiu" (On physical culture). *Xin Qingnian* (New youth), April 1, 1917.

Marcovitz, Hal. *The Munich Olympics, Great Disasters, Reforms and Ramifications*. Philadelphia: Chelsea House, 2002.

Margolick, David. *Beyond Glory: Joe Louis vs. Max Schmeling and a World on the Brink*. New York: Knopf, 2005.

Mason, Tony. "England, 1966." In Alan Tomlinson and Christopher Young, eds., *National Identity and Global Sports Events: Culture, Politics, and Spectacle in the Olympics and the Football World Cup*. Albany: State University of New York Press, 2006.

McGeoch, Rod, with Glenda Korporaal. *Bid: How Australia Won the 2000 Olympic Games*. Sidney: William Heineman, 1994.

Mewett, Peter. "Fragments of a Composite Identity: Aspects of Australian Nationalism in a Sports Setting." *Australian Journal of Anthropology* 10, no. 3 (1999).

Miller, David. *Olympic Revolution: The Biography of Juan Antonio Samaranch* (London: Pavilion, 1992).

Miller, Geoffrey. *Behind the Olympic Rings*. Lynn, Mass.: H. O. Zimman, 1979.

Miller, Toby, Geoffrey Lawrence, Jim Mckay, and David Rowe. "Modifying the Sign: Sport and Globalization," *Social Texts* 17, no. 3 (1999).

Min sheng bao tiyu zu. *Ao Yun Jing Hua Lu*. Taipei: Min sheng bao she, 1984.

Morozek, Donald. *Sport and American Mentality, 1880–1910*. Knoxville: University of Tennessee Press, 1983.

Morris, Andrew D. "'I Can Compete!' China in the Olympic Games." *Journal of Sport History* 26 (1999): 545–566.

———. *Marrow of the Nation: A History of Sport and Physical Culture in Republican China*. Berkeley: University of California Press, 2004.

Morrow, Don, and Kevin B. Wamsley. *Sport in Canada: A History.* Don Mills, Ont.: Oxford University Press, 2005.

Nauright, J. *Sport, Culture and Identities in South Africa.* London: Leicester University Press, 1997.

Ninkovich, Frank A., and Liping Bu. *The Cultural Turn: Essays in the History of U.S. Foreign Relations.* Chicago: Imprint Publications, 2001.

Nixon, Richard. "Asia after Vietnam." *Foreign Affairs* 46, no. 1 (1967).

———. *RN: The Memoirs of Richard Nixon.* New York: Grosset & Dunlap, 1978.

Organizing Committee of Berlin 1936 Games, ed., *The Tenth Olympic Games, Berlin, 1936.* Berlin: Wilhelm Limpert, 1936.

Orwell, George. *Shooting an Elephant and Other Essays.* New York: Harcourt, Brace, 1950.

Park, Roberta. "Sport and Recreation among Chinese American Communities of the Pacific Coast from Time of Arrival to the 'Quiet Decade' of the 1950s." *Journal of Sport History* 27, no. 3 (2000).

Park, Seh-jik. *The Seoul Olympics: A Bridge to the Future and Peace.* Seoul: Tokkon Kim, 1990.

———. *The Seoul Olympics: The Inside Story.* London: Bellew, 1991.

Peng Yongjie, Zhang Zhiwei, and Han Donghui, eds. *Ren wen Ao yun* (People's Olympics). Beijing: Dong fang chubanshe, 2003.

Pope, S. W. "An Army of Athletes: Playing Fields, Battlefields, and the American Military Sporting Experience, 1890–1920." *Journal of Military History* 59, no. 3 (1995).

———. *Patriotic Games: Sporting Traditions in the American Imagination, 1876–1926.* New York: Oxford University Press, 1997.

Pound, Richard. *Five Rings over Korea: The Secret Negotiations behind the 1988 Olympic Games in Seoul.* New York: Little, Brown, 1994.

PRC Foreign Ministry and Zhong gong zhong yang wen xian yan jiu shi, eds. *Zhou Enlai waijiao wenxian* (Diplomatic documents of Zhou Enlai). Beijing: Zhong yang wen xian chubanshe, 1990.

Preston, Diana. *The Boxer Rebellion: The Dramatic Story of China's War on Foreigners That Shook the World in the Summer of 1900.* New York: Walker, 2000.

Public Papers of the United States: Gerald Ford, 1976–1977. Washington, D.C.: U.S. Government Printing Office, 1979.

Qian Jiang. *Xiao qiu zhuan dong da qiu: Ping pong wai jiao bei hou* (The small ball moves the big ball: The inside story of ping-pong diplomacy). Beijing: Dong fang chubanshe, 1997.

Qian Qichen. *Wai jiao shi ji* (Ten main diplomatic events when I was the foreign minister). Beijing: Shijie zhishi chubanshe, 2003.

Qiao Keqin and Guan Wenmin. *Zhongguo tiyu si xiang shi* (The history of Chinese ideas about sports). Lanzhou: Gansu minzu chubanshe, 1993.

Qin fen tiyu yue bao, ed. "Zhu di shi yi jie shi jie yun dong hui kai mu" (Congratulations on the opening of the Eleventh Olympic Games). *Qin fen tiyu yue bao* (Shanghai) 3, no. 10 (July 1936).

Quan guo yun dong da hui xuan chuan zu, ed. *Quan guo yun dong da hui yao lan* (Summary of the [1930] national games). N.p.: Quan guo yun dong da hui, 1930.

Reaves, Joseph A. *Taking in a Game: A History of Baseball in Asia.* Lincoln: University of Nebraska Press, 2002.

Reich, Kenneth. *Making It Happen: Peter Ueberroth and the 1984 Olympics.* Santa Barbara, Calif.: Capra, 1986.

Renmin tiyu chubanshe, ed. *Da di fan zhuan huan xin tian* (The earth turns and the sky is new). Beijing: Renmin tiyu chubanshe, 1965.

———. *Qing chun wan sui* (Long live the young). Beijing: Renmin tiyu chubanshe, 1965.

Riess, Steven A. "The New Sport History." *Reviews in American History* 18, no. 3 (September 1990).

Riordan, James. *Sport and International Politics.* London: E & FN Spon, 1996.

Riordan, James, and Dong Jinxia. "Chinese Women and Sport: Success, Sexuality and Suspicion." *China Quarterly* 145 (March 1996).

Riordan, James, and Robin Jones, eds. *Sport and Physical Education in China.* London: E & FN Spon, 1999.

Riordan, James, and Arnd Kruger, eds. *The International Politics of Sport in the Twentieth Century.* London: E & FN Spon, 1999.

Rong Gaotang, ed. *Dang dai Zhong guo tiyu* (Sports of contemporary China). Beijing: Zhong guo she hui ke xue chubanshe, 1984.

———. *Rong Gaotang tiyu wen lun xuan* (Selected articles and speeches of Rong Gaotang on sports). Shanghai: Huadong shifan daxue chubanshe, 1992.

Rowe, David. *Sport, Culture, and the Media: The Unruly Trinity; Issues in Cultural and Media Studies.* Buckingham, Eng.: Open University Press, 1999.

Samaranch, Juan Antonio. *The Samaranch Years: 1980–1994, Towards Olympic Unity. Interviews Conducted by Robert Parienté with the President of the IOC for the Newspaper l'Equipe.* Lausanne: International Olympic Committee, 1995.

Schaaf, Phil. *Sports, Inc.: One Hundred Years of Sports Business.* Amherst, N.Y.: Prometheus Books, 2004.

Schaffer, Kay, and Sidonie Smith, eds., *The Olympics at the Millennium:*

Power, Politics, and the Games. New Brunswick, N.J.: Rutgers University Press, 2000.

Schwartz, Benjamin Isadore. *In Search of Wealth and Power: Yen Fu and the West.* Cambridge: Harvard University Press, 1968.

Senn, Alfred Erich. *Power, Politics, and the Olympic Games.* Champaign, Ill.: Human Kinetics, 1999.

Seoul Olympic Organizing Committee. *Seoul 1988.* Seoul: Seoul Olympic Organizing Committee, 1985.

Shaikin, Bill. *Sport and Politics: The Olympics and the Los Angeles Games.* New York: Praeger, 1988.

Shao Rugan. "Jian she min zu ben wei de tiyu" (Establish nationalistic sports in China). Guo li zhong yang daxue tiyu yan jiu she, ed., *Tiyu za zhi* (Nanjing) 1, no. 1 (January 1935).

Sharp, Mitchell. *Which Reminds Me . . . : A Memoir.* Toronto: University of Toronto Press, 1994.

Shih, Chi-wen. *Sports Go Forward in China.* Beijing: Foreign Languages Press, 1963.

Shuter, Jane. *The Ancient Greeks.* Crystal Lake, Ill.: Heinemann Library, 1997.

Simon, Vyv, and Andrew Jennings. *Lords of the Rings.* London: Simon & Schuster, 1992.

Smith, Adrian, and Dilwyn Porter, eds. *Sport and National Identity in the Post-War World.* London: Routledge, 2004.

Smith, Anthony D. *National Identity, Ethnonationalism in Comparative Perspective.* Reno: University of Nevada Press, 1991.

Song Ruhai. *Wo neng bi ya: Shi jie yun dong hui cong lu* (Records of the World Sports Games). Shanghai: Shangwu yin shu guan, 1930.

Song Shixiong. *Song Shixiong zi shu: Wo de tiyu shi jie yu ying ping chun qiu* (The story of Song Shixiong: My times with the sports world and television). Beijing: Zuo jia chubanshe, 1997.

Spivey, Nigel Jonathan. *The Ancient Olympics.* New York: Oxford University Press, 2004.

State Department, ed. *Foreign Relations of the United States,* vol. 17: *China, 1969–1972.* Washington, D.C.: U.S. Government Printing Office, 2006.

Su Jinchen. "Jun guomin tiyu zhi ying xiang" (The impact of militarizing citizens' sport). *Tiyu wenshi* 3 (1987).

———. "Zhong guo gu dai ma qiu yun dong de yanjiu" (Polo in ancient China). In *Zhong guo tiyu shi cankao ziliao* (Reference materials on the history of sports in China). Beijing: Renmin tiyu chubanshe, 1958.

Sugden, John Peter, and Alan Bairner. *Sport in Divided Societies.* Lansing, Mich.: Meyer & Meyer Sport, 1999.

Sugden, John Peter, and Alan Tomlinson. *FIFA and the Contest for World Football: Who Rules the People's Game?* Cambridge, Eng.: Polity Press, 1998.

Sun Baojie. "Ao lin pi ke yun dong hui yu zhong guo jindai tiyu" (Olympic movement and sports in modern China). *Tiyu wenshi* 80, no. 4 (1996).

Sun Jinshun. "1936 nian zhong guo zu qiu dai biao dui chu zheng Ao yun hui qian hou de qing kuang" (The background surrounding China's national soccer team's participation in the 1936 Olympic Games). In *Wen shi zi liao xuan ji* 70, ed. Zhong guo ren min zheng zhi xie shang hui yi quan guo weiyuan hui wen shi ziliao yan jiu wei yuan hui. Beijing: Wen shi zi liao chubanshe, 1980.

Sun Yingxiang. *Yan Fu nianpu* (Chronological biography of Yan Fu). Fuzhou: Fujian ren min chubanshe, 2003.

Sun Zhongshan. *Sun Zhongshan quan ji* (Complete collection of Sun Zhongshan). Beijing: Zhonghua shuju, 1985.

Svrluga, Barry. *National Pastime: Sports, Politics, and the Return of Baseball to Washington, D.C.* New York: Doubleday, 2006.

Szymanski, Stefan, and Andrew S. Zimbalist. *National Pastime: How Americans Play Baseball and the Rest of the World Plays Soccer.* Washington, D.C.: Brookings Institution Press, 2005.

Tang Hao. "Shi kao wo guo Sui Tang yi qian de ma qiu" (Preliminary study on polo games in pre-Sui and Tang China). In *Zhong guo tiyu shi cankao ziliao* (Reference materials on the history of sports in China). Beijing: Renmin tiyu chubanshe, 1957.

———. "Wo guo gu dai mou xie qiu lei yun dong de guo ji ying xiang" (The international influence of some Chinese ancient games). In *Zhong guo tiyu shi cankao ziliao* (Reference materials on the history of sports in China). Beijing: Renmin tiyu chubanshe, 1958.

———, ed. *Zhong guo tiyu cankao ziliao ji* (Reference materials on the history of sports in China). Beijing: Renmin tiyu chubanshe, 1958.

Tang Hecheng and Jiang Shan, eds. *Shi ji dang an: 1895–1995 ying xiang er shi shi ji Zhong guo li shi jin cheng de 100 pian wen zhang* (One hundred articles that affected China's historical development in 1895–1995). Beijing: Dang an chubanshe, 1995.

Tang Mingxin. *Tang Mingxin xiansheng fangwen jilu* (Reminiscences of Tang Mingxin, interviewed by Zhang Qixiong and Pan Guangzhe). Taipei: Institute of Modern History, Academia Sinica, 2005.

———. *Wo guo can jia ao yun hui cang sang shi* (The sad history of China's participation in Olympic Games). Taipei: Zhonghua Taipei ao lin pi ke weiyuan hui, 1999–2000.

Tian Zengpei and Wang Taiping, eds. *Lao waijiao guan huiyi Zhou Enlai* (Senior diplomats remember Zhou Enlai). Beijing: Shijie zhishi chubanshe, 1998.

Tie Zhuwei. *Chen yi yuan shuai de zui hou sui yue* (The late years of Marshal Chen Yi). Beijing: Jie fang jun wen yi chubanshe, 1997.

Tomlinson, Alan, and Christopher Young. *German Football: History, Culture, Society.* London: Routledge, 2005.

————, eds. *National Identity and Global Sports Events: Culture, Politics, and Spectacle in the Olympics and the Football World Cup.* Albany: State University of New York Press, 2006.

Tong Le, ed. *Meng xiang yu hui huang: Beijing 2008 Ao yun hui shen ban ji shi yu chang xiang* (Dream and glory: Report on Beijing's bid for the 2008 Olympic Games). Beijing: Min zhu yu jian she chubanshe, 2001.

Ueberroth, Peter. *Made in America: His Own Story.* New York: William Morrow, 1986.

U.S. Congressional Executive Commission on China. *The Beijing Olympics and Human Rights: Roundtable before the Congressional-Executive Commission on China.* 107th Cong., 2d sess., November 18, 2002. Washington, D.C.: U.S. Government Printing Office, 2003.

U.S. Department of State. *Foreign Relations of the United States,* vol. 17: *China, 1969–1972.* Washington, D.C.: U.S. Government Printing Office, 2006.

Van Bottenburg, Maarten. *Global Games, Sport and Society.* Urbana: University of Illinois Press, 2001.

Wakefield, Wanda Ellen. *Playing to Win: Sports and the American Military, 1898–1945.* Albany: State University of New York Press, 1997.

Wan Yan Shao Yuan, *Wang Zhengting zhuan* (Biography of Wang Zhengting). Baoding: Hebei renmin chubanshe, 1999.

Wang Chongli. *Wuhuan ren shi xiang* (Secrets under the five-ring flag). Beijing: Zhong guo wenlian chuban gongsi, 1995.

————. *Zhong guo ti tan re dian xie zhen* (Report on hot topics of Chinese sports). Beijing: Zhong guo wenlian chuban gongsi, 1996.

Wang Daping and Fan Hong. *Tiyu shihua* (The history of sports). Beijing: Kepu chubanshe, 1990.

Wang Jinjun. *Beijing Ao yun 2008* (The 2008 Beijing Olympics). Beijing: Zuojia chubanshe, 2001.

Wang Shi, ed. *Yan Fu ji* (Collections of Yan Fu). Beijing: Zhonghua shu ju, 1986.

Wang Shijie. "Zhong guo tiyu zhi qian tu" (The future of China's sports). *Dong fang za zhi* 30, no. 20 (October 16, 1933).

Wang Zhen. *Bai nian ti tan lüe ying* (A glimpse of sports in China in the last hundred years). Beijing: Zhong guo jing ji chubanshe, 2000.

Wang Zhengya. *Jiu Zhong guo tiyu jian wen* (Observations of sports in pre-1949 China). Beijing: Renmin tiyu chubanshe, 1987.

Wei Jizhong. *Wo kan zhongguo tiyu* (Chinese sports in my mind). Beijing: Sanlian shudian, 2005.

Weiland, Matt, and Sean Willey, eds. *Thinking Fans' Guide to the World Cup*. New York: Harper Perennial, 2006.

Wo men de peng you bian tian xia (China has friends everywhere). Beijing: Renmin tiyu chubanshe, 1965.

Wrynn, Alison M. "'Debt Was Paid Off in Tears': Science, IOC Politics and the Debate about High Altitude in the 1968 Mexico City Olympics." *International Journal of the History of Sport* 23, no. 7 (November 2006).

Wu, Chih-Kang. "The Influence of the YMCA on the Development of Physical Education in China." Ph.D. diss., University of Michigan, Ann Arbor, 1956.

Wu Chongyuan. *Ao yun hui shang de Zhongguo guan jun* (Chinese champions in Olympic Games). Tianjin: Xin lei chubanshe, 1985.

Wu Chongyuan et al. *Liang piao zhi cha: Beijing shen ban 2000 nian ao yun hui shi mo* (Short two votes: The whole story of Beijing's bid for the 2000 Olympic Games). Beijing: Zhong guo ao lin pi ke chubanshe, 1994.

Wu Jingguo. *Ao lin pi ke Zhong hua qing* (My Olympics and China bond). Suzhou: Suzhou daxue chubanshe, 2005.

———. *Ao yun chang wai de jing ji* (Competitions beyond the Olympic Games). Taipei: Tianxia yuanjian chuban gufen youxian gongsi, 2001.

Wu Jisong. *Qin li Ao yun* (Witness to the Olympics). Beijing: Jinghua chubanshe, 2001.

Wu Shaozu et al., ed. *Mao Zedong yu tiyu wenji* (Collected papers on Mao Zedong and sports). Chengdu: Sichuan jiaoyu chubanshe, 1994.

———, ed. *Zhong hua renmin gong he guo tiyu shi* (A history of sports in the People's Republic of China). Beijing: Zhongguo shuji chubanshe, 1999.

Wu Wenzhong. *Tiyu shi* (History of sports). Taipei: Zhengzhong shuju, 1957.

———. *Zhong guo jin bai nian tiyu shi* (A history of sports in modern China). Taipei: Taiwan shang wu yin shu guan, 1967.

Wu Xujun. "Mao Zedong de wu bu gao qi: Da kai zhong mei guan xi da men shi mo" (Mao's five smart moves in improving Sino-American relations). In *Li Shi De Zhen Shi* (Return truth to history), ed. Lin Ke, Xu Tao, and Wu Xujun. Beijing: Zhong yang wen xian chubanshe, 1998.

Wu Yunrui. "Tiyu yu jun shi xun lian zhi guan xi" (The relationship between sports and military training). *Tiyu ji kan* (Shanghai) 2, no. 2 (June 1936).

———. "Wu guo min zu fu xing zhong nu zi tiyu zhi zhong yao" (Importance of women's physical training in China's national revival). *Tiyu za zhi* 1, no. 1 (April 1935).

Wythe, George, Joseph Mills Hanson, and Carl V. Berger, eds. *The Inter-Allied Games.* New York: Games Committee, 1919.

Xia, Yafeng. "China's Elite Politics and Sino-American Rapprochement." *Journal of Cold War Studies* 8, no. 4 (2006).

Xiang, Lanxin. *The Origins of the Boxer War: A Multinational Study.* London: Routledge Curzon, 2003.

Xie Yanlong, ed. *Ao lin pi ke Yanjiu* (A study of the Olympics). Beijing: Beijing tiyu daxue chubanshe, 1994.

Xin hua she tiyu bu, ed. *Cong ling dao shi wu* ([China's gold medals] from zero to fifteen). Beijing: Xinhua chubanshe, 1985.

Xin Jiang. "Zhong Guo Tiyu Yang Wu Yun Dong" (Foreign coaches call the shots in China). *Zhong guo tiyu* 431, no. 5 (2005).

"Xin tiyu" za zhi she, ed. *Guan jun zhi lu* (The road to championships). Hangzhou: Zhejiang ren min chubanshe, 1984.

"Xin tiyu" za zhi she, ed. *Jin pai zai guo ge sheng Zhong shan yao* (Gold medals and singing the national anthem). Beijing: Ren min tiyu chubanshe, 1984.

Xing, Jun. "The American Social Gospel and the Chinese YMCA." *Journal of American–East Asian Relations* 5, nos. 3–4 (Fall–Winter 1996).

Xing Junji and Zu Xianhai. *Bai nian chen fu: Zou jin Zhong guo tiyu jie* (The rise and fall of Chinese sports in the last one hundred years). Zhengzhou: Henan wen yi chubanshe, 2000.

Xinhua News Agency. "China's Sports Relations with Other Countries." In Xinhua News Agency, ed., *China's Foreign Relations: A Chronology of Events (1949–1988).* Beijing: Foreign Languages Press, 1989.

Xiong Xianghui. *Wo de qing bao yu wai jiao sheng ya* (My life in the areas of intelligence and diplomacy). Beijing: Zhong gong dang shi chubanshe, 1999.

Xiong Xiaozheng, Chen Jinzhang, and Lin Dengyuan. "Cong 'Tu Yang' dui li dao 'Jian she min zu ben wei tiyu'" (Confrontations between nationalist sports and western sports regarding the establishment of physical education focusing on China-centered sports). *Tiyu wen shi* 86, no. 4 (1997).

Xu Baoyin. "Tang dai tiyu huo dong zhi yanjiu" (A study of sports in the Tang dynasty). Master's thesis, National Taiwan Normal University, 1977.

Xu Guoqi. *China and the Great War: China's Pursuit of a New National Identity and Internationalization.* New York: Cambridge University Press, 2005.

———. "Historical Memories and China's Changing Views of East Asia."

Journal of American–East Asian Relations 11, nos. 1–4 (Spring–Winter 2002).

Xu Tao. "Mao Zedong de bao jian yang sheng zhi dao" (Mao Zedong's way of staying healthy). In *Li shi de zhen shi* (Return truth to history), ed. Lin Ke, Xu Tao, and Wu Xujun. Beijing: Zhong yang wen xian chubanshe, 1998.

Xu Yinsheng. *Wo yu Ping Pang Qiu: Xu Yinsheng zi zhuan* (Ping Pong and me: Autobiography of Xu Yinsheng). Beijing: Zhongguo she hui ke xue chubanshe, 1995.

Xu Yixiong. "Jindai Zhong guo min zu zhu yi tiyu si xiang zhi xing cheng" (The forming of nationalist sports in modern China). *Tiyu xue bao* 9 (1987).

———. "Wan Qing tiyu si xiang zhi xing cheng: Yi zi qiang bao zhong si xiang wei zhong xin de tan tao" (Creating a theory of sports during the late Qing: The centrality of the ideas of self-strengthening and preserving race). *Tiyu xue bao* 10 (1988).

———. *Zhong guo jindai minzu zhuyi tiyu si xiang* (Thoughts on physical education in modern China). Taipei: Qiying wen hua shi ye you xian gong si, 1996.

Xu Yuanmin. "Yan Fu de tiyu si xiang" (Yan Fu's thoughts on sports). In *Tiyu Xuebao* (Taipei) 18 (December 1994).

Yan, Yuanxiang. "Managed Globalization: State Power and Cultural Transition in China." In *Many Globalizations: Cultural Diversity in the Contemporary World,* ed. Peter L. Berger and Samuel P. Huntington, 19–47. New York: Oxford University Press, 2002.

Yang Xianjiang, "Qing nian dui yu tiyu de zi jue" (Youths' self-conciousness about physical education). *Xuesheng za zhi* (Student magazine) 10, no. 4 (April 1923).

Yao, Ming, with Ric Bucher. *Yao: A Life in Two Worlds.* New York: Miramax Books, 2005.

Ye Xin, ed. *Sheng ming de xuan wo* (Swirls of life). Shanghai: Shanghai renmin chubanshe, 1999.

Ye Yonglie. "He Zhili dui wo shuo" (The story He Zhili herself told me). In Ye Xin, ed., *Sheng ming de xuan wo* (Swirls of life). Shanghai: Shanghai renmin chubanshe, 1999.

———. *Zhong guo ping pang nei mu* (The inside story of Chinese Ping-Pong games). Hong Kong: Minbao chubanshe youxian gongsi, 1995.

Yin Qingyao. *Zhong gong de tong zhan wai jiao* (CCP's united front diplomacy). Taipei: You shi wen hua shi ye gong si, 1984.

Yin Weixing. "Zhong Guo Tiyu Jie" (Chinese sports). *Hua Cheng* 6 (1987).

Young, David C. *A Brief History of the Olympic Games.* Malden, Mass.: Blackwell, 2004.

————. *The Modern Olympics: A Struggle for Revival.* Baltimore: Johns Hopkins University Press, 1996.

Yu Zhuli and Zhang Yihui. *Mu ji er shi nian Zhong guo shijian ji* (Witness to the main events of the last twenty years in China). Beijing: Jingji Ribao chubanshe, 1998.

Yuan Dunru. "Shijie ao lin pi ke yundong hui de jia zhi ji dui wo guo tiyu de ying xiang" (The values of the Olympic Games and their impact on China's sports). *Tiyu zhou bao* (Tianjin) 15 (April 14, 1932).

Yuan He. "Kong Xiangxi yu tiyu" (Kong Xiangxi and sports). *Tiyu wenshi* 98, no. 4 (1999).

Zeiler, Thomas W. *Ambassadors in Pinstripes: The Spalding World Tour and the Birth of American Empire.* Lanham, Md.: Rowman & Littlefield, 2006.

Zhang Caizhen, ed. *Ao yun zhan lue si kao* (Strategic thinking on China's policy regarding the Olympic Games). Beijing: Zhong guo ao lin pi ke chubanshe, 1993.

Zhang Luya and Zhou Qing. *Shi ji qing: Zhong guo yu ao lin pi ke* (Dream of a century: China and the Olympics). Beijing: Renmin tiyu chubanshe, 1993.

Zhang Qixiong. "1960 nian qianhou Zhong hua min guo dui guo ji Ao wei hui de hui ji ming cheng zhi zheng" (The Republic of China's struggle over its name in the International Olympic Committee, circa 1960). *Zhong yang yan jiu yuan jindai shi yanjiu suo ji kan* 44 (June 2004).

Zhang Qiyun, ed. *Xian zongtong Jiang gong quanji* (Complete collections of former president Chiang Kaishek). Taipei: Zhong guo wen hua daxue chuban bu, 1984.

Zhang Zhidong. *Quan xue pian* (Exhortation to learning). Beijing: Zhong hua shuju, 1991.

Zhang Zhijiang. "Hui fu min zu tiyu yu kang zhan zui hou sheng li" (Restoring nationalist sports and the final victory of anti-Japanese war). *Guomin tiyu ji kan chuang kan hao* (September 1941).

Zhao Yu. *Bing bai hang cheng* (China's defeat at the Seoul [Olympics]). Beijing: Zhong guo shehui kexue chubanshe, 1988.

Zheng Jianyuan. "Lun Mao Zedong de tiyu si xiang" (On Mao Zedong's ideas about sports). Master's thesis, National Taiwan Normal University, 1994.

Zheng Zhilin and Zhao Shanxing. "Zhong hua tiyu kao cha tuan fu ou kao cha ping shu" (Comments and narratives on a Chinese sport study tour in Europe). *Tiyu wen shi* 3 (1992).

Zhong gong zhong yang wen xian yan jiu shi, ed. *Deng Xiaoping nianpu* (Chronological biography of Deng Xiaoping). Beijing: Zhong yang wen xian chubanshe, 2004.

———, ed. *Liu Shaoqi nianpu* (Chronological biography of Liu Shaoqi). Beijing: Zhong yang wen xian chubanshe, 1996.

———, ed. *Zhou Enlai nianpu, 1949–1976* (Chronological biography of Zhou Enlai). Beijing: Zhong yang wen xian chubanshe, 1997.

Zhong gong zhong yang wen xian yan jiu shi and Zhong yang dang an guan, eds. *Jian guo yi lai Liu Shaoqi wen gao* (Collection of Liu Shaoqi's writings since the founding of the PRC). Beijing: Zhong yang wen xian chubanshe, 2005.

Zhong guo ao lin pi ke wei yuan hui, ed. *Zhong guo tiyu wen hua wu qian nian* (A five-thousand-year history of Chinese physical culture). Beijing: Beijing tiyu daxue chubanshe, 1996.

Zhong guo ao wei hui Xin wen wei yuan hui. *Zai luoshanji de ri ri ye ye: Zhongguo tiyu dai biao tuan can jia di 23 jie Ao yun hui* (Days and nights in Los Angeles: The Chinese delegation's participation in the Twenty-third Olympiad). Beijing: Zhongguo guang bo dian shi chubanshe, 1984.

Zhong guo di er li shi dang an guan, ed. *Zhong hua min guo shi dang an zi liao hui bian,* di wu ji, di yi bian, wen hua (2) (Collections of archival materials of Republican China, ser. 5, no. 1, culture [2]). Nanjing: Jiangsu gu ji chubanshe, 1994.

Zhong guo shi xue hui, ed. *Xin hai ge ming* (The 1911 revolution). Shanghai: Shanghai ren min chubanshe, 1957.

Zhong guo tiyu fa zhan zhan lue yan jiu hui, ed. *1987 Nian quan guo tiyu fa zhan zhan lue lun wen xuan* (Selected papers on strategies used in Chinese sports in 1987). Beijing: Beijing tiyu xue yuan chubanshe, 1988.

Zhong guo zuo jia xue hui, ed. *Quan guo you xiu bao gao wen xue ping xuan huo jiang zuo pin ji* (Collections of national award-winning journalism). Beijing: Renmin wenxue chubanshe, 1984.

———, ed. *Quan guo you xiu bao gao wen xue huo jiang zuo pin ji, 1985–1986* (Collection of national award-winning journalism, 1985–1986). Beijing: Zuo jia chubanshe, 1988.

Zhong hua min guo ao wei hui, ed. *Official Report of the Republic of China Delegation to the Twenty-first Olympic Games, Montreal, 1976.* N.p.: Republic of China Olympic Committee, Taiwan, 1976.

Zhong hua quan guo tiyu xie jin hui, ed. "Fa kan ci" (Statement of the new journal). *Tiyu ji kan* 1, no. 1 (1935): 1.

Zhong hua ren min gong he guo di yi jie yun dong hui xuan chuan bu, ed. *Zhong hua ren min gong he guo di yi jie yun dong hui* (The PRC's first national games). Beijing: Ren min tiyu chubanshe, 1960.

Zhong hua ren min gong he guo tiyu fa quan min jian shen ji hua gang yao (PRC's sport law and summary of the plan for mass exercises). Beijing: Zhong guo fa zhi chubanshe, 1995.

Zhou Jiaquan. "Jidujiao qingnian hui yu zhong guo jing xian dai tiyu" (The YMCA and sport in modern and contemporary China). *Tiyu wenshi* 90, no. 1 (1998).

Zhou Linyi. "Han dai tiyu xian xiang kao" (Study on sports in the Han dynasty). Master's thesis, National Taiwan Normal University, 1974.

Zhou Xikuan et al., ed. *Zhong guo gu dai tiyu shi* (History of Ancient Chinese sports). Chengdu: Sichuan guji chubanshe, 1986.

Zhuang Zedong and Sasaki Atsuko. *Zhuang zedong yu zuo zuo mu dun zi* (Zhuang Zedong and Sasaki Atsuko). Beijing: Zuojia chubanshe, 1996.

Zwingle, Z. "A World Together." *National Geographic* 196 (1999).

ACKNOWLEDGMENTS

FOR NEARLY A DECADE, my research has focused on the issue of China's internationalization, and this book clearly has benefited from the internationalization of the scholarly community. The staffs of the following libraries have provided invaluable assistance: China's National Library in Beijing; the Shanghai and Tianjin municipal libraries; libraries at National Taiwan University, National Taiwan Normal University, and National Zhengzhi University; libraries at the Institute of Modern History and Institute of History and Philosophy, Academia Sinica, Taiwan, and the Chinese University of Hong Kong; the libraries of Hong Kong University; the special collection libraries at University of California, Los Angeles; the library of the International Olympic Committee, Lausanne, Switzerland; and the libraries of the University of Michigan, Western Michigan University, Kalamazoo College, and Harvard University. The interlibrary loans office at the research library of the University of Michigan deserves special thanks for its incredible ability to find books for me.

Archivists are the best friends of historians. I am grateful to many archivists who helped me gain access to and trace down crucial sources. Among many archivists to whom I am in great debt, the following people deserve special acknowledgment: Wayne Wilson, Michael Salmon, Shirley Ito, and their staffs at the Amateur Athletic Foundation and the Los Angeles sports research library; the dedicated employees of the Guo Shi Guan (National Historical Archives, Taiwan) and Archives of Institute of Modern History, Academia Sinica, Taiwan; Ruth Beck-Perrendound, Patricia Eckert, Khanh Nguyen, and many other wonderful staff members at the IOC's Olympic Studies Centre at Lausanne, Switzerland; Joshua Cochran, Geir Gunderson, and William H. McNitt at the Gerald Ford Presidential Library, who shared with me their amazing knowledge about any sources related to the Ford administration; Mark Fisher and Sally Kuisel of the National Archives, College Park, Maryland; staff members at University of Michigan's Bentley Historical Library; and most importantly, John Widdis and Kristin Fraser of Library and Archives Canada, who helped me gain access to many not-yet-declassified materials.

In the 2006–2007 academic year, the Center for Chinese Studies at the University of Michigan provided a stimulating intellectual environment for me to write this book, and the Telluride House at the University of Michigan offered me a generous faculty fellowship. The house is a dream place for anyone who is working on a book. Its cheerful and cozy environment, delicious food, and extremely motivated and intelligent house members made the sometimes painful writing process bearable and even fun. Thanks to Professor James Lee and all of the members of the Telluride House for the fruitful year. As I made the last dash to wrap up this book, I was fortunate to spend three months at the beautiful campus of the Chinese University of Hong Kong as a Lee Hysan fellow. The university's world-class collection of documents on China, combined with its excellent services, were crucial for helping me to finish the book in a timely fashion. In particular, I would like to acknowledge my deep gratitude to the center's director, H. C. Kuan, as well as to assistant director Jean K. M. Hung.

During my four years of researching and writing this book, many friends and scholars provided invaluable support and help. Chang Li and Liu Sufeng of the Academia Sinica in Taiwan made my research trip in Taipei both fruitful and joyful. Sun Baoli and Li Hongxia of Beijing Sports University, and Wei Wei of the Chinese Academy of Social Sciences, helped me search for access to archival materials in Beijing. Zhang Minqiang of the National Academy of International Studies in Beijing; Liang Kan of Seattle University; John Carroll of the University of Hong Kong; Susan Brownell of the University of Missouri in St. Louis; Barbara Keys of the University of Melbourne, Australia; Sun Yi of the University of San Diego; Wang Guanhua of the University of Connecticut; and Nancy Hearst of Harvard University shared with me historical materials, books, or their own research results. David Nickels of the Historians' Office at the U.S. State Department alerted me to the forthcoming volume of the Foreign Relations of the United States (FRUS) series on Sino-American relations during the Nixon administration, then sent me the e-version of the volume at the very moment it became available. Guy Alitto, Anthony Cheung, Charlotte Furth, Chuck Hayford, Jean Hung, Jin Guantao, Li Jianming, Liu Junxiang, Liu Qingfeng, Liu Xiaoyuan, Ma Jianbiao, Wang Yanan, Yang Lingxia, Yao Ping, You Weijun, You Weimin, and many others, helped me one way or another with this book. To all of them, I am grateful for their support and friendship. I also benefited from advice and comments received from audiences in Boston, Ann Arbor, and Hong Kong when I presented some of my research results.

I first became interested in the issue of sports in China in the fall of 1993, when Beijing lost its bid for the 2000 Olympic Games. At the annual party hosted by the History Department at Harvard University in September 1993, Bill Kirby and I had a very interesting discussion—even a bit of a debate—on the meaning and implications of Beijing's lost bid. Bill has perhaps never realized that our seemingly minor conversation in the lobby of Robinson Hall planted a seed of my interest in the issue. Then I had the good fortune to share an office with my friend Barbara Keys, who was working on her Harvard dissertation on the role of sports in international relations when both of us were graduate fellows at Harvard's Weatherhead Center for International Affairs. Barbara's passionate argument on the importance of sports in international politics helped keep the small seed alive even though at that time I was concentrating on the issue of China and the Great War.

Akira Iriye, Bill Kirby, Andy Markovits, Bob Smolik, and David Strauss all read the manuscript in part or in its entirety and offered priceless comments and suggestions to make the book better. The long and detailed comments from Susan Brownell, Barbara Keys, and John MacAloon were extremely valuable: they saved me from some mistakes and forced me to rethink many issues from different perspectives. Terre Fisher, as always, has contributed enormously to making this book readable in terms of the flow and style of the writing.

My colleagues at Kalamazoo College also deserve a special acknowledgment. They were extremely supportive of my research, granting me an academic leave to jump-start the research in 2004 and then allowing me to take a year-long sabbatical leave in 2006 to bring this book to a timely completion.

I am extremely grateful to Lindsay Waters, a legendary editor at Harvard University Press. Lindsay's confidence in this project when it was still in the early stage and his brilliant advice, inexhaustible wit, and sense of humor were much needed and appreciated. Without Lindsay's generous support and encouragement, this book would not have reached readers until much later. I am also in debt to Phoebe Kosman, Lindsay's able assistant, who was very efficient in getting my questions answered and forcing me to stay on track whenever she sensed I was going astray. In addition, I was fortunate to have Julie Carlson as my manuscript editor. She has a super-sharp eye for errors and an excellent sense of style; this book reads much better thanks to her efforts. Thanks also go to Elizabeth Gilbert, for her efficient supervision of the project, and to Lisa Roberts, for her beautiful design.

My two mentors, Akira Iriye and Yang Shengmao, have played a crucial role in my career development. Without their encouragement, support, and inspiration, this book would have never been written in the first place. This book is dedicated to them as a small token of my profound gratitude.

Finally I would like to express my debt to Ann for all of her sacrifices to support my work on this book and her invaluable help in checking my pinyin errors—and to my children, Margaret, Julia, and Tom, for understanding their daddy's frequent absences. They are the best kids one could have in the world.

ACKNOWLEDGMENTS

★ ★ ★ ★

All of these people and organizations deserve whatever credit this book may garner, but I alone take responsibility for any errors. Note that while every effort has been made to secure permission to reproduce the illustrations in this book, we may have failed in a few cases to trace the copyright holder. Should the copyright holders contact us after publication, we would be happy to include a suitable acknowledgment in subsequent reprints.

ILLUSTRATION CREDITS

31, 46, 94, 113, 115, 200, 206, 217, 220, 241, 253, 258, 266	Courtesy of the IOC Archives.
43	Courtesy of the Los Angeles Sports Library.
47	From *XIth Olympic Games: Berlin, 1936* (official report of the Eleventh Olympic Games), 2:1097.
67	From *Di liu jie quan guo yun dong da hui bao gao* (Report of the Sixth National Games), Shanghai, October 1935.
72	From Zhong hua ren min gong he guo di yi jie yun dong hui xuan chuan bu, ed. *Zhong Hua Ren Min Gong He Guo Di Yi Jie Yun Dong Hui* (The PRC's first National Games) (Beijing: Ren min tiyu chubanshe, 1960).
130, 133, 139	From *You Yi Zhi Hua Bian Di Kai: Zhong Guo Ping Pong Dai Biao Tuan Can Jia Di San Shi Yi Jie Shi Jie Ping Pong Qiu Jin Biao Sai She Ying Ji* (Friendship flowers are everywhere: Official photos of the Chinese table tennis delegation's participation in the Thirty-first World Table Tennis Championships). Hong Kong: You yi chuban gong si, 1971.